Where In The
WORLD?
United States & Capitals, Plus Physical Features!

Designed and Authored by Amanda Predmore

A Classically Based Geography Curriculum On
UNITED STATES AND CAPITALS and US PHYSICAL FEATURES
with HISTORICAL, CULTURAL, SCIENTIFIC, & ENVIRONMENTAL TID-BITS

Part of the **Where in the World** Geography Series
Where the student's learn to memorize through drawing and discussion.
http://bit.ly/WhereInTheWorldGeo

Copyright © 2020 by Amanda Predmore

Where in the World?
United States and Capitals, Plus Physical Features!

Memorize and Engage Geography Through
Repetition and Discussion

http://bit.ly/WhereInTheWorldGeo

All rights reserved. See restrictions and allowances below.

This book or any portion thereof may not be reproduced and is licensed by purchase
for the use of educational material for one homeschool family, or one student in a
classroom. Copy of maps for personal use in your family is permitted. Beyond this
you may not transmit or distribute without express written permission of the
author/designer except for brief quotations in a book review.

ISBN 978-1-7325085-2-1

Printed in the United States of America

Where In The WORLD?

United States & Capitals, Plus Physical Features!

Designed & Authored by Amanda Predmore

Horseshoe Bend in Glen Canyon in Arizona - Featuring the Colorado River

TABLE OF Contents

A Note from Amanda Predmore ix
Learning Levels + Tips on How to Teach 1
Activities, Incentives, and Review Games 3
All the Parts - Get to Know the Curriculum 4
Map: Post French & Indian War 6
Map: Louisiana Purchase 7
Summary Map for Lessons 1-10 8
Summary Map for Lessons 11-24 9
Map: Where in the World? 10

LESSON DIRECTORY

Lesson 1 11
Lesson 2 21
Lesson 3 31
Lesson 4 53
Lesson 5 71
Lesson 6 80
Lesson 7 90
Lesson 8 99
Lesson 9 111
Lesson 10 125
Lesson 11 136
Lesson 12 143

Lesson 13 149
Lesson 14 159
Lesson 15 171
Lesson 16 176
Lesson 17 186
Lesson 18 196
Lesson 19 204
Lesson 20 216
Lesson 21 225
Lesson 22 240
Lesson 23 249
Lesson 24 262

Each lesson begins with Parts 1 & 2 (See full description of the "Parts on Page 4).

Following the last lesson, there are additional Part 1 "Closer Look" Maps that reflect the TrueReview 6 week schedule. These maps are labeled as "TrueReview 1, 2, 3, 4, 5, 6"

"Closer Look" maps show the geography that needs to be reviewed for the lesson you are currently in.

Closer Look / TrueReview Pages

Closer Look / TrueReview 1 274
Closer Look / TrueReview 2 275
Closer Look / TrueReview 3 276
Closer Look / TrueReview 4 277
Closer Look / TrueReview 5 278
Closer Look / TrueReview 6 279

Blank Blackline United States Map 281

Mount Rushmore National Memorial - George Washington, Thomas Jefferson, Theodore Roosevelt, and Abraham Lincoln

Dedication

First, and always, I thank you, Lord, for knowing me so wholly, so intimately. As this blessing unfolds, I am in awe of not only your love but your good and wonderful gifts, thank you.

To my children, Elijah, Ethan, and Isabella.

In my zeal, I began this journey to teach you all about the United States. You were only four years old. Little did I know that the worksheets would turn into a book, then two, then three. Thank you for your inspiration, patience, and proud smiles on your faces. I want you to know this world that our Lord created for us and I look forward to exploring it with you!

I also wish to thank all the homeschool parents that initially reached out to say, "Hey, can you do more of these?" My answer was always, "yes" and from that point, you have encouraged me to better this teaching tool at every turn.

Your loyalty is humbling, and I take profound responsibility in doing well for you all.

Thank you,

Amanda

Autumn in the Ozarks

Homeschool Mama of elementary aged triplets and creator of the "Where in the World?" Geography Series

One additional thought...

Subjects within the book are repeated many times over, such as the Louisiana Purchase, Reconstruction of the Southern States after the Civil War, and various wars. This is an opportunity as an educator to teach these historical events over and over from a state and physical entity perspective. If you find that your child reports that they "already know this" then it is optimal to utilize this as a catalyst for oral quizzes as you go through the text as well as dialectic conversation.

A note from Amanda Predmore

Creator of the *"Where in the World?"* Geography Curriculum
Where students memorize geography through drawing and discussion!

Keeping it simple, endless possibility for creativity with gentle memorization!

This year we'll be going on a journey to learn about the United States of America. With her states and capitals and unique and distinctive physical features throughout the land - it will be an exciting journey!

Geography serves as a launchpad to a deep understanding of the world in which we live. In this book, our students learn where different states are and the capitals that govern them. Alongside this, students learn the history that shaped our country since the Jamestown and Plymouth colonies. How many other nations fought and died over this land that America prevailed in governing. They learn about landmark decisions by the U.S. Supreme Court and the bravery of some to dream and inspire others to change hearts towards fairness and unity. Students will look at the plight of the Native Americans and how they lived, and their journey after Europeans came to this land. Throughout the book, ecology will be taught through topography, plants, animals, and man's influence over the earth, for good or ill. It is fantastic information that, as educators, we have the unique and awesome responsibility to make it come alive for our student's sake.

The classical method in learning has so much to do with repetition, intensity, and duration. However, this process doesn't have to be daunting or terrible for our students. We can walk through learning together, discovering together, have fun imagining what it would be like to be there, and experience that together!

My heart's desire is that, within this book, you will find the right tools for your classroom or family to launch into a remarkable discovery of the United States. And hopefully, stepping through this method with a bit of creativity and discussion will make the geography come alive! And in the end, if they have the locations memorized, bonus! But first and foremost, have fun with discovery!

With prayer and blessings,

Amanda Predmore

Sunrise Over Crown Point in the Columbia River Gorge. Oregon state on the left, Washington state on the right, with the only break in the Cascades.

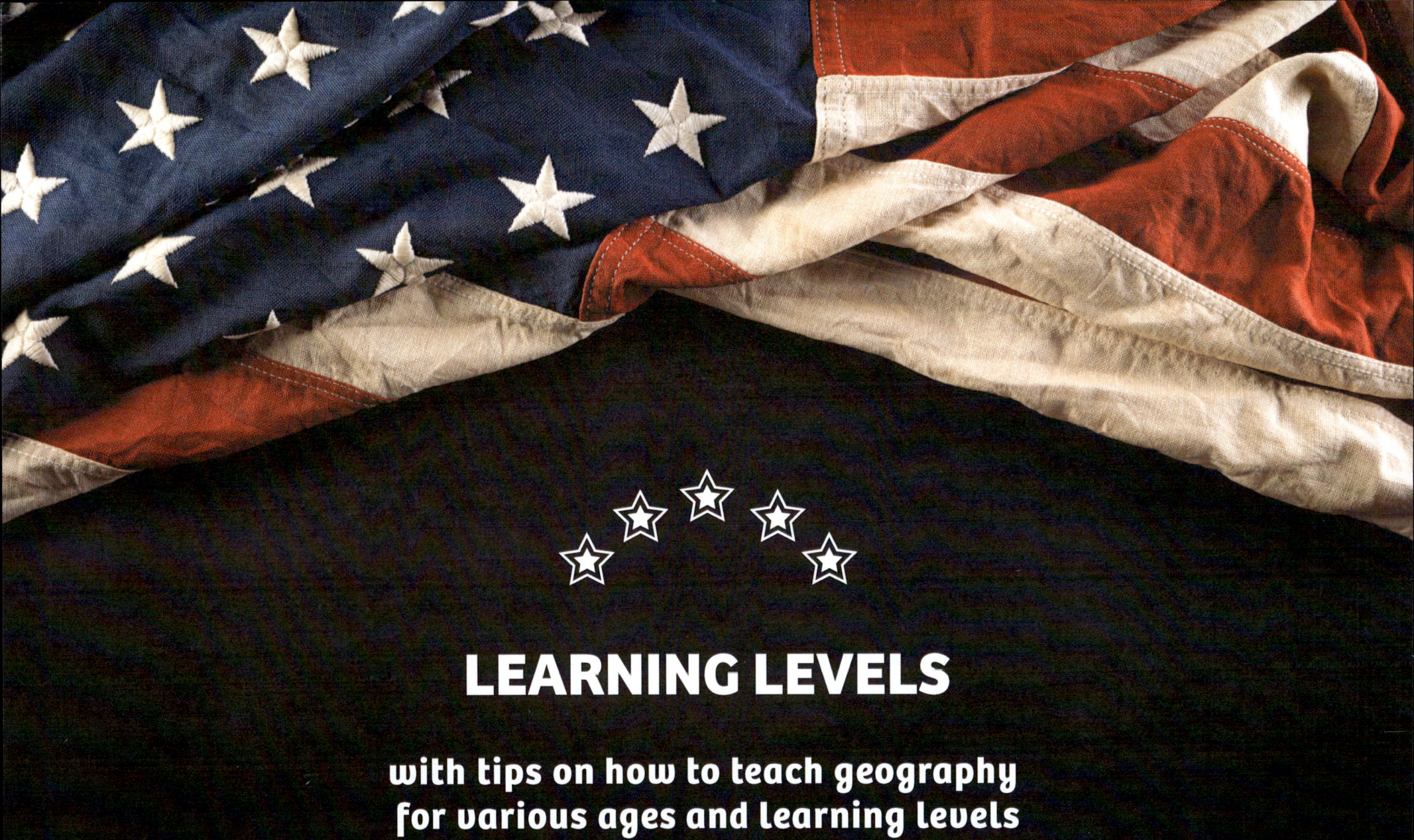

LEARNING LEVELS

with tips on how to teach geography for various ages and learning levels

Learning Levels with Tips on How To Teach Geography

Learning Level 1

Learning geography can be done as early as 4 years of age. How? The fun way! Make up a song or chant to a rhythm while you and your student place cheerios on the geography being learned. Pick whichever map in each lesson that works best for your student. If they have writing skills learned, even a little, you can have them write the initials of the geography (i.e., "M" for Maine) on the fill-in sheet if it doesn't cause too much angst for the student. Or, use the cut and paste labels. Although, with little hands and challenged motor skills, the names are small and they will need help in this process. You may even need to cut and apply the glue, and the student can stick it in the right place. Be sure not to stick it on, they need to learn where it goes!

Look up 2-3 points of interest that your student will think is interesting about the geography you are studying. If it is a good fit, have them draw a picture of one aspect of what is being taught about the geography. Take a look at the "Discussion Dive" pages for tips and examples on how you can make geography more engaging. Lightly discussing the geography with your littlest learners will undoubtedly add to their learning experience. Also, be sure to get some photos that will draw visual intrigue of the places they are learning about. With this level and advanced levels of learning, activities are always fun too! Check out some of the suggested geography activities to bring life to learning this material. Depending on your student, doing one geography project per week is enough to give them exposure. You may be surprised what they will learn and retain!

Learning Level 2

As the students get older and their motor skills develop, you can begin to utilize the step-by-step process in each lesson. As you learn along with your student the pages provided in each lesson starts with a complete world picture, then a closer look and then zooming right in. Just follow the instructions along with your student, helping them in the process. As with Level 1 and Level 3 learners, it is gainful to sing or chant the lesson's geography at the beginning and near the end of the experience to help pound in the memory pegs. The "Memorization through Repetition" should be done 2 times weekly in addition to the "Now Let's Trace, Shade & Label" worksheet, which is used as an introduction to the lesson's geography. Both of these tools will help solidify the whereabouts of these places through tracing, shading, and labeling.

Like Level 1 Learners, look up 2-3 points that your student will think is interesting. If it is a good fit, have them draw a picture of one aspect of what is being taught about the geography. Take a look at the "Discussion Dive" and "Dig Deeper" pages for tips and examples on how you can make geography more engaging. This gives exposure to the dialectic and research skills your students will need. Also, be sure to get some photos that will draw visual intrigue. If it is a good fit for your home and educational style, find kid-friendly videos that talk about these places and their unique history.

Learning activities are always fun too! Check out some of the suggested geography activities to bring life to learning this material.

Learning Level 3

For advanced, self-directed students, as with all learning levels, the goal is to memorize all areas of geography. Through repetition of drawing, your student will create a visual memory of this geography.

It is encouraged to engage in discussion about the geography that your student is learning through current events and structured dialogue. Take a look at the "Discussion Dive" and "Dig Deeper" pages for tips and examples on how you can make geography more engaging while practicing the dialectic and research skills your students need. For memory retention, it is good to do twice-weekly review utilizing the tools within the lesson pages, through geography games and/or point and name review.

Don't forget that these advanced learners love activities too! Check out some of the suggested geography activities to bring fun into learning this material.

NEW GRAMMAR!
For all levels of learning there are new vocabulary words throughout this book! Be sure to look for learning opportunities!

Great for homeschooling where multiple age children can learn from the same lessons!

Why we learn geography!

Geography is a foundational stepping stone in learning culture and social influences, the physical environment, political climate, and the "where" of the events of the world and how they shape and influence our society. To have a mental map of your country and the entire world opens the mind to understanding the relationships between countries and the world's interdependence.

Did you know

that drawing improves memory by encouraging a seamless integration of semantic, visual, and motor aspects of a memory trace? *Fun tip for making it stick!*

And this curriculum specializes in "making it stick" by utilizing three classical memorization techniques: **repetition, intensity, and duration.**

Activities

These activities need preparations and are offered here as ideas to launch from - utilize online searches if needed to fuel creativity while trying to stay simple to avoid getting overwhelmed.

- Scavenger hunts (with or without learning to use a compass).
- A puppet show to act out a scene from history, i.e. the Pilgrams landing in Plymouth.
- Learning how to use a compass by placing a geography related treasure and instructions on how many steps North, East, West and South to find it!
- Mapping out how many miles it is to go from here to geography being learned, how would they get there, and how long would it take to get there.
- Finding out something worth researching in the geography being learned and dig deeper!
- Recreate state shapes with play-doh.
- Create an itinerary for travel to a far-away state and how much would that cost (and why did they choose that state?).
- Map the student's USA footprint by checking to see what products they use that are created in the USA.
- Pick a state and explore a dish that is known to come from there.
- Learn about time zones within the United States. What time is it in Hawaii, New York, Ohio?
- Utilizing a globe or map, have the student share what can be learned about a state of their choice. Can they tell what the topography is, the capital, who are the neighboring states.

Incentives

Most all children need incentives and rewards to stay on track. Here are just a few ideas to help educating your students a bit easier!

- Lots of encouragement and praise!
- Make a paper airplane out of their geography drawing from the day's lesson and throw towards a globe or map... wherever it lands you can briefly teach them about that area - bonus geography!
- End with a game for accomplishing the goal. It could be a geography game, or just any game the student loves best!
- Dominoes/Magformers/Legos/Building Blocks, etc. For every question answered or every goal (big or small) accomplished - the student gets 5 (more or less) pieces to slowly build their own creation.
- Food or Fun Passes - Use an "I got caught being good" jar and place a little something in every time they accomplish the goals that you set for them. At the end of the lesson or school day, they get to reap their reward or accumulate for a bigger reward like a special trip!
- Trinkets Treasure Chest (or rewards basket) Fill a miniature treasure chest with trinkets, stickers, seeds, mystery presents, for the choosing at the end of a successful school day.
- Your child teaching class or being the teacher's assistant.

And the list goes on... check online for homeschool incentives and rewards.

Review Games

Use review games in your homeschool to build relationships, connect with your children, make memories, and pound the memory pegs in a bit further while having fun!

Where in the World! First step is to number a blank map in order of being taught (for instance: Augusta, Maine (1), Concord, New Hampshire (2), Boston, Massachusettes (3). Make geography named labels and place them into a bowl, basket, hat or bag and pick a geography location for the student to find on the numbered map. If the student gets the number location on the map correct they get a point!

Geo Bingo! Based on the same idea as "Where in the World!" Number your blank maps in order of being taught. Then make the same numbers on little pieces of paper and place them into a bag or basket for drawing from. Call one number (Not the Geography Name!) out at a time and have your student(s) find the number and name the geography. If they get it right they get to color that country or get a point! Once all geography for that board (map) are colored in, you win! If you have multiple students, they can all win!

We homeschool parents generally like to "DIY" most everything - however if you don't have the time or inclination to prepare these games, I've taken some of the work out of it and made it available for purchase as a download (you just have to cut) combined with a variety of enlarged maps including numbered maps and answer keys!

http://bit.ly/WhereInTheWorldGeo

All the Parts
Get to Know the Curriculum!

There are 2 books that work as a team!
These two books, together, have 5 parts for each lesson.
Take a look below to understand each part and where they can be found!

BOOK 1

Book 1 is the Teaching Resource Guide. This guide includes parts 1, 2, & 3 for each lesson.

BOOK 2

Book 2 is the Worksheet Book. This book includes parts 4 & 5 for each lesson.

Parts of each Lesson

1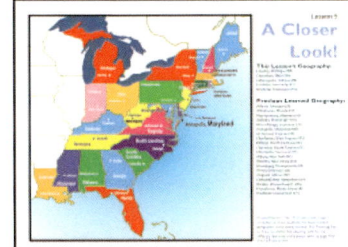

Closer Look! A map showing new geography being learned, alongside geography learned over the last 6 lessons! This map is located in the Teaching Resource Guide (Book 1) to be used as a reference when doing review work.

2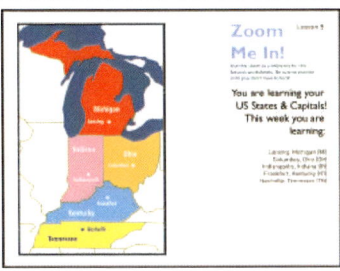

Zoom me in! A map zoomed in to show just the new geography being learned. This map reflects the worksheet called "Now, let's trace, shade, & label!" This map is a great reference when first learning the geography. This map is located in the Teaching Resource Guide (Book 1) to be used as a reference as needed.

3

Tid-Bits! This is the place where you find all of the tid-bits of history, culture, geographical information, science, animals, and more, relating directly to the geography being learned! This section is located in the Teaching Resource Guide (Book 1).

4

Worksheet - 1 per lesson: "Now, let's trace, shade, & label!" This worksheet is the first introduction to the geography being learned! A gentle way to become familiar with the geography while learning about these places through the tid-bits of information available in the teaching resource guide. This section is located within the Worksheet Book (Book 2).

5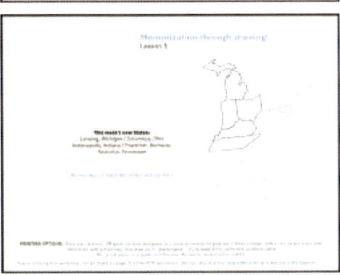

Worksheets - 2 per lesson: "Memorization Through Repetition" This worksheet includes the new geography PLUS geography for the last 6 lessons. A gentle way to memorize. Before you know it, the "Closer Look!" map won't be needed! This section is located within the Worksheet Book (Book 2).

TIPS FOR BEING PREPARED!

Having the right tools makes a difference in the quality of drawing and labeling. It is recommend that tracing and coloring be done with colored pencils.

In addition, a fine point sharpie works well over the colored pencil, it is suggested to have a blue for rivers, a black for geography labeling and red for cities. Most geography is the same grouping of colors. Pre-grouping the needed colored pencils and pens into a geo-kit will be helpful.

Recommended Product:
Sharpie Pen Stylo Fine Point

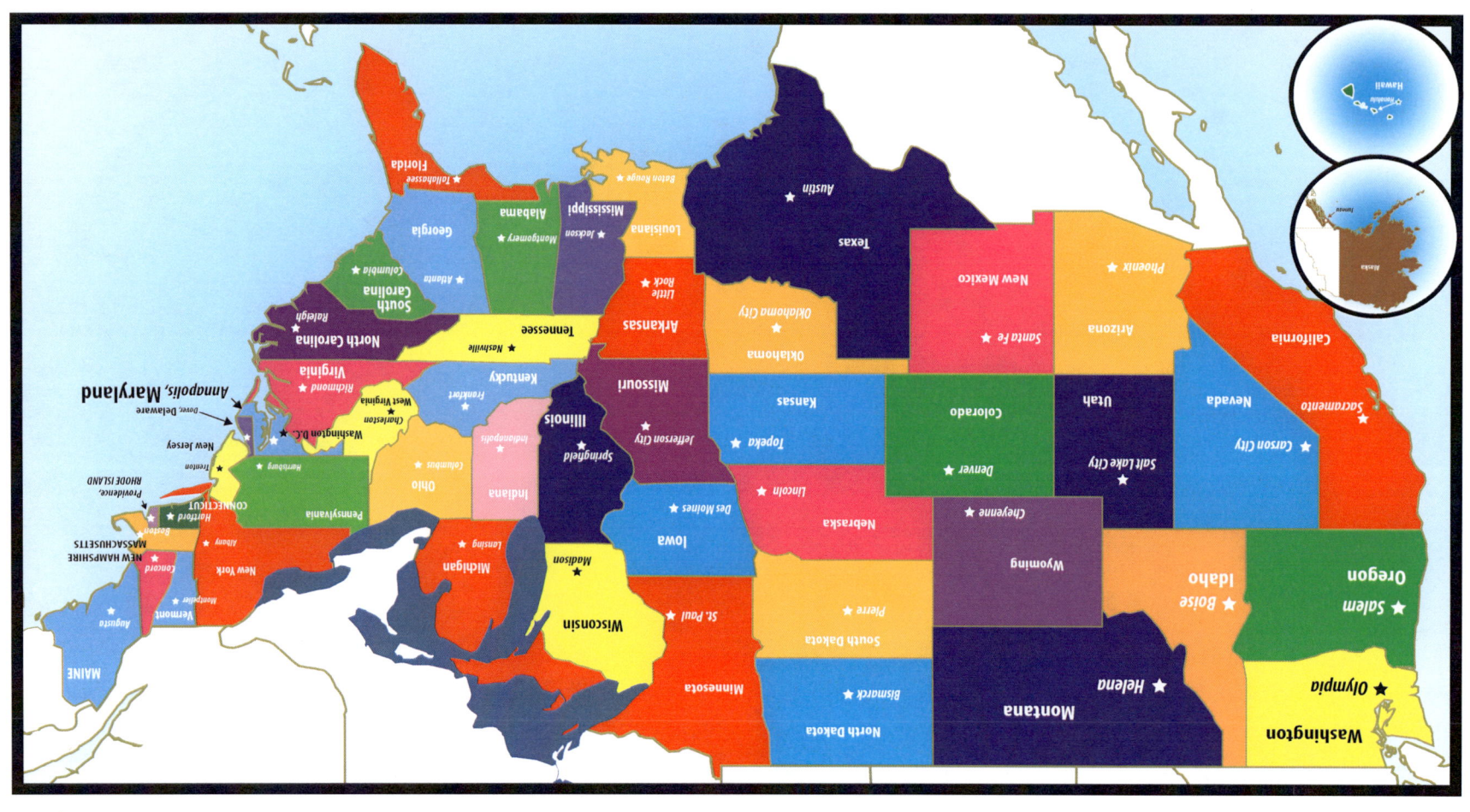

Summary Map for Lessons 1-10

Lesson 1
Augusta, Maine (ME)
Concord, New Hampshire (NH)
Boston, Massachusetts (MA)
Providence, Rhode Island (RI)
Hartford, Connecticut (CT)

Lesson 2
Montpelier, Vermont (VT)
Albany, New York (NY)
Trenton, New Jersey (NJ)
Harrisburg, Pennsylvania (PA)
Dover, Delaware (DE)

Lesson 3
Annapolis, Maryland (MD)
Richmond, Virginia (VA)
Charleston, West Virginia (WV)
Raleigh, North Carolina (NC)
Columbia, South Carolina (SC)
Washington, D.C.

Lesson 4
Atlanta, Georgia (GA)
Tallahassee, Florida (FL)
Montgomery, Alabama (AL)
Jackson, Mississippi (MS)
Baton Rouge, Louisiana (LA)

Lesson 5
Lansing, Michigan (MI)
Columbus, Ohio (OH)
Indianapolis, Indiana (IN)
Frankfort, Kentucky (KY)
Nashville, Tennessee (TN)

Lesson 6
Madison, Wisconsin (WI)
Springfield, Illinois (IL)
Des Moines, Iowa (IA)
Jefferson City, Missouri (MO)
Little Rock, Arkansas (AR)

Lesson 7
St. Paul, Minnesota (MN)
Bismarck, North Dakota (ND)
Pierre, South Dakota (SD)
Cheyenne, Wyoming (WY)
Lincoln, Nebraska (NE)

Lesson 8
Topeka, Kansas (KS)
Oklahoma City, Oklahoma, OK
Austin, Texas (TX)
Denver, Colorado (CO)
Santa Fe, New Mexico (NM)

Lesson 9
Salt Lake City, Utah (UT)
Phoenix, Arizona (AZ)
Carson City, Nevada (NV)
Sacramento, California (CA)
Honolulu, Hawaii (HI)

Lesson 10
Helena, Montana (MT)
Boise, Idaho (ID)
Olympia, Washington (WA)
Salem, Oregon (OR)
Juneau, Alaska (AK)

Summary Map for Lessons 11-24

Lesson 11
- White Mountains
- Green Mountains
- Adirondack Mountains
- Allegheny Mountains

Lesson 12
- The Great Valley
- Blue Ridge Mountains
- Great Smoky Mountains
- Cumberland Mountains
- Mt. Mitchell

Lesson 13
- Rocky Mountains
- Pikes Peak
- Mt. Elbert
- Sierra Nevadas
- Mt. Whitney

Lesson 14
- Cascade Mountains
- Mt. Rainier
- Mt. St. Helens
- Denali

Lesson 15
- Lake Superior
- Lake Michigan
- Lake Huron
- Lake Erie
- Lake Ontario

Lesson 16
- Chesapeake Bay
- Hudson Bay
- San Francisco Bay
- Puget Sound
- Pamlico Sound

Lesson 17
- St. Lawrence River
- Ohio River
- Mississippi River
- Missouri River
- Arkansas River

Lesson 18
- Colorado River
- Red River
- Rio Grande River
- Columbia River
- Great Salt Lake

Lesson 19
- Cumberland Road
- Santa Fe Trail
- Mormon Trail
- Gila Trail
- Old Spanish Trail
- California Trail
- Oregon Trail

Lesson 20
- Erie Canal
- Pennsylvania Canal
- Chesapeake & Ohio Canal
- Ohio & Erie Canal
- Miami & Erie Canal

Lesson 21
- Eastern Woodlands
- Plains
- Plateau
- Northwest Coast
- California
- Great Basin
- Southwest

Lesson 22
- Mojave Desert
- Sonoran Desert
- Colorado Desert
- Painted Desert
- Great Salt Lake Desert

Lesson 23
- Grand Canyon
- Black Hills
- Ozark Highlands
- Okefenokee Swamp
- Olympic Rainforests
- Niagara Falls

Lesson 24
- Mississippi Delta
- Mammoth Cave
- San Andreas Fault
- Gulf of Mexico
- Death Valley

Where in the World?

Most* lessons in this book are centered on the United States of America.

*Lesson 16 we learn about Hudson Bay in Canada

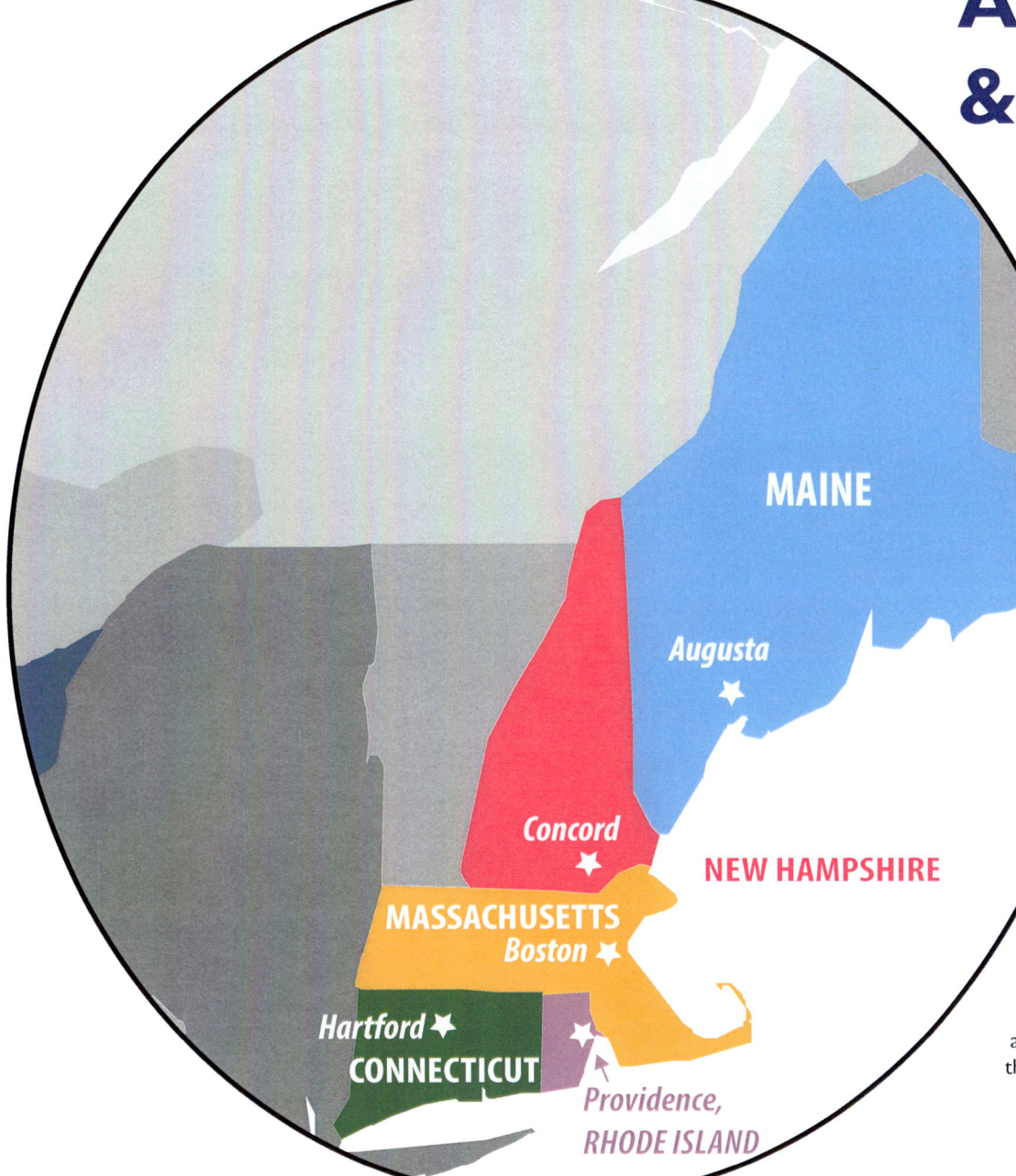

A Closer Look & Zoom Me in

Lesson 1

Use this sheet as a reference for this lessons worksheets - be sure to practice until you don't have to look!

You are learning your US States & Capitals! This week you are learning:

Augusta, Maine (ME)
Concord, New Hampshire (NH)
Boston, Massachusetts (MA)
Providence, Rhode Island (RI)
Hartford, Connecticut (CT)

Hint: The geography found on this page, is also the geography that you will be reviewing this week. Refer to this map as needed when doing your "Memorization Through Repetition" worksheets.

Parent/Teacher: The "A Closer Look" page is intended to show students the accumulated geographic areas being learned. Lesson 1, however is the first map and therefore this page doubles with "Zoom Me In!" For Teaching Tips on how to utilize these two teaching aides for the different learning levels please, refer to page 1.

This Lesson's Geography:
US States and Capitals

Augusta, Maine (ME)
Concord, New Hampshire (NH)
Boston, Massachusetts (MA)
Providence, Rhode Island (RI)
Hartford, Connecticut (CT)

Tid-Bits

New England, as it was named, was established initially as England's territory in today's states of Maine, Vermont, New Hampshire, Massachusetts, Rhode Island, and Connecticut.

This week, you will learn about five out of six of these states and the remaining state of Vermont next week. Collectively, we call these states the New England states. This is where America began and where historically significant eras were defined.

The New England colonies are the oldest land of the United States, predating the American Revolution by more than 150 years. It began with the Puritan Pilgrims that fled England's religious persecution. In 1620, the Mayflower carried them to the land we now call Massachusetts, establishing the Plymouth Colony, the first colony in New England. For twenty years after the Pilgrims landed, a multitude of Puritans settled in this area. Those that survived did so by farming and fishing, plus lumbering, whaling, and trading.

Writers from New England and essential events in the area helped influence and support the American Revolutionary War. Notable writers from the area or those that wrote many works in New England states include Emerson, Thoreau, Longfellow, Twain, Alcott, Stowe, Dickenson, Bates, and Frost. Be sure to look these authors up and read some of their influential writings!

New Hampshire Colony

New York Colony

Massachusettes Colony
(Partly Modern Maine and All of Modern Massachusettes)

Rhode Island Colony

Pennsylvania Colony

Connecticut Colony

New Jersey Colony

Delaware Colony

Virginia Colony

Maryland Colony

North Carolina Colony

South Carolina Colony

Georgia Colony

The original 13 colonies are listed on map by name.

Secondary categorization by color:

- New England colonies
- Middle colonies
- Chesapeake colonies
- Lower South colonies

By the 1840s, New England was front and center with their anti-slavery message as well as leading the way in American Literature as well as elevating higher learning.

The Industrial Revolution was led by New Englanders, having established numerous textile mills and machine shops in operation by 1830. This gave way to much of the manufacturing monopoly that the area had in the nineteenth century as well as playing

---

Lesson 1

an integral role in the American Civil War.

Today, the New England states have changed their focus to technology, weapons manufacturing, scientific research, and financial services.

The New England region was part of a broader area referred to as the Thirteen Colonies. Until July 4th, 1776, when the American Revolutionary War was won, and America was born, no longer under British rule.

For religious freedom from Britain, the New England colonies were founded. In contrast, the other colonies were created for economic prosperity. All thirteen were Britain's in the New World and included colonies in Canada, Florida, and the Caribbean.

Augusta, Maine

Augusta, Maine is the first state in America that we are learning about. As this state is found at the tippy-top of the eastern side of the United States, the people in the area called West Quoddy Head, situated on the coast, are the first in our country to see the sunrise!

Of the New England region, Maine is the largest state. In fact, Maine's land size equals all of the remaining areas of New England put together. However, the population is smaller when compared to the other states.

The state of Maine leads the country in growing and exporting blueberries as well as catching and shipping "bugs" around the world. Wait a minute, what "bugs" are we talking about? Well, in Maine, they call lobsters "bugs!"

In 1754, a trading company had built Fort Western in Maine to protect the region from attacks of area native tribes. Around this fort, people started to set up their dwellings, and soon, a village came into being. This village came to be known as Augusta, in 1797. In 1827, Augusta, earlier known as Harrington, became Maine's capital.

Do you like donuts? Have you ever had those poppable sweet donut holes? If you have and do, then you can thank the inventor of the donut hole who came from Maine. He was a sixteen-year-old named Hansen Gregory, who was trying to find a way to improve on the Dutch pastry by making sure that the center of the treat was cooked through when fried. So what did he do? He removed the center and fried up the pieces. Wa-La! The donut hole was born, and he had sweet success!

Concord, New Hampshire

Concord, New Hampshire is also known as the "Granite State" due to its large number of quarries and granite formations. Within, they have Petersborough Town Library, the first public tax-supported library in the United States was established in 1833.

Also a New England state, in 1776, New Hampshire was the first of the thirteen colonies to have a government and a constitution of its own, independent of British control. Later, in 1788, it ratified, that is, accepted the United States Constitution, becoming the ninth state of America.

Summiting Mount Monroe, White Mountains, New Hampshire - © nhmountainhiking.com

The White Mountains of New Hampshire are an attraction to anyone who visits the state. These are the northern portion of the Appalachian range. There are plenty of lakes and river valleys in New Hampshire, which give the beautiful state appeal for visitors and residents alike. While the winters in the region are long and bitterly cold, the summers are pleasantly warm.

Before the Europeans started settling in the region, the lands were occupied by the Abenaki tribes, who spoke Algonquian. Later, English and French traders and explorers began coming to New Hampshire with the first permanent settlement by London fishmongers at Hilton's Point in 1623. In case you don't know, a fishmonger is a market or a person that sells fish.

Leading up to the American Revolution, there was a raid by the Patriots on the British Fort named "Fort William and Mary." This critical event that leads up to the war has patriots trying to steal gunpowder from the fort through trickery and marked the beginning of American revolutionary activities. Five months after this, the Battles of Lexington and Concord were fought.

The first seen sunrise in the United States behind West Quoddy Head Lighthouse in Lubec, Maine. Photo by Ray Hennessy

Boston, Massachusetts

The Massachuset tribe that resided in the Great Blue Hill gave the state its name. Massachusetts too, is a part of New England.

Well known for the dedicated development in the field of education, universities like the Massachusetts Institute of Technology (MIT), Harvard University, and Tufts University are located here.

In Plymouth, Massachusetts, there is a story worth knowing. Not only for understanding but retelling, so that we don't lose the divinity at the center of America's beginning. There are many whose feet walked the land in what was to become America before it was settled by Europeans. They were the various indigenous tribes who made this land home, as well as explorers from Spain, France, England, and Russia, to name a few.

In the area of what was to become Massachusetts, there was a man named John Smith, who had a successful history as a soldier, explorer, colonial governor, Admiral, and author. He played an essential role in the colonization of Jamestown in Virginia in 1607. There he made a name for himself by being saved by Pocahontas. Later, in 1614, John Smith and ships under his command arrived to map Cape Cod and the vicinity. After Smith was done exploring and mapping, he set out, leaving behind his trusted associate, Thomas Hunt, to trade with the local tribes. Engaging in trade

Detail of John Smith from an illustration in The Generall Historie of Virginia, New England, and the Summer Isles. Public Domain

relationships, he hoped, would assist in colonizing in the area.

Turns out, however, that Thomas Hunt was not worthy of anyone's trust. In the name of friendship and trade, he lured twenty-four Nauset and Patuxet Indians to board his ship. Then took them captive.

Later, after learning of his treachery, John Smith wrote: "most dishonestly, and inhumanely, for their kind usage of me and all our men, carried them with him to Malaga, and there for a little private gain sold those silly salvages for rials of eight."

Hunt had the Indians below deck as he sailed to the Straits of Gibraltar. Upon arrival to Malaga, he sold as many as he could as slaves. Local Friars in town discovered his evil plan. They took custody of the remaining Indians, instructing them in the Christian faith. It was written of the Friars "so disappointed this unworthy fellow of the hopes of gain he conceived to make by this new and devilish project." Of the Indians that the Friars took in, a man named Tisquantum was among them, most would come to call him Squanto. Back to Squanto in a moment...

Do you remember the Nauset and Patuxet tribes that Indians were stolen from? Well, as you can imagine, they were outraged by the kidnappings and became extremely hostile. In fact, trading and exploration ships from England and France arriving in Plymouth and Cape Cod were no longer welcome to trade for valuable beaver pelts. Unfortunately for a French trading vessel, they found this out too late as their burning ship sank into the deep. All but a few perished except a few who were enslaved by the Nauset.

Between 1618 and 1619, the tribe's anger was distracted. A hostile enemy killed many and drove them out of the area. It was not a human enemy but a pandemic that took hold of the entire area affecting many tribes and significantly reducing their population.

During this time, Squanto had traveled from Spain up to London, England, where

he learned the English language and worked as an interpreter and expert on North American natural resources for the Newfoundland Colony. As luck would have it, he met a gentleman named Captain Dermer who worked for the New England Company. This Company had hope that they would be able to profit from beaver trade with the Indians of Massachusetts. Despite this challenge, Squanto, with his expertise, gave new confidence to their mission. His ability to

Squanto or Tisquantum teaching the Plymouth colonists to plant corn with fish. By The German Kali Works, New York - Bricker, Garland Armor. New York: Macmillan, 1911. Page 112., Public Domain

interpret between the English and the Indians and set forth peaceful intentions was just what they needed. Besides, Squanto wanted to go home, and they were his ride!

In 1619, Captain Dermer and Squanto sailed to New England. Upon arriving, they discovered the sad truth that Squanto's tribe, the Patuxet, died from the plague. All he found on the land were graves. He found his brother with the neighboring Massasoit Tribe, making his home with them.

Squanto's return was just in time for the Mayflower Pilgrims, who pulled into Provincetown Harbor in November of 1620. In sending out scouting parties from the ship, they found that there were hostile Indians there. So, they moved on around Cape Cod, landing in the abandoned Patuxet territory. This area, named by John Smith, was Plymouth.

From the time they anchored in the fall all the way through wintertime into spring, the Pilgrims built shelters and storehouses, taking care of the dying and sick. Not many survived, women and children were especially hard hit with illness. Fear of tribal presence persisted, but they saw only fires in the distance, no Indians. The Indians, however, knew about them. One day on March 16th, an Indian by the name of Samoset decided to pay the Pilgrims a friendly visit to welcome them. His English wasn't all that good, but he was able to explain that there was another Indian that knew English well and that they should meet him.

By William Halsall - Pilgrim Hall Museum, Public Domain

Six days later, Squanto introduced himself, bringing along his new tribe the Massasoit as well as another tribe named Quadequina. This meeting was friendly, out of which came a peace treaty and establishment of trading.

Squanto was now an essential ally to the Plymouth Colony. He translated and negotiated between tribal leaders and Plymouth's governors, which began as John Carver, and later became William Bradford. Peace was made with the Nauset, with whom they had their initial conflict on Provincetown Harbor as well as friendship with other Indian leaders within the Wampanoag Confederation.

Also, Squanto was a devoted guide in more than one sense. Firstly, he took the Pilgrims to various tribes, helping to establish trading relations. He also helped the Pilgrims learn how better to utilize natural resources like how to catch eels, and how to use fish caught for fertilizer to plant corn. It is speculated that without Squanto, the success of the Plymouth Colony would not have developed as it did, or possibly not at all.

About one hundred fifty years later, Britain had established a total of 13 colonies that were led by royally appointed governors. Not to say that when Britain had begun creating their colonies that they were the only ones... In fact, there were plenty of French, Spanish, Dutch, and even Russian colonies. But, only the English colonies united together to fight for unity and independence from England. At the time, England was a hard place to thrive. There was religious persecution as well as a lack of food because businessmen were making more money from wool than food. Going to America was a light in the darkness. However, Britain's Parliament still had a grip on the colonies from across the Atlantic Ocean.

In 1765, the Parliament of Britain, the controlling government body that passed laws in England, voted in the Stamp Act, which was the first tax on the thirteen colonies. Many in the colonies felt that they should have been represented at the Parliamentary level to vote on any issue that directly affected them. However, they had no representation. England was making decisions on taxing the people based on England's needs, not those of the colonials. They called this "taxation without representation." To the colonials, this was a serious matter, it was tyranny. Tyranny means that a government is

By Karl Anton Hickel, The House of Commons, Parliament, London, England

being cruel and oppressive in its rule over the people.

In response to the Stamp Act, the colonies refused to buy British goods, enacting a boycott. In 1766, Parliament's response was to repeal the act and immediately vote in the Declarative Act. This allowed Parliament to make laws and impose taxes on the colonists without the colonists' voice being represented in Parliament. This gave the Parliament total control, like a dictatorship over the thirteen colonies. In essence, it legalized the way that they wished to operate, the way they were already leading.

Next, Parliament voted in a tax on the colonies for glass, paper, and tea

The Boston Massacre on March 5th, 1770 - By Alonzo Chappel - New York Public Library. Public Domain

called the Townshend Act. The colonists did not like this, and the anti-British feelings burned. The colonists responded by circulating a letter to all colonies in an attempt to gather consensus against this law, and against Britain. They determined that they alone, not Parliament, could pass legislation that affected the colonies. Parliament then instructed the royally appointed governors to dissolve all assemblies that agreed with this letter, and this stance against Britain.

As time passed, it was clear that Parliament was unable to enforce any laws or taxes upon the colonies. The acts were all repealed, with exception to one tax on tea to show Parliament's power. At the same time, Parliament sent soldiers to the Massachusetts colony to stamp out any anti-British feelings. However, this only fueled the hatred that was growing against England.

On March 5th, 1770, residents gathered around a customs house, surrounding a soldier. Worried, the soldier called for help. When reinforcements came, they gathered together, and without an order to fire, they did. When the smoke cleared, five colonists lay dead. From that fateful day on, this event was referred to as "The Boston Massacre." News of the massacre spread to all of the colonies, and disdain for Britain strengthened.

In 1772, various colonists, beginning with Samuel Adams of Massachusetts, organized a system of correspondence with the other colonies. Other colonies followed this example and set up their own communication system. The ability to communicate easier began to bring solidarity to the people.

Britain's next move proved unwise. In 1773, they passed the British Tea Act. This law made it so that only the British East India Company could sell tea to the colonies - which, as you may recall, was also taxed.

When the tea ships arrived in Boston Harbor, the dockworkers refused to unload the tea or pay the tax. The royal governor of Massachusetts declared, "pay the tax by September 16th at

midnight with or without the tea being unloaded, or reap consequences!" This did not go over well with the colonists, as you can imagine. They gathered together and devised a plan that they hoped would get the attention of Parliament.

That night, these men of Boston disguised themselves as Mohawk Indians, crept silently onto the ship that held the tea, then together, with purpose and conviction, they unloaded that tea. Not, however, onto dry land; instead, they threw it into the deep blue ocean. This became known to all as "The Boston Tea Party." Do you think they received Parliament's attention? They sure did!

The Boston Harbor got shut down. The entire Massachusetts colony was put under the control of the "Red Coats," which was what the colonies called the British military.

This iconic 1846 lithograph by Nathaniel Currier was entitled The Destruction of Tea at Boston Harbor; the phrase "Boston Tea Party" had not yet become standard. Public Domain

All thirteen colonies were outraged. In turn, the colony delegates gathered together in Philadelphia, Pennsylvania, to meet and discuss the situation. This session was the first meeting of the Continental Congress. Notable members included John Adams, Samuel Adams, George Washington, Richard Henry Lee, and Patrick Henry. Together, they concluded that the actions of Britain were intolerable. They would put off discussions until spring to resolve their response to their grievances.

In March of 1775, they convened in Virginia. Patrick Henry gave his famous and convicting words to promote taking up arms against Britain.

"Besides, sir, we shall not fight our battles alone. There is a just God who presides over the destinies of nations, and who will raise up friends to fight our battles for us. The battle, sir, is not to the strong alone; it is to the vigilant, the active, the brave. Besides, sir, we have no election. If we were base enough to desire it, it is now too late to retire from the contest. There is no retreat but in submission and

slavery! Our chains are forged! Their clanking may be heard on the plains of Boston! The war is inevitable — and let it come! I repeat it, sir, let it come. It is in vain, sir, to extenuate the matter. Gentlemen may cry, Peace, Peace — but there is no peace. The war is actually begun! The next gale that sweeps from the north will bring to our ears the clash of resounding arms! Our brethren are already in the field! Why stand we here idle? What is it that gentlemen wish? What would they have? Is life so dear, or peace so sweet, as to be purchased at the price of chains and slavery? Forbid it, Almighty God! I know not what course others may take; but as for me, give me liberty or give me death!"

FULL SPEECH LOCATED AT THIS LINK:
https://bit.ly/GiveMeLibertyOrDeath

War was looming, and Patrick Henry was the brave man willing to make it clear that this was the only course of action if they were to be free of Britain.

Learning that the Massachusetts colony was stashing guns and ammunition in Concord, Britain sent 700 soldiers to seize their stockpile. On their way, they were ordered to go to Lexington to capture Samuel Adams and John Hancock. Upon learning this, a man by the name of Paul Revere rode the streets on horseback in the dead of night, warning his fellow colonists that the British were coming!

Patrick Henry's "Treason" speech before the House of Burgesses in an 1851 painting by Peter F. Rothermel, Public Domain

Just 70 colonist volunteers assembled to defend their position against the British in Lexington. These men were called Minutemen because of their dedication and sworn oath to fight at a minute's notice.

The brave 70 stood, instructed not to fire unless fired upon. Tensions ran high, the British poised for the battle, and there was a shot. Who fired? No one knew, but this was the "shot heard around the world" that began the American Revolutionary War. From this point forward, Boston would be under attack for close to a year, and the war would rage even longer.

The Continental Congress met on the primary business of the day: war. This war was highly supported by the northern colonies, but the south remained skeptical about parting ways with the British.

To bridge this gap in support of the war, on June 15th, 1775, the Continental Congress voted in a Virginian military leader with a succesful record from the French and Indian War. His name was George Washington, and that day he became Commander and Chief of the military.

"The British are coming!" Paul Revere's Ride - By Office of War Information - This media is available in the holdings of the National Archives and Records Administration, cataloged under the National Archives Identifier (NAID) 535721., Public Domain

There were many notable battles fought where each side had victory. Amid these battles, a document circulated among the colonies entitled "Common Sense" addressed to the "Inhabitants of America" authored by Thomas Paine. Within, it called the colonies to declare independence from Britain. This encouraged the people and spurred a motion written on June 7th, 1776, by Richard Henry Lee that called for a Declaration of Independence. Some colonies weren't a hundred percent sure about this. Before moving forward to vote, the Continental Congress wanted everyone on board - so they waited. In the meantime, a committee was formed to draft the anticipated Declaration. This committee included John Adams, Benjamin Franklin, Roger Sherman, Robert Livingston, and Thomas Jefferson. Jefferson, was asked to put pen to paper for the first draft in what he called "An Expression of the American Mind." After a few revisions by the committee, a draft was presented to the Continental Congress on June 28th, 1776.

During this time, the British showed up with thirty-two thousand soldiers on fleets of ships with sites on the New York colony - specifically, Long Island.

The Declaration of Independence was voted on and approved on July 2nd. On July 3rd, minor revisions were made. Then, all assembled on July 4th, 1776, to sign, therefore enacting the Declaration of Independence. America was no longer under British rule. The war, however, still raged, and we were not yet free.

First U.S. President, George Washington, Public Domain

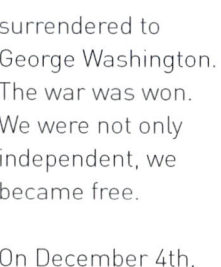

John Trumbull's famous 1818 painting is often identified as a depiction of the signing of the Declaration, but it actually shows the drafting committee presenting its work to the Congress.

Portrait of Thomas Jefferson while in London in 1786 by Mather Brown, Public Domain

The battle in the New York colony on Long Island happened on August 27th, 1776, with more than a thousand American lives lost. George Washington's troops with many battles won and lost had dwindled down in number to only eleven thousand. Then, after a cruel winter in Valley Forge, Pennsylvania, sickness took so many lives. By February, only four thousand remained.

Relief and support were on the way from Prussia and France. An army officer named Baron Friedrich Wilhelm Von Steuben came and trained the remnant, giving strength, strategy, and hope to their numbers. At this time, France recognized America as a newly independent country and threw their

support behind the fight for independence.

Many joined the ranks over time, knowing what and why they fought. On October 6th, 1781, sixteen-thousand American soldiers attacked, and on October 19th, the Red Coats

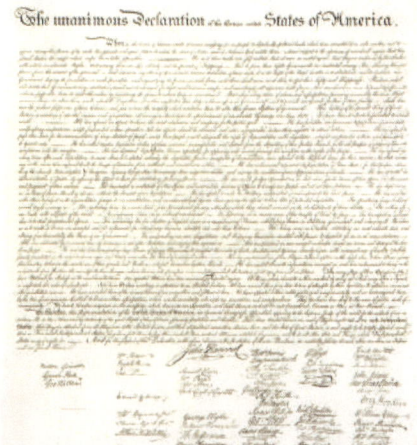

U.S. Declaration of Independence, Public Domain

surrendered to George Washington. The war was won. We were not only independent, we became free.

On December 4th, 1783, General George Washington resigned from the Continental Congress to return to the quiet life with his wife Martha in Mt. Vernon, Virginia.

No more than six years later, George Washington was again called upon for his courageous leadership, becoming our first President of the United States of America.

Providence, Rhode Island

This state has a rather long official name- The State of Rhode Island and Providence Plantations. Despite its lengthy name, the state is actually the smallest of all the states of America.

Before being colonized, the dominant native group in Rhode Island was the Narraganset tribe. In the 1500s, explorers and traders started arriving from Europe- they were Portuguese, Dutch, and Italian. In 1663, Rhode Island officially became a British colony. When the states united, Rhode Island was the last to join the union. It ratified the American Constitution only

after the Bill of Rights had been included in it.

During the colonial period, a minister by the name of Roger Williams set up the Providence Plantation in Rhode Island. He was the first to officially use the name Rhode Island. However, today the specific origin of Rhode Island's name is not fully known. It is said that an explorer named Giovanni da Verrazzano saw the island near Narrangansett Bay and thought it looked like the Greek island, Rhodes. Another explorer, Adriaen Block, remarked that the land had a reddish appearance. The Dutch phrase that he used was 'een rodlich Eylande.' The name for the island could have been a result of any of these. In 2009, the General Assembly of Rhode Island considered removing the 'and Providence Plantations' from the state's official name; however, felt keeping it reflected the colonial past.

A monument called "King Philip's Seat" is situated on top of Mount Hope and commemorates the death of the Wampanoag chief Metacomet. King Philip's War, which is sometimes referred to as the First Indian War, was a conflict between New England Indians and New England colonists and their Indian allies. The war is named after Metacomet, which was the Wampanoag chief that went by the name Philip because of the excellent relationship between his father (named Massasoit) and the Mayflower Pilgrims. Metacom became tribal chief in 1662 after Massasoit's death. Metacom, did not, however, maintain the alliance with the colonists. In 1671, during peace treaty negotiations, colonists required the Indians to surrender their guns.

To make matters worse, three Wampanoags were hung for murder in Plymouth Colony in 1675. In retaliation, Indian raids attacked homesteads and villages throughout Massachusetts, Rhode Island, Connecticut, and Maine over the next six months. The colonial militia retaliated. The colonies assembled the most massive army that New England had yet mustered, consisting of 1,000 militia and 150 Indian allies. They burned Indian villages in the territory of Rhode Island. The war raged as Indians pushed the colonizers in Massachusetts Bay, Plymouth, and Rhode Island colonies, burning towns as they went, including Providence. In the end, the colonial soldiers overwhelmed the Indians, almost completely destroying the Wampanoags and their Narragansett allies. On August 12th, 1676, Metacom retreated to Mount Hope, where he was killed by the militia.

Metacom, also known as King Philip - Wampanoag Confederation Chief. Line engraving, colored by hand, by the American engraver and silversmith Paul Revere.

Don't get scared when you see this most massive bug. This blue termite, aptly named 'Nibbles Woodaway" is endemic to Providence, the capital of Rhode Island. Endemic means that this bug can be found nowhere else in the whole world. This termite is 58 feet long, and if it were real, it could swallow houses with just a couple gulps! 'Nibbles Woodaway' is the mascot for a pest control company and has become an iconic symbol of the area. I think it is safe to say that all are relieved "Nibbles" is completely unreal! Also unique in Rhode Island is Cumberlandite, a rare rock, which is exclusive to Rhode Island. This, unlike 'Nibbles Woodaway,' is very much real. The Cumberlandite is the state rock, and it owes its name to the specific town it can be found, Cumberland. Notable industries that help support the Rhode Island economy include shellfish and fish harvesting as well as the manufacturing of silverware.

Hartford, Connecticut

Connecticut has its share of history, not only as a New England state as part of colonial America but also with many "firsts." In Connecticut, a company called New Haven

'Nibbles Woodaway' on Rhode Island - The resident termite

produced the first-ever phone book, which was published and distributed in 1878.

Connecticut contributed an essential piece in the history of nuclear-powered submarines with the first-ever built, the USS Nautilus, made in Connecticut in 1954.

The state is named for the Connecticut River, the longest river in the New England region of the United States. It flows to the south for 406 miles through four states. The native Algonquian Indians get credit for originating the name, "Quinnehtukqut," but we spell it quite differently today. "Quinnehtukqut," in their language, meant 'land on the long tidal river'. Among the Algonquian Natives who resided in

Rhode Island Coastal Skyline - Licensed through Creative Commons

Connecticut, the most powerful was the Pequot tribe. In the 1630s, Europeans from the colonies near Connecticut started making their way to this region. In 1633, Fort Hoop was built by the Dutch in the area that is now Hartford. Present areas of Wethersfield and Windsor was where the British set up their forts. However, the Dutch fort in Hartford was taken over by the British and made into a colony in 1662.

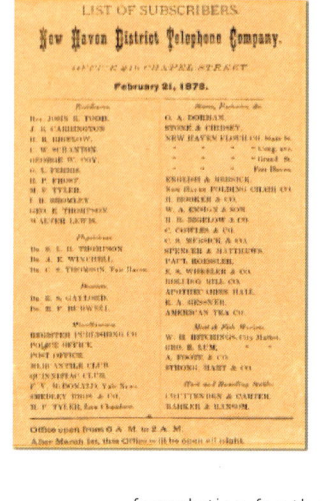

Connecticut is known as the 'Constitution State' because the first settlers who arrived wrote down a set of laws and rules which were initially meant for governing themselves. This set of rules, called the "Fundamental Orders of Connecticut," provided a foundation for the writers of America's Constitution.

Downtown Hartford, Connecticut - Public Domain

Early on, the USS Nautilus broke numerous records. In May of 1955, the submarine headed south sailing from New London to Puerto Rico, the transit was the longest ever by a submerged submarine and achieved the highest sustained submerged speed. In 1958 she recorded her famous voyage under the North Pole. In the spring of 1966, she again entered the record books when she logged her 300,000th mile underway.

Maiden Voyage of the nuclear-powered USS Nautilus

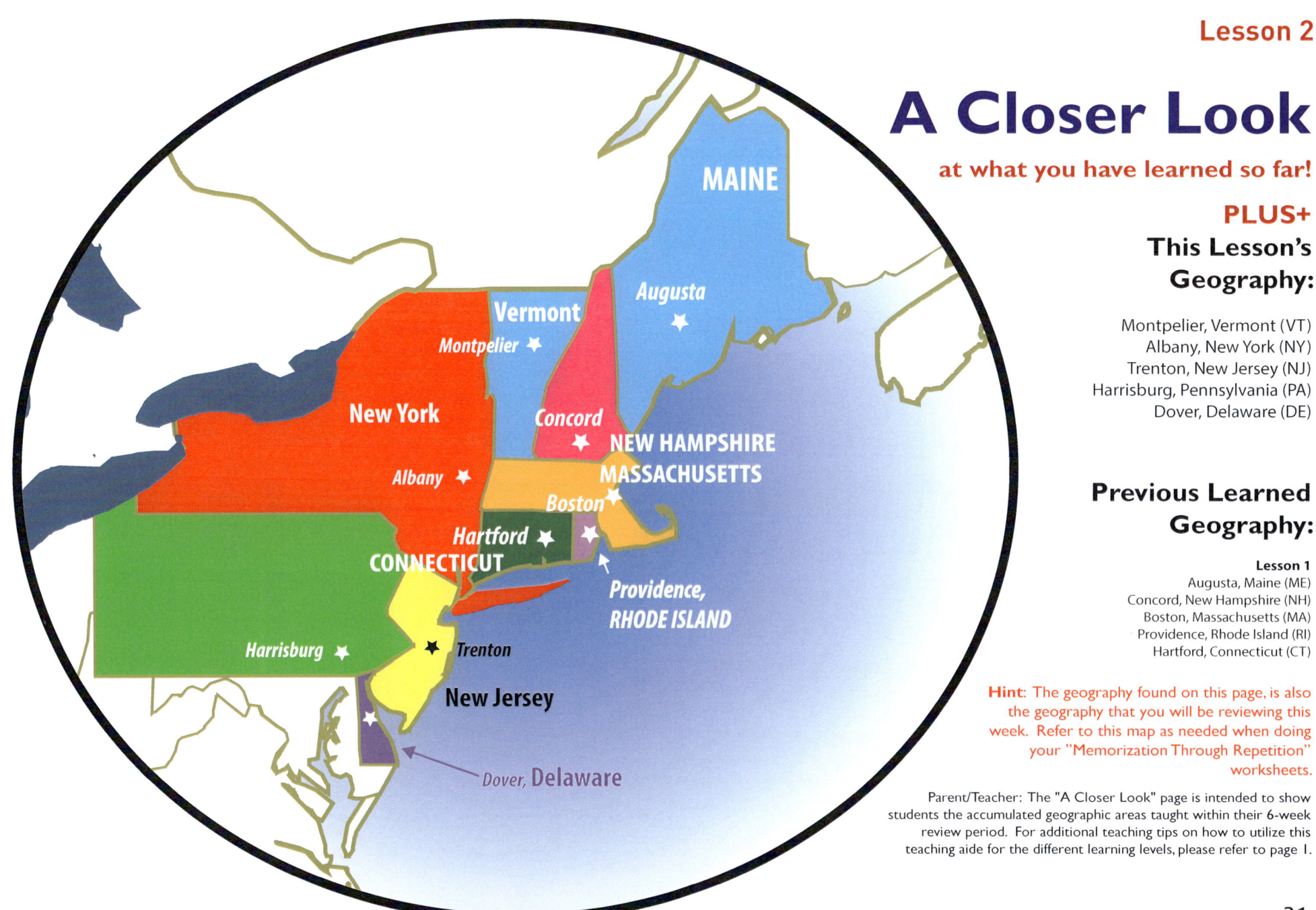

Lesson 2

A Closer Look

at what you have learned so far!

PLUS+
This Lesson's Geography:

Montpelier, Vermont (VT)
Albany, New York (NY)
Trenton, New Jersey (NJ)
Harrisburg, Pennsylvania (PA)
Dover, Delaware (DE)

Previous Learned Geography:

Lesson 1
Augusta, Maine (ME)
Concord, New Hampshire (NH)
Boston, Massachusetts (MA)
Providence, Rhode Island (RI)
Hartford, Connecticut (CT)

Hint: The geography found on this page, is also the geography that you will be reviewing this week. Refer to this map as needed when doing your "Memorization Through Repetition" worksheets.

Parent/Teacher: The "A Closer Look" page is intended to show students the accumulated geographic areas taught within their 6-week review period. For additional teaching tips on how to utilize this teaching aide for the different learning levels, please refer to page 1.

Lesson 2

Zoom Me In!

Use this sheet as a reference for this lesson's "Now, let's trace, shade & label" worksheet. Be sure to practice until you don't have to look!

You are learning your US States & Capitals!

This week you are learning:

Montpelier, Vermont (VT)
Albany, New York (NY)
Trenton, New Jersey (NJ)
Harrisburg, Pennsylvania (PA)
Dover, Delaware (DE)

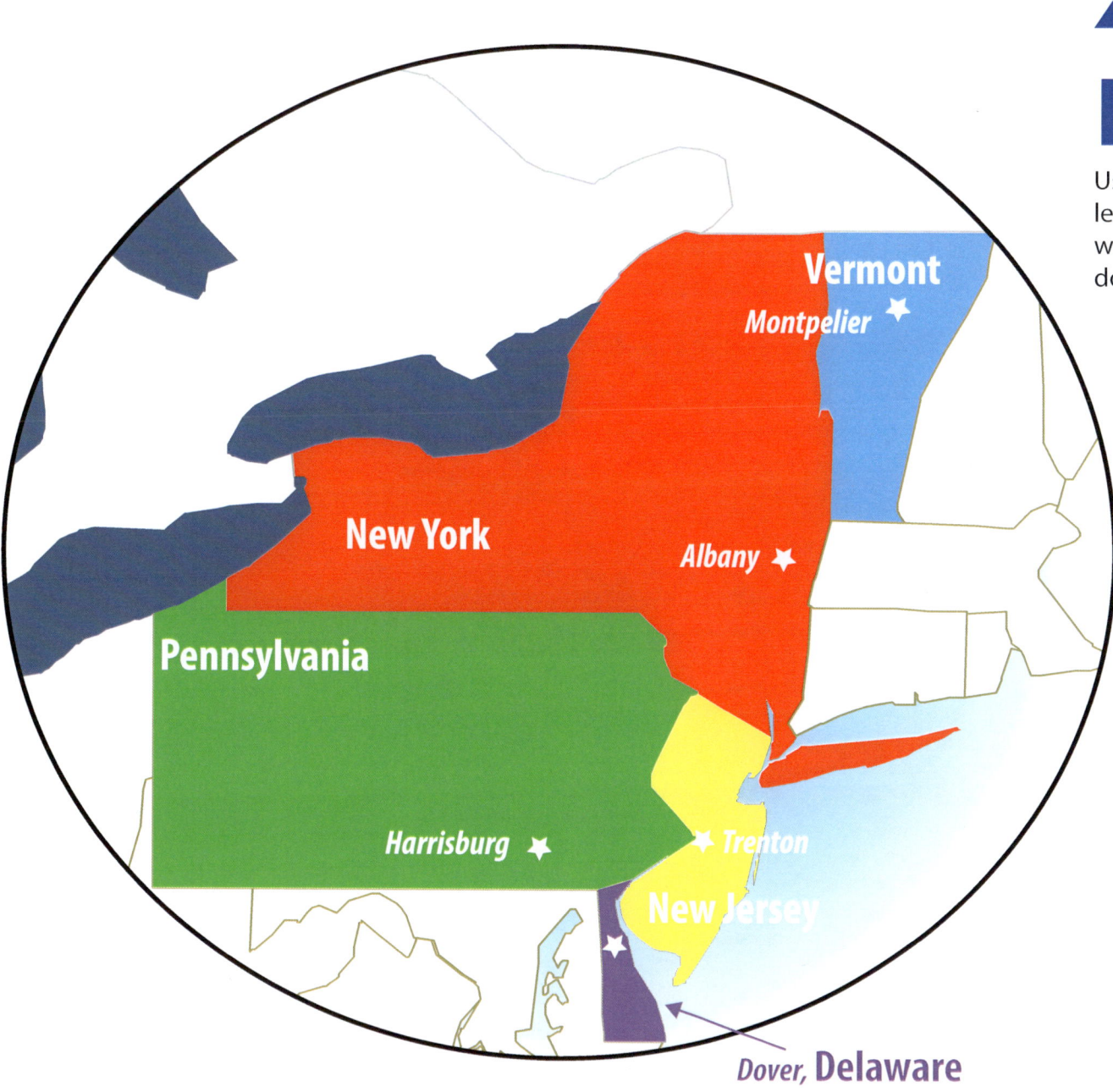

This Lesson's Geography:
US States and Capitals

Montpelier, Vermont (VT)
Albany, New York (NY)
Trenton, New Jersey (NJ)
Harrisburg, Pennsylvania (PA)
Dover, Delaware (DE)

Tid-Bits

Montpelier, Vermont

In 1609, Vermont, our last New England state that we are learning about, was first explored by a French man by the name of Samuel de Champlain. He was the first European to set foot on the land that would eventually become Vermont.

Later, during the 1600s, a few French military settlements were established, then abandoned. The area became a separation point, through which settlers would travel. The French and Native Americans moved through to the north, and English settlers were southbound.

As time marched on, there were boundary disputes in the early 1700s by two countries that didn't like each other much, Britain and France. Their disagreements eventually led to the French and Indian War, where England defeated France.

You may have noticed that Vermont was not one of the thirteen New England colonies. Instead, this territory was split between the two, and some of the lands were under dispute with New Hampshire and New York laying claim to Vermont. This was a time of confusion and fighting because settlers had claimed land that was already claimed. In other words, land ownership overlapped. In the years leading up to the American Revolution, many acts of rebellion took place in Vermont that were not against Britain but against the New York colony. There was a group of settlers named "Green Mountain Boys" that were from New Hampshire. The

Champlain and his Indian guide in Isle La Motte, Vermont, at the site Champlain is said to have first set foot in Vermont (and encamped) in 1609. Lake Champlain is in the background. Sculptor E.L. Weber, 1967; Photo by Matt Wills, 2009 - By Mfwills - Own work, Public Domain

1875 engraving depicts the capture of Fort Ticonderoga by Ethan Allen on May 10, 1775 - By Heppenheimer & Maurer - The New York Public Library digital library. Image ID: 808517, Public Domain

group was organized by Ethan Allen in 1770-71. They harassed and attacked new Vermont settlers with land titles issued from New York. However, these issues were put to rest when news of the Revolution reached them. In 1775, Allen and the "Green Mountain Boys" captured key British forts in the north. The group's efforts were crucial to the Patriots

Lesson 2

fighting for the cause, as it gave them confidence that the Revolution indeed was a united American front.

As mentioned, the American Revolution got underway with not much attention given to the boundary issue. Then, the Continental Congress declared independence from Britain on July 4th, 1776. Vermont did not want to be a part of it; in fact, they wanted to be recognized as a separate country, and so declared in 1777. They called themselves the State of Vermont, which existed for 14 years as an unrecognized independent country, considered by New York to be a district in rebellion. Later in 1790, negotiations between New York and Vermont removed Vermont's barriers to enter the Union in 1791.

Vermont is covered with the Green Mountains that are cut through with beautiful large rivers and valleys. They extend through the center of the state and are the most prominent natural feature.

Green Mountains in Vermont - by Jose, adobe stock

The French had a part in naming the state. "Ver" is the French word for "green," and "mont" is the French word for "mountain." "Ver-Mont" means "Green Mountain," which is why the state's nickname is the "Green Mountain State." The area is a popular destination for visitors that like to ski, snowboard, and hike. Many small towns and villages are dispersed along the valleys of the Green Mountains.

In the center of Vermont is the capital city, Montpelier. Those that live and visit here experience moderate temperatures. The summer can reach a high in the mid-'80s. In the autumn and spring months, highs average in the mid-50s and lows in the 20s and 30s during the wintertime. Vermont receives quite a lot of precipitation with an average of 40 inches a year that comes in the form of rain and snowfall. The heaviest snowfall in the state is in Washington County, with an average of ten feet each year!

In Montpelier, there are fewer than 9,000 people, which makes this capital the lowest populated in America. This city feels like a small town, especially since they prefer local businesses over chains such as McDonald's, which is nowhere to be found.

Do you like maple syrup? Well, Montpelier is the largest producer of maple syrup in the U.S. So, if you eat real maple syrup on your pancakes, chances are it was shipped from Vermont!

For the ratio of cows to people, Vermont has the highest number of dairy cows in the country, which must be why Ben & Jerry's make their yummy ice cream in Vermont! Ben & Jerry's Ice Cream company donates their leftover ice cream to local farmers who give it their hogs. The hogs like all the flavors, except Mint Oreo.

Vermont, home to the Ben & Jerry's ice cream company factory.

Albany, New York

The Dutch were the first Europeans to settle in the New York area; they called it New Netherland. Their colony extended from modern-day Albany, New York, in the north to Delaware in the south. They also had settlers in areas that are now New Jersey, Pennsylvania, Maryland, Connecticut, and Delaware. Their initial stop to colonization was along the Hudson River in 1624. In 1664, Britain took control of the land and renamed it New York. King Charles II of Britain gave the area to his brother, James, the Duke of York, from which the name came. As one of the original 13 colonies, New York played a crucial political and strategic role during the American Revolutionary War.

From 1892 until 1954, there was an enormous migration of people that arrived in New York Harbor, passing through Ellis Island

Downtown Albany, New York

toward their pursuit of the American dream. Some estimate that up to

Immigrants upon arrival at Ellis Island - Public Domain

forty-percent of America can trace at least one family member to Ellis Island.

As immigrants neared New York westbound across the Atlantic Ocean, the first sight they saw as they approached the

Immigrants nearing Ellis Island can see Lady Liberty on Liberty Island

harbor was the Statue of Liberty. For them, she marked a sigh of relief that they had made it to America. Lady Liberty represented America the Free, and symbolized a safe haven from oppressive countries from which many came. Emma Lazarus framed this sentiment in her iconic poem, 'The New Colossus.' (below)

"Lady Liberty," or "Mother of Exiles," as she is called by many, is a colossal statue standing tall on Liberty Island facing the New York Harbor. Her design was inspired by the Roman goddess named Libertas. The torch she holds high above represents the enlightenment of the world. There are broken chains at her feet, symbolizing America's people breaking free from Britain's tyranny. In her left hand, she holds a tablet representing our laws with the date July 4th, 1776 inscribed in Roman numerals.

From her feet to the tip of the torch, she stands 151 feet and 1 inch. If you include all of Lady Liberty, down to her foundation, she is 305 feet 1 inch tall. Her head is 17'3", her nose is 4'6" and her index finger is 8' long! She is made out of copper, and it takes 354 steps to climb to the top of the crown upon her head, where seven rays represent the seven continents of the world!

She was a gift bestowed on America's people by France. Her full, official name is "Liberty Enlightening the World." She took 10 years to build in France. They began shipping her in pieces to America in 1885 with assembly starting in April of 1886; completion for all to enjoy was on October 28th, 1886, when she was dedicated to the American people.

On September 11th, 2001, the twin towers in downtown New York City were hit by a Muslim terrorist group called al-Qaeda. The attack on the Twin Towers was one of three targets that day intended to bring down America's economic, military, and government centers, and to shake America's confidence in our safety. This attack began America's war on terrorism.

The al-Qaeda group took over four commercial airplanes, utilizing them as weapons to crash into buildings. The first two planes' targets were the Twin Towers. The third was the Pentagon; the fourth target is thought to have been the White House or the Capitol Building in Washington D.C. However, the fourth plane had brave passengers aboard that fought the terrorists, foiling their evil plans. Unfortunately, the plane crashed in Shanksville, Pennsylvania.

In New York City, the people went about life, as usual, that morning, until the first plane slammed into the North Tower. Most thought it was a horrible accident.

"Give me your tired, your poor,
Your huddled masses yearning to breathe free,
The wretched refuse of your teeming shore,
Send these, the homeless, tempest-tossed to me,
I lift my lamp beside the golden door!"

by Emma Lazarus
American poet and essayist best known for her sonnet "The New Colossus," written for the Statue of Liberty.

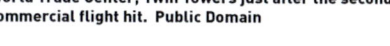

World Trade Center, Twin Towers just after the second commercial flight hit. Public Domain

However, that thought was erased when the second plane hit. All of America knew at that moment: we were under attack. There stood the twin towers, with many dead, where the aircraft had crashed. There was panic for those trying to get out, and many stayed in their offices under unwise orders to wait.

New Yorkers flee as the towers collapse. Public Domain

Airplane fuel caused an intense fire and extreme heat in the structure of the Twin Towers. Eventually, the buildings could take no more stress, and both buildings collapsed. First, the South Tower, followed by the North Tower about thirty minutes later. The intensity of the blast from the buildings collapsing made many other buildings and skyscrapers around the Twin Towers fall as well.

America stood still, paralyzed in watching this atrocity unfold before our eyes. The devastation of life lost from the attacks on the World Trade Center was 2,606 souls. Together, the passenger planes upon crashing lost 246 lives. At the Pentagon, there were 125 deaths.

There were so many heroes that day. Many of the heroes gave their lives to save as many people as they could. They were running into the burning buildings while everyone was running out. The heroes that lost their lives that day were 343 firefighters, 72 police officers, and 55 military personnel.

Firefighter takes an emotional break from the chaos. Getty Images

September 11, 2001 - New Yorkers amidst the rubble. Public Domain

All this death was caused by 19 terrorists that were members of the Islamic terrorist group al-Qaeda, which was led by Osama bin Laden. It is believed that his motivations varied. They may have included the U.S. support of Israel, American immorality, sanctions imposed against Iraq, the presence of the U.S. military in Saudi Arabia, and support of allies against Muslims in various countries.

Osama Bin Ladan - Public Domain

The effects of the attacks were experienced for many years. America's stock market crashed, creating an economic struggle. In New York,

everything was much worse, for they were dealing with the tremendous mess of dust and debris from the many buildings that collapsed. The cleanup was horrendous and ugly. New Yorkers were dealing with the loss of loved ones, and many had to cope financially with the loss of businesses and jobs. Our government during that time was being led by President George W. Bush, who, as our Commander-in-Chief retaliated with a "War on Terror." In Afghanistan, our

President Bush talks with those brave heroes from the Fire Department of New York after the attacks. Public Domain

military sought out and attacked the Taliban and searched for members of al-Qaeda. Their leader, Osama bin Laden, hid well in caves for many years before we successfully hunted him down and ended his life.

In New York City, it is believed that approximately 37% of the population are from other countries. Many think that there are over 200 languages spoken. Those that live and work in New York City pay a lot for rent: the average payment is $3,400 per month! When driving in this city, it is illegal for you to "block the box" and honk your horn.

New York's Federal Reserve Bank has the most abundant storage of gold in the whole world! Approximately 7,000 tons of glittering gold bars are there, 5% of all the world's gold ever mined.

Empire State Building - New York City

The Empire State Building, the tallest building in New York, gets hit by lightning on average 23 times per year and is home to over 1,000 businesses.

Trenton, New Jersey

As you may remember, New Jersey was one of the original 13 British colonies and served as an important battleground during the American Revolution. In fact, the area was known as the "Crossroads of the Revolution," for there were more than a hundred battles in New Jersey during the fight for American independence.

In New Jersey, there are a lot of people! In fact, it boasts the highest population density of any U.S. state. Named for the island Jersey in the English Channel, this state has an extensive and scenic coastline that makes New Jersey a magnet for visitors that vacation here mainly during the summertime months, especially Atlantic City! In 1870, the very first boardwalk was built in Atlantic City because the businesses wanted to reduce the amount of sand that visitors tracked in from the beach. The sidewalk remains the longest in all the world, which stretches for six miles. In the late 1800s, there was a candy shop that sold taffy, the store's owner was named David Bradley. In 1883, a significant storm flooded his business, along with many others on the boardwalk. All his taffy was soaked with the Atlantic Ocean's saltwater! A young girl visiting the shop asked if there was any taffy that she could buy. In joking laughter, he offered her some of his

Atlantic City, New Jersey - Waterfront Boardwalk

"saltwater taffy!" After trying a piece, she bought much more to share with friends and family. Turns out, saltwater was an excellent addition to the recipe! Besides candy shops, along the boardwalk are hotels, restaurants, gift shops, and casinos, to name a few.

Saltwater Taffy

Besides Atlantic City and its boardwalk, New Jersey is known for being an industrial town. Also, it is a leading producer of cranberries, blueberries, and tomatoes, which leads to its nickname the "Garden State."

In New Jersey, in 1858, the first, almost complete, dinosaur skeleton in the North American continent was found by a man named William Parker Foulke. He unearthed it in Haddonfield, New Jersey. This dinosaur came to be called Hadrosaurus Foulkii and was the first dinosaur skeleton in the world to be mounted for display.

During the last twenty-five years of the 1800s, inventor Thomas Edison created

Hadrosaurus Foulkii

many devices in his Menlo Park lab. His ideas paved the foundation of some luxuries we enjoy today. They include the phonograph, which allowed a user to record sound and play it back. He was most well known for perfecting the incandescent light bulb utilizing bamboo filament, and he provided a system to distribute electricity for everyone to have! While these were what he was most known for, Edison had more than a thousand patents during his lifetime on his inventions.

A few fun facts on New Jersey... This state is the "Diner Capital of the Country" with an estimated 525 diners! New Jersey had the first baseball game, the first college

Thomas Alva Edison in his laboratory - Public Domain

football game, and the first drive-in movie theater.

Harrisburg, Pennsylvania

Pennsylvania's name means "Penn's Woods" after William Penn's father, Sir William Penn.

William Penn left London to search out a place in the Americas where he could be free to worship without persecution. He was also a writer, early member of the Quakers, and founder of the English North American colony, the Province of Pennsylvania. Under his leadership, the city of Philadelphia was planned and developed as a safe place for his fellow Quakers, becoming one of the original 13 British colonies.

Initially, Pennsylvania's capital was Philadelphia, which also served as the site for the first and second Continental Congresses in 1774 and 1775. The latter Congress produced the Declaration of Independence amid the American Revolution.

After we won our independence from Britain, Pennsylvania ratified the Constitution, becoming the second state in the Union.

Although the patriot and inventor Benjamin Franklin was born in Boston, the city of Philadelphia likes to claim him as one of their own, for he moved there at the age of 17. He worked for Pennsylvania to make many civic improvements, including founding the Library Company of Philadelphia in 1731, which today has accumulated one of the most significant collections of historically valuable manuscripts and printed material in the United States. He also organized the Union Fire Company in 1736, which was also known as the "Bucket Brigade." This was the first

Benjamin Franklin, Public Domain

organized all-volunteer fire company in the colonies. Also, Benjamin Franklin founded the Philadelphia Zoo, the first public zoo in the United States.

The "Bucket Brigade" Union Fire Company in 1736

During an Assembly of the Province of Pennsylvania in 1751, the Speaker ordered to get a 2,000-pound bell from England. He asked that a Bible verse be inscribed "Proclaim LIBERTY throughout all the Land unto all the inhabitants thereof" (Leviticus 25:10).

The bell celebrated the anniversary of William Penn's Charter. The 2,000-pound bell, however, cracked while it was being tested. In its early years, the bell was used to summon lawmakers to legislative sessions and to alert citizens about public meetings and proclamations.

During the American Revolutionary War, on the night of September 18th, 1777, the Patriot soldiers fighting for America against Britain, seized the Liberty Bell because they believed that the British would melt it down for ammunition. Two hundred soldiers in a caravan transported

Liberty Bell, Philadelphia, Pennsylvania

the bell from the Philadelphia State House to the basement of the Zion Reformed Church in Allentown. It remained there until the British left in June of 1778.

The largest city in Pennsylvania is Philadelphia. For a time, it was the capital for Pennsylvania and our nation, until the permanent capital was established in 1800 within Washington, D.C. In Philadelphia, the Declaration of Independence and the U.S. Constitution were signed.

After Philadelphia was the capital of Pennsylvania, then came Lancaster for a short time, and finally Harrisburg.

During the American Civil War, which was fought from 1861 to 1865, the Battle of Gettysburg took place in Pennsylvania. In this battle, the Union led by General George Meade, defeated Confederate General Robert E. Lee. This brought an end to the northern invasion by the Confederacy. This also was the place where President Lincoln gave his famous Gettysburg Address. Visitors from all over come to Pennsylvania to take in a significant amount of American Revolutionary and Civil War history. Monuments that draw in visitors by the thousands each year include Independence Hall and the Liberty Bell.

In 1952 at the University of Pittsburgh, a scientist named Jonas Salk developed the first polio vaccine from the dead polio virus. He first tested it

Artist rendering of President Abraham Lincoln giving the Gettysburg Address

on himself and his family. After which the vaccine was made available nation wide a few years later. His discovery reduced the number of polio cases from nearly 29,000 in 1955 to less than 6,000 in 1957, just two years later.

Here are some fun facts:
The first-ever baseball stadium in the United States was built in Pittsburgh in 1909. A town named Hershey in

Battle of Gettysburg

Pennsylvania is considered to be the Chocolate Capital of the U.S.

The first daily newspaper was published in Philadelphia on September 21st, 1784. Do you know what a newspaper is?

In a town called Hazleton in Pennsylvania, there is a law prohibiting teachers from sipping a carbonated drink while lecturing students in a school auditorium. In Philadelphia, Betsy Ross made the first American flag. The Rockville Bridge in

Modern Day Polio Victims, Public Domain

Harrisburg is the longest stone arch bridge in the world. Pittsburgh is known for manufacturing steel, which lends to the name of their professional football team, the Pittsburgh Steelers. Lillle League Baseball's first World Series was held in 1946 in Williamsport. During the Depression in the 1920-30s, canned goods served as admission to The Star Theater in Mercersburg to help supply the local soup kitchen.

Hershey, Pennsylvania - A little town history! - Public Domain

Dover, Delaware

Of the original 13 colonies, Delaware earned its official state nickname "The First State," by being the first to ratify the Constitution, becoming the first state of the Union. Another nickname refers to Delaware as the "Diamond State," for Thomas Jefferson, spoke about Delaware being a "jewel among the states" as he thought Delaware had an incredibly beautiful coastline.

Rockville Bridge in Harrisburg, Pennsylvania - Public Domain

While this state is the second smallest in the country, it is densely populated, especially in the north, where most people work in various industries. In Delaware, there are only three counties in the whole state! Their names are New Castle, Kent, and Sussex. The entire state is 96 miles long and varies from 9 to 35 miles in width. Can you think of a state that is smaller in the United States?

In 1638, down in the Delaware Valley was located the first European colony established by settlers from Sweden. Between the years 1698 to 1699, descendants of these early settlers built a church called the "Old Swedes Church," which still stands today and is one of the oldest churches still in use.

Bethany Beach, Delaware - Public Domain

After World War II began, many tall observation towers were erected along the coastline to protect the coastal town and bay from German warships. Today, just eleven towers remain.

More than anywhere else in the world, the Delaware Bay serves as the home to horseshoe crabs. These creatures were used by the Native American Indians for fertilizer as well as for food. This practice was taught to the early colonial settlers,

Horseshoe crabs by the thousands on the Delaware seashore

which was then passed down through the generations until the 1960s.

Interestingly, the state of Delaware does not have a National Park System presence: no national parks, seashores, historic sites, battlefields, memorials, or monuments.

A part of an enduring symbol of American pioneers is the log cabin, which originated in Finland. When Finnish settlers came to America, settling in Delaware in the mid-1600s, they brought the log cabin plans. One such log cabin still remains within the Delaware Agricultural Museum in Dover, the capital of Delaware. One man named Thomas Garret gave all he had, losing his entire fortune in the battle against slavery. Over his lifetime, this brave man helped more than 2,000 slaves move through Delaware, which was a vital stop on the Underground Railroad. He worked closely with Harriet Tubman, who is a famous abolitionist. He was sued by a slave owner in Maryland and fined for helping a black family escape.

Thomas Garret, hero of the Underground Railroad

Lesson 3

A Closer Look
at what you have learned so far!

PLUS+
This Lesson's Geography:
Annapolis, Maryland (MD)
Richmond, Virginia (VA)
Charleston, West Virginia (WV)
Raleigh, North Carolina (NC)
Columbia, South Carolina (SC)
Washington, D.C.

Previous Learned Geography:
Montpelier, Vermont (VT)
Albany, New York (NY)
Trenton, New Jersey (NJ)
Harrisburg, Pennsylvania (PA)
Dover, Delaware (DE)
Augusta, Maine (ME)
Concord, New Hampshire (NH)
Boston, Massachusetts (MA)
Providence, Rhode Island (RI)
Hartford, Connecticut (CT)

Hint! The geography found on this page, is also the geography that you will be reviewing this week. Refer to this map as needed when doing your "Memorization Through Repetition" worksheets.

Parent/Teacher: The "A Closer Look" page is intended to show students the accumulated geographic areas taught within their 6-week review period. For additional teaching tips on how to utilize this teaching aide for the different learning levels, please refer to page 1.

Zoom Me In!

Lesson 3

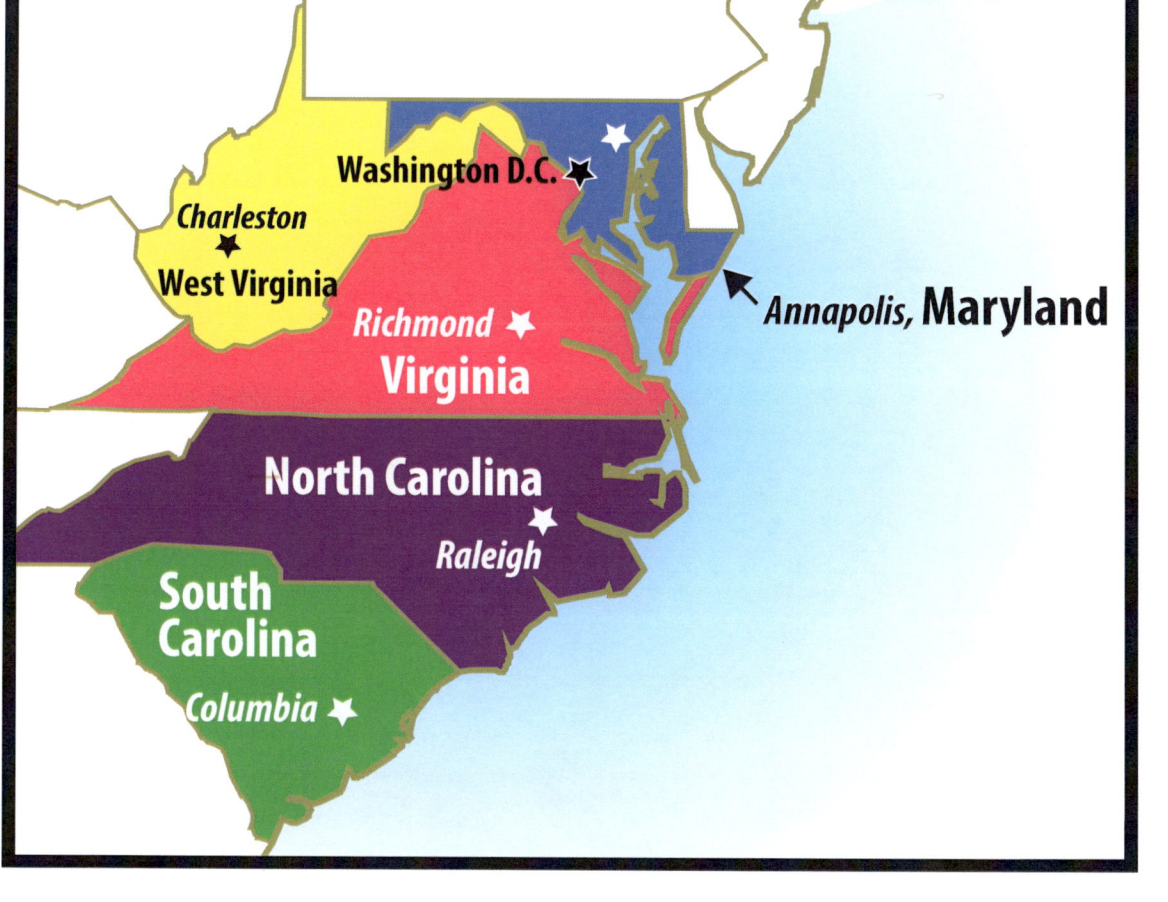

Use this sheet as a reference for this lesson's worksheets. Be sure to practice until you don't have to look!

You are learning your US States & Capitals! This week you are learning:

Annapolis, Maryland (MD)
Richmond, Virginia (VA)
Charleston, West Virginia (WV)
Raleigh, North Carolina (NC)
Columbia, South Carolina (SC)
Washington, D.C.

This Lesson's Geography:
US States and Capitals

Annapolis, Maryland (MD)
Richmond, Virginia (VA)
Charleston, West Virginia (WV)
Raleigh, North Carolina (NC)
Columbia, South Carolina (MS)
Washington D.C.

Tid-Bits

Annapolis, Maryland
St. Mary's City - 1634 An English Colony is founded & America's first Civil War A man named George Calvert was supposed to sail from England to America, to create a settlement north of the Potomac River. He was the first Lord Baron of Balti-

Cecilius Calvert, Lord Baron II of Baltimore

more and he had applied for a royal charter from the King of England, of which he was granted the rights to the land east of the Potomac River by King Charles I in 1632. This royal charter was given with an agreement that profit from the land would be shared with the King. However, before a settlement could get underway, George Calvert died in London. His son Cecilius Calvert, the second Lord Baron of Baltimore, took up his father's cause, seeking to establish the area as a safe

Replica of the ship, the "Dove" that the first settlers of St. Mary's City arrived on.

place for Catholics to worship without persecution, as they felt in England. These first settlers arrived at the shore of a small island called St. Calvert on two small ships named "Ark" and "Dove" in March of 1634. A mix of both Protestants and Roman Catholics were aboard. Unfortunately, this mix led to religious conflict and political power struggles that eventually brought the two sides into a civil war. Over the next 50-60 years, continued struggles between the Catholics and Protestants (also referred to Anglicans) persisted. In the mid to late 1680s, following the rise of a Protestant monarchy in England, people against the Catholic government in Maryland overthrew them and took power. Lord Baron of Baltimore lost his ability to govern the province. Maryland was then designated as a royal province of Britain. That is, until 1715 when Benedict Calvert, the 4th Lord Baron of Baltimore, was granted rights to the land and leadership over the province. This change was due to his long Baltimore family line and his conversion to Anglicanism, which was England's official religion. However, before the Baltimores regained their rights to the land, in 1695, the royal Governor, Francis Nicholson, moved the government from St. Mary's City

Lesson 3

(where the Baltimore family reigned - the first settlement) to Ann Arundell Town. He renamed the town to Annapolis after Princess Anne, who later became Queen Anne of Great Britain. Today, Annapolis remains the capital of Maryland. The original colony of St. Mary's City now serves as an archaeological site with a small tourist center.

The original settlement of St. Mary's City

Maryland and their "Assembly of Freemen" and the America's Revolution
Generations later, Maryland entered the Revolutionary period, where Americans called Patriots were fighting to be free of England's rule. However, Maryland was initially against declaring independence.

The eighth session of their convention called "Assembly of Freemen," which assembled to govern Maryland, convened July 3rd, 1776. During this convention, Maryland concluded that they needed their first state constitution, which should not refer to Parliament or the King of England. It would, however, be a constitution that would be "of the people only." On August 1st, 1776, the Assembly of Freemen gathered once more. This ninth and final convention was also known as the Constitutional Convention of 1776, where they drafted Maryland's state constitution. When they adjourned the convention on November 11th, there was no need to meet again. The "Assembly of Freemen" conventions were replaced by the Maryland Constitution of 1776. A new government had been established. Thomas Johnson was their first elected governor.

During the American Revolution, many people from Maryland joined the fight against England. After Maryland ratified the "Articles of Confederation and Perpetual Union," and the "U.S. Constitution" on April 28th, 1788, Maryland became the seventh state to join the Union.

In 1791, Maryland gave land to form a portion of the District of Columbia. This district is referred to as Washington D.C. and now serves as the nation's capital.

Chesapeake Bay, Maryland

Francis Scott Key and The Star Spangled Banner during The War of 1812
Our beloved "Star-Spangled Banner" is the national anthem of the United States. This song was written by a man from Maryland named Francis Scott Key, who was a 35-year-old lawyer and apparently, a poet! He wrote this poem on September 14th, 1814, while watching Fort McHenry in Baltimore Harbor being attacked by the Royal Navy of Britain during the War of 1812. He was inspired by the large U.S. flag, with 15 stars and 15 stripes, known as the Star-Spangled Banner, flying triumphantly above the fort during the U.S. victory. The War of 1812 was between America and Britain once again. We fought to ensure our liberty from Britain's tyranny.

Civil War, Chesapeake Bay, and the National Aquarium
During the American Civil War, which was fought between 1861 and 1865, Maryland remained part of the Union. During that period, some Marylanders owned slaves. A few Maryland men joined the Southern cause and fought against the Union.

Maryland's nickname is the "Old Line State." This comes from the American Revolutionary War troops from Maryland that was referred to as the Maryland Line. A second nickname is "Little America," for the land has several different terrains, including mountains, beaches, sand dunes, farmland, forests, and more!

One of Maryland's most notable features is the Chesapeake Bay. This large body of saltwater partially separates the state

Francis Scott Key, Author of the "Star Spangled Banner"

The original flag upon which Francis Scott Key gazed while writing his famous poem that became our national anthem - The Star Spangled Banner

O! SAY CAN YOU SEE, BY THE DAWN'S EARLY LIGHT,
WHAT SO PROUDLY WE HAIL'D AT THE TWILIGHT'S LAST GLEAMING,
WHOSE BROAD STRIPES AND BRIGHT STARS THROUGH THE PERILOUS FIGHT
O'ER THE RAMPARTS WE WATCH'D WERE SO GALLANTLY STREAMING!
AND THE ROCKETS' RED GLARE, THE BOMBS BURSTING IN AIR,
GAVE PROOF THROUGH THE NIGHT THAT OUR FLAG WAS STILL THERE;
O! SAY, DOES THAT STAR-SPANGLED BANNER YET WAVE,
O'ER THE LAND OF THE FREE, AND THE HOME OF THE BRAVE?

from the south to the north. In this bay, fishermen catch more blue crabs than any other U.S. state. In fact, during lunch at the Chesapeake Bay, more crab cakes are sold than hamburgers and hot-dogs combined!

An attraction for locals and visitors alike is the National Aquarium in Baltimore. The aquarium displays over 750 species in 2.2 million gallons of water. They also have interactions between trainers and dolphins for all to see!

Richmond, Virginia

Virginia was one of the original 13 colonies. Virginia has the nickname "Mother of Presidents" because eight men who became president were born in Virginia. Virginia became the 10th state to ratify the Constitution, at a vote on June 25th, 1788.

Jamestown, John Smith, and Pocahontas

Virginia's capital is Richmond, which began as a village of the Powhatan Confederacy, and was initially settled by English colonists in Jamestown beginning in 1607. The Powhatan Confederacy was a union of over 30 Algonquian speaking Native American tribes that resided in the Chesapeake Bay, within both Virginia and Southern Maryland. This confederation provided military support and paid tributes to its powerful chief, Powhatan. Powhatan had a daughter named Pocahontas. She is notable for her association with the Jamestown colony and for saving the life of colonist and explorer, John Smith.

Captain John Smith and a hundred others sailed to the coast of Virginia in April 1607. There they built a fort on the James River. There were friendly as well as hostile encounters with Indians of the area. One such meeting was led by a close relative of Powhatan's, where they captured John Smith while he was exploring the Chickahominy River. John Smith describes the account differently in different communications with England, stating initially "that there was a great feast followed by a long talk with Powhatan." In a separate report, many years later, Smith wrote that his capture wasn't at

Pocahontas saves the life of John Smith - By New England Chromo. Lith. Co. circa 1870
Library of Congress, Prints & Photographs Division, Public Domain

all friendly and that there was a threat to his life. He stated, "at the minute of my execution, she (Pocahontas) hazarded the beating out of her own brains to save mine; and not only that but so prevailed with her father, that I was safely conducted to Jamestown." Many years after the death of Pocahontas, Smith explained that he was captured and taken to the paramount chief. Where "two great stones were brought before Powhatan. Then as many, as could lay hands on him, dragged him to them, and thereon laid his head, and being ready with their clubs, to beat out his brains, Pocahontas the Kings dearest daughter, when no treaty could prevail, got his head in her arms, and laid her own upon his to save him from death." Early accounts establish that Pocahontas became friends with John Smith and the Jamestown colony. History tells us that she went to the settlement often to play games with the boys. She also helped the colony survive starvation by bringing them enough food to get through hard times.

As colonists continued to enlarge their settlement, the Powhatans began to feel that their lands were being threatened. This brought about conflicts. In the summer of 1609, the First Anglo-Powhatan War began. The Powhatans had captured many colonists and plundered their posses-

Painted by John Gadsby Chapman, "The Baptism of Pocahontas" 1840
A copy is on display in the Rotunda of the US Capitol, Public Domain

sions. In response, the colonists felt that they need to take drastic action. In a treaty with a tribe that didn't like Powhatan, they plotted to trick Pocahontas into boarding a ship. They held her for ransom, demanding the release of colonial prisoners and the return of various stolen weapons and tools. For the love of his daughter, Powhatan returned the prisoners. However, he kept a number of weapons. A long standoff ensued, during which the colonists kept Pocahontas captive.

During her year-long captivity, she was held at Henricus in Chesterfield County, Virginia. Little is known about her life there, although we know that a minister, Alexander Whitaker, taught Pocahontas about Christianity and

helped her improve her English. Upon her baptism, she took the Christian name "Rebecca." During that year, she also met John Rolfe. Rolfe was an English-born man who had a wife and child that had died on the way to Virginia after the wreck of the ship Sea Venture. He was a pious man and Pocahontas had accepted the Christian faith. In a long letter to the governor requesting permission to wed her, expressed his love for Pocahontas. He wrote that his desire to marry Pocahontas was for the good of his plantation, the honor of our country, Glory of God, and for salvation. He wrote, "Pocahontas, to whom my hearty and best thoughts are, and have been a long time so entangled, and enthralled in so intricate a labyrinth that I was even a-wearied to unwind myself thereout." The couple was married

on April 5th, 1614, and had a single son named Thomas, born in January 1615.

In March 1614, a standoff escalated to a violent confrontation between hundreds of colonists and Powhatan men on the Pamunkey River. The colonists encountered a group of senior Indian leaders at Powhatan's capital of Matchcot. The colonists allowed Pocahontas to talk to her tribe when Powhatan arrived, and she reportedly rebuked him for valuing her "less than old swords, pieces, or axes." She said that she preferred to live with the colonists "who loved her."

Pocahantas went back to live with her husband. Their marriage created a peaceful relationship between the colony of Jamestown and Powhatan people. The era is marked as the "Peace of Pocahontas," lasting eight years. For the Powhatan people, this marriage was controversial, for their princess had married a commoner. In March 1617, Rolfe and Pocahontas were on a trip returning to

Virginia after a visit with John Smith in London. They sailed briefly on the river Thames when Pocahontas became very sick. She was taken ashore and sadly passed away. Pocahontas was only about 21 years old.

The Jamestown settlement flourished for nearly a hundred years as the capital of the Virginia colony. When the capital moved to Williamsburg in 1699, Jamestown became abandoned.

Thomas Jefferson & the Virginia Statute for Religious Freedom
Thomas Jefferson, a founding father of our great nation, wrote the Virginia Statute for Religious Freedom. The Virginia Statute for Religious Freedom is a proclamation of freedom of conscience as well as the principle of separation of church and state. This legislation was passed by the Virginia General Assembly on January 16th,

Colonial Jamestown About 1614
By Sidney King, Public Domain

1786, and served as the basis for the Constitution's protections for freedom of religion.

Virginia & The American Civil War

The American Civil War was between the United States of America and the Confederate States of America. A collection of eleven southern states that left the Union in 1860 and 1861.

On April 4th, 1861, Virginia held a state convention to address the issue of seceding from the Union. The vote to secede failed to pass, but not for long. Eleven days later, opinion shifted when President Abraham Lincoln ordered troops to put down the rebellion of the states that had seceded and joined the fight against the north in the American Civil War, effectively seceding from the Union and becoming a state within the Confederacy. However, not everyone in Virginia felt the same. Fifty counties in Virginia responded by creating a Union-based state government of their own in Wheeling, Virginia. An act passed in Congress confirmed that West Virginia was now a state of their own and forevermore separated from Virginia. Virginia was the only state to experience a consequence of land loss during the war.

Initially, the capital for the Confederate States was in Montgomery, Alabama. However, many believed that Virginia's capital was critical to their survival. Thus, they moved the Confederacy capital to Richmond, Virginia. Many

General Ulysses S. Grant of the Union Army, Public Domain

battles were fought in Virginia in defense of Richmond.

After four bloody years of conflict and over 600,000 dead soldiers, the United States defeated the Confederate States with the surrender of the Commander of the Confederate Army, Robert E. Lee, to General Ulysses S. Grant at the Appomattox Courthouse in Virginia. Afterward, the rebellious states were readmitted to the Union, and the institution of slavery was abolished nationwide.

West Virginia

Beautiful West Virginia has, like so many other states, a vibrant and intriguing history, especially in how

Commander of the Confederate Army, Robert E. Lee, Public Domain

they came to be a state. You've learned that the land now called West Virginia was apportioned to the English Virginia colony in the 1600s until the end of the American Revolutionary War. Then, after independence was won from Britain, Virginia became a state.

John Brown's Revolt
Nearly a hundred years later, in 1859, a town in Virginia called Harpers Ferry was the site of John Brown's raid on the federal armory. Brown's plan was to arm as many enslaved men as possible with guns and ammunition for a revolt. Together they captured the city, cutting off railroad bridges, and securing the federal arsenal of weapons. Soon, John Brown was surrounded by federal troops that were led by Lieutenant Colonel Robert E. Lee. Brown was arrested, tried for treason, found guilty and hanged. While Brown's plans ultimately failed, the raid contributed significantly to the coming of civil war as it succeeded in fueling a fear of slave rebellions. This brought an increasing tension between the North and the South.

Slavery
The North's economy relied on various industries, whereas the South primarily depended on growing crops. These crops required workers to sow the seeds, pluck the cotton, and various other duties. These workers were not paid; they were owned like property, and called slaves. Because they were considered property, the property owners could treat them however they wished, good or bad.

John Brown, Public Domain

TREASON!

All TRUE CHRISTIANS who believe in "Immortality through Jesus Christ alone," are requested to pray for

CAPT. JOHN BROWN.

who now is under sentence of death, and is to be hung next month for righteousness sake, and doing justly with his fellow man, his country and his God.

By request of one who loves the Truth, and feels for the man that is to die a martyr to it.   J.

Somersworth, Nov. 4, 1859.

"Treason" Broadside, 1859 November 4th - By unattributed, Somersworth - Executive Papers of Virginia Governor Henry A. Wise, 1856-1859. Accession 36710. State Government Records Collection, The Library of Virginia, Richmond, Va., Public Domain

There were laws called "Slave Codes" that governed how the slave owner's property was dealt with. For an extensive article covering how slaves were treated, and the rights of the property owners go to:

https://bit.ly/ TreatmentOfSlaves

Teacher/Parental Caution: Some content in the article may be unsuitable for your students/children. However, the material can be filtered to teach what is appropriate based on your discretion.

When Virginia changed their minds and voted to secede from the Union during the Civil War, the people in the north and northwest Virginia disagreed with their decision. They were called Unionists. They began a plan to leave Virginia. Both the Union and the Confederacy wanted control of the region, for there were railroads that connected Washington, D.C. and Ohio that could be utilized to move troops and weapons. The Unionists worked on writing a new constitution that

included an anti-slavery clause, and on June 20th, 1863, President Abraham Lincoln and Congress admitted West Virginia to the United States.

Adena People, The Mound Builders

Moving back in time, there were the mound builders. Between 250 and 150 BC, the Adena people built the Grave Creek Mound and the Criel Mound, among others. The Grave Creek Mound was found in Marshal County in West Virginia. A circular mound 240 feet across and 62 feet tall. This conical mound serves as an ancient burial ground that is the largest in the United States. While hunting in the area in 1770, a man named Joseph Tomlinson happened upon the mound. Later, he and his brother built a log cabin 300 feet nearby. Thirty-three years later, Meriwether Lewis wrote about the mound in his journal when he saw it in 1803 on his way to meet with his friend William Clark in Louisville, Kentucky. Upon their meeting, they would head out on an adventure to explore the Louisiana Purchase and beyond. All those that knew about the mound didn't know what was buried in there until 1838. The nephew of the original landowner who built his cabin nearby, Abelard Tomlinson and his brother-in-law, excavated the mound. At approximately 111 feet in, they found the first of four burial chambers with skeletons and jewelry.

GRAVE CREEK MOUND
This world-famous burial mound was built by the Adena people sometime before the Christian Era. The mound was originally 69 feet high, 295 feet in diameter, and was encircled by a moat. There were many mounds in the area—hence the city's name: Moundsville. In 1838, the Grave Creek Mound was tunnelled into and two log tombs with several burials and grave offerings were found.

WEST VIRGINIA HISTORIC COMMISSION, 1961

Once the excavation of the mound was complete, they expanded the lower chamber and created a museum inside the mound. That was abandoned in 1847. In 1964, the Grave Creek Mound was declared a National Historic Landmark. Over the next years, approximately 450,000 relics were transferred to a local museum for all to learn from.

Greenbrier History

During World War II, an upscale resort in the Allegheny Mountains called "The Greenbrier" served to detain diplomats from Germany, Italy, and Japan. They were kept until American diplomats were returned home safely in exchange. Shortly after that, in 1942, the U.S. Army purchased the hotel, converting it into a hospital where more than 24,000 soldiers were cared for.

First Amendment Rights

In 1942, West Virginia passed a law requiring teachers and their students to recite the Pledge of Allegiance while saluting the American flag. This created a problem for Walter Barnette, who was a practicing Jehovah's Witness. He refused to obey this law, stating that it went against his religious beliefs. For this, he was expelled from school. On June 14th, 1943, it was ruled by the U.S. Supreme Court in West Virginia that forcing citizens to salute the United States flag and recite the pledge was in violation of their freedom of

The Greenbrier Resort, West Virginia - Public Domain

speech and religion, which is guaranteed in the First Amendment to the Constitution of the United States.

U.S. Constitution First Amendment states:

"Congress shall make no law respecting an establishment of religion, or prohibiting the free exercise thereof; or abridging the freedom of speech, or of the press; or the right of the people peaceably to assemble, and to petition the government for a redress of grievances."

Bridge Day In West Virginia, there is a bridge called "New River Gorge Bridge." This bridge spans 1,700 feet and is the longest steel arch bridge in the Western Hemisphere. During October on the third Saturday, the people host a festival on the bridge, called "Bridge Day!" Traffic is shut down, and a celebration is thrown. Hundreds of base and bungee jumpers plunge 876 feet down to the river bank below! This event hosts close to 100,000 visitors each year!

Western Hemisphere In case you were wondering what the term Western Hemisphere means, it is a geographical reference for the half of Earth, which lies west of the prime meridian and east of the anti-meridian. Can you find these meridian lines to locate the Western Hemisphere? Get your globe or map out! Hint: The Prime Meridian is located at 0 degrees Longitude, going through the western portion of Europe and west Africa.

Coal Wars West Virginia is a major coal-producing state, supplying 15 percent of the nation's coal. During the Civil War, the region had just a few active coal mines. However, the coal mining industry grew substantially

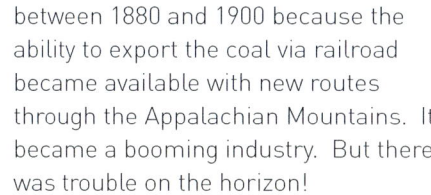
Bridge Day, West Virginia - Public Domain

West Virginian Coal Miners - Public Domain

between 1880 and 1900 because the ability to export the coal via railroad became available with new routes through the Appalachian Mountains. It became a booming industry. But there was trouble on the horizon!

From 1912 to 1921, the West Virginia coal wars were fought between the coal companies and their employees. The employees mined the coal and felt unfairly treated for the work they performed. They desired better pay and better work conditions. They wanted the right to buy food and supplies where they pleased, not having to buy from the coal mining companies that had a monopoly on them. Also, they demanded that the coal mining companies recognize and accept the workers as a single voice within a union. Their union was called the United Mine Workers (UMW).

Well, the coal mining companies didn't take these demands well. The employees decided to strike. In response, the coal mining companies hired guards armed with rifles to guard the entrances to the mines. The coal companies also threw their employees out of the housing that they rented to them. With nowhere to go, the miners moved into coal camps that were being supported by their union. About 35,000 miners resided in these camps. Conflict and hostile feelings began to get worse with the arrival of the guards that teased and taunted the strikers. The Socialist Party activists supplied the miners with thousands of weapons. Then, about 6,000 miners declared their intent to destroy the companies and kill the guards. On

Armed Coal Miners, Public Domain

September 1st, 1912, the miners were armed and ready for war. In response to this threat, the coal companies hired more armed guards. Thankfully, West Virginia's Governor declared martial law to be in effect. One day later, the government seized 1,872 rifles, 556 pistols, 6 machine guns, 225,000 rounds of ammunition, 480 blackjacks (a weighted bludgeoning weapon), many daggers, bayonets, and brass knuckles. This held off the inevitable.

"There was a time when many U.S. children toiled in factories for 70 hours a week, until child labor laws went into effect in the 1900s. In 1924, Congress proposed a constitutional amendment prohibiting child labor, but the states did not ratify it. Then, in 1938, Congress passed the Fair Labor Standards Act." Source: scholastic.com

Eight years later, on May 19th, 1920, tensions erupted between the armed guards and local miners that sparked what became known as the Battle of Blair Mountain. From August 20th, 1921, miners began rallying together. On August 24th, between 5,000 and 20,000 miners began marching towards Logan County. The local sheriff had gathered together a fighting force of approximately 2,000 county police, state police, state militia, and armed guards to stop the miners. On August 25th, the war began. The sheriff's men were equipped with machine guns and rented aircraft, from which they dropped bombs on the attacking miners.

On August 30th, 1921, President Warren G. Harding declared martial law for the entire state of West Virginia and sent 2,500 federal troops that arrived on September 2nd. Knowing that they were now facing a large, well equipped and trained force, the miners surrendered.

West Virginian Coal Camps Public Domain

Around 550 miners and labor activists were convicted of murder, insurrection, and treason for their participation in the Battle of Blair Mountain. This battle was the largest insurrection within the United States since the

President Warren G. Harding

American Civil War.

Raleigh, North Carolina

On the western side that borders Tennessee, North Carolina is covered with a couple major Appalachian ranges, including the Blue Ridge Mountains and the Great Smokies. Moving easterly to central North Carolina, the landscape turns into beautifully forested rolling hills. However, the largest region is a coastal plain, where the summers are warm, and the people enjoy mild winters. Off the coast, at the outer edge of Pamlico Sound, is a long chain of islands known as the Outer Banks.

As one of the original 13 states of the Union, North Carolina has, along with the others, a rich history filled with challenges, mistakes, triumph and sadness.

The Lost Colony
When European

settlers first arrived in present-day North Carolina, the largest group of Native Americans was the Cherokee Nation. In the warm summer month of August 1587, the first British colony in North America was established. This colony is shrouded by mystery, the oldest, most intriguing unsolved mystery indeed. A ship sailed with about 115 colonists from Plymouth, England, landing on Roanoke Island off the coast of North Carolina. There, shortly after their arrival, a baby girl was born. Her name was Virginia Dare, the first child born of English parents in America. Virginia Dare's grandfather was named John White, and served as the governor of the new colony. Later that same year, he sailed back to England to gather supplies for the colony, leaving his daughter and granddaughter behind. Some speculate that he would not have gone if he knew what was happening across the vast ocean. Upon his arrival to England, a major naval war had broken out between England and Spain. Queen Elizabeth I called on every available vessel to go to battle with the Spanish Armada. Three years passed, and finally, in August of 1590, John White made his long-awaited journey back to his family and colony. But

Cape Hatteras, North Carolina - Public Domain

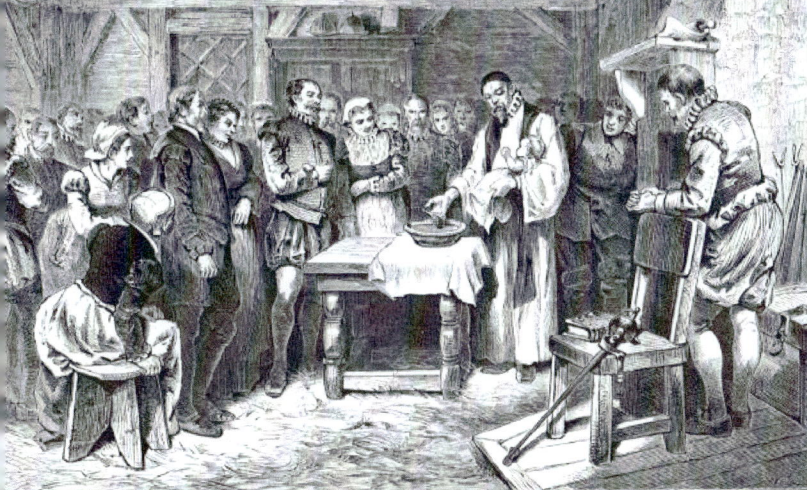
Baptism of Virginia Dare, wood-engraving, 1880 - By William Ludwell Sheppard, Public Domain

what he found was not what he expected. What he found was devastating. There was simply no trace of the colony. No family, no settlement, no daughter, no 3-year-old granddaughter, Virginia. There was a clue. A clue that would lead nowhere except unprovable theories. A single word "Croatoan," carved into a wooden post.

This site became known as the "Lost Colony of Roanoke." Investigations into the unknown fate of these people have continued over the centuries. No one has solved the mystery. "Croatoan" was the name of a local island just south of Roanoke and a Native American tribe had the same name. It is speculated that whatever happened to the colonists was directly related to the tribe. Another says that they attempted to sail back to England and perished along the way either by being swallowed by the sea or sunk down at the hands of the Spanish Armada. Other theories exist, but the mystery continues.

Colonial North Carolina Ratifies the U.S. Constitution

In 1663, Britain granted the Carolina region to eight Englishmen, making North Carolina a royal colony in 1729. During the American Revolutionary War, in 1775, the colony of North Carolina was the first to vote in favor of declaring independence from Great Britain.

With the beginning of the American Revolution, people in North Carolina were divided on the issue. Those that supported independence were called Patriots. Those that sided with Britain

The Lost Colony, design by William Ludwell Sheppard, engraving by William James Linton. - Public Domain

were called Loyalists. North Carolina ratified the U.S. Constitution and joined the Union as the 12th state in 1789.

Cherokee Trail of Tears
At the onset of the 1830s, about 125,000 Native American Indians lived their lives, raised their families, and cultivated their land for food on millions of acres in Georgia, Tennessee, Alabama, North Carolina, and Florida. This land had been lived on by the Indians for hundreds of generations. White settlers wanted to grow cotton on the Indians' land. The federal government, under the Indian Removal Act imposed by Andrew Jackson, forced the Indians to abandon their homelands, walking thousands of miles to "Indian territory" that was designated by the U.S. government across the Mississippi River. This treacherous and deadly journey is known as the Trail of Tears.

(Read more about the Trail of Tears in Lesson 4)

Slavery and the Civil War
With the lands available, North Carolina developed an extensive plantation system based on slave labor. After 1835 their economy was booming! They became a leading exporter of tobacco and cotton.

North Carolina, along with other southern states, had created an economy that depended on slavery. Despite this, North Carolina was not quick to join the Confederacy before the American Civil War. Out of the eleven states, they were tenth to secede, which happened after the war began. North Carolina was responsible for sending more soldiers to fight than any other Confederate state, although very few battles were fought within the state.

Reconstruction of the Southern States
The Civil War began on April 12th, 1861, and after concluding on April 9th, 1865, a different kind of war began. Reconstruction of the southern states was at hand. This meant reintegrating the southern states into the Union as well as 4 million newly freed black Americans. While this primarily had to do with the reconstruction of the South in terms of economy, this was a social reconstruction. People's hearts and minds were rooted deeply in their way of life, in the form of superiority over black people.

While the Civil War goal was clear, and the 13th Amendment made slaves free, a plan

Cunne Shote, the Indian chief, a great warrior of the Cherokee Nation. - The Miriam and Ira D. Wallach Division of Art, Prints and Photographs: Print Collection, The New York Public Library. 1750 - 1799.

for reconstruction didn't fully exist. On April 11th, 1865, President Abraham Lincoln gave a speech regarding reconstruction in Louisiana, mentioning that some blacks should have the right to vote. He referred to those that were already free, and those that enlisted to fight for the freedom of all. Three days later, Abraham Lincoln was assassinated, and Vice President Johnson was sworn into office as our seventeenth President. During the years that Johnson was President, he believed that the states needed to run reconstruction at the state level. Unfortunately, this didn't work out well. Left to themselves, the South put in

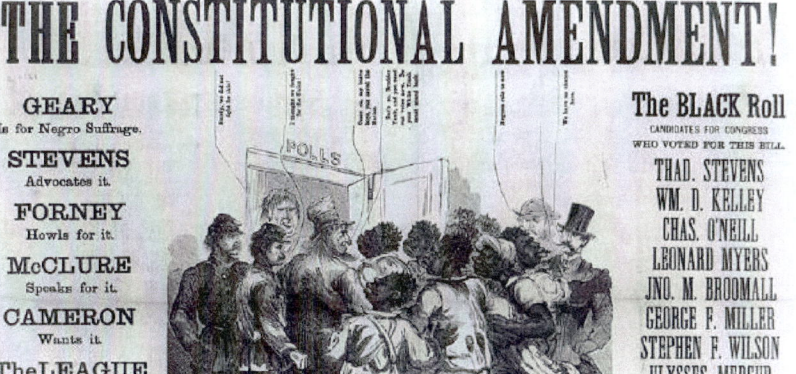

place laws called "black codes" that restricted ex-slaves' activities and ensured their availability as a labor force.

This angered the North, and Congress worked to pass legislation to hold the states accountable to a higher standard of reconstruction. Johnson vetoed just about everything the Congress put forth. Congress then worked to override the vetoes, which they successfully did 15 out of 21 times. In fact, Johnson was the most thwarted

President of all time. Despite Johnson's best efforts to allow the states to govern themselves, the "Radical Republicans" in Congress crafted their own Reconstruction Plan, placing southern states under martial law and passing other legislation to restrict the powers of the President. In February 1868, Johnson moved to dismiss Secretary of War Edwin M. Stanton without Senate approval. This violated the Tenure of Office Act, which had been passed by Radical Republicans a year earlier, vetoed by Johnson, and then overridden by Congress. Stanton's dismissal triggered impeachment proceedings, and the House voted to convict Johnson on eleven articles of impeachment.

The combination of Congress' control of the reconstruction plan and the election of Radical Republican and former Civil War General Ulysses S. Grant, brought about necessary changes that would lead the South into a dark and turbulent era. With the Reconstruction Act of 1867, the South was temporarily divided into five military districts and given the structure to govern each state's organization of the black male suffrage. This law required southern states to ratify the 14th Amendment before they could rejoin the Union. The 14th

17th U.S. President Andrew Johnson By Mathew Brady - c. 1870-1880, Library of Congress, Public Domain

Amendment redefined citizenship by granting "equal protection" for all under the Constitution, including former slaves. Also, Congress approved the 15th Amendment, guaranteeing that a citizen's suffrage would not be refused "on account of race, color, or previous condition of servitude."

The "Radical Republican's" Reconstruction Plan had a progressive effect on southern society - that is, initially. African Americans were elected to state governments in the South and to the U.S. Congress during this period. The South created the first state-funded public school systems, laws against racial discrimination in public transport, and more. Despite conforming for a brief time, change of heart towards equality was not widespread.

This was evident as many southern whites became violent in response to the reconstruction that was so revolutionary to their previous way of life. Groups such as the Klu Klux Klan targeted both black and white Republican leaders, as well as other blacks who challenged white people's authority. Federal legislation was passed aiming at these types of supremacist groups during the administration of President Ulysses S. Grant in 1871, as they were interfering with black suffrage and other civil rights. However, white supremacy gradually tightened its hold on the South just a few short years later. Racism dangerously persisted, and the eradication has proven to be a slow and painful progression across generations. **(More coming on the Civil Rights movement with Reverend Doctor Martin Luther King, Jr. in Lesson 4).**

By now, you have heard the word suffrage. In case you don't know what it means: it means the right to vote. The 15th Amendment made it so all men, regardless of race, color, or previous condition of servitude, can vote. Women at this time did not have suffrage. What does that mean? If you said that at this time in history, women cannot vote, you would be right!

Taking Flight Two clever, and mechanically inclined young brothers named Orville and Wilbur Wright, once dreamed of machines with the power of controlled flight!

These two brothers, originally from Dayton, Ohio, took up aeronautics for fun in 1896, also carrying out their work in North Carolina. In this letter (below), Orville Wright describes the most exciting and significant event in the process leading up to the historic first flight on December 17th, 1903 in Kitty Hawk, a seaside town in North Carolina:

Ku-Klux-Klan (KKK) - Public Domain

"Our experiments at Kitty Hawk in 1901 proved conclusively to us that the tables of air pressure then in existence were entirely unreliable. From this we were led into the designing and construction of a wind tunnel and apparatus to be used in the tunnel for measuring the lift and drift and the center of pressure on airfoils This was in the Fall and Winter of 1901-02... Our early experiments at Kitty Hawk were conducted for the purpose of developing a method of maintaining equilibrium in the air and also to learn something about soaring flight. It was from reading accounts of Lilienthal's experiments that we became interested in this.

Reconstruction Era Illustration representing black mens suffrage - Entitled "The First Vote" - Printed in Harper's Weekly - Public Domain

43

At Kitty Hawk we had the opportunity of witnessing daily the soaring flight of buzzards, fish and chicken hawks, and eagles. Attempts to imitate their flights without a motor have not been very successful, although in 1902 and 1903 we made a dozen or more flights in which we remained in the air for a minute with no, or scarcely any descent; and in 1901, Mr. Alex Ogilvie and I continued the soaring experiments at Kitty Hawk and succeeded in making a number of flights of more than five minutes duration (the longest of which was nine and three-quarter minutes) without any loss of height at all. In many cases we landed at a higher point than the one from which we started. I see no reason why flights of several hours duration cannot be made without use of a motor. But, of course, these flights

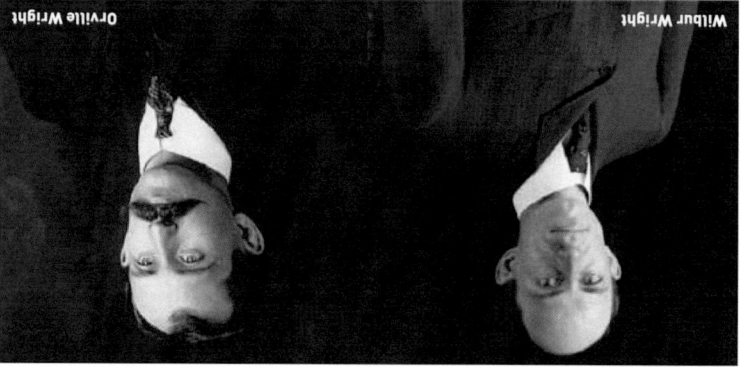

Wilbur Wright   Orville Wright

The Wright Brothers - Public Domain

must be made in rising trends of air — a condition required by all birds for soaring flight.

The most remarkable example of soaring that I have ever seen was witnessed by Wilbur and myself near Kitty Hawk in 1900. The remarkable feature of the flight was in the intelligence or the instinct of the birds which led them to create for themselves a soaring condition where it did not already exist. One morning after a cold night we saw a number of buzzards, probably fifteen in number, and several fish hawks, begin by flapping their wings vigorously and flying together in a small circle, not more than fifty or seventy-five feet in diameter, at a height of twenty-five or thirty feet from the ground. They all kept well together in the circle, gradually working upward. When at an altitude of approximately fifty feet they suddenly quit flapping and ground, which was a

stratum of air immediately above the ground. The warm sun had no doubt created a warm stratum of air of an aeroplane. The angle of the buzzard is not better than that fact the gliding altitude. In all lost circle they leaving the After line, straight a in off gliding each separate, thousand feet began to about one they reached an altitude of When they spread out into larger circles. The birds through concerted action made an opening through the cold stratum above and started a rush of warm air upward, and then used this upward rush of air to gain altitude.

As you can tell, not only were the Wright brothers mechanically inclined, they also had to rely on their obser-

"Wright Brothers' 1903 Machine." The New York Public Library Digital Collections. 1860 - 1920.

The Miriam and Ira D. Wallach Division of Art, Prints and Photographs: Photography Collection,

rose higher as they wings. station- ary then rose rapidly

"Wright brothers gliding at Kitty Hawk, N.C. 1900-1903." The New York Public Library Digital Collections. Public Domain.

The Miriam and Ira D. Wallach Division of Art, Prints and Photographs: Photography Collection,

vations of their environment - specifically, of birds, the air, and even temperature. You see, what the Wright brothers observed in these birds, was that they changed the angle of the tips of their wings to make their bodies roll right or left. This was a crucial insight into their success.

And, on December 17th, 1903, the Wright brothers first-ever piloted-and-powered-airplane-flight made history. As they took off from a cliff near Kitty Hawk, their flying machine went for about 120 feet and lasted in the air only 12 seconds. While we've come a long way since then in the science of flight, we have the Wright brothers to thank for being the first brave men to achieve this feat. So when you get on an airplane and fly up into the great blue beyond, remember to think about the Wright brothers that first learned to fly high in the sky!

Columbia, South Carolina

Native Americans, Settlers, and the American Revolutionary War

Native American tribes, including the Cherokee, the Catawba, and the Yamasee, lived in the region when Europeans arrived. The first permanent English colony was Charles Town, which was settled in 1670. In 1729, the territory was divided into North Carolina and South Carolina.

In this region, planters prospered during the colonial period, but by 1775, the people of South Carolina were unhappy being ruled by Britain. They joined with other British colonies fighting against England for their independence in the American Revolutionary War. Many of the war's battles were fought in South Carolina.

The Antebellum Era -
America was a young nation that had structure within the Constitution. Still, tensions were developing that was culturally and economically separating entire regions, namely, the north and the south. South Carolina, since the beginning of America, has had consistent disagreements with the federal government. The time called the Antebellum Era, best describes how this nation became divided, leading to the Civil War.

The Cotton Gin and Slave Labor -
The Antebellum Era begins after the War of 1812, lasting until the Civil War. Just before and during the Antebellum Era, South Carolina's economy and the population grew. The southern states, including South Carolina, had cotton plantations which were worked by slave labor. Then, in 1794, cotton became, not just important, but the most important crop. Why this change? After Eli Whitney invented the cotton engine, more commonly referred to as the "cotton gin," the ability to separate the raw cotton from the seeds was ten times faster than done by hand. The cotton gin revolutionized the cotton industry, and suddenly, cotton became a very profitable crop. This meant more plantations, more cotton to pick, and more slave hands needed for picking it.

While Eli Whitney may not have intended his cotton gin to lead to more slavery, the number of slaves rose by 70%. In the south, including South Carolina, the 1790 census reported that there were 697,897 slaves. By 1810, there were 1.2 million. Historians believe that the cotton gin in large part, inadvertently led to the Civil War because of the economic dependency on slave labor. **(More on the Eli Whitney and his legacy in Lesson 4)**

Nullification of the U.S. Constitution
Years go by, and in 1828 and again in

"Antebellum" is a Latin word that means "before the war." The Antebellum Era in America is marked by the cultural and economic separation of the northern and southern regions, the westward expansion of the nation, and a spirit of reform. The Antebellum Era are the years between the War of 1812 and the Civil War, 1815-1860.

1832, Congress passed two high Tariffs on British goods. This helped the north, as it discouraged buying from Britain and encouraged buying from U.S. manufacturers, which were located in the north. In the south, however, these Tariffs were difficult to pay, creating hardship and negative feelings towards the federal government, which they believed was favoring the north.

South Carolina had advocates that wanted more control at the state level, limiting the

Cotton Plantation, Adobe Stock, by Mailsonpignata

these Tariffs imposed on South Carolina null and void. This was during the Presidency of Andrew Jackson. He responded by lowering the Tariffs and enacting the Nullification Proclamation and the Force Bill, which threatened to send federal troops to enforce the tariffs. South Carolina, facing the military threat, backed down and obeyed the law. However, tensions continued to grow.

Cotton harvesting by slave labor - By Unknown, Public Domain

federal government's power. They wanted unrestricted imports and exports, also referred to as "free trade," and they believed in the nullification of the U.S. Constitution. Nullification is the idea that since the states formed the Union, and subsequently, the federal government, the state has the final authority to determine the limit of power that the federal government has within the states. Therefore, many in South Carolina believed they had the right to reject federal laws that they considered beyond the federal government's constitutional powers. With this belief, South Carolina passed "Ordinance of Nullification," which made

Voting in South Carolina - In correlation with what is happening between South Carolina and the Federal Government, you need to also understand how people were able to vote within South Carolina. From 1790 until 1865, wealthy landowners were in control of South Carolina. That is, men could not be seated in the State House of Representatives unless he owned at least 500 acres of land and 10 Negroes. It was believed that any man incapable of being of this stature would otherwise taint the electoral vote that counted towards federal elections, such as the President of the United States. In addition to this controlled election process, the ordinary voter did not participate in presidential elections in the popular vote; rather, the state house of representatives chose 8 electors to vote for them. The 1860 Presidential election was the last time that South Carolina voted this way and didn't vote in another Presidential election again until 1868, whereas Ulysses S. Grant became President.

The 1860 Presidential Election and South Carolina Secedes From The Union - 1860 was an election year, there were four candidates: Republican Abraham Lincoln, Southern Democrat John C. Breckinridge, Democrat Stephen A. Douglas, and Constitutional Union candidate John Bell. On November 6th, 1860, the votes had been counted, and Abraham Lincoln was declared the winner, a landslide victory.

When Abraham Lincoln won the Presidential election in 1860, South Carolina, along with many other southern states, believed what came next was the demise of their slavery-based economy and social structure. President Lincoln was anti-slavery. He did not acknowledge the idea of any state to secede from the Union. He did, however, believe that his duty was to uphold the Constitution of America and defend the Union.

Three days after Lincoln was sworn in as President of the United States, the House of Representatives in South Carolina passed the "Resolution to Call the election of Abraham Lincoln as U.S. President a Hostile Act." Within just weeks, they were the first to secede from the Union on December 20th, 1860.

This act of rebellion was the beginning of the standoff between the north and the south. The first shot came just shy of 4 months later.

The First Shot of the Civil War - The Union's federal troops occupied a fort in the south called Fort Sumter. South Carolina threatened these forts. In the north, many believed that they would not be able to hold the fortification. Therefore, they should just pull out. Others thought that if supplied

Lincoln taking the oath at his second inauguration, March 4, 1865. Lincoln with hand on Bible, Chief Justice Salmon P. Chase administering oath of office. - By Unknown author - Illus. in: Harper's weekly, v. 9, 1865 March 18, p. 161., Public Domain

adequately that they should go on the offense and attack. In the middle ground of these two opinions is what President Abraham Lincoln decides.

At the time, the men stationed at Fort Sumter were in need. Lincoln has decided to peacefully send food and supplies only, no additional troops or weapons. His decision was filled with hope that the Confederates would not attack, especially if he were to alert them of their peaceful intentions.

On April 6th, Lincoln sent a letter to the Governor of South Carolina stating that he was going to send three unarmed ships loaded with only food and supplies, intending to boost the troops' spirits.

On April 11th, South Carolina's Governor received the letter. As you may suspect, Lincoln's hopes for this peaceful exchange were dashed. The Governor of South Carolina ordered his General to call on the men at Fort Sumter to surrender by 4 a.m. on April 12th, 1861. Union Major Robert Anderson responded:

"I have the honor to acknowledge the receipt of your communication, demanding the evacuation of this fort, and to say, in reply thereto, that it is a demand with which I regret that my sense of honor and my obligations to my Government prevent my compliance."

Without compliance on April 12th, 1861, in the early morning coolness, before the sun awoke, the men of Fort Sumter roused to the startling sound of an explosion overhead. This shot that they heard was fired from a nearby fort to signal the Confederate Army to begin firing on Fort Sumter, and that they did. The Confederacy was positioned all around Fort Sumter, on land and water. General Pierre Beauregard of the Confederacy had organized enough ammunition needed for a full-scale bombardment on Fort Sumter for up to 48 hours. That is if he timed the assault properly. Every two minutes, another mortar was shot going counterclockwise at Fort Sumter.

Major Robert Anderson, U.S. Army, By Unknown, Public Domain

Fort Sumter was built for a naval assault and was strong enough to withstand direct hits on the side. At the time, warships couldn't shoot at an arc above the fort, where the fort was most vulnerable. But here, the Confederacy was not utilizing warships. The fire was coming from 43 guns and mortars stationed at Fort Moultrie, Fort Johnson, a floating battery, and Cummings Point. The capabilities of the offense allowed for an arching assault that hit directly overhead.

The Confederate Army Bombardment on the U.S. Army Stationed at Fort Sumter, South Carolina
The first battle of the Civil War. By Unknown, Public Domain

Although Fort Sumter was mostly made out of brick, there were wooden buildings within. The Confederates with this knowledge took cannonballs heating them red hot in a furnace before shooting them on top of the fort. These cannon balls were so hot that when they hit the fort, the wooden structures within were instantly ablaze. This proved to be more dangerous to the Union soldiers than anything.

The Union's Surrender -

The bombardment continued for 34 hours, with very few return shots fired by Fort Sumter. On the afternoon of April 13th, the fort's central flagpole was knocked down at 1 p.m. Colonel Louis Wigfall, a former U.S. Senator, decided that the fort had had enough punishment. In a small boat, he approached Fort Sumter, waving a white handkerchief from his sword. In a meeting with Major Anderson, he said, "You have defended your flag nobly, Sir. You have done all that it is possible to do, and General Beauregard wants to stop this fight. On what terms, Major Anderson, will you evacuate this fort?" Anderson was low on ammunition, and the fires were burning out of control. To add to this, his men were exhausted and hungry. He was satisfied that they had defended their post honorably, without losing a single soldier, and agreed to a truce at 2:00 p.m.

The Confederate Army Bombardment on the U.S. Army Stationed at Fort Sumter, South Carolina
The first battle of the Civil War. Published in Harper's Weekly on April 13, 1861, By Unknown, Public Domain

No men had lost their lives in this battle, on either side, that is until the 100 gun salute, which was one of the conditions that Anderson had for withdrawal. 50 shots into the 100 gun salute, a premature explosion of a cartridge killed one soldier with another dying a few days later.

Anderson and his soldiers were allowed to leave back to the north. The Civil War had officially begun.

In an excerpt from "Mary Chestnut's Diary," she recounts her testimony of when the battle began, she writes:

"I do not pretend to go to sleep. How can I? If Anderson does not accept the terms at four, the orders are, he

Painted Portrait of Mary Chestnut, Unknown Artist, Public Domain

shall be fired upon. I count four, St. Michael's bells chime out and I begin to hope. At half-past four, the heavy booming of a cannon. I sprang out of bed, and on my knees prostrate I prayed as I never prayed before."

Mary Chesnut, who lived from 1823 until 1886, was the author of "A Diary from Dixie." The book began as her journal that detailed her insightful view of Southern life and leadership during the American Civil War. She was married to James Chesnut, Jr., who served as a U.S. senator from South Carolina, that is until he resigned to take a leadership role in the secession movement for the Confederacy.

Washington, D.C.

Our nation's capital, established on July 16th, 1790, by our founding fathers, is a dynamic city that has had many highs and lows within its place in history.

Temporarily, the capital was hosted in Philadelphia from 1790 until 1800, while Washington City was being built. Now known as Washington, D.C., the district is a unique city in our nation, for it was created by the Constitution of the United States to serve as the nation's capital.

(To review an excerpt of the Constitution, and an excerpt from the Federalist Papers No. 43 written by James Madison, as well as a definition of the Federalist Papers, see the last portion of this article beginning with the sub-titled "Article I, Section 8, Clause 17.")

President George Washington had the honor of choosing the site for the capital city, to which it is named for. He decided on a border area along the Potomac and Anacostia Rivers with the need for Maryland and Virginia to donate land to the new district. This city was to be very different, distinguished from all states. To do this, they needed to design the city. Pierre Charles L'Enfant was the visionary appointed to oversee the creation of this distinct city. Pierre created a modern city with grand boulevards, the capital building in the center, and monuments throughout. When he presented his ideas for Washington City, Pierre, who was from France, had in mind another significant capital, Paris. It was a beautiful vision that had almost been fully built, until the War of 1812.

Washington City Burns The War of 1812, considered by some to be the second war for independence, happened because the U.S. needed to reassert their position as a sovereign nation and defend the desire to trade and expand, which Great Britain was attempting to undermine. On August 24th, 1814, the British invaded Washington City (now called Washington, D.C.), setting fires to several of the buildings. Much of the city burned down to the ground, including the White House (then called the Presidential Mansion), the Capitol building, and the Library of Congress.

In response to the devastation, some in Congress wanted to move the capital.

Northern Congressmen pushed for Philadelphia or other prominent northern cities for reconstruction. While Southern congressmen argued that moving the capital would hurt the people's sense of dignity and strength. Decided with a vote on September 21st, 1814, they struck down the proposal to relocate by a margin of 83 to 54.

In 1847, the capital's boundaries were reduced. Virginia took back the land initially donated to the city as the voters believed that they had been left out of the development. However, over the years, the district has grown based on various factors, and in 1901, the city proposed the McMillan Plan. This plan was to fully realize L'Enfant's original vision, which included a redesign and expansion of the National Mall. Washington D.C. continued to expand

The Burning of the White House During British Invasion in the War of 1812, By Unknown, Public Domain

and develop during the rest of the 20th century.

Interestingly, residents of Washington D.C. don't have the same voting rights that all other states have. Representation of the Washington D.C. at the Congressional level is a non-voting delegate to the House of Representatives and a shadow senator. However, for the first time in 1964, D.C. residents were allowed to vote in Presidential elections, and in 1973 they voted in their first mayor.

In Washington D.C., the nation's most important government buildings and monuments are arranged around a large landscaped park called the National Mall. Here you will find the Capitol building, where U.S. laws are made, the White House, where the President lives. Most notably, there are over 300 monuments and statues, including Franklin Delano Roosevelt Memorial, Korean War Veterans Memorial, Thomas Jefferson Memorial, Vietnam Veterans Memorial, and Martin Luther King, Jr. Memorial, National World War II Memorial, Washington Monument, and the Lincoln Memorial. Also, The Smithsonian Institution operates many large national museums in Washington, and the city is home to the world's most extensive library, the Library of Congress, which was burnt down during the British invasion. Thomas Jefferson resupplied their inventory with his library of books in 1815 for a cost of $23,950 for 6,487 volumes.

Politics back then were not much different from today, in that, with the proposed sale of Jefferson's library, there was opposition from some at the Congressional level. Cyrus King argued "that Jefferson's books would help disseminate his "infidel philosophy" and were "good, bad, and indifferent ... in languages which many can not read, and most ought not." After much debate, the bill passed with a narrow margin along party lines.

Article I, Section 8, Clause 17 - Although the words may be hard to understand, here in Article I, Section 8, Clause 17, the Constitution states the establishment of Washington, D.C.:

"To exercise exclusive Legislation in all Cases whatsoever, over such District (not exceed-

Thomas Jefferson Memorial, TOP LEFT: Exterior, BOTTOM RIGHT: Interior, both by Unknown, Public Domain

Franklin Delano Roosevelt Memorial, By Unknown, Public Domain

Seat of Government of the United States, and to exercise like Authority over all Places purchased by the Consent of the Legislature of the State in which the Same shall be, for the Erection of Forts, Magazines, Arsenals, dock-Yards, and other needful Buildings;"

(SOURCE: https://constitution.congress.gov-/browse/article-1/section-8/clause-17/)

"Excerpt In The Federalist No. 43, whereas James Madison explained the need for a "federal district," subject to Congress's exclusive jurisdiction and

Vietnam Veterans War Memorial, By Unknown, Public Domain

ing ten Miles square) as may, by Cession of particular States, and the Acceptance of Congress, become the

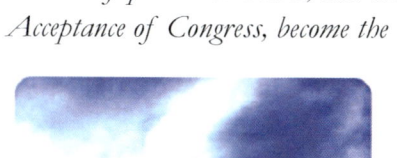

OUT OF THE MOUNTAIN OF DESPAIR, A STONE OF HOPE

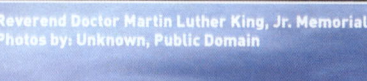

Reverend Doctor Martin Luther King, Jr. Memorial, Photos by: Unknown, Public Domain

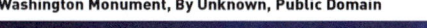

National World War II Veterans Memorial, By Unknown, Public Domain

separate from the territory, and authority, of any single state:

"The indispensable necessity of compleat authority at the seat of Government carries its own evidence with it. It is a power exercised by every Legislature of the Union, I might say of the world, by virtue of its general supremacy. Without it, not only the public authority might be insulted and its proceedings be interrupted, with impunity; but a dependence of the members of the general Government, on the State comprehending the seat of the Government for protection in the exercise of their duty, might bring on the national councils an imputation of awe or influence, equally dishonorable to the Government, and dissatisfactory to the other members of the confederacy."

(SOURCE: https://www.heritage.org/re-port/the-constitution-and-the-district-columbia)

"The Federalist Papers is a collection of 85 articles and essays written by Alexander Hamilton, James Madison, and John Jay under the pseudonym

"Publius" to promote the ratification of the United States Consti-tution. The collection was commonly known as "The Federalist" until the name "The Federalist Papers" emerged in the 20th century. The original plan was to write a total of 25 essays, the work divided evenly among the three men. In the end they wrote 85 essays in the span of six months. Jay wrote five, Madison wrote 29, Hamilton wrote the remaining 51."

(DIRECT QUOTE FROM WIKIPEDIA: https://en.wikipe-dia.org/wiki/The_Federalist_Papers)

Washington Monument, By Unknown, Public Domain

Abraham Lincoln Memorial, INTERIOR LEFT: Exterior, LARGE PHOTO: Interior, both by Unknown, Public Domain

Martin Luther King, Jr. was born in 1929, in a prosperous region of Atlanta, Georgia, to a family of black Baptist preachers. King encountered racism from a young age, experiences which made him determined he would stand up to the segregation laws in the South. In 1955, he participated in a successful campaign against bus segregation in Montgomery, and his influence grew from there.

In 1963, he was arrested in Birmingham, Alabama. During his time in prison, he wrote a letter explaining his belief in nonviolent protest to achieve his goals.

The White House, TOP: North Entrance, BOTTOM: South Entrance, Both by: Unknown, Public Domain

Library of Congress, TOP: Exterior, BOTTOM: Interior, Both by Unknown, Public Domain

Capitol Hill, Washington, D.C. The United States Capitol, often called the Capitol Building, is the home of the United States Congress and the seat of the legislative branch of the U.S. federal government. Photo by: Unknown, Public Domain

200,000 Civil rights protesters at the Mall in front of Lincoln's Memorial on August 28, 1963 - Washington D.C.

In his letter, he wrote: "'You may well ask: "Why direct action? Why sit-ins, marches, and so forth? Isn't negotiation a better path?" You are quite right in calling for negotiation. Indeed, this is the very purpose of direct action. Nonviolent direct action seeks to create such a crisis and foster such a tension that a community which has constantly refused to negotiate is forced to confront the issue.'"

leaders that day to deliver a speech to 200,000 protesters beneath the Lincoln Memorial. King was unsure of what to say and had been adjusting his speech in the hours beforehand. As he spoke to the crowds and the television cameras, Mahalia Jackson, a gospel singer, shouted from behind him, 'tell them about the dream Martin!' Hearing this, King departed from his planned speech and started

> " *I have a dream that my four little children will one day live in a nation where they will not be judged by the color of their skin but by the content of their character.* **I have a dream today!** "

–Reverend Doctor Martin Luther King, Jr. at the March on Washington on the steps in front of the Lincoln Memorial - Quote from his speech entitled "I have a dream" A full script and recording of this speech can be found here: https://bit.ly/Dream-MLKjr

His efforts in Birmingham drew national attention when police turned dogs and fire hoses on the demonstrators. Not only was King jailed, but also a large number of his supporters, including hundreds of school-children.

That same year, leaders of six large civil rights groups joined together to organize a 'March on Washington.' King was amongst them and was one of several

Reverend Doctor Martin Luther King, Jr. overlooking the mall prior to his epic speech "I Have a Dream!"

improvising the part that would become most famous; 'I have a dream.'

King's passionate speech and vision for a fair and equal society touched the hearts of people across America. The massive support proved the government could no longer delay desegre-gation. In 1964, President Lyndon B. Johnson signed the Civil Rights Act. The next year, the National Voting Rights Act ensured the right to vote for African-Americans.

A Closer Look
at what you have learned so far!

Lesson 4

PLUS+
This Lesson's Geography:
Atlanta, Georgia (GA)
Tallahassee, Florida (FL)
Montgomery, Alabama (AL)
Jackson, Mississippi (MS)
Baton Rouge, Louisiana (LA)

Previous Learned Geography:
Annapolis, Maryland (MD)
Richmond, Virginia (VA)
Charleston, West Virginia (WV)
Raleigh, North Carolina (NC)
Columbia, South Carolina (SC)
Washington, D.C.
Montpelier, Vermont (VT)
Albany, New York (NY)
Trenton, New Jersey (NJ)
Harrisburg, Pennsylvania (PA)
Dover, Delaware (DE)
Augusta, Maine (ME)
Concord, New Hampshire (NH)
Boston, Massachusetts (MA)
Providence, Rhode Island (RI)
Hartford, Connecticut (CT)

Hint: The geography found on this page, is also the geography that you will be reviewing this week. Refer to this map as needed when doing your "Memorization Through Repetition" worksheets.

Parent/Teacher: The "A Closer Look" page is intended to show students the accumulated geographic areas taught within their 6-week review period. For additional teaching tips on how to utilize this teaching aide for the different learning levels, please refer to page 1.

Lesson 4

Zoom Me In!

Use this sheet as a reference for this lesson's worksheets. Be sure to practice until you don't have to look!

You are learning your US States & Capitals! This week you are learning:

Atlanta, Georgia (GA)
Tallahassee, Florida (FL)
Montgomery, Alabama (AL)
Jackson, Mississippi (MS)
Baton Rouge, Louisiana (LA)

This Lesson's Geography:
US States and Capitals

Atlanta, Georgia (GA)
Tallahassee, Florida (FL)
Montgomery, Alabama (AL)
Jackson, Mississippi (MS)
Baton Rouge, Louisiana (LA)

Tid-Bits

Atlanta, Georgia

Georgia Terrain In Georgia, you can aim your sights in any direction to find distinctly different terrains. Sweeping from the tail end of the Appalachians in the north to the southeast where long beaches border the Atlantic coastline and the coastal plain covers 60% of the state. Off the coast are the Sea Islands, a chain of over 100 tidal and barrier islands that go along the coastlines of

Georgia "The Peach State" - Public Domain

South Carolina, Georgia, and a little bit of Florida. Then going off to the south in Georgia is where the Okefenokee Swamp is found. Two well-known rivers make up borders in Georgia. The Savannah River on the east boundary and the Chattahoochee River runs along the western edge. Georgia is a uniquely diverse region where people experience mild winters and hot, humid summers.

Georgia's Nicknames Like many states, Georgia has nicknames that characterize what has been unique or distinctive. The first nickname is the Peach State. You're sure to guess that Georgia is the country's number one grower of peaches! They are also big producers of peanuts, pecans, and Vidalia onions. The Vidalia onions have a reputation as the sweetest in the world, and they can only be grown in Georgia. A second nickname is the Empire State. For, like New York is a vital economic center for the northeast portion of the United States, Georgia's financial strength is equally important to the south.

Atlanta's Beginning Atlanta, Georgia's capital city, had its begin-

Downtown Atlanta, Georgia - Public Domain

nings in 1837, the year the area was selected to be the end of the railroad line. At that time, railroads were vital for importing and exporting goods and comfortably transporting people to and from the area. So, when that railroad line went in, settlement of people grew up. In 1845, it was named Atlanta, which is located in the foothills of the Blue Ridge Mountains.

Jimmy Carter After serving as Georgia's governor, Jimmy Carter, went on to serve one term as the 39th U.S. President from 1977 to 1981. Each presidency is marked by their ability, or inability, to manage the inevitable challenges that they face at home and abroad, to defend and protect our Union. Jimmy Carter's presidency was marked by mediating peace talks between Egypt and Israel in 1978 that led to the Egypt-Israel Peace Treaty. Then in 1979, he oversaw the Iranian hostage crisis, whereas 66 Americans were taken hostage at the American Embassy in Iran. This happened, in part, because Carter made a humanitarian decision to allow the Shah (exiled leader of Iran) to receive healthcare for cancer in America. 444 days after the crisis began, the hostages were set free just hours after President Ronald Reagan, the nation's 40th president, delivered his inaugural address.

Lesson 4

Northern Georgia in the valley at the foot of the Blue Ridge Mountains - Public Domain

U.S. President Jimmy Carter

Many historians believe that the hostage crisis cost Jimmy Carter a second term as President. Today (2020), Carter continues to reside in Plains, Georgia, the same state and city of his birth.

Colonial Georgia When Europeans from Spain first arrived in 1540, they encountered mostly Cherokee and Creek Indians. The explorer to account for interaction with the Indians was Hernando de Sota, who claimed the territory for Spain. However, by the second half of the 1600s, the British were also in the area. As history reveals, Georgia was named for King George II of England, who granted permission for the land to become a colony. This made Georgia the last and the youngest of the 13 English colonies, being founded in 1732. Initially, when

Artist Rendering of Colonial Georgia, by Unknown - Public Domain

England was looking to establish this colony, it was thought to be the perfect place for London's indebted prisoners. However, it was not meant to be. In fact, it was colonies around the Chesapeake Bay in both Maryland and Virginia that received about 50,000 indebted prisoners. Many years later, Britain established

another penal colony on a newfound continent named Australia, whereas they shipped roughly 164,000 convicts beginning in 1788. Instead, the Georgia colony, whose boundaries were larger than what they are today with much of present-day Alabama and Mississippi, was ultimately established to protect South Carolina and other southern colonies from Spanish invasion coming from Florida.

Trail of Tears At the beginning of French and British colonial settlement, the Indians that had lived on the land had both good and bad relationships with the Europeans grounded primarily in trade and camaraderie. When things went badly, selfishness and fear were the cause that led to territorial issues, deceitful practices, and the belief that one is either inferior or superior.

European's intentions were not always clear to the Indians. Some approached the tribes peacefully, others approached the Indians with violence. In turn, many Indians approached Europeans with both friendship and brutality. Many U.S. citizens feared the Indians and looked upon them as unrefined, inferior savages.

Fear and selfishness can lead to anger, the consequence can be hatred. After the American Revolutionary War, within our newly formed nation, fear mixed with greed was aimed at the Tribal Nations.

The white men termed this the "Indian Problem." George Washington, America's first President believed that this "Indian Problem" could be dealt with by influencing the tribes to be "civilized" to become more "like us." This meant leading the Indians to adopt European ways in Christianity, economic practices, and speaking the English language. Tribal nations in the southeast, namely, Choc-

Cherokee woman and child - Public Domain

taw, Chickasaw, Seminole, Creek, and Cherokee, embraced these customs, becoming known as the "Five Civilized Tribes."

Land in the states of Georgia, Alabama, North Carolina, Florida, and Tennessee was valuable, with prime plantation land. In Georgia, there was farmland, but there was also gold!

Gold was initially discovered by Hernando de Soto, the Spanish explorer, back in the 1540s. After Spain was run out of the area by the English, the gold was not mined until it was rediscovered in 1819. The gold, however, ran through the land

of the Cherokee Nation, the farmland also theirs.

This "civilized tribe" didn't seem so civilized anymore to the thousands of settlers that poured into the area wanting to profit from the Indian's land. To get the Indian's property, the white man stopped at nothing to get it for themselves. They burned and looted homes and towns, stole their livestock, squatted on land that did not belong to them, they even committed mass murder.

State Government felt compelled to act. The Federal Government, all the way up to the President, got involved in the "Indian Problem." During this time, the U.S. presidency was held by Andrew Jackson from 1829-1837, who was the first Democratic President. His successor was Martin Van Buren, who held office from 1837-1841. The state governments wanted the tribal nations gone to open up their land. President Andrew Jackson agreed. The states passed laws that limited the Tribal Nation's sovereignty and rights within their territory. In retaliation, Native Americans brought their injustice to the Supreme Court in a case entitled Worcester v. Georgia in 1832.

In contrast, the Supreme Court disagreed with Georgia and made it clear with their ruling that "the laws of Georgia and other states can have no force." It was deemed illegal for the state to interfere with the Tribal Nations, at all; they are sovereign, and not under control of the U.S. Government.

Georgia and other southern states disagreed with the Supreme Court ruling, so did President Andrew Jackson. He proceeded despite the verdict, passing the "Indian Removal Act," signed into law in 1830. This law gave the federal government the power to exchange Native lands east of the Mississippi River

President Andrew Jackson - Public Domain

for property west of the Mississippi River, so called the "Indian Colonization Zone."

Twenty-nine years earlier, this land was a portion of the land purchased from France in the Louisiana Purchase. This law required the government to negotiate removal treaties in a fair, voluntary, and peaceful way and disallowed any level of government to coerce the Tribal Nations to give up their land. Although President Jackson was able to get this bill passed, he ignored the law and put forth forceful efforts to remove Indians from their property.

In 1831, under threat of the U.S. Army invasion, the Choctaw Nation was the first to be expelled from their land, which spanned Alabama, Florida, Mississippi, and Louisiana. Some were bound in chains, were not given food, supplies, or other help from their oppressors, thousands perished. Other nations were systematically removed from their land. Notably, in 1836, the Creeks were driven from their homeland who set out on foot to present-day Oklahoma. Out of 15,000 Creeks, 3,500 died along the way.

Of the "Five Civilized Tribes," most had given up their lands. The Cherokee Nation, was the second-largest in all of America, and the largest east of the Mississippi River. At the height of their population in the south they numbered 285,000 spread out among the southern states. The Cherokee

Painting of the "Trail of Tears." By: Unknown, Public Domain

Nation was divided on the issue of being relocated. Many wanted to war with the United States to retain sovereignty over their land. Others thought that working with the U.S. to arrive at an agreement was best. This way, they would negotiate payment for their property, have access to relocation assistance, and money for their lost land.

There was a delegation (group) of Cherokee people assembled to discuss the "Indian Removal Act" with the U.S.,

Cherokee Nation Indians - Public Domain

which included the Principal Chief John Ross. That delegation left the meeting with no resolution. The U.S. wanted to initiate new talks, but with a more receptive audience. In 1835, self-appointed representatives from a minority Cherokee political faction met with President Jackson to discuss a treaty.

President Jackson's terms included western land titles, self-government, relocation assistance, and several other long-term benefits—all conditioned on a total Cherokee removal. There was a clause initially included that would allow a small number of Cherokee to stay if they accepted state authority over them. However, this was struck down by President Jackson by the final draft of the treaty.

Our nation believed that this was a done deal, knowingly deceptive as it were. Before the signing of the treaty, the U.S. Senate received a letter from John Ross, the elected Principal Chief of the Cherokee Nation. Within, he stated that what

Cherokee Nation, Principle Chief John Ross

An excerpt from the letter to the Senate from Principal Chief John Ross, dated July 2, 1836:

"The delegation must repeat, the instrument entered into at New Echota, purporting to be a Treaty, is deceptive to the world and a fraud upon the Cherokee people. If a doubt exists as to the truth of their statements, a Committee of Investigation can learn the facts, and it may also learn that if the Cherokees are removed under that instrument, it will be by force.

This declaration they make in sincerity, with heart-sickening at the scenes they may be doomed to witness; they have toiled to avert such a calamity; it is now with Congress, and beyond their control; they [control]; they hope they are mistaken, but it is hope against a sad and almost certain reality. It would be uncandid to conceal their opinions, and they have no motive for expressing them but a solemn sense of duty. The Cherokees cannot resist the power of the United States, and should they be driven from their native land, then will they look in melancholy sadness upon the golden chains, presented by President Washington to the Cherokee people, as emblematical of the brightness and purity of the friendship between the United States and the Cherokee nation."

A concluding paragraph from the same letter:

"The faith of the United States being solemnly pledged to the Cherokee nation for the guarantee of the quiet and uninterrupted protection of their territorial possessions forever; and it being an unquestionable fact, that the Cherokees love their country; that no amount of money could induce them voluntarily to yield their assent to a cession of the same. But, when under all the circumstances of their peculiar situation and unhappy condition, the nation see the necessity of negotiating a treaty for their security and future welfare, and having appointed a delegation with full powers for that purpose, is it liberal, humane, or just, that a fraudulent treaty, containing principles and stipulations altogether objectionable, and obnoxious to their own sense of propriety and justice, should be enforced upon them? The basis of the instrument, the sum fixed upon, the commutation of annuities, and the general provisions of the various articles it contains, are all objectionable. Justice and equity demand, that in any final treaty for the adjustment of the

**Artist Rendering - Indian Removal Act in action
By Unknown - Public Domain**

Cherokee difficulties, that their rights, interests, and wishes should be consulted; and that the individual rights of the Cherokee citizens, in their possessions and claims, should be amply secured; and as freemen, they should be left at liberty to stay or remove where they please."

After returning from a trip to Washington City, John Ross found himself without a home. In a separate letter found in historical archives reveals a second-hand testimony of John Ross' departure from Georgia.

"Mr. John Ross, the principal chief of the Cherokee nation. He was at Washington city, on the business of his nation. When he returned, he travelled till about 10 o'clock at night, to reach his family; rode up to the gate; saw a servant, believed to be his own; dismounted, ordered his horse taken; went in, and to his utter astonishment, found himself a stranger in his own house, his family having been, some days before driven out to seek a new home. A thought then flitted across his mind, that he could not, under all the circumstances of his situation, reconcile it to himself to tarry all night under the roof of his own house as a stranger, the new host of that house

being the tenant of that mercenary band of Georgia speculators, at whose instance his helpless family had been turned out and made homeless.

Upon reflecting, however, that "man is born unto trouble," Mr. Ross at once concluded to take up lodgings there for the night, and to console himself under the conviction of having met his afflictions and trials in a manner consistent with every principle of moral obligation towards himself and family, his country and his God. On the next morning he arose early, and went out into the yard, and saw some straggling herds of his cattle and sheep browsing about the place. His crop of corn undisposed of. In casting a lookup into the widespread branched of a majestic oak, standing within the enclosure of the garden, and which overshadows the spot where lies the remains of his dear babe, and most beloved and affectionate father, he there saw, perched upon its boughs, that flock of beautiful pea-fowls, once the matron's care and delight, but now left to destruction and never more to be seen. He ordered his horse, paid his bill, and departed in search of his family, after traveling amid heavy rains, had the happiness of overtaking them on the road, bound for someplace of refuge within the limits of Tennessee. Thus have his houses, farm, public ferries, and other property, been seized and wrested from him."

By 1838, there were 16,000 Cherokees left in Georgia, and when the treaty was enacted, only 2,000 relocated from their homeland to the Indian territory west of the Mississippi. President Jackson's term was over, and President Van Buren now oversaw the "Indian Removal Act," who sent 7,000 soldiers to expedite the removal process. The Cherokee people were forced into stockades at bayonet point while the white people looted their homes and belongings. They were forced to march 1,200 miles. Many faced health challenges, including typhus, dysentery, cholera, and starvation. Historians estimate that more than 5,000 died as a result of the journey.

It was one Choctaw leader that told an Alabama newspaper, this was a "trail of tears and death." In the 1830s, the U.S. military evicted about 100,000 eastern Native Americans forcing them to march westward. It is believed that about a quarter of the Native Americans died along the way. This sad event is now memorialized as the "Trail of Tears."

Eli Whitney and the Cotton Gin

Eli Whitney was born in 1765 in Westboro, Massachusetts. Whitney enjoyed making things from an early age. As a young man, he designed and built a machine to prepare cotton, which was able to do a day's work in less than an hour. This invention was called the cotton engine, more commonly referred to as the cotton gin that he invented in Georgia. Eli's invention revolutionized the cotton industry, allowing cotton plantations in the south to strengthen its economy and expand its operations.

While being known primarily for his cotton gin, Eli Whitney ended up solving a problem that had nothing to do with the cotton industry. One with a solution that would impact industry forever. In the late 1790s, America was at risk of a war with France. The problem for the army was that each musket had to be made by an individual craftsman. This meant that production was slow – they needed 40,000 but had only produced 1,000 weapons. Each musket was unique, and, if a part broke, the replacement had to be made specially.

Whitney had an idea. Instead of craftsmen making the musket themselves, workers would make each individual part, based on a single design. In the end, the parts would be put together to create a musket.

Eli Whitney, inventor of the Cotton Gin
Public Domain

Illustration depicting the use of the cotton gin on the plantation - Public Domain

This meant that muskets could be made faster, could be repaired quickly, and workers didn't have to be skilled at making them. This was known as an 'interchangeable parts' system.

Whitney's idea did not go to plan. He had promised to make 10,000 muskets in two years but barely made any. It took him 10 years in total. But the army was so impressed that they ordered 15,000 more muskets anyway.

It is unknown whether Whitney was able to make a fully functioning interchangeable parts system. Still, after his death, other inventors expanded on his ideas. Industries could now create items faster, with less skill required using a standardized design. This step forward in production still helps us today. First, there was the craftsman, then interchangeable parts. This led directly to the age of the Industrial Revolution that thoroughly changed the world. It turned economies upside down and reinvented how society gets by.

which increased the desire for this valuable land. Once obtained, these cotton plantations demanded more slave labor, which resulted in the Civil War.

By the mid-1800s, Georgia had the highest number of cotton plantations of any southern state. The idea of taking away slave labor would undermine their very way of life. Therefore, Georgia was the fifth of the southern states to secede from the Union and served as a significant battleground during the Civil War. The Union Troops led by General William T. Sherman left a 200-mile path of destruction in their "March to the Sea" that began with capturing of Atlanta, burning down much of the city, then going forth all the way to Savannah.

Cotton Plantation with Slave Laborers Pictured
By Unknown, Public Domain

Civil War on the Horizon

Throughout Georgia, the Native Americans are now gone. Their property was ready for the taking, and take they did. While the minority of the area was now available for mining gold, which lasted from 1829 until the early 1840s, the real treasure was the millions of acres of cotton plantations. At this point in history, the cotton gin had made the cotton industry explode,

The Union Troops led by General William T. Sherman "March to the Sea"

Reverend Doctor Martin Luther King, Jr.

Fast forward now, from the marked end of the failed reconstruction of the southern

states in 1877. Fifty-two years later, on January 15, 1929, in Atlanta, the capital city in Georgia, a baby was born. His name was Michael King, Jr. Later, in 1934, Michael King Sr. was sent on a multinational trip by his church backed by the Baptist World Alliance (BWA) with the last stop in Berlin, Germany, where he witnessed first hand the rise of Nazism. The BWA put out a resolution which said: *"This Congress deplores and condemns as a violation of the law of God the Heavenly Father, all racial animosity, and every form of oppression or unfair discrimination toward the Jews, toward colored people, or toward subject races in any part of the world."* What Michael King, Sr. witnessed on his trip coupled with the position of his church made him think of a man named Martin Luther, who in 1517, began the Protestant Reformation by posting the Ninety-Five Theses that led to Pope Leo X excommunicating him from the Catholic Church. Michael King Sr.'s heart was so impressed upon, that he changed both his name and his five-year-old son's name to Martin Luther King to display his convictions to stand firm, be brave, and courageous in the sight of racism.

While growing up, Martin Luther King, Jr., along with his brother Alfred, and sister Christine, would read the Bible aloud. After dinner, the children's grandmother Jennie, who little Martin affectionately referred to as "Mama," would tell lively stories from the Bible.

Martin Luther King, Jr. as a young boy - Pubic Domain

Martin became friends with a little boy that regularly visited his father's business across the King family home. When the boys turned about six years old, they began going to school. The little boy went to an all-white school, while Martin went to an all-black school. Sadly, the little boys' parents didn't allow them to play together anymore, stating that "we are white and you are colored." Martin's parents, learning of this, sat him down to discuss at length America's history of racism and slavery.

Later, in looking back at his childhood, Martin shared that he was "determined to hate every white person." However, his parents instructed him that it was his Christian duty to love everyone.

Martin witnessed his father standing up against segregation that happened all around him. Once, his father was stopped by a police officer who called King Sr. "boy." In protest, King's father responded respectfully yet sharply that Martin was a boy, but he was a man. Another time the two were shopping for shoes when the clerk instructed them to sit in the back. Martin's father responded, "we'll either buy shoes sitting here, or we won't buy any shoes at all." After leaving the store, without shoes, he told his son, "I don't care how long I have to live with this system, I will never accept it." In 1936, when Martin was about 7 years old, his father led hundreds of African-Americans in a civil rights march to the city hall in Atlanta to protest voting rights discrimination. Martin later said of his father that he was "a real father" to him.

When Martin skipped the ninth grade and was enrolled in Booker T. Washington High School. The high school was the only one in the city for African American students. It had been formed after local black leaders, including Martin's Grandpa, urged Atlanta to create it. King became known for his public-speaking ability and was part of the school's debate team.

During his junior year, in a speech that he won first prize for, he stated, "black America still wears chains. The finest Negro is at the mercy of the meanest white man." On the ride home to Atlanta by bus, he and his teacher were ordered by the driver to stand so the white passengers could sit down. King initially refused but complied after his teacher told him that he would be breaking the law if he did not submit. During this incident, King said that he was "the angriest I have ever been in my life."

During Martin's junior year, Morehouse College in Atlanta, Georgia, announced that if any high schoolers could pass the entrance exam that they would be admitted. During World War II, many students abandoned higher education to enlist, and Morehouse College was eager to have students fill the classrooms. This was a challenge that Martin was ready for. At the age of 15, he passed the exam, enrolled in Morehouse, choosing ministry as his ultimate goal, and graduating with a Bachelor of Arts in sociology in 1948 when he was just 19 years old. From there, Martin continued his education at Crozer Theological Seminary in Chester, Pennsylvania, earning a Bachelor of Divinity. After, he set his sights on obtaining a doctoral degree in systematic theology at Boston University. Where he met Coretta Scott, who would become his wife on June 18, 1953. They were married on the lawn of her parent's home in Alabama, wherein 1954, Martin became the pastor at the Dexter Avenue Baptist Church in Montgomery, Alabama.

In 1957, Reverend Doctor Martin Luther King, Jr. with like-minded civil rights advocates established in Atlanta, Georgia, the Southern Christian Leadership Conference (SCLC). This organization dedicated its efforts, led by Martin, to attain equal rights for African Americans. (More on Reverend Doctor Martin Luther King Jr. under Washington D.C. in Lesson 3, under Alabama herein Lesson 4, and under Tennessee in Lesson 5)

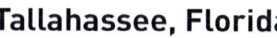

Martin Luther King, Jr. and his bride Coretta King Wed on June 18, 1953 - Public Domain

Tallahassee, Florida

When people think of Florida, images of pristine beaches with white sands, palm trees, and a lot of sunshine come to mind. It is a place where people, like everywhere in the world, live, work, and play. However, it is also a place where people travel for vacation and retirement. The southernmost city in the U.S. is a place called Key West, which is just 90 miles from Cuba. Florida is a subtropical paradise and unique combination of history, climate, natural beauty, cultural diversity, architecture, and romantic appeal.

Florida has many nicknames! Known as the Sunshine State, the Southernmost State, the Everglades State, the Orange State, the Alligator State, and the Peninsula State, the Flower State, and more. In Spanish, Florida is translated to "flowery." Spain had the privilege to name the area for they were the first European settlers to colonize the land. Upon their arrival were the indigenous Native Americans of the Seminole Nation, who still live in the area.

Eviction of the Seminoles and Taking of Florida

Before his presidency, General Andrew Jackson invaded the Seminole territory in 1817 to drive out the Seminole that was causing trouble with settlers in Georgia. At the time of the invasion, the Seminole resided in Florida, which

Andrew Jackson with Seminole Indian
Seminole War I - Public Domain

The Seminole War - By U.S. Marine Corps - National Archives and Records Administration, Public Domain

was owned by Spain. Today, this is referred to as the first of two Seminole Wars.

Even though Spain owned Florida, they were fighting a losing battle against revolutions in South America, where they also held land. This caused the Spanish military power to be concentrated in South America, making it impossible to defend Florida against the U.S.

While Spain didn't have the military force to persuade the U.S. to stay within their bounds, they did send

"fighting words." The Spanish Minister demanded evacuation and "suitable punishment" for Jackson.

U.S. Secretary of State John Quincy Adams' reply scolded the Spanish for not restraining the Indians. Essentially stating, "Keep the inhabitants of Florida in line, or we'll do it for you."

Eventually, Spain negotiated with Adams a Treaty to sell Florida to the U.S. for $5 million. After which, Jackson served as the military governorship in Florida while it was being integrated as a U.S. territory. Later, in 1845, Florida became the 27th state of the Union.

During the Second Seminole War in Florida, the United States government ordered Native Americans to leave Florida. This was done because of the Indian Removal Act in 1830, which demanded indigenous Americans to be confined to the Indian territory marked off for them by the government, west of the Mississippi River.

Present-Day Florida Today, while tourism is the leading industry, the citrus business comes in at a close second. When you bite into a juicy orange, or another citrus fruit like grapefruit, it is a good chance it comes from Florida!

In the city of Orlando, Disney World and Sea World reside. The cities in Florida also include Palm Beach, Fort Lauderdale, and Key West to name a few hot tourist sites. There is also Daytona Beach that has the Daytona International Speedway close by!

John Glenn standing in the cockpit of a F-106B
By U.S. Navy - OSU Archives, Public Domain

John Glenn entering his spacecraft, Friendship 7, prior to the launch of Mercury-Atlas 6 on February 20, 1962.
By NASA - Public Domain

Exploration of a New Kind Florida is not only known for the sunshine and good times, but in the race to space, Florida came in first place!

On February 20th, 1962, John Glenn and a crew of 6 others became the first American men to orbit around the Earth, launched from Cape Canaveral, Florida. After three years of training, the men, led by John Glenn rocketed into space aboard the Mercury capsule Friendship 7. This was the third American crew in space and the first to orbit Earth. In 4 hours and 56 minutes, John Glenn circled the globe three times, reaching speeds of more than 17,000 miles per hour. The successful mission concluded with a splashdown and recovery in the Atlantic Ocean, 800 miles southeast of Bermuda.

Neil Armstrong Seven years later, in 1969, marked a turning point for not only America, but for all the world. This mission was fueled by America's will to send the first man to the moon. At the core of that historic moment, however, lay the story of one man whose strength, perseverance and personal conviction brought him to the moment his foot would leave the indelible and iconic imprint on the lunar surface. His name was Neil Armstrong he was the commander on the Apollo 11 moon landing for exploration and discovery.

Florida coastline attracts locals and tourists year round - Adobe Stock

On July 16, 1969, he spoke these famous words as he took the first step on the moon, "That's one small step for man, one giant leap for mankind." His crew consisted of two other men, Command Module Pilot, Michael Collins, and Lunar Module Pilot, Edwin "Buzz" E. Aldrin, Jr. All three men had been to outer space and back once before, and the landing on the moon was their final mission.

> "That's one small step for man, one giant leap for mankind."

Today, NASA continues their efforts in the field of space exploration and discover at the Kennedy Space Center on Merritt Island, Florida. This facility is the country's primary site for human space-launching. The various buildings were built on over 144,000 acres of land, which is next door to the Cape Canaveral Air Force Station. The two facilities often collaborate and share resources concerning spaceflight.

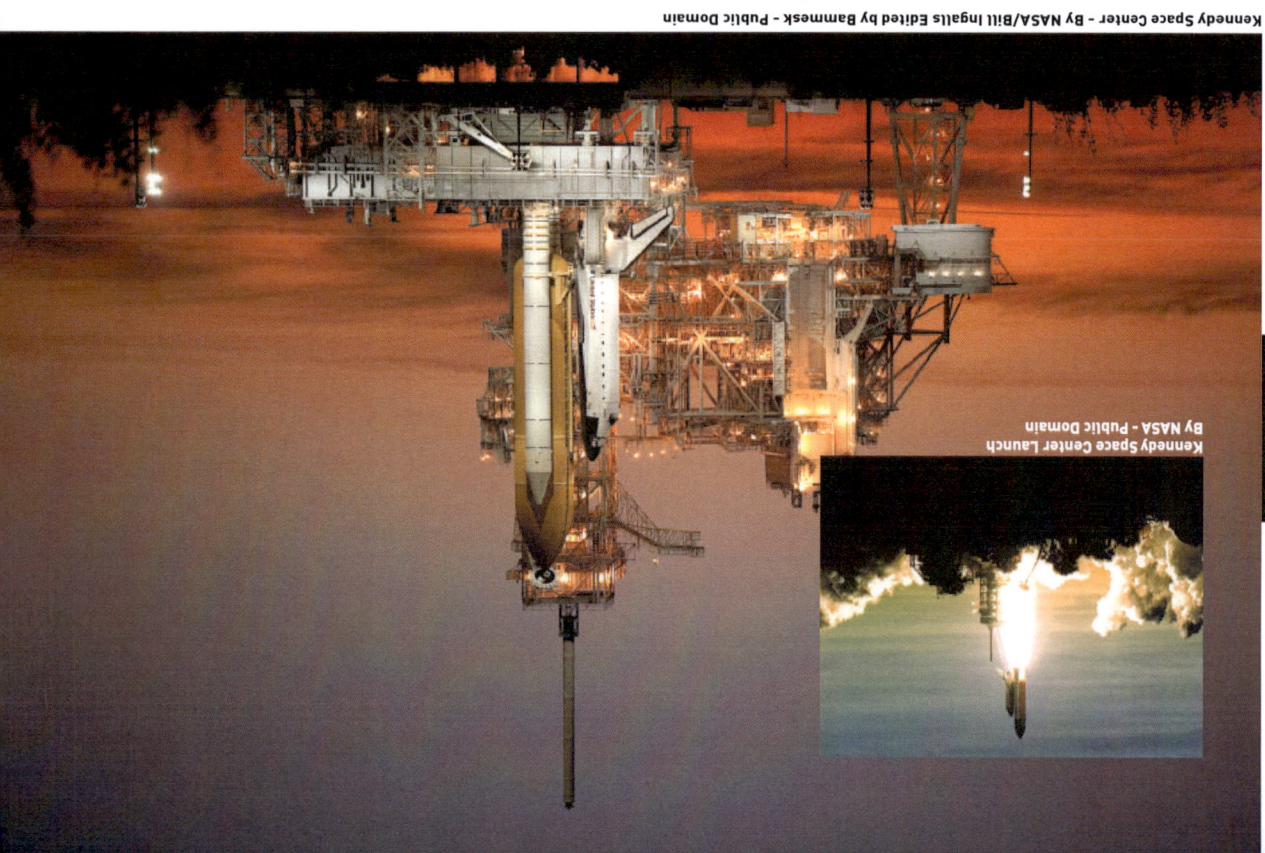

Kennedy Space Center - By NASA/Bill Ingalls Edited by Bammesk - Public Domain

Kennedy Space Center Launch
By NASA - Public Domain

By NASA
Astronaut Buzz Aldrin on the Moon
Public Domain

By NASA
Buzz Aldrin's Footprint on the Moon
Public Domain

By NASA
Eagle's ascent stage approaching Columbia
Public Domain

From Left: Commander, Neil Armstrong
Command Module Pilot, Michael Collins
Lunar Module Pilot, Edwin "Buzz" E. Aldrin, Jr.
By NASA, Public Domain

Montgomery, Alabama

The northern part of the state of Alabama is made up of the very southern portion of the Appalachian Mountains. The land is rugged with lots of forests and hills, filled with untamed creatures of many kinds. On the flip side, in the south of Alabama is mostly flat. The climate is mild in the summer, and the winters are short. The capital of Alabama is Montgomery. It's known for its role in the American Civil War and the Civil Rights Movement of 1961.

Early Indigenous People In the early history of Alabama, before America was even a country, some people lived there with the same name as the Mississippi River. They left behind earthen mounds, which are still investigated by archaeologists. When the European explorers arrived in the 1600s, the mound-building

French Slave Ship Bound for the America's
By Unknown, Public Domain

people were gone, but other Indian groups lived there; the Cherokees, Choctaws, Creeks, and Chickasaws.

In 1830, President Andrew Jackson decided to move all the Indian tribes to another area. As you have learned, this trek has come to be known as the Trail of Tears. Indians were displaced from their homes and moved to unwelcoming land.

When Andrew Jackson passed the Indian Removal Act, he made room for cotton plantations and tobacco plantations to flourish in the southern part of the country. The landowners needed workers for the fields, so they bought slaves from slave traders who stole people from Africa, forcing them aboard their ship bound for the Americas.

The Need For Slavery: North vs. South The northern states did not allow slavery. Their way of life did not require slaves to survive economically. In other words, people made money lots of different ways that did not rely upon agriculture alone - their economy was diverse. The north's economy was based in textiles and lumber. Textiles is the process of making cloth, and lumber is the process of cutting down trees and processing the trees into usable wood products. They also were in the business of furs, mining, and shipping. All this they did without slave labor. Much of the work went to immigrants that would work for lesser pay. The north made money based on industry, not plantations. They likened slavery to what their forefathers ran from in Britain. However, in Alabama, they had built an economy that relied on agriculture.

They believed their crops required slaves to pick and process the cotton from the fields. Together, the nation elected President Abraham Lincoln, who was solidly against slavery. Alabama, knowing that slavery was on the chopping block, broke apart from the Union with the other southern states to create a new government called the Confederate States of America. Lincoln, to protect the Union from breaking up, sought to reunite the states that were in rebellion. He did not want America divided. This led to the Civil War that began in April of 1861. There were 7 battles within Alabama, all were won by the Union. Most notable of the conflicts is the battle of Mobile Bay.

Even though Lincoln passed the 13th Amendment in 1864, which abolished slavery, the African American people were still treated as though they were slaves and were heavily discriminated against. This treatment continued into the 20th century.

The Montgomery Bus Boycott In the 1950s, a man named Reverend Dr. Martin Luther King, Jr. formed a civil rights activist group called The Southern Christian Leadership Conference (SCLC). Their goal was to inspire civil rights reform through non-violent protests. He modeled this reform after the inspiration of Billy Graham and Gandhi. Gandhi created a movement called "Passive Resistance" that effectively ended Britain's rule in India.

In action, what does "Passive Resistance" look like? Arm in arm, with hundreds of like-minded followers, Martin Luther King, Jr. would walk down the streets in protest. Any civil authority, like police officers, that required them to stop, was peacefully refused. Many times, the protesters were arrested for "crimes" that were baseless. For instance, once, King was arrested for driving 30 miles an hour in a 25 mile an hour zone. King was arrested 29 times through the course

An Arab Slave Ship in the Red Sea, with British Cruiser in sight - By H. Haveal, Public Domain

of the Civil Rights Movement.

December 1st, 1955, was a day like any other, where many people took the bus to get where they needed to go. On the buses in the south, based on the Jim Crow laws of segregation, a white section and a black section indicated where one sat based on their skin color. Should the white section of the bus in the front become full, then white passengers would take seats in the black section in the back, even if someone was already sitting there. A woman named Rosa Parks, a civil rights activist, decided that day, she was not going to move when the bus driver asked.

Peacefully, she sat in defiance until she was arrested and taken to jail. Upon learning of Rosa Parks' arrest, local Civil Rights leader JoAnn Robinson jumped into action. She assembled a powerful group of people, including Martin Luther King, Jr. of the SCLC, and Rosa Parks, to organize a boycott against the bus system. A boycott is where people decide not to purchase a service or product, bringing attention to a perceived injustice. In this case, that injustice was discriminatory lawful segregation. This became known as the Montgomery Boycott.

The entire black community in Montgomery, about 50,000 people, did not ride the bus for over a year. Instead, they walked, biked, and carpooled with transportation provided by the Civil Rights leadership. The black population represented 75% of bus ridership. Without them paying for bus service, the system crippled. However, it was not enough to influence the city to make the change that the protesters peacefully demanded. To the courthouse, the protesters went! At a Montgomery federal court, on June 5th, 1956, it was ruled that any law requiring segregation by race for seating on buses violated the 14th Amendment to the U.S. Constitution. That Amendment was adopted following the Civil War in 1868. It guarantees that all citizens, regardless of the color of their skin, have equal rights and equal protection under state and federal laws. The city of Montgomery appealed to the U.S. Supreme Court, which upheld the lower court's decision on December

Rosa Parks has been arrested and is booked into the Montgomery jail - By Unknown - Public Domain

Mug Shot - Public Domain - Public records

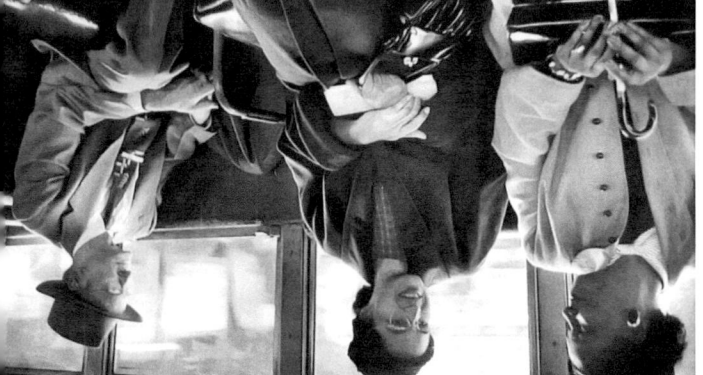

Rosa Parks enjoys a seat on the bus, where she chooses.
By Unknown, Public Domain

During the Montgomery Boycott - Alternative Transportation
By Unknown, Public Domain

During the Montgomery Boycott - By Unknown, Public Domain

A fully boarded, segregated bus in Montgomery, Alabama
By Unknown, Public Domain

20th, 1956. Finally, after 381 days, the boycott came to an end. Montgomery's buses were forevermore desegregated on December 21st, 1956.

The Supreme Court handed down this landmark ruling that said "separate but equal" is not lawful in this land. At this moment, the Civil Rights Movement had momentum that significantly changed laws in the south bringing more equality and justice for all.

Jackson, Mississippi

Hernando De Soto was the first Spanish explorer to find the land of Mississippi in 1540. In 1682, French explorer Sieur de La Salle claimed France's territory and built the first settlement in 1699. Over 100 years later, Mississippi joined the Union as the 20th state in 1817. Jackson is the capital and Mississippi's largest city.

The Choctaw Indians were the largest Native American tribe living in the Mississippi area. The original name of the capital was Le Fleur's Bluff. In 1822, it was renamed after Andrew Jackson because of his victory in the Battle of New Orleans. He was the seventh President of the United States.

Mississippi is a Native American word that means "great waters" or "father of waters." This describes the great Mississippi River flowing down the edge of the state of Mississippi all the way to the Gulf of Mexico. Mississippi is called the "Magnolia State" named for the flower that grows so well in both the flood and coastal plains, which make up the entire region.

During the 1800s, like all other southern states, Mississippi depended on the cotton plantation system for its economic prosperity. The level of money made by the plantation owners was gained by slave labor.

Seceding from the Union and fighting in the Civil War is Mississippi's story as well. On January 9, 1861, Mississippi was the second, following South Carolina, to form the Confederate States of America.

Hope from the "Spirituals" in the Shadow of Slavery and the Blues

In the darkness before the Civil War, Christianity had spread throughout the slave community. While not all slaves were Christian, the doctrines, symbols, and vision of life taught from the Bible by the Christian Church was familiar to most. Christianity for the slaves was visible and invisible. That is, it was organized by slave owners with Church on Sunday with a hired pastor. The invisible came spontaneously by adapting the church for themselves. Weekly Sunday service was encouraged by some owners and forbidden by others. Regardless, slaves would gather for illegal prayer meetings. Most slaves were unable to read; therefore, they would take the Lord's word from the "spirituals." These "spirituals" were songs that were adapted from the words spoken from the Bible in Sunday service. These meetings and the ability to simply pray were so important to the slaves that they risked floggings to pursue their relationship with the Lord, and community with each other.

**Illustration of Slaves Singing the "Spirituals"
By Unknown - Public Domain**

Choctaw Village near the Chefuncte, by Francois Bernard, 1869, Peabody Museum—Harvard University. The women are preparing dye in order to color cane strips for making baskets. Public Domain

"My people told stories, from Genesis to Revelation, with God's faithful as the main characters. They knew about Adam and Eve in the Garden, about Moses and the Red Sea. They sang of the Hebrew children and Joshua at the battle of Jericho. They could tell you about Mary, Jesus, God, and the Devil. If you stood around long enough, you'd hear a song about the blind man seeing, God troubling the water, Ezekiel seeing a wheel, Jesus being crucified and raised from the dead. If slaves couldn't read

Painting of Slaves Singing the "Spirituals" - By Unknown

Illustration of Slaves Singing the "Spirituals"
By Unknown - Public Domain

the Bible, they would memorize Biblical stories they heard and translate them into songs."

Quote by Velma Maia Thomas in her book "No Man Can Hinder Me: The Journey from Slavery to Emancipation through Song" (New York: Crown Publishers, 2001), p14.

Illustration of Slaves Singing the "Spirituals"
By Bricher Conant - Public Domain

During the day, they would sing these "spirituals" while they worked, and within, there was a message to each other about their invisible church.

From his own experience of the "invisible institution" was recalled by former slave Wash Wilson:

"When de niggers go round singin' 'Steal Away to Jesus,' dat mean dere gwine be a' ligious meetin' dat night. De masters ... didn't like dem' ligious meetin's so us natcherly slips off at night, down in de bottoms or somewhere. Sometimes us sing and pray all night."

-Wash Wilson, as part of the Slave Narratives from the Federal Writer's Project 1936-1938, Library of Congress

They would sing out in the fields with their secret code. Then they would steal away and gather in a secret place in the dark of night to learn and worship the Lord. This is where they found their hope in the dark shadow of slavery.

Established from the "spirituals" sung by slaves was born a musical style we call "The Blues," which originated in the Mississippi Delta after the Civil War. "The Blues" offered an escape from oppression and a means of expression for many African Americans.

Spirituals were created spontaneously and were passed orally from person to person. On record, there are over 6,000 spirituals. However, because slaves were not allowed to be taught to read or write—meant that the actual number of songs is unknown.

Some of the best-known spirituals include: "Sometimes I Feel Like a Motherless Child," "Nobody Knows The Trouble I've Seen", "Steal Away," "Swing Low, Sweet Chariot," "Go Down, Moses," "He's Got the

Bear formerly owned by Kermit Roosevelt, thought to be made by Michtom, early 1900s; Smithsonian Museum of Natural History, 2012

Whole World in His Hand," "Every Time I Feel the Spirit," "Let Us Break Bread Together on Our Knees," and "Wade in the Water."

Civil War & Civil Rights Many of the battles of the Civil War were fought in Mississippi. One of the worst battle spots was at Vicksburg in 1863. When the Civil War was over, Mississippi was readmitted to the United States in 1870. Many of the residents of Mississippi were African Americans. As this story goes, they were denied many rights available to whites. However, that story began to change when the Civil Rights Movement in the mid-1900s helped change laws and hearts.

Present-Day Mississippi Today, the state of Mississippi has many different avenues for income. The climate is suited for farming, and the primary crops are cotton and soybeans. Valuable livestock consists of chickens and cattle. In the Gulf of Mexico, fishermen catch shrimp selling them in the marketplace and catfish are raised in artificial ponds. Lumber from the forests provides for many kinds of wood products, everything from furniture to homes.

The Teddy Bear One interesting tid-bit pulled from our past tells of the story where President Theodore (Teddy) Roosevelt refused to shoot a bear that had been captured and tied to a tree while on a hunt in Mississippi. Someone made an editorial cartoon about the event, which inspired the making of a children's toy called a "Teddy Bear" named for President "Teddy" Roosevelt.

U.S. President Thomas Jefferson
Public Domain, Library of Congress

Map of the Louisiana Purchase - Sources: Natural Earth and Portland State University, By William Morris

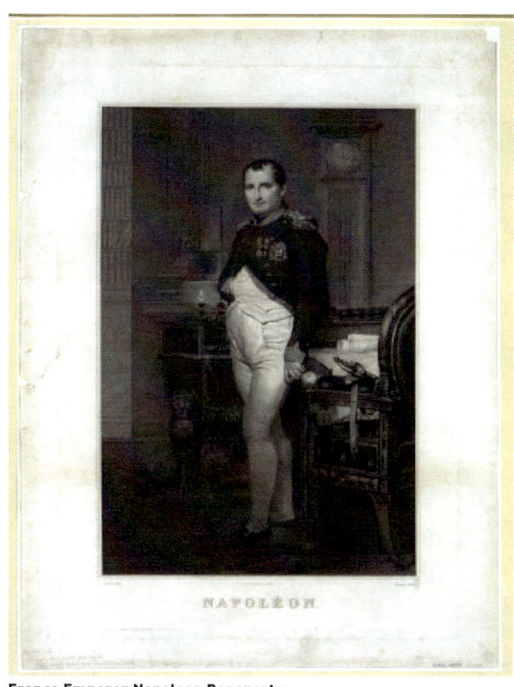
France Emperor Napoleon Bonaparte
Public Domain - Library of Congress

Louisiana

Thomas Jefferson, President of the United States, bought over 800,000 square miles of land from France, which came to be known as the Louisiana Purchase. The purchase added 13 more states to our nation. The very first state was called Louisiana, and its capital is Baton Rouge.

Here is the back story of how America doubled in size overnight!

Around the 1660s, French explorers, traders, and missionaries began colonizing North America's interior from their foothold in modern-day Canada. By the middle of the 18th century, France held a vast territory known as 'La Louisiane' or Louisiana, stretching down the length of the Mississippi River, then to the west. Be sure to check out the map of the Louisiana Purchase. In the north part of the land, "La Louisiane' went as far west as present-day Montana. Then, the west side of the territory diagonally southbound to present-day Louisiana.

At the same time, the valley above the Ohio River that goes along the southern boundary of present-day Ohio, Indiana, and Illinois was a disputed territory. Both the British colonies and France wanted this land. This sparked the North American portion of a nine-year war that began in 1754, we call this the French and Indian War. However, the more complex phase of this war is called the Seven Year's War, which was fought from 1756-1763 between France and Britain. This war was fought on five continents, affecting the Philippines, West Africa, North and South America, India, and Europe. The tide of the war turned against France, and in 1762 they secretly ceded all of Louisiana west of the Mississippi to Spain, their allies. At the close of the war, in 1763, Britain acquired the disputed territory of the Ohio River basin through the Treaty of Paris.

A few years go by, and another war pervades the land, where the British colonies fight Britain for their independence. This was the American Revolutionary War that concluded in 1783. At the end of this war, Britain ceded land to the newly formed United States of America. Now, just to mention here, this does not include the "Louisiana" land that France secretly gave to Spain. Eventually, however, the United States learned of who owned Louisiana.

As the United States grew, the Mississippi River became an important economic center. The U.S. signed agreements with Spain to allow free use of the river and storage of goods in Spanish New Orleans.

Then, something rather unexpected happened. In 1801, the French empire, ruled by Napoleon, convinced the ailing Spanish empire to hand back Louisiana to France. This was very troubling for America, who worried that Napoleon would not allow us to use the Mississippi River any longer, and possibly create trouble.

In Paris, the U.S. minister, Robert Livingstone, had one desperate tactic: working with the British – stressful, but potentially disastrous for Napoleon. Having limited control of Louisiana and facing potential invasion from Britain, Napoleon agreed to opened negotiations. These negotiations led to the Louisiana Purchase.

The Louisiana Purchase is considered the greatest real estate deal in history. The purchase would come to include the modern states of Arkansas, North Dakota, South Dakota, Iowa, Louisiana, Missouri, Nebraska, and Oklahoma. Most of present-day Colorado, Kansas, Minnesota, Montana, and Wyoming were also included. The size of the U.S. had been effectively doubled!

For this vast domain, the United States agreed to pay $11,250,000. With Interest, the total price came to $27,267,622. The Louisiana Purchase was concluded in 1803.

The purchase opened the door for broader American expansion westwards and is seen by some historians as the beginnings of Manifest Destiny. As economic opportunities in the east declined, the west looked ever more tempting.

The War of 1812 Not too many years later, once again, we had problems with Britain that seemingly threatened our sovereignty. The U.S. desired good trade relationships with France and Britain; however, bad blood between the two was getting in the way! Britain didn't want the U.S. to trade with their enemy.

Britain set up blockades in enemy ports. Blockades are acts of war where a country blocks anyone from coming in or going out from enemy territory, most often coastlines.

In this case, Britain was blocking American ships from trading with France. Not only this, Britain made-up rules that if enemy supplies were being delivered, Britain could take the goods as contraband of war. This led to Britain seizing goods from American ships, many times even boarding the vessel and seizing Americans as well, claiming that they were searching for "deserters." Deserters are people that are trying to escape their duty in fighting in a war for their country.

Britain going after American ships, in part, led to the War of 1812, which ended with the Battle of New Orleans, fought on December 20th, 1814. This last battle was led by General Andrew Jackson, who later became the 7th President of our country.

Present-Day Louisiana has a mix of many cultures with two notable groups. Firstly, are the Cajuns that descend from a French-speaking group of Canada. Secondly, the Creoles are people with a mix of French, Spanish, Caribbean, African, or American Indian background.

Baton Rouge is the capital of Louisiana and sits on the Mississippi River, that continues to be an essential port for the United States. Its primary industries process natural gas and oil.

One of the main tourist attractions in the city is a big festival called Mardi Gras. This festival lasts several weeks, starting in January and ending Tuesday night before Ash Wednesday, the first day of Lent.

Louisiana Bayou - By Unknown, Public Domain

Louisiana is one of the nation's flattest states and borders the Gulf of Mexico. Nearly all the land is below sea level. Within, are miles of swampland and waterways known as bayous. It has a humid climate that is hot in the summer, mild in the winter, with hurricanes that hit the coastline. In 2005 the city of New Orleans was severely damaged by Hurricane Katrina. It was the deadliest hurricane to strike the Gulf Coast since 1928.

(More on Hurricane Katrina under the Mississippi Delta in Lesson 24)

Painting of the War of 1812 - U.S. and Britain ships fighting in the Atlantic. By Unknown Public Domain

Above: General Andrew Jackson within the War of 1812 at the Battle of New Orleans By Unknown Public Domain

Devastation caused by Hurricane Katrina in New Orleans, Louisiana - By Unknown, Public Domain

A Closer Look
at what you have learned so far!

Lesson 5

PLUS+
This Lesson's Geography:
Lansing, Michigan (MI)
Columbus, Ohio (OH)
Indianapolis, Indiana (IN)
Frankfort, Kentucky (KY)
Nashville, Tennessee (TN)

Previous Learned Geography:
Atlanta, Georgia (GA)
Tallahassee, Florida (FL)
Montgomery, Alabama (AL)
Jackson, Mississippi (MS)
Baton Rouge, Louisiana (LA)
Annapolis, Maryland (MD)
Richmond, Virginia (VA)
Charleston, West Virginia (WV)
Raleigh, North Carolina (NC)
Columbia, South Carolina (SC)
Montpelier, Vermont (VT)
Albany, New York (NY)
Trenton, New Jersey (NJ)
Harrisburg, Pennsylvania (PA)
Dover, Delaware (DE)
Augusta, Maine (ME)
Concord, New Hampshire (NH)
Boston, Massachusetts (MA)
Providence, Rhode Island (RI)
Hartford, Connecticut (CT)

Hint: The geography found on this page, is also the geography that you will be reviewing this week. Refer to this map as needed when doing your "Memorization Through Repetition" worksheets.

Parent/Teacher: The "A Closer Look" page is intended to show students the accumulated geographic areas taught within their 6-week review period. For additional teaching tips on how to utilize this teaching aide for the different learning levels, please refer to page 1.

Lesson 5

Zoom Me In!

Use this sheet as a reference for this lesson's worksheets. Be sure to practice until you don't have to look!

You are learning your US States & Capitals! This week you are learning:

Lansing, Michigan (MI)
Columbus, Ohio (OH)
Indianapolis, Indiana (IN)
Frankfort, Kentucky (KY)
Nashville, Tennessee (TN)

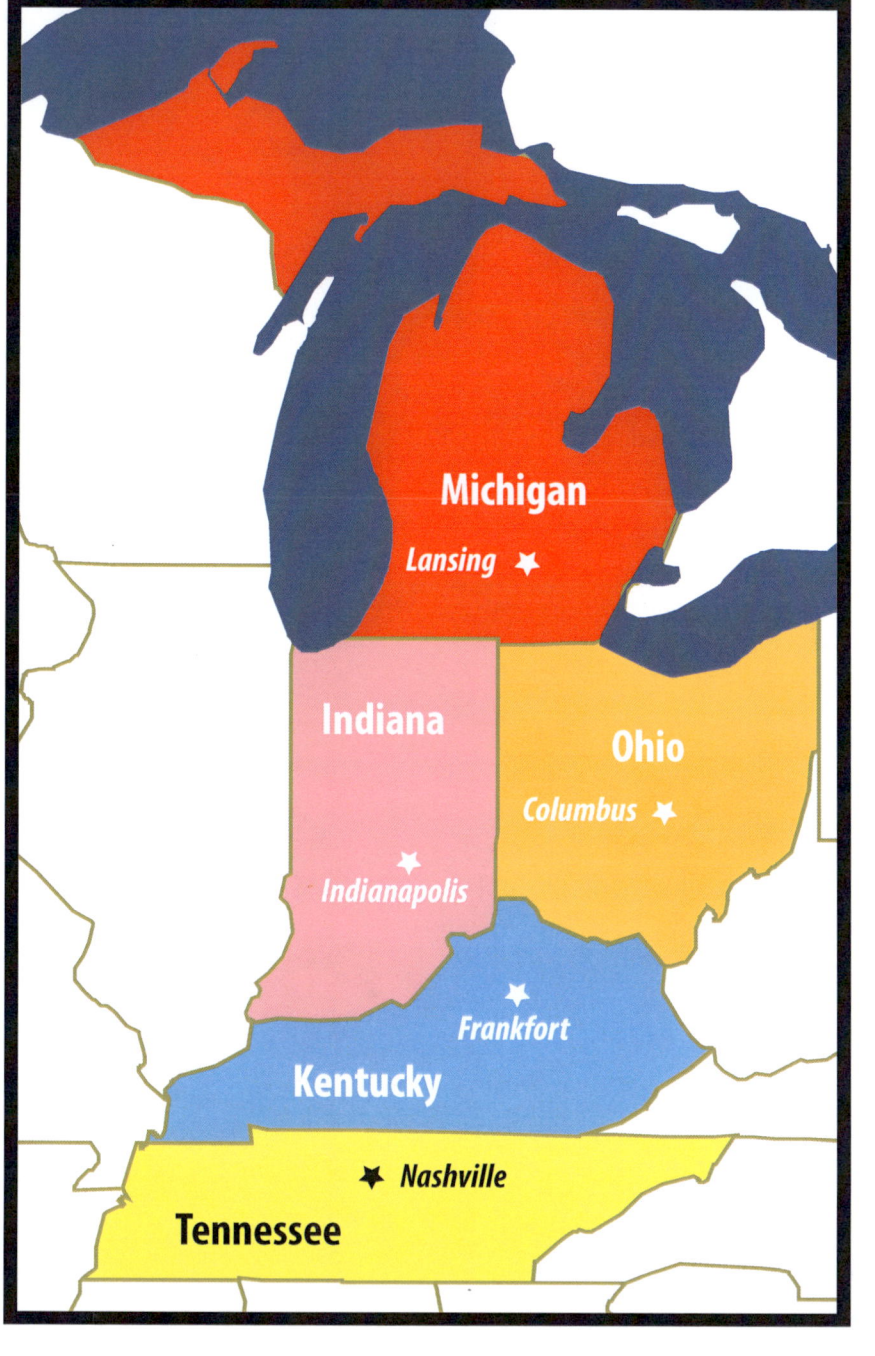

This Lesson's Geography:
US States and Capitals

Lansing, Michigan (MI)
Columbus, Ohio (OH)
Indianapolis, Indiana (IN)
Frankfurt, Kentucky (KY)
Nashville, Tennessee (TN)

Tid-Bits

Lansing, Michigan

Michigan is a Native American word meaning large lake. This is no surprise, for Michigan borders the largest freshwater lake in the entire world! This particular body of water is called the Great Lakes.

Michigan's European settlers came in the early 1800s from various countries, including Germany, Ireland, Netherlands, Italy, and Poland.

Lake Michigan of the Great Lakes - By Unknown, Public Domain

Ford Model-T - By Unknown, Public Domain

Ford Model-T Assembly Line - By Ford Motor Company

In 1796 the new United States took full control of the Northwest Territories. The people in Michigan decided against slavery and helped slaves move to Northern Michigan and Canada through the Underground Railroad.

Detroit was the state capital until 1847 and then moved to Lansing. Although Michigan is primarily known for the automobile industry, they are also an agricultural state that produces cherries, apples, grapes, pears, plums, and peaches.

Portrait of Henry Ford (c.1919) By Hartsook, photographer Library of Congress's

The "Big Three" Motor Companies -

During the First Industrial Revolution, which began around 1760 and lasted until somewhere between 1820-1840, Detroit became an industrial powerhouse. Michigan became the nation's leading manufacturing state, dominated by the automobile industry. The state is home to three major manufacturers: General Motors, Ford, and Dodge. Mass production on assembly lines was the most significant development of the early 1900s.

In 1908, Henry Ford created the Ford Motor Company. He began the production of automobiles that could be mass-produced on a moving assembly line. It was the first time anything like that existed. From 1913 to 1927, Henry Ford produced over 15 million Model T automobiles.

Lesson 5

Even though other companies began experimenting with gasoline-powered vehicles, Ford was the person who made them work. Throughout the industry, assembly-line production became the accepted mode for car manufacturing.

Henry Ford's Motor Company became the world's largest and most profitable automobile company. The Ford family continues to own and operate the company as it has done for more than 100 years.

There are many successful stories of automobile companies, including the Buick Motor Company, that began in 1903. The REO Motor Company opened in 1904. Then General Motors Company came along a year later. A man named Durant dreamed of owning his own company, and in 1911 he formed Chevrolet with the help of a race car driver named Louis Chevrolet.

John and Horace Dodge opened a shop in Detroit to produce parts for automobiles. Henry Ford contracted with them to build engines,

B-24 Bomber Assembly Line at the Ford Motor Company - Public Domain

axles, and transmissions. In 1913 these brothers started their own Dodge Motor Company. In 1925, the Chrysler Corporation became famous for mid-priced cars that performed well.

When World War I broke out, Ford motor company helped British automobile companies make cars and trucks for the war effort. Many American car companies joined to fight the battle on the assembly line by creating airplane engines and vehicles equipped for war.

The Ford Company, Chrysler Company, and the Dodge Motor Company were called the Big Three because they made 75% of the automobile sales in America.

In 1940, when the U.S. was anticipating their part in World War II, William Knudsen, the president of General Motors, was asked by President Roosevelt to help produce tanks and cars for the war. Knudsen called upon the "Big Three" to build tanks. In addition to tanks, Ford began building aircraft. They went on to make B-24 bombers using the auto-industry assembly line for their production.

Columbus, Ohio

The French explorer Sieur de La Salle came to the area of Ohio in 1669 and claimed it for France. Two years later, the French lost it to Great Britain in the French and Indian War. As you've learned, the British then suffered the loss of this land in the American Revolutionary War, effectively beginning the United States of America. After this, Ohio, Indiana, Illinois, Michigan, Wisconsin, and a portion of Minnesota, became known as the Northwest Territory beginning in 1787.

When Ohio became a state, a site was chosen for the capital and named Columbus. Before the American Civil War, Columbus was considered a safe place for slaves who had escaped their masters in the South.

The Myaamiaki tribe that spoke the Algonquian language named the river "Ohio" that runs along the southern boundary of the state. Ohio state is named for this river, which means "great river." "The Buckeye State" is Ohio's

Ohio's namesake - Buckeye Tree

nickname, and it comes from a tree found throughout the Ohio land.

Ohio has three natural regions. Part of it is the Appalachian Mountains. The western part has gently rolling plains, known for good soil and crops, and the third part stretches along the southern shore of Lake Erie, with warm summers and cold winters. Manufacturing has been an essential part of Ohio's

economy, especially in making motor vehicles and metal products. They are known for making automobile tires.

Harriet Tubman & The Underground Railroad After our independence was won in the American Revolutionary War and up until the Civil War, slavery was a big issue in our young country. The southern States relied on slavery, and the northern States didn't. The people who wanted to help slaves find their way to freedom formed many secret escape routes to get them from the South into the North. The network became known as the Underground Railroad.

Around 1830, in the deep darkness of night, the Underground Railroad began to work, helping slaves move north in secret. It was active throughout the first 20 years before the Civil War.

The Underground Railroad had networks throughout the country. It is believed that Ohio was the most active of all systems compared to other parts of the North. Within Ohio, the Quaker population was invaluable in hiding slaves as they moved their way north. In addition, there was a

Southern Slaves Seeking Freedom Along the Underground Railroad, By Unknown, PD

Harriet Tubman, A Conductor on the Underground Railroad
By Unknown, Public Domain

Slaves on their way to freedom on the Underground Railroad - By Unknown, Public Domain

hero for the cause: her name was Harriet Tubman. She was initially freed through the Underground Railroad. She then became famous for going back for more... not just once, but many times. It is believed that she led at least 70 and possibly as many as 300 slaves to freedom. She had lots of secret ways to move people through the night. Sometimes farm owners would use signals, like blankets on their roofs, to help her know whether it was safe to come to that house to stay the night or stay away in the woods because it wasn't safe. Harriet would always have her shotgun with her - not so much for safety from masters looking for their runaway slaves, but for the slaves that might change their minds and turn back. Once the decision was made to run, there was no turning back.

Because it was called the Underground Railroad, some of the code words had to do with trains. Slaves were called passengers, hiding places were called stations, guards that led them were called conductors, and people who helped them were called agents.

The slaves needed to hide in the woods during the day and travel only at night. The journey was difficult, and they had to find shelter along the way. Winter was the best time for slaves to escape because the Ohio River would freeze, enabling them to run across.

A Ride for Liberty – The Fugitive Slaves – By Eastman Johnson
Online Collection of Brooklyn Museum; Public Domain

Harriet Tubman inspired freed slaves to help others, even at the risk of their own safety and freedom. With the end of the Civil War, over 100,000 "passengers" rode the train to freedom.

Indianapolis, Indiana

Indiana is in the Midwest of the United States. It is known as the Crossroads of America, and its citizens are Hoosiers. No one really knows what a Hoosier is, but historians believe the word comes from the east and means someone who is backward-thinking.

On December 11, 1816, Indiana became the nineteenth state in the US. It is a relatively small state. In fact, the only state smaller west of the Appalachians is Hawaii. The name of the state means "Indian land." Governmental leaders believed that the center of the state was an excellent place for the capital, and in 1825 Indianapolis became the capital. With rolling hills in the north, sand dunes by Lake Michigan, a vast plain in the middle that is perfect for farming, and the fertile Ohio River valley, Indiana has quite a diverse geography. The summers are humid and hot, but the winters can be icy cold.

Like so many other states, Indiana has a shared history with neighboring states. The land was first explored by Sieur de La Salle, who was French, in 1679. France made a claim to the area and others, like

Ohio, but after the French and Indian War, it became a part of Great Britain. In 1783, it became a territory of the United States after the American Revolution.

Battle of Tippecanoe – The area eventually thrived because of William Henry Harrison, the territory's first governor and the 9th President of the United States. He led and won the Battle of Tippecanoe in 1811, making the area safer for settlers. You see, the Native Americans living in the area were hostile to people moving into their lands west of the northern Appalachians. With the battle won, settlers began to arrive to build their lives there and by 1840, over 680,000 people were living in the state.

On October 6, 1866, the first-ever train robbery happened in Indiana

William Harrison as painted by Rembrandt Peale in 1814

when the Reno Brothers gang stole $13,000 in Jackson County. They broke into one safe and tipped the other off the train before jumping off.

The notorious bank robber, John Dillinger, escaped his holding cell on March 3, 1934, in Crown Point, even though it was supposed to be escape-proof. He fooled his prison guards with a wooden pistol before he stole the sheriff's car to cross into Illinois. The federal government had to intervene. Dillinger was killed by FBI agents on July 22, 1934.

Many runaway slaves found their way to Indiana through the Underground Railroad. Levi and Catherine Coffin helped make Newport, which is now Fountain City, become known as "Grand Central Station of the Underground Railroad" because they helped save 2,000 people. Indiana was an essential stopping point for many runaway slaves on their way to freedom in the north.

Indy 500 – One of the most notable things for which Indiana is known is the Indy 500, an auto race. Every Memorial Day weekend, more than

Simon Pagenaud and others racing in the Indy 500, By Unknown

250,000 people go to the Indianapolis Motor Speedway to watch Indy cars zip around the track for 500 miles. It is the biggest, one-day sporting event in the world, and it earned the title "The Greatest Spectacle in Racing." The very first race was in May 1911. Ever since the track was built in 1909, the competition has happened every year.

Quaker abolitionist Levi Coffin and his wife Catherine helped more than 2,000 slaves escape to freedom. Public Domain

Frankfurt, Kentucky
Kentucky became the first state west of the Appalachian Mountains on June 1, 1792, but it was the 15th state of the United States. The capital is Frankfort, but the largest city is Louisville. Kentucky

Kentucky prairie land – By Unknown, Public Domain

is the "Bluegrass State." Its nickname comes from its blue-green grass, and not bluegrass music. Kentucky has warm summers and cool winters. Kentucky was named for the beautiful land it sits on, which comes from a Native American word meaning "prairie." It always has been and continues to be a significant agricultural area. It has a long history as one of the largest coal-producing regions as well.

Before settlers moved into Kentucky, the Cherokee, Shawnee, and Iroquois nations lived on the land. American settlers weren't able to live there because mountain ranges made it impossible until Daniel Boone, a famous American explorer, discovered the Cumberland Gap in 1750. After he found a way through, people began emigrating to Kentucky and surrounding areas. In 1774, the very first settlement was founded. Daniel Boone founded another in 1775 and called it Boonesboro. It was a part of Virginia before Kentucky became a state in 1792.

Frankfort, the state capital, was founded in 1786 by an American general when he bought the land. It was established as the capital in 1792. Louisville and Lexington tried to become the capital cities, but Frankfort managed to stay the capital.

Abraham Lincoln was born in Hodgenville, Kentucky, on February 12, 1809.

The War of 1812 had a significant impact on American lives at the time. More than half the people lost in the war were from Kentucky, though no battles were actually fought in the state.

During the Civil War, Kentucky sided with the Confederacy, but Kentuckians were very torn. Many people fought for the North, and others fought for the South. President Abraham Lincoln and Jefferson Davis, the Confederacy's President, were both born in Kentucky. The state never officially seceded from the Union.

"Riders Up!" is the traditional call jockeys hear to mount their horses at The Kentucky Derby, the most well-known piece of Kentucky history and culture. It is an annual horse race in Louisville on the first Saturday of May and the first race of the American

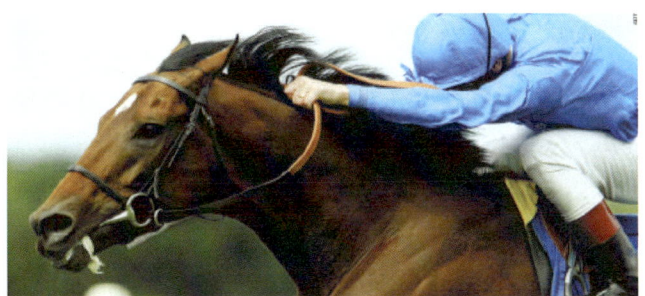

Riders Up! Compliments of Churchill Downs Race Track

Triple Crown. The Kentucky Derby Festival with fireworks and an airshow starts two weeks before the one-and-a-quarter mile race, which is run by three-year-old Thoroughbreds. The winner is draped with a blanket of roses, and the race was nicknamed "The Run for the Roses." The race only lasts about two minutes, and people have called it "The Most Exciting Two Minutes in Sports." The Kentucky Derby was started by Bill Monroe and was run every year for 144 years. 2020 was the first year it wasn't held because of the COVID-19 pandemic. The race track is named after John and Henry Churchill; but the name officially became Churchill Downs in 1937.

"The Triple Crown" is awarded based on winning all three important races for Thoroughbreds. The first horse to win The Kentucky Derby, Preakness Stakes, and Belmont Stakes was Sir Barton in 1919. Gallant Fox was the second horse, and the first time the term "The Triple Crown" was used was by sports-journalist Charles Hatton to describe the races. The Kentucky Derby made their race date the first Saturday of May, so the Triple Crown would always be run in the same order.

The Thoroughbred named Secretariat ran the fastest Kentucky Derby in 1973 with a time of 1:59.4 minutes. The purse, or winnings, offered at the Derby is $3 million (2020). Each year, millions of people watch and bet on the race around the world.

Nashville, Tennessee

Tennessee entered the Union on June 1, 1796, as the sixteenth state. It is 432 miles wide but only 112 miles north-to-south. Of the 6.89 million people that live in

Kentucky Derby (left & below) compliments of Churchill Downs Race Track

Secretariat, Triple Crown Winner
By Unknown, Public Domain

Helen Penny Chenery with Secretariat, Public Domain

after Tanasi, a Cherokee village. Tennessee is nicknamed the Volunteer State because so many people volunteered for the War of 1812. Tennessee is in the southern Appalachian range, notably the Blue Ridge Mountains and the Great Smoky Mountains. There are also low ridges, rolling hills, and plains. Tennessee borders the great Mississippi River and experiences moderate weather with cool winters and warm summers.

Memphis and Nashville are its most well-known cities. Both have deep roots in the music of blues and country. People go to Memphis in May for their famous barbecue competition, but it is also home to Elvis' estate: Graceland. Nashville is the capital and has The Grand Ole Opry, a renowned music hall and home to the longest running radio show.

Tennessee, there have been some that found fame, like Elvis, Johnny Cash, and Dolly Parton. The state was named

Initially, both the French and English wanted this land. So both moved in! Britain won control of the area from France after the French and Indian War in 1763.

In 1775, Richard Henderson got the land for the middle of Tennessee from Cherokee Indians. Now known as Nashville, he settled Fort Nashborough along the Cumberland River in 1779. It was named for an American Revolution officer, Francis Nash. Established as a city in 1806, it then became the state capital in 1843. It is known as "Athens of the South" because it is a center for art and learning, and there are a lot of buildings with ancient Greek architecture influence. Not only is it home to the Grand Ole Opry, but also the Country Music Hall of Fame and Museum.

Memphis means "place of good abode" and was named after an ancient Egyptian city. It was founded on May 22, 1819, by Andrew Jackson, a future president, James Winchester and John Overton.

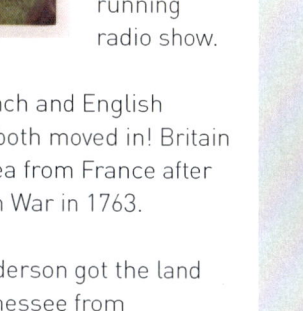

Elvis Presley, By Unknown, Public Domain

Tennessee became a hub of commercial importance when railroads arrived in the 1850s, making it easier for goods and people to come and go.

Families were divided during the Civil War. The east sided with the North, but the west sided with the South. Tennessee was home to famous battle sites, like Shiloh.

Reverend Dr. Martin Luther King, Jr., Final Days -
So far, you've learned about the Civil Rights movement and Reverend Dr. Martin Luther King, Jr. A portion of that story ends here.

The Civil Rights Movement is a massive part of American history between the 1950s and 1960s. At the center of this was Martin Luther King, Jr. - who was killed in Memphis, Tennessee, in 1968. Black Sanitary Public Works employees had been striking for better pay and treatment since March 12th, 1968. They were not paid or treated the same as white employees. On April 3rd in Memphis, Martin Luther King, Jr. gave his last speech, "I've Been to the Mountaintop," at a rally. He said:

"And then I got to Memphis. And some began to say the threats, or talk about the threats that were out. What would happen to me from some of our sick white brothers?

later, Martin Luther King, Jr. was shot at 6:01 pm on April 4, 1968, by James Earl Ray. He was rushed to St. Joseph's Hospital for emergency surgery but died at 7:05 pm. He is buried in the Martin Luther King Jr. National Historical Park.

Martin Luther King, Jr. was a humanitarian and leader. He lived his life outside of fear to fight for people's rights even when there were threats to his life. He spent time in prison, suffered violence, and worked endlessly to end oppression, ignorance, and violence. He did all these things through nonviolent protests, speeches, education, and kindness. He dreamed of an America where all people could live their lives equally. Instead of giving into violence, he stood for nonviolence. He worked with other civil rights activists to achieve a national influence for the greater good. His work is honored in monuments, foundations, and hearts, in the United States and around the world.

Well, I don't know what will happen now. We've got some difficult days ahead. But it doesn't matter with me now. Because I've been to the mountaintop. And I don't mind. Like anybody, I would like to live a long life. Longevity has its place. But I'm not concerned about that now. I just want to do God's will. And He's allowed me to go up to the mountain. And I've looked over. And I've seen the promised land. I may not get there with you. But I want you to know tonight, that we, as a people, will get to the promised land. So I'm happy, tonight. I'm not worried about anything. I'm not fearing any man. Mine eyes have seen the glory of the coming of the Lord."

He was staying at the Lorraine Motel in Room 306, a room he often stayed in. He stood on the balcony and said, "Ben, make sure you play 'Take My Hand, Precious Lord' in the meeting tonight. Play it real pretty." Moments

Martin Luther King Jr. stands on the balcony of the Lorraine Hotel, where moments after this photo was taken, he was assassinated. By Unknown, Public Domain

Martin Luther King Jr. and Coretta Scott King sarcophagus within the Martin Luther King Jr. National Historic Site-By Sjkorea81

A Closer Look
at what you have learned so far!

Lesson 6

PLUS+

This Lesson's Geography:

Madison, Wisconsin (WI)
Springfield, Illinois (IL)
Des Moines, Iowa (IA)
Jefferson City, Missouri (MO)
Little Rock, Arkansas (AR)

Previous Learned Geography:

Lansing, Michigan (MI)
Columbus, Ohio (OH)
Indianapolis, Indiana (IN)
Frankfort, Kentucky (KY)
Nashville, Tennessee (TN)
Atlanta, Georgia (GA)
Tallahassee, Florida (FL)
Montgomery, Alabama (AL)
Jackson, Mississippi (MS)
Baton Rouge, Louisiana (LA)
Annapolis, Maryland (MD)
Richmond, Virginia (VA)
Charleston, West Virginia (WV)
Raleigh, North Carolina (NC)
Columbia, South Carolina (SC)
Montpelier, Vermont (VT)
Albany, New York (NY)
Trenton, New Jersey (NJ)
Harrisburg, Pennsylvania (PA)
Dover, Delaware (DE)
Augusta, Maine (ME)
Concord, New Hampshire (NH)
Boston, Massachusetts (MA)
Providence, Rhode Island (RI)
Hartford, Connecticut (CT)

Hint: The geography found on this page, is also the geography that you will be reviewing this week. Refer to this map as needed when doing your "Memorization Through Repetition" worksheets.

Parent/Teacher: The "A Closer Look" page is intended to show students the accumulated geographic areas taught within their 6-week review period. For additional teaching tips on how to utilize this teaching aide for the different learning levels, please refer to page 1.

Zoom Me In!

Lesson 6

Use this sheet as a reference for this lesson's worksheets. Be sure to practice until you don't have to look!

You are learning your US States & Capitals! This week you are learning:

Madison, Wisconsin (WI)
Springfield, Illinois (IL)
Des Moines, Iowa (IA)
Jefferson City, Missouri (MO)
Little Rock, Arkansas (AR)

This Lesson's Geography:
US States and Capitals

Madison, Wisconsin (WI)
Springfield, Illinois (IL)
Des Moines, Iowa (IA)
Jefferson City, Missouri (MO)
Little Rock, Arkansas (AR)

Tid-Bits

Madison, Wisconsin

Wisconsin became the thirtieth state in the Union on May 29, 1848. It had been a territory right after the American Revolution, with settlers arriving for the mining, lumber, and dairy industries. Here in the state of Wisconsin, there are 5.82 million Cheeseheads. People here are called "Cheeseheads" because they produce more dairy than any other and have excellent cheddar cheese. The license plates even say, "America's Dairyland."

Wisconsin, "America's Dairyland" - Photo by: Unknown

Madison is the state capital, known as the "City of Four Lakes" because it touches lakes Monona, Mendota, Waubesa, and Kegonsa.

Wisconsin Dells - Photo by: Unknown - Public Domain

The state was named after the Wisconsin River, which is Native American for "gathering of waters." Wisconsin touches the vast Lake Superior. It has long and cold winters and warm summers.

Wisconsin has a large tourism industry. More than 300,000 people work in tourism, which makes the state over $9 billion a year. The Wisconsin Dells is a popular place for families to vacation in the summers.

Wisconsin was initially inhabited by the Chippewa, Winnebago, and Potawatomi tribes. Then Jean Nicolet, a Frenchman and explorer, studied the land when he arrived in 1634 in Green Bay. Over a hundred years later, the English gained the territory from the French in 1763 after the French and Indian War. The region became American land in 1783 after the Revolutionary War.

Settlers were slow to arrive in Wisconsin in the early 1800s. They were mostly immigrants from Germany, Poland, Scandinavia, and other European countries. More came when it officially became a territory in 1836. Madison was founded in the same year and was chosen as the capital, named for President James Madison, our 4th President.

Lesson 6

Before the Civil War, the Underground Railroad was an essential part of Wisconsin's history. Many runaway slaves made their way through Wisconsin on their way to freedom in Canada.

The worst forest fire in American history, called the Great Peshtigo Fire, started in October 1871 in Wisconsin. Over twelve hundred people died, and two billion trees burned to ash. It is America's deadliest fire.

Farming, dairy, and lumber became the most critical industries for Wisconsin in the late 1800s. While today, lumber and agriculture are less important, dairy has remained a valuable industry for the state.

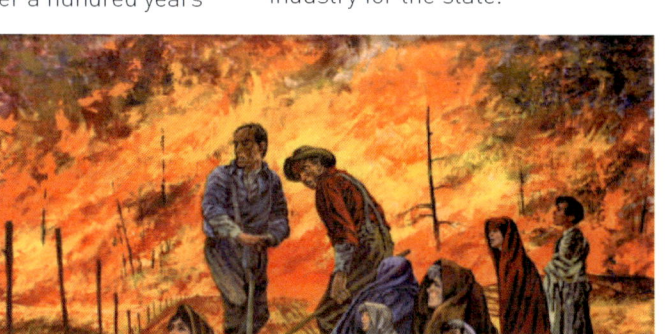
Painting of the Great Peshtigo Fire of 1871 in Wisconsin
By Unknown, Public Domain

In 1968, Mayor Henry Maier created Summerfest in Milwaukee. Every year, over a million people go to Milwaukee for an eleven-day music festival, which is often called "World's Largest Music Festival." There are eleven stages, and more than 700 bands play.

Native American tribes called Wisconsin home long before European explorers and white settlers arrived. Their history was not kept the way Europe's was. Archaeologists have found clues about their pasts by digging. What they found was that over 1,000 years ago, there was an era called Mississippian. The people who lived then are called Oneota. They farmed and lived in villages, depending on corn, bean, and squash crops to survive. The Oneonta were experienced gatherers, and hunters. They also had large trade networks. Their culture was rich in traditions and familial respect, and it was passed down through tribal elders. When Europeans arrived, the way of life for Native Americans changed.

The first explorer, Jean Nicolet, and a missionary, Jacques Marquette, arrived in 1634. The explorers were interested in trading for furs, and the missionaries worked with the Native Americans for over 150 years. The settlers and the American government changed their way of life even more. As more settlers went further and further west, the population grew. As you might guess, this led to conflict between settlers and the tribes. The Sauk and Fox tribes were forced to give their land to the United States in 1804, which caused the Black Hawk War.

Today, the Native Americans have tribal councils, to help keep their culture alive and fight for their right to make their own laws. They also work to keep the history alive.

Springfield, Illinois

Illinois became the twenty-first American state on December 3rd, 1818. It was named after the Illinois Native American tribe. It is the 25th largest state and sixth most populated with 12.67 million people. Eight million live in Chicago and the surrounding area. The state capital is Springfield, which Abraham Lincoln lived in from 1844 until he left in 1861 to become our 16th President, and Illinois is often called "Land of Lincoln."

As the third-largest city in the United States, Illinois is thought of in two sections: Chicago and everywhere else. Although Illinois is primarily known for Chicago's business, transportation, culture, and education center, farming is a big part of Illinois' economy, which mostly depends on livestock. Northern Illinois sits on Lake Michigan, and there are few hills. The state almost entirely rests at 600 feet above sea level, but the south does have the Ozark Mountains near Missouri. The winters are cold, and the summers are hot.

Like all other areas of the country, indigenous people lived in Illinois for a long time before white settlers arrived. The first known Native American people to live there were the Mississippians, which was a mound-building civilization. Several tribes were living in Illinois when French explorers arrived, including the Cahokia, Kaskaskia, Michigamea, Peoria, and Tamaroa.

The French explorers Louis Jolliet and Jacques Marquette were the first to arrive in 1673. After the French and Indian War, the land became English instead of French. Then in 1783, Illinois became a Union territory after the American Revolution. Springfield was settled in 1818 by Elisha Kelly, and the land became a state within the Union.

Our 16th President, Abraham Lincoln, moved to Illinois with his family in 1830. Lincoln showed interest in the law, which he began to explore as a hobby. He would visit courthouses to listen to examples of excellent oratory. Before long, Lincoln started reading law books. In 1836, he passed an oral exam conducted by a panel of lawyers and received his law license. While he did not attend law school, Lincoln pursued his cases with diligence, for which he was often rewarded. He practiced law in Springfield, becoming a politician and a husband to his wife Mary Todd in 1842. Later, he ran for President in 1860, winning the vote and being sworn in as U.S. President in 1861. He then moved from Springfield, Illinois, to Washington, D.C.

Downtown Chicago as seen from Lake Michigan - Photo by: Unknown - Public Domain

A younger Abraham Lincoln, possibly around 1845
By Unknown - Public domain

During the Civil War, 250,000 Illinoisans fought for the Union.

In the 1830s, John Deere invented the steel plow, which made Illinois prairie land more fertile and valuable.

Chicago was positioned exactly right to become an American hub for transportation. First, it is in the middle of the country with access to the Great Lakes and the Ohio River. The St. Lawrence Seaway makes it possible for people and goods in the Midwest to make it all the way to the Atlantic Ocean. In 1848, the Illinois and Michigan Canal opened transportation even more, because goods could travel between the Mississippi River and the Great Lakes.

People continued to move to Chicago because of the fast-growing industries. A labor movement began in the late 1800s, because many workers were treated poorly and wanted better work environments. There were violent moments between people and the police. Haymarket Square Riot was one of the most famous, which happened in Chicago, Illinois, in 1886.

Following the Civil War and the "Long Depression" (1873 to 1879), industrial manufacturing was rapidly expanding in the United States. Chicago was a major industrial center, where tens of thousands of immigrants were employed at a wage of about $1.50 a day. American workers worked between 60 to 100 hours weekly. The city became a center for many attempts to organize labor's demands for better working conditions. Employers responded with anti-union measures that included firing union members, recruiting strikebreakers, employing spies, and private security forces to divide the workers.

Conversely, socialist and anarchist organizations were actively militant. They believed that successful operations against the police and taking major industrial centers would lead to public support. This in turn would cause a revolution, destroy capitalism, and establish a socialist economy. There also existed the Noble and Holy Order of the

The Haymarket Riot, By Harper's Weekly-Public Domain

Knights of Labor. They did not believe in socialism or anarchy. They promoted the social and cultural uplift of the working man and demanded the eight-hour workday.

During the Industrial Revolution, in the late 1800s was a time when America exploded in economic size and wealth, which led to all these labor concerns. The voices of the masses were heard in what we call today the "Labor Movement," of which the labor unions were the backbone. In 1938, Congress passed a law called the "Fair Labor Standards Act." This law set the 40-hour workweek, regulated child labor, and set minimum wage and overtime pay standards. Later, these unions negotiated health care benefits. Now... what is a labor union? A labor union is a group of like-minded people joined together for the common welfare of employees related to working conditions, pay, and benefits. The first Monday of each September is Labor Day. In 1894, it became a federal holiday created initially for the public to celebrate the workers of the trade and labor organizations. Today, it is thought of as the last long weekend before the end of summer, where families and friends enjoy a bit more time together in the sun.

One of the most devastating fires in American history is known as the Great Chicago Fire. Between October 8th and October 10th, 1871, over a third of the city was destroyed after a small fire started in Catherine and Patrick O'Leary's barn. There is a legend about a cow kicking

An artist's rendering of the Great Chicago Fire of 1871
By John R. Chapin, died 1907 - From [1]. Originally from Harper's Weekly., Public Domain

Des Moines, Iowa

One of the most productive agricultural regions in the United States, from high above Iowa is a checkerboard pattern of farms, towns, and cities. Often referred to as the "Tall Corn State," its official nickname has a distinct meaning - they have flourishing cornfields, of course! Also known as the Hawkeye State, it honors the Native American leader, Black Hawk, who lived among a small group of Indians in the area.

Skyline of Des Moines, Iowa's capital and largest city - By Tim Kiser - Self-photographed

over a lantern, but it's just a story. Almost 300 people died, and 18,000 were buildings destroyed. Four square miles burned to ash. The fire was so devastating because Chicago's buildings, streets, sidewalks, and more were all built out of wood. The fire started in the middle of the night, spread quickly, and devoured everything in one day's time. It was not until October that things began to calm down, but the city was in a disastrous state. People did not know what to do, and they were homeless.

Thankfully, it did not take long for the people of Chicago to start rebuilding their beloved city. It cost over $200 million to rebuild. As Chicago was rebuilt, people continued to move to the town because there were even more jobs than before. Luckily, the city didn't lose everything. Transportation and the city's organization were still usable. Nine years after the fire, the town gained over 170,000 people. The Chicago Fire Department's training academy at the site of the O'Leary barn where the Great Chicago Fire began. In 1997, Catherine O'Leary and her cow were forgiven for the fire.

The state consists of many small communities, founded on fertile soils with plenty of rainfall. These communities are primed for farming. Around 90 percent of the land is utilized for agriculture, specializing in corn, soybeans, and livestock. The production of dairy is also very prominent in the northeast part of the state.

Native Americans were the original settlers in modern Iowa, dating back from 300 AD all the way to the 1600s. Native Americans inhabited the eastern lands, building big earth mounds over time. In 1803, the Union purchased land from the French in the Louisiana Purchase. Then later, in 1838, the state of Iowa was part of an organized territory of the U.S. until entering the Union in 1846. Iowa had a strong stance against slavery and fought on the side of the Union during the American Civil War between 1861 and 1865.

A Midwestern state, Iowa blends grasslands of the high prairie plains from the west to dense forests of the east. This land has a gently rolling landscape that steadily rises moving westward from the mighty Mississippi River, which forms the eastern boundary. Parallel, on the other side of the state, the muddy Missouri River and its tributary, the Big Sioux, form the western border of Iowa.

1871 illustration from Harper's Magazine depicting Mrs. O'Leary milking the cow
By Anonymous - Harper's Magazine, 1871, Public Domain

Central Iowa cornfield and dairy in June
By Christiane Tas - Own work, Public Domain

A Tid-Bit of Agriculture History

During the mid-1800s to mid-1900s, most farmers used draft horses for hard labor. The 1,800-pound animals plowed the earth for corn and oats, planted the crops, and cultivated the fields. They brought in the hay crop, pulled wagons of field corn, and hauled manure. The horse was of great importance to the success of a farm. No farm could survive without horse labor. However, there were considerable changes on the horizon that would enable farmers to grow more by working more land into crops for harvest; not only this, but changes in the kitchen as well. These farming changes came in the form of innovative farming equipment, automation of automobile manufacturing, and diversification of crops to meet the needs of society. Transportation through various means such as waterways allowed shipment of food to places near and far. In the kitchen, the wood-burning cook-stove, the Mason jar, and the refrigerator immensely helped prepare and preserve food. With the preservation of food, there was less waste. People became willing to stock up on foods. All of these progressive and very efficient methods reinforced the agricultural system. This made life more productive and profitable for farmers.

Jefferson City, Missouri

Sitting along the Missouri River, Jefferson City started as a small settlement called Lohman's Landing before the settlement became Missouri's capital in 1826. A son of the famous American pioneer Daniel Boone mapped out the city in 1822, naming it after Thomas Jefferson, our third President of the United States. The name of Missouri comes from a local Native American tribe that once lived in the area. The French gave the name to the local river, which seemed like an excellent state name too!

The Missouri River broadly divides the landscape, with the northern side of the river mostly consisting of rolling hills, open plains, and prairie country. In contrast, just south of the river, the land is primarily rough and hilly. Here again, the landscape displayed evidence of a native Mississippian culture that built large cities and mounds, before diminishing in the 14th century. Then European explorers in the 1600s came upon the Osage and Missouria nations. The French settlers established Louisiana, purchased by the United States in 1803.

In 1804, the city of St. Louis saw Lewis and Clark set out on their famous expedition, which was established to explore the area of the Louisiana Purchase and beyond.

The story begins like this...

On the early eve of a dreary December day in 1803, a group of men huddled in a boat drifting slowly along the edge of the Mississippi River. With their destination in sight, they readied themselves to go ashore at the Wood River's mouth in present-day St. Louis, Missouri. They set up camp amongst the trees. While the weather was mean - with wind, snow, hail, and bitter cold - they had prepared for this and could not turn back. Bad weather was just one danger among the many they would overcome in this epic adventure.

The expedition was led by two men named Meriwether Lewis and William Clark. The country's president, Thomas Jefferson, was curious about this new land that they had just purchased called "Louisiana." Since he could not go on this adventure, he chose his

Lewis and Clark statue with their dog Seaman in St. Charles, Missouri By NOAA Photo Library - Public Domain

childhood friend and personal secretary Meriwether Lewis to lead the exploring party. Lewis put together a group of men, and to be his co-leader, he chose his trusted colleague William Clark, who had served alongside him in the Army. Both men knew the western frontier that they were going to explore and they had survival skills that they had learned in the Army. Lewis spoke several Native American languages. This expedition had goals: explore the territory, learn all they could about the natives living in the region, learn about the terrain, plants, animals, and geology. They were to map out and journal everything that they found and

Lock and Dam No. 15, is the largest roller dam in the world Davenport, Iowa; Rock Island, Illinois. (1990) By US Army Corps of Engineers, Carol Arney - US Army Corps of Engineers Digital Visual Library. Public Domain

Statue of Sacagawea and her baby boy.
By Unknown - Public Domain

The adventure was named the Voyage of Discovery, and the name given to this select group of 45 men was the Corps of Discovery.

After they made camp upon their arrival at St. Louis, they decided to spend the winter there. Come spring of 1804, the weather was good for travel. They left St. Louis with their sights set on exploring all the way to the Pacific Ocean. They took about a year to get there and a year to get back, leaving St. Louis, Missouri, by boat and then traveling westward through present-day Missouri, Iowa, Nebraska, and South Dakota.

In November, they reached present-day North Dakota and met a young Shoshone Native American woman whose name is forever synonymous with Lewis and Clark. Her name was Sacagawea (Sa-kuh-juh-WEE-uh). She and her fur-trader husband, Toussaint Charbonneau (Too-SAHNT SHAR-bon-oh), joined the expedition as interpreters. That wasn't the only thing she would do, however. She helped the group find horses, identify edible plants and herbs, and obtain essential supplies. While on this trek, Sacagawea gave birth to a baby boy that she named Jean. As she carried her baby, with her husband by her side, she also served as a powerful symbol of peace to tribes along their way, which kept them safe.

The expedition was hard, as they endured exhaustion, freezing temperatures, braved rough rivers and dangerous mountains, and crossed canyons, all while surviving on little food. At last, in November of 1805, they reached the Pacific Ocean—over a year after they left Missouri. After surviving a harsh winter on the coast, they began their journey homeward. At the end of their adventure in March of 1806, they shared their tales with President Jefferson, delivering maps created of the unchartered land, rivers, and mountains. They also presented all the journals filled with every facet of their exploration, which detailed their experiences with Native American tribes, and scientific observations on plants and animals that they had never seen before. They also told stories that made other adventurous Americans want to go west—and west they went, for the next century. Manifest Destiny was on the rise.

experienced. Their adventure was an epic 8,000-mile-long trek that was a major step in westward expansion for the young United States of America.

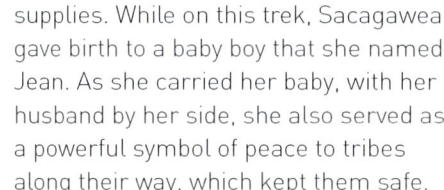

Corps of Discovery meet Chinooks on the Lower Columbia, October 1805 (Charles Marion Russel, c. 1905)
Humanities Texas, Public Domain

LEWIS AND CLARK EXPEDITION 1804-1806

By Victor van Werkhooven
Own work, Public Domain

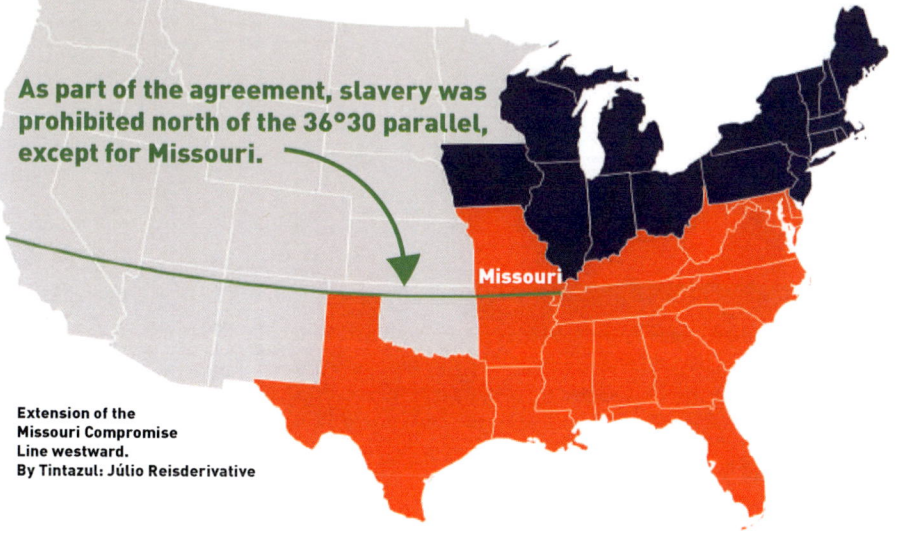

As part of the agreement, slavery was prohibited north of the 36°30 parallel, except for Missouri.

Missouri

Extension of the
Missouri Compromise
Line westward.
By Tintazul: Júlio Reisderivative

The Missouri Compromise

The establishment of slavery became especially prominent in the area following two significant events: the invention of the cotton gin by Eli Whitney in 1793, and the Louisiana Purchase. These two milestones in history led to the westward migration of slave-owning settlers into the area of present-day Missouri and Arkansas, then known as Upper Louisiana. The majority of slave owners had moved north to Missouri from worn-out agricultural lands in North Carolina, Tennessee, Kentucky, and Virginia. Still, cotton cultivation, arguably the industry to which slave labor was the most important, was never as well-suited to Missouri's climate as to the rest of the southern United States and was limited entirely to the southern parts of the state.

As time marched on, Missouri requested statehood within the Union; this posed a problem with the balance of power within the House of Representatives, based on the three-fifths rule. By this rule, for every five slaves, three would be counted in the population, and the population of each state determines how many representatives the state has in Congress. If Missouri were to become a state, the south would then have the majority. Still, there were objections to the expansion of slavery into the Louisiana Purchase territory-based solely on egalitarianism, which is believing that all people are created equal and deserve equal rights and opportunities. The problem was without a solution, a stand-still on both sides of Missouri's desire to become a state.

Then came an unexpected turn of events... Maine offered its petition for statehood. Seizing the opportunity, the Senate linked both bills, making Maine's admission into the Union a requirement for Missouri to enter the Union as a slave state. The balance was restored. However, not in the eyes of all; an egalitarian society would have to wait.

The Missouri Compromise was passed in 1820. Maine became a state that same year; Missouri, followed in 1821. Maine was admitted into the Union as a free state, Missouri as a slave state. As part of the agreement, slavery was prohibited north of the 36°30 parallel, except for Missouri. It also disallowed any more of the Louisiana Territory being admitted as slave states.

Missouri, a central player in the westward expansion of the United States, is memorialized today by the Gateway Arch. Here in Missouri, the Pony Express, Oregon Trail, Santa Fe Trail, and the California Trail began. As a border state, Missouri's role in the American Civil War was complicated, and there were many conflicts within.

Little Rock, Arkansas

Arkansas became the 25th state on June 15th, 1836. Little Rock is the capital and has been from the time it was a territory. When French explorers came to the area, they named it after the Arkansas River, which is a word from the local Quapaw tribe. It is known as the Natural State because there are so many beautiful mountains and lakes. The north and west have highlands, the Ouachita Mountains, and the Ozark Mountains covered in forests. The south and east have lowlands and plains for farming. Arkansas has mild winters with hot summers.

Initially, the French explorers created a trading post at Little Rock in 1722 along the Arkansas River. Then this territory changed hands from the French to the Spanish and back to the French before our third President, Thomas Jefferson, bought the area from France in the Louisiana Purchase of 1803. Then Arkansas became a U.S. territory in 1819.

The Quapaw tribe was the predominant tribe in the area before Europeans and settlers moved in. Many Native Americans were forcibly removed from their homeland between 1821 and 1836 to make room for settlers.

Slavery was a critical and difficult topic when Arkansas applied to become a state. The south wanted to own slaves, and the north didn't. Arkansas entered the Union in 1836 as the thirteenth slave state. Years later, in 1860, just before the Civil War, 25% of Arkansas' population were slaves.

During the American Civil War, Arkansas seceded from the Union to join and fight

Attempting to go to school - The "Little Rock Nine" By Unknown - Public Domain

Little Rock Nine - By Unknown - Public Domain

Done with the first day of school - The "Little Rock Nine" By Unknown - Public Domain

with the Confederacy. Because Arkansas is next to the Mississippi River, it was an essential state for the Confederacy. Having control over the Mississippi meant they could control trade and travel. Along the Mississippi, they were able to move troops, ammunitions, and supplies for the war effort. Three years after the Confederate rebellion was put to rest with the North winning over the South, Arkansas returned to the United States in 1868.

The "Little Rock Nine"

The U.S. Supreme Court made it illegal to segregate public schools based on skin color with the landmark case of Brown v. Board of Education in 1954. With this decision, schools across the south were, by law, supposed to begin integrating. In Little Rock, Arkansas, in 1957, nine black students tried to go to a school that had not yet been integrated. Only white students went there. Arkansas state troops were sent to stop the nine students from entering the school. Each day for weeks, they tried to go to school and weren't allowed. Word reached all the way to the White House that the state of Arkansas was going against the law that the Supreme Court had handed down. In response, federal troops arrived to enforce the law. Finally, after weeks, the "Little Rock Nine" were able to enter the school, enroll as students and be taught alongside white students.

Why were these students separated in the first place? The answer is in a set of laws called "Jim Crow" laws that began being passed in southern states a few years after the Civil War ended. These laws were created to segregate, or keep separate, black and white people. These laws stayed in place until 1954, with the Supreme Court decision to integrate schools. Jim Crow laws meant black people could not use the same public places that white people did. These laws were protected in 1896 in the Supreme Court case Plessy v. Ferguson because the Supreme Court said the designated areas were "separate but equal," even though they were not. Schools, buses, bathrooms, restaurants, hospitals, drinking fountains, and everything else were separate. White people had theirs, and black people had theirs.

During the era of Jim Crow laws, black people sometimes lived in fear for their lives in the south. It was a very difficult and dangerous time because they were not allowed to live freely. These rights that they deserved, but did not have the freedom to exercise, are called Civil Rights.

Many Jim Crow laws were in place for almost a hundred years, making it hard for black people to vote. In 1964, the Civil Rights Act passed, and in 1965, the Voting Rights Act passed. These two laws were fundamental in making life better and more equal for all Americans.

Representation of the racist south at the idea of school integration. By Unknown, Public Domain

A Closer Look
at what you have learned so far!

Lesson 7

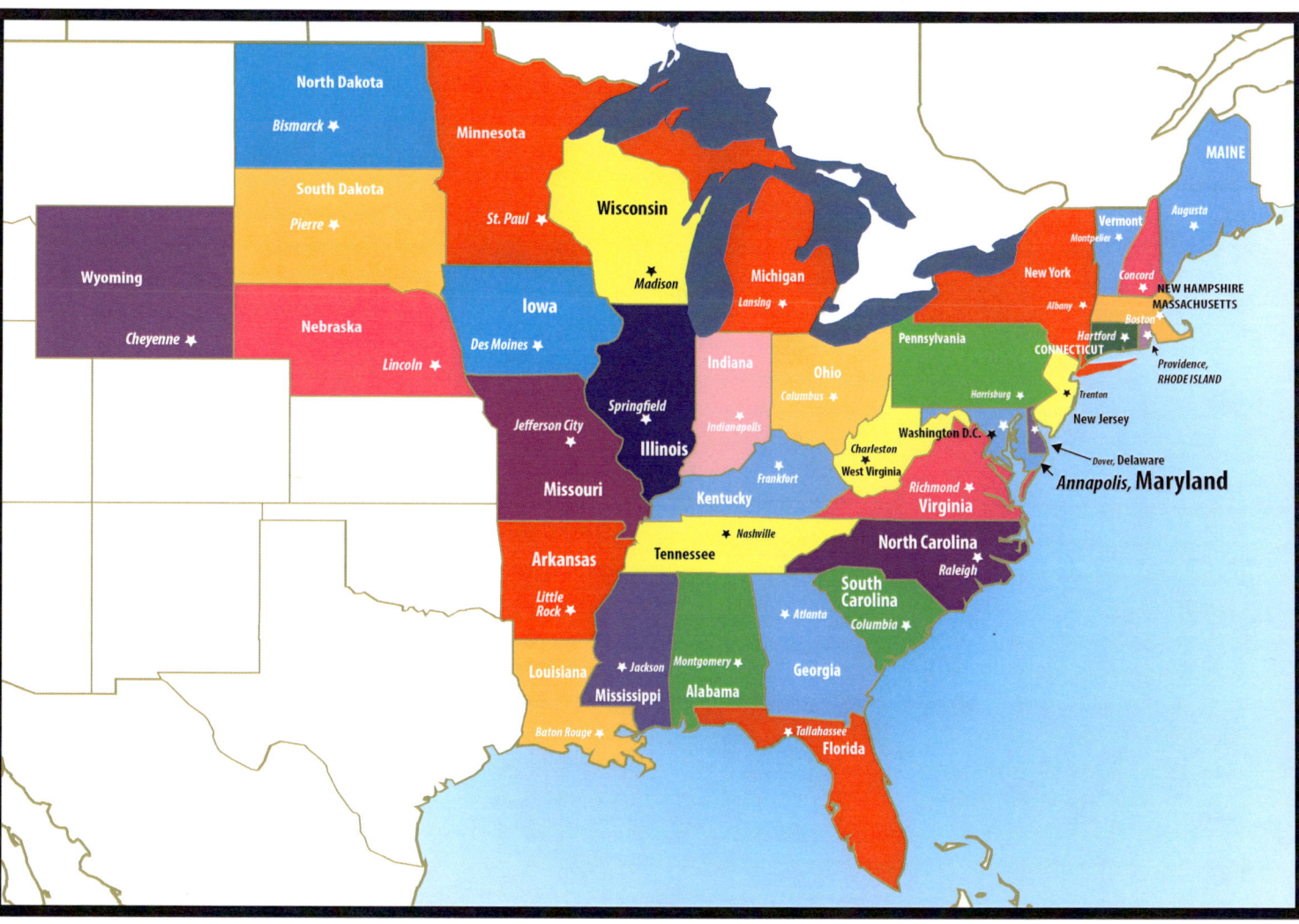

PLUS+
This Lesson's Geography:

St. Paul, Minnesota (MN)
Bismarck, North Dakota (ND)
Pierre, South Dakota (SD)
Cheyenne, Wyoming (WY)
Lincoln, Nebraska (NE)

Previous Learned Geography:

Madison, Wisconsin (WI)
Springfield, Illinois (IL)
Des Moines, Iowa (IA)
Jefferson City, Missouri (MO)
Little Rock, Arkansas (AR)
Lansing, Michigan (MI)
Columbus, Ohio (OH)
Indianapolis, Indiana (IN)
Frankfort, Kentucky (KY)
Nashville, Tennessee (TN)
Atlanta, Georgia (GA)
Tallahassee, Florida (FL)
Montgomery, Alabama (AL)
Jackson, Mississippi (MS)
Baton Rouge, Louisiana (LA)
Annapolis, Maryland (MD)
Richmond, Virginia (VA)
Charleston, West Virginia (WV)
Raleigh, North Carolina (NC)
Columbia, South Carolina (SC)
Montpelier, Vermont (VT)
Albany, New York (NY)
Trenton, New Jersey (NJ)
Harrisburg, Pennsylvania (PA)
Dover, Delaware (DE)
Augusta, Maine (ME)
Concord, New Hampshire (NH)
Boston, Massachusetts (MA)
Providence, Rhode Island (RI)
Hartford, Connecticut (CT)

Hint: The geography found on this page, is also the geography that you will be reviewing this week. Refer to this map as needed when doing your "Memorization Through Repetition" worksheets.

Parent/Teacher: The "A Closer Look" page is intended to show students the accumulated geographic areas taught within their 6-week review period. For additional teaching tips on how to utilize this teaching aide for the different learning levels, please refer to page 1.

Zoom Me In!

Lesson 7

Use this sheet as a reference for this lesson's worksheets.
Be sure to practice until you don't have to look!

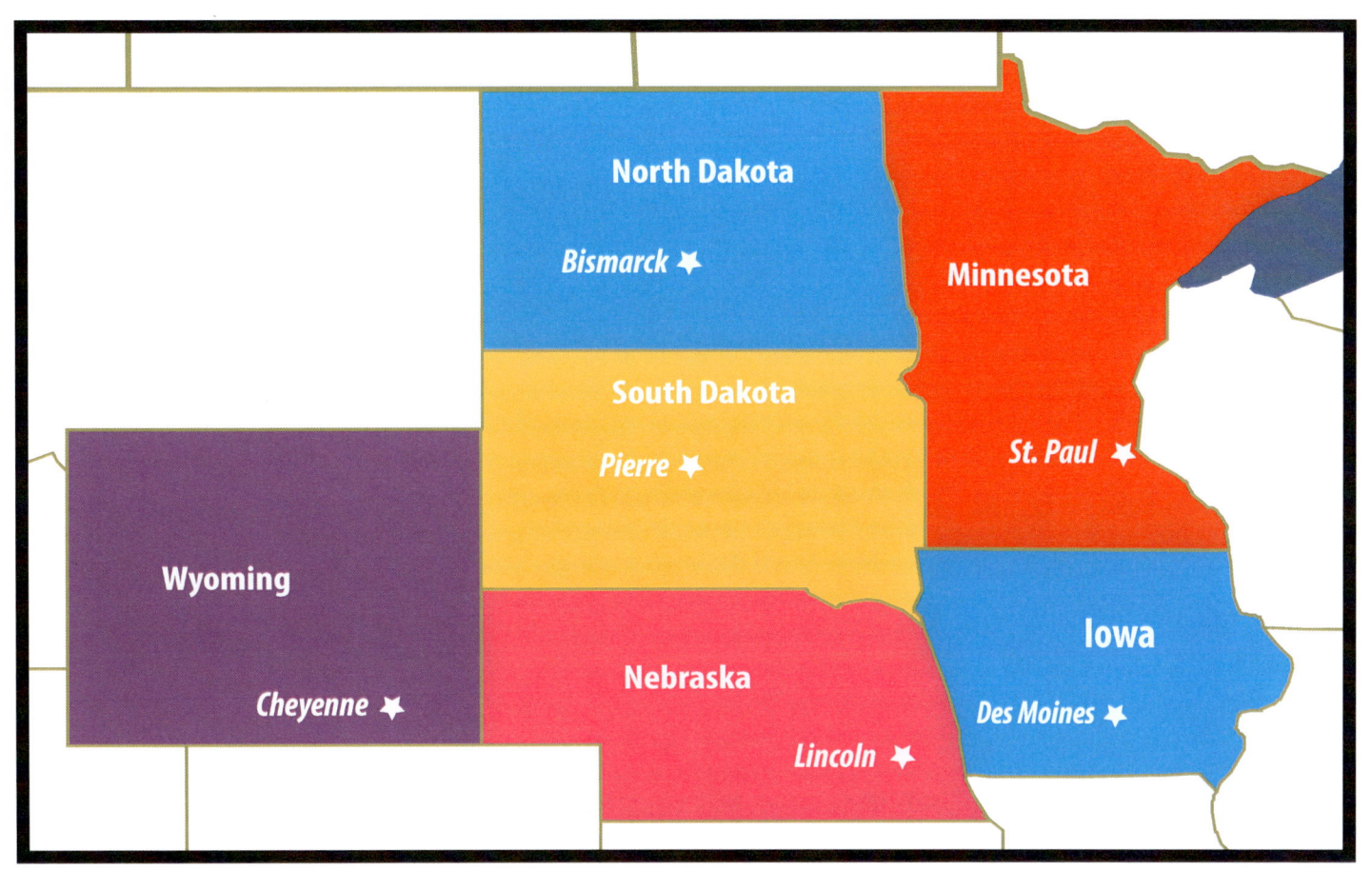

You are learning your US States & Capitals!

This week you are learning:

St. Paul, Minnesota (MN)
Bismarck, North Dakota (ND)
Pierre, South Dakota (SD)
Cheyenne, Wyoming (WY)
Lincoln, Nebraska (NE)

This Lesson's Geography:
US States and Capitals

St. Paul, Minnesota (MN)
Bismarck, North Dakota (ND)
Pierre, South Dakota (SD)
Cheyenne, Wyoming (WY)
Lincoln, Nebraska (NE)

Tid-Bits

Saint Paul, Minnesota
Indian History – Dakota/Sioux

On May 11th, 1858, Minnesota became the 32nd state. Saint Paul is the capital. Of the lower 48 states, it reaches the farthest north. It borders Canada and Lake Superior. Minnesota was named after the Minnesota River. The Dakota Sioux named the river Minnesota because it means "sky-tinted waters." It is a big state with a lot of lakes, which is why people call it the "Land of 10,000 Lakes," even though there are actually 11,842 lakes. Among these lakes are many forests, hills, plains, valleys, and wildlife living in

Land of 10,000 Lakes - Minnesota - By Unknown, Public Domain

Minnesota. It has cold winters and warm summers.

The Dakota tribe was part of the Sioux Nation. They lived in Minnesota along with the Chippewa tribe a long time before French explorers came in the 1600s. French fur traders arrived in the 1600s to trade for furs with the local tribes. Many of these French traders created strong relationships with the Native Americans. The bonds were so strong that they fought beside them during the French and Indian War against Britain. After that war, Britain took control of Minnesota. When the U.S. defeated Britain in the Revolutionary War, part of Minnesota was turned over to the U.S. The rest of Minnesota was bought from the French in the Louisiana Purchase of 1803. In 1849, Minnesota became a territory. Nine years later, it became a state.

The Dakota people were not happy that the U.S. was taking their land without keeping their promises or making payments for the property. The Dakota started one of the worst Native American wars in 1862 in the Minnesota River Valley by killing several settlers. The fighting lasted four months. When it was over, several Dakota were hung in Mankato, Minnesota, and those left were driven from their homeland.

Attractions

In 1992, the Mall of America opened just outside Minneapolis. The mall has over 4.2 million square feet and has more than 400 stores. There is even a theme park in the middle of the mall. Over 40 million people visit every year.

Minneapolis is home to the longest continuous indoor walkway, connecting 73 blocks. It is eight miles long and is called the Skyway System. It was built because the winters are so cold in Minneapolis that it's hard for people to walk outside. The Skyway lets people go to work, shop, eat, and more without leaving the system.

The Great Depression

The Great Depression was a devastating economic crisis in the 1930s. What began in the United States

Mall of America, Minnesota - By Unknown, Public Domain

Lesson 7

ended up affecting the entire world. The Great Depression started because prices in the stock market began falling in September 1929. Then on Tuesday, October 29th, 1929, the market crashed - this dark day is now called "Black Tuesday." The world's economic productivity fell by 15% between 1929 and 1932, which is a lot. Some economies didn't recover until World War II.

No one was spared from the Great Depression; everyone's way of life changed.

Skyway System, Minneapolis, Minnesota - By Unknown, Public Domain

Skid Row, Minneapolis, Minnesota - During the Great Depression in the 1930s - By Unknown, Public Domain

Regardless of economic status, both the rich and the poor and everywhere in between lost their jobs and their savings. The unemployment of Americans reached an all-time high at 23%. Farming communities were hit really hard because they could not sell their crops for enough money to feed their families or plant crops for the following year. No one had money to buy anything, so people in manufacturing and other industries weren't working because no one could buy what was being made. Minnesota's economy relied on farming and industry.

During World War II, the economy was stimulated once again, enabling people to find jobs and make money. This allowed them to buy the things they needed, which got manufacturing rolling once again. Farming technology was improved, which helped farmers tremendously. Everything got better and better after the war.

Bismarck, North Dakota

North Dakota became the 39th or 40th state on November 2, 1889. No one knows which state was 39th and 40th because North Dakota became a state at the same time South Dakota became a state. There is a rivalry between the two sibling states. When signing, President Benjamin Harrison thought it would be funny to shuffle the papers so no one would ever know which came first. While geographically it is the 19th largest state, it is the 47th most populated state with just a little over 762,000 residents.

**Depression hit family, Minnesota
By Unknown, Library of Congress
Public Domain**

North Dakota borders Canada, where it got its nickname, "Peace Garden State," because it is a symbol of friendship between our two countries. It was named for a Native American word "Dakota," meaning friends. The capital is Bismarck, and the state has rolling hills and buttes, which are hills with flat tops. The Missouri River is the biggest river in this state. The Badlands are a famous rugged area in the southwest; they are part of a National Park named for Theodore Roosevelt, our 26th President. These lands have been called by this strange name, Badlands, for a long time - not just here in North Dakota but also in other places with similar features.

Badlands... what does this name mean? Where did it come from? Are the lands really that bad?

Modern tribes like the Lakota called this land "mako sica" (mah-koh see-kah). When translated means "badlands." Some European explorers came up with similar terms like the French, who called it a "bad land to travel." As settlers moved westward, they would see flat, rolling, grass-covered land for miles. This is easy to travel through, but then... their wagon begins going over loose rock and mud, and in the distance, they would see canyons, no more grass, no more flat ground. The road ahead, filled with unusual landforms and hills, is unfriendly. A challenging trip indeed, with no end in sight. Little water and not much to eat. Do you think that they have looked at it as bad land?

North Dakota Badlands, By Unknown, Public domain

It might have been difficult to traverse, harsh to live in, but since it is full of color and strange shapes, the Badlands is a beautiful place to visit. Theodore Roosevelt said the Badlands do not seem to belong to this earth.

North Dakota has a dry climate with hot summers and frigid winters. Most people live on farms or in small towns. Here, farmers grow more wheat than anywhere else in the U.S.

Before Europeans and settlers arrived, a lot of Plains tribes lived on the land for thousands of years, like the Mandan, Sioux, and Chippewa tribes.

French Canadians explored the area starting in 1738. Spain held the region from 1762 to 1802. It was quickly sold to the U.S. in the Louisiana Purchase in 1803. Sent in an expedition by Thomas Jefferson, Lewis and Clark were the first Americans to explore the region.

The Dakota Territory was created in 1861 and included present-day North and South Dakota. Settlers did not move here quickly - that is until the railroad came through. Then, people started moving in more in the 1870s and 1880s.

The 1930s were hard on North Dakota because of the drought. Many of the farms and farming communities did not survive. Many people moved away. People started coming back in the 1960s when the military built several missile sites, air bases, and military facilities in North Dakota.

North Dakota tried to rename their state Dakota in 1947 and 1989. Both times, they were not allowed to.

A "dinosaur mummy" was discovered on a ranch outside of Marmarth, North Dakota, in 1999 by a teenager. A duck-billed hadrosaur was found with bones and tendons still intact because it was so well preserved.

International Peace Garden

The International Peace Garden is made up of 2,339 acres between North Dakota and Manitoba, Canada. There are over 100,000 flowers. The Peace Chapel has an 18-foot tall clock made out of flowers.

International Peace Garden - North Dakota. By Unknown, Public Domain

Speaking of flowers, here in North Dakota, there are more sunflowers grown than anywhere else in the U.S.

The very center of North America is in Rugby, North Dakota. A monument 21 feet high is made out of stone to let everyone know.

Salem Sue is the largest Holstein Cow in the world. She lives in New Salem, North Dakota. She is made of fiberglass and is 38 feet tall, 50 feet long, and weighs six tons. Jamestown has the world's most giant buffalo. Smaller than Salem Sue, it is 26 feet tall, 36 feet long, and weighs sixty tons.

Don't lie down and fall asleep in your shoes in North Dakota. It's illegal! Although in case North Dakota has its first earthquake while you are sleeping, those shoes may come in handy. Up to this point, there have been no known earthquakes in North Dakota, the only state in the U.S. where that is true!

There are a lot of rodeos in North Dakota every year. Hundreds of cowboys compete at more than fifty local and regional rodeos every year.

Theodore Roosevelt and the Rough Riders

Before Theodore Roosevelt became President, he lived in North Dakota. While he lived there, the Spanish-American War broke out. He wanted to do something to help, so he helped organize the First Volunteer Cavalry in 1898. They were nicknamed the Rough Riders. There were two other regiments like it, but the Rough Riders were the only ones to go to battle.

Colonel Theodore Roosevelt - By Unknown, Public Domain

The Spanish-American War was fought because Spain had colonized Cuba and was not treating it well. Cuba was rebelling against Spain because they wanted their independence. Roosevelt sided with the Cubans. After the first commander of the regiment transferred to a different division, Roosevelt became the Rough Riders commander. Many men from all different backgrounds joined the cavalry. College athletes, singers, Texas Rangers, and Native Americans all volunteered to follow Roosevelt. Everyone had to be skilled horsemen and ready to go to battle.

The Rough Riders were sent to Cuba to fight against the Spanish. The Rough Riders were sent early, but there wasn't enough room on the

Colonel Theodore Roosevelt and the Rough Riders- By Unknown, Public Domain

ships for their horses to go, too. As a cavalry regiment, they needed their horses to fight. Many men were left behind also. The Rough Riders had low spirits because they didn't have their horses, and their fellow soldiers. Additionally, many were sick when they arrived in Cuba.

The Battle for Las Guasimas was the first for the Rough Riders. They had to march and fight on foot. The Spanish had the advantage and should have kept their outpost, but the Rough Riders fought them back. Eventually, they took control of the Las Guasimas outpost.

Santiago was a critical city to hold. It meant control over Cuba and victory in the war. To take control of Santiago, a battle was fought on San Juan Hill. On July 3, 1898, the Rough Riders began the eight-mile march to Santiago from Las Guasimas. When they stopped at the foot of San Juan Hill, the Spanish started shooting at the Rough Riders. They quickly looked for cover. Slowly and safely they made it to the rest of the military, to fight the Battle of San Juan Hill. Roosevelt rode on horseback and led his men, who still didn't have their horses, to victory. The battle was fought uphill, which added to the difficulty. It was a hard-won battle—a victory over Spain.

The Rough Riders earned a legendary reputation at the Battle of San Juan Hill. It was a turning point in the war. The Spanish left Cuba a few weeks after surrendering. Theodore Roosevelt came back to the United States, a military hero for leading the Rough Riders to victory.

Pierre, South Dakota

South Dakota became a state on November 2, 1889. Pierre is the capital. South Dakota was named after the Dakota tribe who lived there. Eastern South Dakota is flat prairie, and the western part are plains that are higher in elevation than the prairies. This area's landscape is broken by hills and canyons. The western plains have large, rugged, and forbidding land called the Badlands. The dense forested Black Hills are in the west and serve as the home to Mount Rushmore and Black Elk Peak. Black Elk Peak is the nation's highest point east of the Rocky Mountains at 7,242 feet tall. The state is sometimes called "The Mount Rushmore State." The Missouri River flows through the middle of the state

South Dakota Scenery - By Unknown, Public Domain

before it becomes part of the border between South Dakota and Nebraska. South Dakota has warm winters and cold summers.

Before Europeans and settlers arrived in the area, Arikara, Sioux, and Cheyenne people lived there. By the 1800s, the only remaining tribal nation were the Sioux.

This land was part of the territory referred to as "Louisiana." While it changed hands a few times, eventually in 1803, the U.S. purchased "Louisiana" from the French. Then, in 1804, Lewis and Clark explored South Dakota. The first permanent settlement was created in 1817 along the Missouri River. Dakota was made into a territory in 1861. In 1874, people came in hopes to strike it rich as there was gold found in the Black Hills.

In 1832, John Jacob Astor built Fort Pierre Chouteau for his American Fur Company. The fort was the largest and best trading post in the northern Great Plains.

Mount Rushmore - South Dakota - By Unknown, Public Domain

Here also, Native Americans fought wars against settlers from the 1850s to the 1890s because they did not want to lose their land and way of life. In 1890, 200 Sioux people were killed at the Battle of Wounded Knee. After the battle, the remaining Native Americans were forced to live on reservations.

Mount Rushmore National Memorial is one of the biggest tourist attractions in South Dakota. It is a huge sculpture of four presidents carved into the granite mountain. The presidents on Mount Rushmore are George Washington, Thomas Jefferson, Abraham Lincoln, and Theodore Roosevelt. The memorial was finished in 1941. It took fourteen years to build with a cost of over a million dollars.

Crazy Horse was a Lakota tribe leader. A memorial in his honor is being designed and built in the Black Hills. It will be the biggest statue in the world when it is completed at 563 feet tall and 641 feet long.

South Dakota shares "The Badlands" with North Dakota which you've learned a bit about. Within, some of the richest deposits of fossils in all the world have been found. In fact, there are so many it would cover over 244,000 acres. Among those fossils are some very unique finds! For instance, a camel the size of a dog, a horse with three toes, a saber-toothed cat, and a Tyrannosaurus Rex.

General George Armstrong Custer is an important man in American history. He was an officer and calvary commander in the Army. He fought during the Civil War, including the battle of Gettysburg. After that, he went west to fight in the Indian Wars. In 1874, he confirmed gold in the Black Hills, which created a lot of change in the Dakota Territory. The Sioux Nation had been given rights to stay on their land in the Treaty of Fort Laramie in 1868. When people found out there was gold in South Dakota, they started moving into the area and onto Sioux land. This started the Black Hills War of 1876.

General Custer and his troops were fighting in the Montana Territory. On June 25, 1876, they fought in the Battle of Little Bighorn, which has become known as Custer's Last Stand because he died there. General Custer led five companies of men against the Lakota tribe. There were more than 3,500 people involved in the fight. As soldiers died, the Lakota took the guns from the dead men, which meant Custer's forces had less ammunition while the Lakota gained more. The Lakota killed all of Custer's men at the Battle of Little Bighorn. In 1886, this battleground was designated a national cemetery.

TOP: Crazy Horse Monument (while under construction) By Unknown, Public Domain
BOTTOM: Crazy Horse - By Unknown, Public Domain

General George Custer - By Unknown, Public Domain

Cheyenne, Wyoming

Wyoming became the 44th state in the U.S. on July 10, 1890. It is the tenth largest state but has the least amount of citizens with only 550,000 people. Cheyenne is the capital of Wyoming. It is nicknamed the "Equality State" because it gave women the right to vote and hold elected offices before any other state. Wyoming is a big state with a lot of mountains and plains. It is very dry with winters that are cold and long, the summers are warm and short. Ranching is a big part of Wyoming's culture. Ranches have cattle and sheep on them, but they also grow crops, like potatoes, beans, corn, wheat, and more. The Native American tribes: Crow, Arapaho, Lakota, and Shoshone lived on the land before Europeans and settlers arrived. The name Wyoming comes from a Munsee word, meaning "at the big river flat."

Various Images of Yellowstone National Park - All by: Unknown - Public Domain

Old Faithful

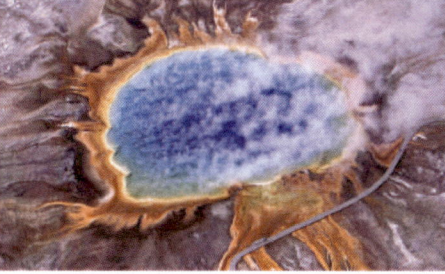

Yellowstone National Park and the geyser, Old Faithful, are in Wyoming. There is also a lot of wildlife, like coyotes, bears, eagles, moose, and more. With millions of people traveling to Wyoming to take in the national parks, hike, and experience the cowboy culture, tourism is vital to Wyoming's economy. Every summer in Cheyenne, there is a festival called Frontier Days, which hosts the world's largest rodeo. It is a place people like visiting to escape from busy lives and see Wyoming's breathtaking scenery.

Part of the territory was first claimed by Spain for its Mexican territory. After the Mexican-American War in 1848, it became an American territory. The other part belonged to France, but it became American as part of the Louisiana Purchase.

In 1834, Fort William, which was later called Fort Laramie, was the first settlement in Wyoming.

Yellowstone National Park

Wyoming is so beautiful, people knew they wanted to keep it that way. That it needed to be protected. In 1872, Ulysses S. Grant, our 18th President, made Yellowstone National Park the first national park. The establishment of Yellowstone originated the concept of natural preservation and the importance of wildlife conservation. Today, there are many national parks in Wyoming, including Devil's Tower, the first national monument. More people moved to Wyoming for bounty and beauty after the railroad was built in Cheyenne in 1867.

The Wild Bunch - Butch Cassidy & the Sundance Kid

Wyoming is in the west, the wild west. A man by the name of Henry Longabaugh once stole a horse in a town called Sundance within Wyoming. He got caught and went to prison. There he was nicknamed "Sundance Kid." Around 1896 he was released from prison and met Butch Cassidy and joined his gang called the "Wild Bunch." This gang had the longest run of successful bank and train robberies in American history.

The law was hot in pursuit, but Butch Cassidy and the Sundance Kid fled the United States. First to Argentina and then to Bolivia, where they were killed in a shootout in November 1908. Their story became famous when Hollywood made a film about them much later.

Women's Suffrage

Women's suffrage is a big part of American history. Women did not always have the right to vote and hold elected office. They had to fight for a very long

TOP: Women's Suffrage Protest Wyoming – By Unknown, Public Domain

Documentation Photo of some of the first votes in Wyoming By Unknown, Public Domain

time to be able to vote. Wyoming is known as the "Equality State" because they were the first to recognize those rights for women.

In the 1820s, women started forming groups that fought for their right to vote and other things like, anti-slavery, religious movements, and more. They wanted the same rights and freedoms that white men had. In 1848, many women gathered at Seneca Falls, New York, for a convention to share their ideas, which encouraged them, adding vigor to their civil rights fight.

Wyoming became a U.S. territory in 1868. A year later, in 1869, they gave women the right to vote and unrestricted suffrage. When they became a state in 1890, women were able to vote and hold office. That is fifty-one years before the United States made it a law for all states. The entire United States allowed women to vote and hold office when the 19th Amendment was added to the U.S. Constitution on August 18, 1920. In 1924, Wyoming was the first state to elect a female governor. Her name was Nellie Tayloe Ross.

The Wild Bunch - By Unknown, Public Domain

A Closer Look
at what you have learned for the last 6 lessons!

Lesson 8

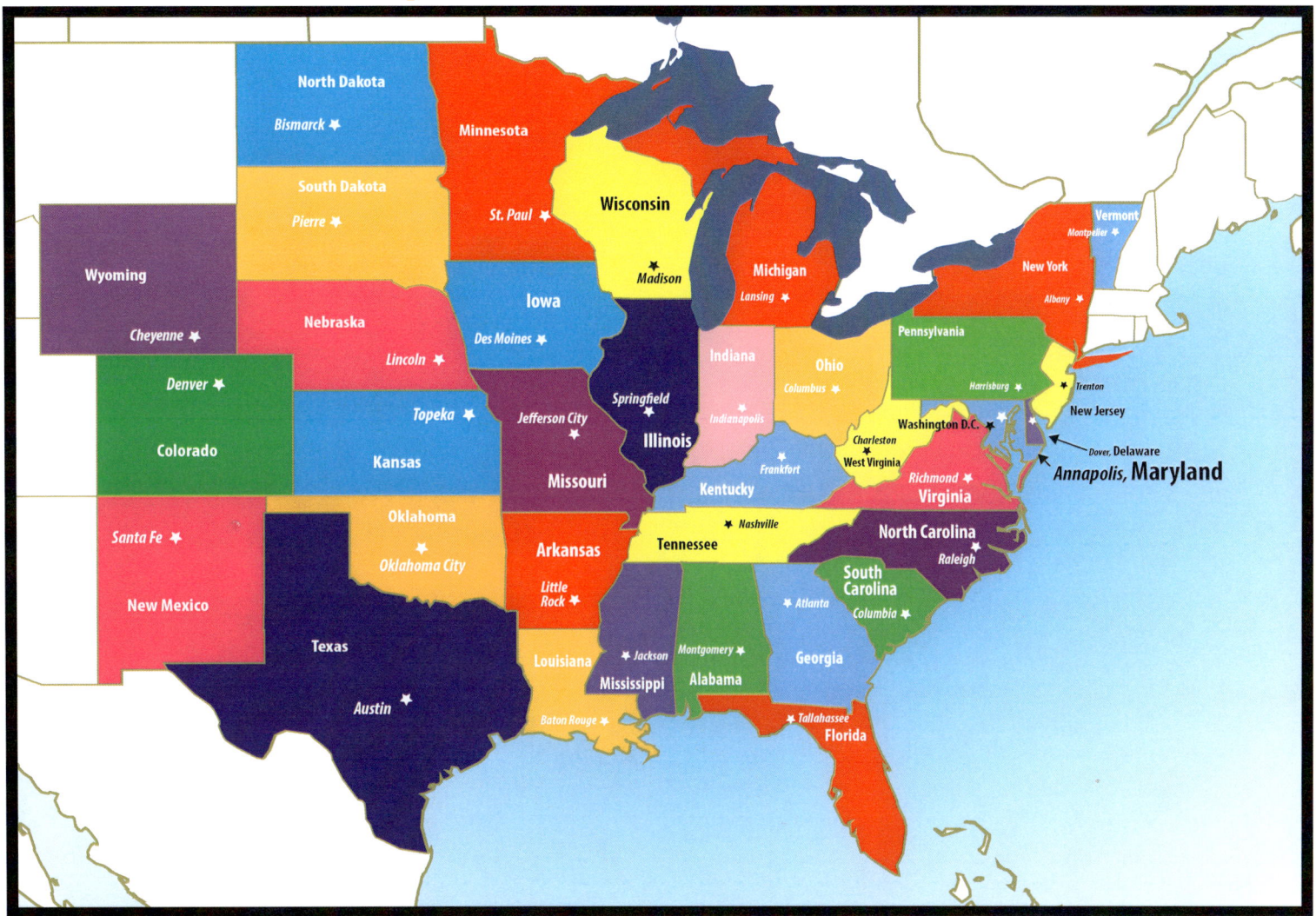

Hint: The geography found on this page, is also the geography that you will be reviewing this week (except states in gray). Refer to this map as needed when doing your "Memorization Through Repetition" worksheets.

Parent/Teacher: The "A Closer Look" page is intended to show students the accumulated geographic areas taught within their 6-week review period. For additional teaching tips on how to utilize this teaching aide for the different learning levels, please refer to page 1.

PLUS+
This Lesson's Geography:

Topeka, Kansas (KS)
Oklahoma City, Oklahoma (OK)
Austin, Texas (TX)
Denver, Colorado (CO)
Santa Fe, New Mexico (NM)

Previous Learned Geography

Listed here is the geography learned over the last 6 lessons. All lessons learned before the last 6 lessons are no longer on the map.

St. Paul, Minnesota (MN)
Bismarck, North Dakota (ND)
Pierre, South Dakota (SD)
Cheyenne, Wyoming (WY)
Lincoln, Nebraska (NE)
Madison, Wisconsin (WI)
Springfield, Illinois (IL)
Des Moines, Iowa (IA)
Jefferson City, Missouri (MO)
Little Rock, Arkansas (AR)
Lansing, Michigan (MI)
Columbus, Ohio (OH)
Indianapolis, Indiana (IN)
Frankfort, Kentucky (KY)
Nashville, Tennessee (TN)
Atlanta, Georgia (GA)
Tallahassee, Florida (FL)
Montgomery, Alabama (AL)
Jackson, Mississippi (MS)
Baton Rouge, Louisiana (LA)
Annapolis, Maryland (MD)
Richmond, Virginia (VA)
Charleston, West Virginia (WV)
Raleigh, North Carolina (NC)
Columbia, South Carolina (SC)
Montpelier, Vermont (VT)
Albany, New York (NY)
Trenton, New Jersey (NJ)
Harrisburg, Pennsylvania (PA)
Dover, Delaware (DE)

Zoom Me In!

Lesson 8

You are learning your US States & Capitals!

This lesson you are learning:

Topeka, Kansas (KS)
Oklahoma City, Oklahoma (OK)
Austin, Texas (TX)
Denver, Colorado (CO)
Santa Fe, New Mexico (NM)

This Lesson's Geography:
US States and Capitals

Topeka, Kansas (KS)
Oklahoma City, Oklahoma (OK)
Austin, Texas (TX)
Denver, Colorado (CO)
Santa Fe, New Mexico (NM)

Tid-Bits

Topeka, Kansas

Kansas became the 34th state on January 29th, 1861. It is located in the Midwest in a region called The Great Plains. The state is made up of various biomes, including steppe, grassland, and prairie; overall, it is very flat. Topeka is the capital. However, Kansas City is the most famous city that curiously straddles the border between Kansas and Missouri along the confluence of the Kansas and Missouri Rivers. In other words, Kansas City is in both states.

Kansas is known for its barbecue, smooth jazz music, and the Kansas born author L. Frank Baum, who wrote the children's classic The Wizard of Oz. The name Kansas comes from the Native American Kansa, or Kaw, tribes, who lived along the Kansas River. Kansas has two nicknames: The Sunflower State and the Cyclone State. In Kansas, there are lots of tornadoes! Summers are warm, and the winters are cold.

Before Europeans and settlers arrived, Cheyenne, Pawnee, Kaw, and other Native American tribes lived on the land.

Spain was the first country to explore Kansas in 1541. French explorers came in the late 1600s from Canada. Kansas was bought from France as part of the Louisiana Purchase.

In 1853, Fort Riley was built on the Kansas River, so settlers and traders had a place to go when traveling along the Oregon Trail and Santa Fe Trail. Several years later, it became the home of General George Armstrong Custer's 7th Cavalry. They led an attack on the Sioux and Cheyenne tribes known as the Battle of Little Bighorn.

Kansas became a territory in 1854. Before this, in 1820, the Missouri Compromise was passed. As you learned in Lesson 6, the Missouri Compromise was an act of Congress made to keep the balance of power of slave states vs. free states in the Senate. As part of the agreement, slavery was prohibited north of the 36°30' parallel, excluding Missouri. Kansas was above that line. Many people didn't like this because it meant that the transcontinental railroad would cost more money and time, as they were not allowed to use slave labor. Others didn't agree with this law because it was a drastic change to their way of life.

Kansas-Nebraska Act - Then enters the Kansas-Nebraska Act of 1854. This act was created to overturn the Missouri Compromise, allowing the territories to decide if they wanted slavery, or not. From the north, settlers poured into the area that didn't wish for slavery. From the south, many settlers came that wanted slavery. This caused trouble, lots of trouble. People were so angry that battles broke out over the ownership of slaves.

An example of this was the "Sack of Lawrence" that happened on May 21st, 1856. A pro-slavery mob wrecked and burned a hotel and newspaper office in a antislavery town. In doing this, they had hoped to wipe out this "hotbed of abolitionism." Three days later, John Brown and a group of antislavery people retaliated in the "Pottawatomie Massacre," which happened three days later. After this, Kansas was known as "Bleeding Kansas." This was one more chink in the chain, pushing America towards Civil War. As for Kansas, the question was finally settled when Kansas was admitted as a free state in January 1861.

The Old West - The Frontier Region is also known as The Old West, where cowboys lived and worked. Kansas was a big part of that region and depended on cattle to survive. To keep the peace, frontiersmen depended on lawmen. Wyatt Earp, William B.

Lesson 8

Beautiful Kansas Sunflower Field - By Unknown, Public Domain

Painting of John Brown, Abolitionist - Pottawatomie Massacre

"Bat" Masterson, and James Butler "Wild Bill" Hickok became legends for protecting people of wild frontier towns like Abilene, Dodge City, Hays, Wichita, and Ellsworth.

After the 1880s, cattle were necessary but less critical when wheat farming became the most significant industry for Kansas. However, cattle are still a big part of Kansas' economy today. The only state that produces more cattle than Kansas, is Texas. Kansas is still the biggest producer of wheat in the country. Sumner County is called "The Wheat Capital of the World."

Kansas was the birthplace of a few inventions that have changed our world. The dial telephone was invented by Almon Stowger in 1889. Mr. Stowger was from El Dorado, Kansas. The helicopter was developed in Goodland, Kansas, by William Purvis and Charles Wilson in 1909.

Like other states in the Midwest during the drought of the 1930s, farmers had to leave Kansas because the farmland wasn't growing anything. 80,000 people moved away during this time. Then, during World War II (1939-45), people came back because the state started building airplanes for the war effort.

Helium was once thought to be a very rare element. The University of Kansas in Lawrence proved that idea wrong. They did lots of experiments on a gas well in Dexter, Kansas, finding that helium was one of the most common elements. Because it is so common, we use it to fill up balloons, so they float. Then we suck the helium out of the balloons to sound like cartoon characters!

Every state has silly laws that were passed at some point. Kansas is no exception. Apparently, Kansas didn't want people to enjoy cherry pie with ice cream, so they made it against the law for a while.

As you probably know, but may not have thought about, maps are really important to find our way in places that are unfamiliar to us. Everyone must use the same measuring tools to create maps and boundaries between places like states, towns, and even your home. So, everyone uses the same spot to anchor their maps and measures from. All of North America, with the countries of the United States, Canada, and Mexico, all use this same spot. That place is called the Geodetic Center of North America, and it is on Meade's Ranch in Osborne County, Kansas.

Tornado Alley - The Great Plains, as the name indicates, is very flat. Flat areas invite tornadoes. The U.S. has more than 1,000 each year, making it the hot spot for tornado activity. The area has been appropriately nicknamed Tornado Alley. At the heart of Tornado Alley lies Kansas. Together with other states in this area there are more destructive tornadoes than anywhere else in the world.

A Kansas tornado captured on its path, 2015. Public Domain

Kansas ratified the 15th Amendment to the U.S. Constitution before any other state. This amendment gave black men the right to vote. Women's suffrage and the 19th Amendment would come several years later.

Brown v. Board of Education - As you've learned from the Civil Rights Movement... After the Civil War, segregation of blacks from whites was a regular part of people's lives in the South. However, that didn't mean it was right, or that everyone was okay with it.

In 1951, nine-year-old Linda Brown was not allowed to go to an all-white elementary school in Topeka, Kansas. Her dad was very upset. He and thirteen other families took the school's board of education to court because he wanted his daughter to get a good education. He

believed that schools for black children were not equal to the schools for white children. Under the 14th Amendment, everyone has the right to equality under the law. The schools were separating whites from blacks, which was discriminatory, therefore not equal.

These thirteen black families decided to legally fight the board of education for their children's right to receive an equal education in the case called Brown v. Board of Education. The District Court in Kansas agreed with the public school. Linda Brown's dad did not agree, so he took the case to the U.S. Supreme Court. Thurgood Marshall, a lawyer and future Supreme Court Justice fought the case and won on behalf of Linda Brown.

Landmark case, Brown v. Board of Education - Newspaper on display. By: Unknown - Public Domain

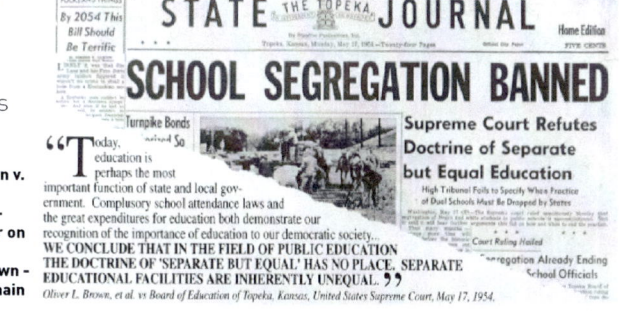

Landmark case, Brown v. Board of Education - Newspaper on display.
By: Unknown - Public Domain

was legal to racially segregate public places. Black people were not allowed to use the same buses, schools, restaurants, and even water fountains as white people. These laws became known as Jim Crow laws under the idea of "separate but equal." Things started changing in the 1950s when organizations and lawyers began working to desegregate public schools by taking them to court. Brown vs. The Board of Education was not the first case, but it was the landmark case that led to positive changes in the south, and the crumbling of the Jim Crow laws.

This landmark case decision by the Supreme Court in 1954, made it illegal to segregate public schools. The Supreme Court justices, or judges, made their decision unanimously. Everyone in the court agreed that racial segregation in public schools is unconstitutional. All the justices rarely agree. Up until that point, people believed "separate but equal" was a good argument to keep people apart. The fundamental problem with this idea is that if they were truly equal, why segregate?

The Supreme Court was not always of this mindset. Fifty-eight years earlier, in 1896, Plessy vs. Ferguson was another case put in front of the Supreme Court. During that case, the justices decided it

Brown vs. The Board of Education is a significant part of American history, and it happened in Kansas. The case became a turning point in the Civil Rights Movement. Not all public schools allowed black students right away, as you learned with the "Little Rock Nine" in Lesson 6. The Civil Rights Movement would continue fighting for these rights for many years to come. It wasn't until 1976 that the Supreme Court made it illegal for private schools to segregate their students.

Amelia Earhart - You might have heard of Amelia Earhart. She was born in

Amelia Earhart (Top and Left), By: Unknown, Public Domain

Atchison, Kansas. She was the first woman to fly alone across the Atlantic Ocean. She also was the first person to fly from Hawaii all the way to the mainland of the United States.

During World War I, she was a nurse in Canada for the Red Cross. She fell in love with airplanes there, but she didn't ride in her first airplane until December 1920. A month later, she started taking flying lessons, working as a filing clerk to pay for them. Within the year, she bought her first plane and named it "The Canary." In 1932, she was the first woman to fly nonstop across the United States, flying from Los Angeles to New Jersey in nineteen hours.

Amelia was a talented pilot, setting many records. In fact, Congress gave her the "Distinguished Flying Cross," a military award, for her heroism and extraordinary achievements.

Her career was filled with big milestones and awards, but it was a short career. In 1937, Amelia Earhart decided to fly around the world. She had tried once before without success. Amelia wanted to be the first person to ever fly around the world. She took off from Oakland, California, on June 1st, 1937. Amelia did not fly this exhibition alone. She had a navigator by the name of Fred Noonan, with her. Earhart and Noonan flew 22,000 miles; they only had 7,000 more to go before they made it back to Oakland. They stopped in New Guinea for fuel on July 2nd. It was the last time anyone ever saw them. People searched for two weeks to find them, but they were never found.

There are many theories as to what happened during their flight, but we will never know. It is a great mystery because nothing was found of Amelia, Noonan, or the plane. They were declared lost at sea after two and a half weeks of searching.

Oklahoma City, Oklahoma

Oklahoma became the 46th state on November 16th, 1907. It is known as the "Sooner State" because settlers claimed the land sooner than it officially became an American territory. Oklahoma City is the capital. It is made up mostly of plains with some hills and mountains. The weather can be hot in the summers, but winters are mild. Spring can bring a lot of tornadoes as Oklahoma is located within Tornado Alley.

Francisco Vasquez de Coronado was the first Spanish explorer to arrive in 1541. In 1682, France claimed the land when René-Robert Cavelier explored it. The United States bought the area in the Louisiana Purchase. It became a place for fur traders to do business. In 1823, the first American settlement, a trading post, was constructed where Salina is today.

Before Europeans and settlers arrived,

Native American tribes Caddo, Wichita, Pawnee, Kiowa, Arapaho, Osage, and others lived on the land. They hunted buffalo and grew crops like corn, beans, and squash. Choctaw words "okla" means people and "humma" means red; Oklahoma in Choctaw means "red people."

After President Andrew Jackson passed the "Indian Removal Act" of 1830, the Native Americans were sent from their land and led to the area of present-day Oklahoma. At the time, these federally owned unsettled lands west of the Mississippi were to be exchanged for Indian lands in the south. A few tribes went peacefully, but many resisted the relocation policy. The understanding was that the Native Americans would reside, untouched, in this federally owned land, forever.

Homestead Act of 1862 & the Oklahoma Land rush -
Thirty-two years later, signed into law by Abraham Lincoln, the Homestead Act of 1862 allowed settlers to own federal land.

In a July 4th, 1861 speech, Lincoln said that America's government was

"to elevate the condition of men, lift artificial burdens from all shoulders, and give everyone an unfettered start and a fair chance in the race of life."

Initially, nothing much happened with the Homestead Act. It was signed into

Downtown skyline view of Oklahoma City in Oklahoma
By: Unknown, Public Domain

law just before the Civil War, which was quite a distraction for some time.

With overcrowding in the east and the war over, the west became attractive for those with an adventurous spirit.

Free is the best price of all, which is what The Homestead Act promised. It is considered by many historians to be one of the longest-running and most impactful piece of legislation in America's history. The Homestead Act remained active for 124 years until it was repealed in 1976. During the

homestead era, about 270 million acres of federal land was claimed in 30 states, from Florida to Michigan to Alaska. Thousands of people over many years would claim federal land as their own, under the Homestead Act. It was this legislation that contributed to massive amounts of people going westward, all at once. Wherever there was land to be acquired for free, towns would spring up! Manifest Destiny was at hand!

A "Homestead" was made up of 160 acres, and they could be given to any citizen who wanted to settle and farm. Normally, to apply for land, a person had to be a citizen of at least 21 years old or the head of their household. Upon approval, the landowner

Homestead Certificate for 160 Acres

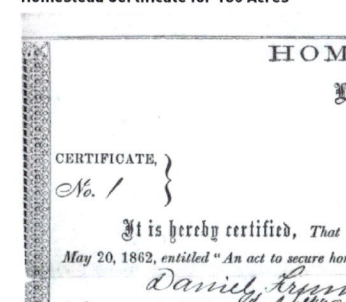

Oklahoma Land Rush, 1889 - By Unknown, Public Domain

U.S. land office after the Land Rush of 1889. - By Bain News Service, publisher - Library of Congress Catalog, Public Domain

It is a spring day, the date is April 22nd, 1889. Under the sun that approaches high noon, is a restless mass of settlers hungry for land. Every minute the tension increases as they listen for the cannons to blast, signaling the start of the Oklahoma Land Rush. As the minute hand notches over the hour, noontime has come. The cannons boom, pistols are fired, and bugles blare across the landscape. In a million chaotic maneuvers, horseback riders spurring their horses forward and wagon drivers cracking whips. 50,000 strong, they set forward a thunderous clash with the ground, a frenzied sprint filled with exhilaration as they race to stake their claim to a hope-filled homestead.

was to improve the land, file a patent or deed, and live on it for at least five years. The only people not eligible were those who had fought against the U.S. during the Civil War. 1.6 million homesteads were given away. That's 10% of the United States' land, which is over 420,000 square miles.

Eventually, the land in Oklahoma became available for the taking. Although, the road to this destination was fraught with complexity. Briefly explained, this included loss of Indian land owned by Seminole and Creek Indian tribes because they fought against the Union in the Civil War. Other Indian territory was protected federally by mandate from President Rutherford B. Hayes. Who issued a proclamation on April 26th, 1879, forbidding trespass into the area described by treaties and laws of the United States as Indian Country.

However, the federally protected Indian Country had "Boomers."

These 'Boomers' as they were called, would not stop squatting on Indian land. Eventually, it became such a problem that the government decided that it would be best to negotiate with the Creek Indian Nation for their land. The Creeks ceded the territory being paid $2,250,000. The region was then designated as federal "unassigned land" that could be opened up to white and Indian settlement under the Homestead Act.

Although legally prohibited from voting, women were eligible to participate in the Oklahoma Land Rush, and in this case, there was no citizenship requirement either. Immigrants from Ireland, England, France, and Scotland were among the thousands ready for free land.

On that first day, 2 million acres of land was staked for claiming. Those that tried to claim land before noon were called "Sooners," which is how Oklahoma got its nickname "The Sooner State." Unfortunately, there were casualties from the chaotic nature of the rush and those who were

"The Oklahoma Land Rush, April 22, 1889", by John Steuart Curry
U.S. National Archives and Records Administration, Public Domain

simply willing to kill for land. Other ugly confrontations happened between those that legally rushed out and illegal claim jumpers hidden in the thickets with horses staged to look like they had run the race.

Austin, Texas

Looking at a map, everyone can easily spot Texas among the states for its sheer size! While it is not the largest, it is by far the biggest of the lower 48 states. It is so large that characterizing the landscape is challenging to do with 10 different climatic zones. The range of climate in this vast land includes arid areas, meaning little or no rain, where it is too dry and barren to support vegetation. Other regions are semi-arid, which has a bit more rain. These arid, semi-arid landscapes are in the west. To the east, the landscape changes to humid and subtropical. Yearly the arid areas get only as much as 15" of rain. However, the mountains receive heavy snowfall.

A river called the Rio Grande separates Texas from Mexico. The Gulf of Mexico lies in the southeast.

The most significant portion of the region is a coastal plain, which covers southern and eastern Texas. The coastal plain has flat and low valleys that go inward from the Gulf of Mexico. The central and western parts of Texas are made up of hills and plateaus.

Before Europeans arrived, Native Americans made up the population of Texas. These tribes included the Jumano, Caddo, and Comanche tribes, among others.

The Spanish started exploring the region in the early 1500s. In 1685, a French explorer, Sieur de La Salle, began exploring a part of the area and tried to establish a settlement there. At the same time, Spain was in the area, building settlements and missions. San Antonio became the main settlement of Texas, while the Spanish ruled the area beginning around 1680.

The natives in Texas were unwelcoming and hostile towards outsiders that wished to create a life there. Ultimately, this delayed settlement of Texas. Much later, Mexico declared its independence from Spain in 1821. As a result, the Texas land became part of Mexico. The

The Alamo Mission in Texas - By: Unknown, Public Domain

local Mexican government allowed U.S. citizens to immigrate to the land and establish settlements. After this, a sharp rise in population occurred, causing friction between Texas and the people in Mexico City. After several small disputes, this region broke off from the Mexican government in a rebellious revolution.

The Alamo - During the war for independence, about 200 Texan volunteers were held up at the Alamo, a Spanish built Catholic Mission near San Antonio. These men were attacked by an immense number of Mexican troops. The siege began on February 23rd, 1836. It lasted for 13 days before the Mexican forces finally managed to break through the courtyard and kill most Texans, including a past congressman from Tennessee, Davy Crockett.

The Texans lost at the Alamo that fateful day. Moving forward into other battles, the expression "Remember the Alamo" was used as a battle cry to rally the rebels. Ultimately the rebels defeated the Mexican Army during a clash on the coast of the San Jacinto River. With this win, Texas became an independent republic in 1836. Sam Houston was made the first president of the newly founded republic.

A vast majority of the new republic desired Texas to become part of the United States. Shortly after their independence was won, the people of

One of many beautiful landscapes of the great state of Texas. By Unknown, Public domain

Texas voted for annexation. However, most people in the United States did not wish to take on Texas because Mexico had threatened war with the U.S. if they did.

Eight years passed, and in 1844, U.S. President John Tyler helped reach an agreement so Texas could join the Union. Congress approved of the negotiation in 1845. But, there was a problem. Mexico believed that a portion of the Texan land was still theirs and they continually argued with the U.S. about the border.

Ten years after the Texas rebellion and one year after Texas joined the Union, these arguments erupted into the Mexican-American War, beginning in 1846, lasting until 1848.

When the war was drawing to a close, the two governments met in Mexico City to sign the Treaty of Guadalupe Hidalgo. It is officially known as the Treaty of Peace, Friendship, Limits, and Settlement between the United States of America and the Republic of Mexico.

Mexican territory prior to the Mexican-American War and the signing of the Treaty of Guadalupe Hidalgo.

In this treaty, Mexico ceded an enormous piece of land to the United States. Present-day states that were ceded include all of California, Nevada, Utah, Arizona, New Mexico, Texas, and parts of Wyoming, Colorado, Kansas, and Oklahoma. This was a big deal. The Louisiana Purchase doubled our young country's size in 1803 with the purchase of 828,000 square miles. Now, in 1848, the acquisition from Mexico was the third-largest in U.S. history, totaling 529,000 square miles of land.

Johnson Space Center "Houston, we have a problem!" a familiar quote that many know. The Johnson Space Center, which resides in Houston, is the official Mission Control site. The flight controllers oversaw Apollo 11, the first mission to land on the moon's surface on July 20, 1969. Neil Armstrong was the commander of the ship, Edwin E. Aldrin, Jr., otherwise known as Buzz Aldrin, served as the Lunar Module Pilot for the flight. There was a third man as well, Michael Collins, the Command Module pilot. Mission Control watched and assisted these three on their trip and oversaw their safe return.

Denver, Colorado

Colorado was the 38th state admitted into the Union, on August 1st, 1876. 100 years after the colonists declared independence from Britain! Forming the United States as we

Apollo 11 Crew: Neil Armstrong (left) and Buzz Aldrin (right) in training at the Johnson Space Center - By: NASA - Public Domain

now know it took quite a lot of time. The "Colorado" name was passed onto the state from the well-known Colorado River. This river begins at a small lake high in the Rocky Mountains within Colorado, flowing all the way to the Gulf of California.

Colorado has the Rocky Mountains in the west and the

Johnson Space Center - Mission Operations Control Room 2 at the conclusion of Apollo 11 in 1969 - By: NASA, Public Domain

Battle of Churubusco by J. Cameron, published by Nathaniel Currier. Hand tinted lithograph, 1847. Digitally restored.

Great Plains in the east. Across the eastern plains, where the land is flat and empty, much of it is used for farming crops or cattle ranches. Traveling further east, the plains give way to the region known as the Colorado Piedmont, which is a broad, hilly prairie. At the foothills of the Rockies, this region houses most of Colorado's population and industry, including the capital, Denver, and other cities like Boulder, Colorado Springs, and Aurora. In the remaining portion of Colorado, about half of its total land lies the Rockies with less than two people per square mile living there. The economy in the Rockies is dependent on small farms and tourism around the national parks.

The first European explorers and settlers started to venture through present-day Colorado in the 1540s. Spain soon claimed the region as part of its empire. The area changed

Colorado Great Plains - By: Unknown, Public Domain

occupation a few times over many years. In 1803, France sold Louisiana to the U.S. A portion of present-day Colorado was part of that Louisiana territory. The other part would be included in the U.S. much later after the Mexican-American war.

In 1858 Colorado's fortunes changed forever when gold was discovered. Thousands of people traveled to the region hoping to make their fortune. This led to increased conflicts with the Native American residents. In 1864,

these conflicts were brought to a bloody climax when Colonel John Chivington with 675 U.S. troops betrayed a large gathering of 750 Cheyenne and Arapaho. Chivington ordered his troops to fire on them, even though they were under a white flag of truce. More than 230 men, women, children, and elderly were killed, despite surrendering. This event has become known as the Sand Creek Massacre that led to the Arapaho-Cheyenne War. Historians suggest that the massacre had far reaching consequences leading to the Plains Wars over the next decade.

As gold dried up, many towns were left abandoned as 'ghost towns.' The economy of Colorado since moved to focus on agriculture. Though, during the Second World War, the region became crucial for military bases.

Colorado has an ancient history of

St. Elmo, a Ghost Town in Colorado By: Unknown, Public Domain

people that lived and thrived in this region. Notable groups were the Pueblo, also known as the Anasazi, who moved to modern-day Colorado in 100 AD. Pueblo is preferred over the name Anasazi, because 'Anasazi' comes from the Navajo word for 'ancient enemies,' referring to the old conflict between the Pueblo and Navajo peoples.

The name 'Pueblo' was given to them by Spanish settlers – Pueblo meaning

Colorado Piedmont, a broad, hilly prairie. At the foothills of the Rockies - By: Unknown, Public Domain

Anasazi Ruins in Mesa Verde National Park in Colorado
By: Unknown, Public Domain

Carlsbad Caverns - By: Unknown, Public Domain

Santa Fe, New Mexico

New Mexico is one of the largest states in the Union, at over 120,000 square miles. The capital is Santa Fe. Much of New Mexico is so dry and desolate that even cacti cannot survive in some places. As you travel northward through New Mexico's rugged terrain, you will encounter more rainfall and a greater variety of plants and animals, like rattlesnakes and coyotes. Where pine forests cover areas around mountains, animals like black bears, mountain lions, minks, foxes, and many species of birds are common.

A vast portion of New Mexico's economy – around half - is based on tourism and services. People from across the U.S. enjoy spectacles like the Native American ceremonies and the Albuquerque International Balloon Fiesta, which is the largest in the world. Natural beauty spots draw visitors, such as the Carlsbad Caverns, which is a large and beautiful cave system. The caverns are also home to around a million bats. The bats contributed a boost to the economy. How, you might ask? Well, the bats provide fertilizer through their guano or excrement!

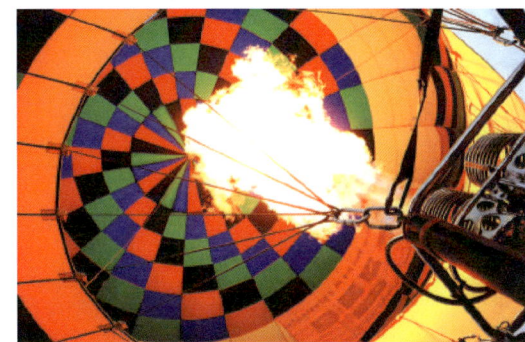
Top/Bottom: Albuquerque International Balloon Fiesta.
By: Unknown, Public Domain

'village' and referring to the type of house they lived in, which were built in the cliffs. Thousands of Pueblos inhabited these cliff dwelling that resemble modern apartment blocks. Their artwork can still be seen drawn on the cliffs where they lived. They illustrated their artwork in dark areas where the sun did not shine, preserving the art for thousands of years.

They were farmers and hunters. However, it seems that the Pueblo people were affected by changes in climate or soil, making the area far more challenging to thrive in. They likely dispersed to other places as a result.

The first Europeans to visit were Spaniards, searching for the Seven Cities of Cíbola. These cities were rumored to contain gold and other splendors. After wandering the area for two years, they found nothing – the cities had never existed. Slow settlement began, but attempts to convert the resident Pueblo people to Christianity caused a rebellion and expulsion of Europeans in 1680.

The Gadsden Purchase

Following the conquest of the vast region of Mexico in 1848, the U.S. peacefully gained the land south of the Gila River in southern New Mexico and Arizona in 1853. The Mexican government was short of money, partly because of the war

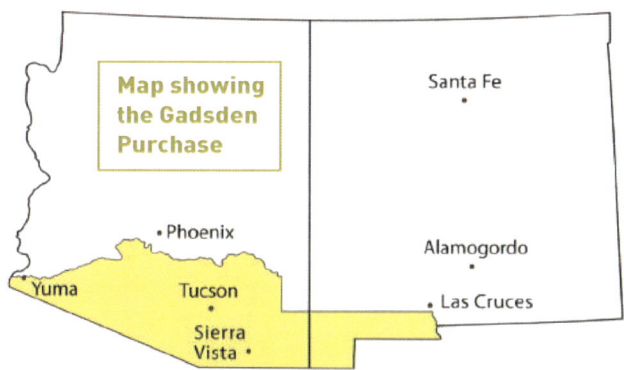
Map showing the Gadsden Purchase

they had just fought against the U.S. Through the Gadsden Purchase, Mexico agreed to sell this land to the U.S. for $10 million.

The land was used to build the Southern Pacific Railroad, which for the first time, enabled people to travel from Los Angeles to El Paso, San Antonio, and New Orleans. The introduction of the railways meant that New Mexico became increasingly accessible.

New Mexico landscape, By Unknown, Public Domain

The notorious "Billy the Kid" – By: Unknown, Public Domain

This accessibility invited settlers to make their way into the New Mexico territory. The settlement of the land led to intensified conflicts with Native Americans. Apache hostilities went strong until 1886. This, combined with disputes between local landowners, known as range wars, gave New Mexico something of a violent reputation. Billy the Kid, one of New Mexico's most famous resident outlaw, came to prominence at this time and participated in various battles with law enforcement before being killed at the age of 21.

In 1912 New Mexico achieved statehood, and its population has continued to grow ever since.

The Manhattan Project

In World War II, scientists in America began developing an atomic bomb. This type of bomb is hundreds of times more powerful than an ordinary bomb. These scientists needed a remote area where there were no people, so that they could test their new bomb. The open expanse of New Mexico seemed an ideal place. On July 16th, 1945, the first atomic bomb was detonated. The explosion was so massive it left a crater 250 feet wide and could be felt 100 miles away.

This successful test enabled the use of atomic weapons in war. In August 1945, nuclear bombs were dropped on the Japanese cities of Hiroshima and Nagasaki. The death toll reached 140,000, with many more made sick from the radiation. Despite this horrific toll, the bomb is thought to have forced the Japanese government to surrender, effectively ending World War II.

The Trinity test of the Manhattan Project was the first detonation of a nuclear weapon. Photo provided by the United States Department of Energy Trinity and Beyond: The Atomic Bomb Movie Public Domain

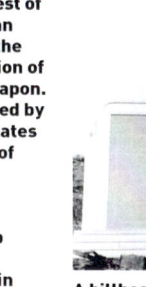

A billboard encouraging secrecy among Oak Ridge workers – By: James E. Westcott, Public Domain

World War II, United States of America drops two atomic bombs.
"Little Boy" explodes over Hiroshima, Japan, August 6th,1945 (left);
"Fat Man" explodes over Nagasaki, Japan, August 9 ,1945 (right)

A Closer Look!
at what you have learned for the last 6 lessons!
PLUS+
This Lesson's Geography:
Salt Lake City, Utah (UT)
Phoenix, Arizona (AZ)
Carson City, Nevada (NV)
Sacramento, California (CA)
Honolulu, Hawaii (HI)

Previous Learned Geography:
Listed here is the geography learned over the last 6 lessons. All lessons learned before the last 6 lessons are no longer on the map.

Topeka, Kansas (KS)
Oklahoma City, Oklahoma (OK)
Austin, Texas (TX)
Denver, Colorado (CO)
Santa Fe, New Mexico (NM)
St. Paul, Minnesota (MN)
Bismarck, North Dakota (ND)
Pierre, South Dakota (SD)
Cheyenne, Wyoming (WY)
Lincoln, Nebraska (NE)
Madison, Wisconsin (WI)
Springfield, Illinois (IL)
Des Moines, Iowa (IA)
Jefferson City, Missouri (MO)
Little Rock, Arkansas (AR)
Lansing, Michigan (MI)
Columbus, Ohio (OH)
Indianapolis, Indiana (IN)
Frankfort, Kentucky (KY)
Nashville, Tennessee (TN)
Atlanta, Georgia (GA)
Tallahassee, Florida (FL)
Montgomery, Alabama (AL)
Jackson, Mississippi (MS)
Baton Rouge, Louisiana (LA)
Annapolis, Maryland (MD)
Richmond, Virginia (VA)
Charleston, West Virginia (WV)
Raleigh, North Carolina (NC)
Columbia, South Carolina (SC)

Lesson 9

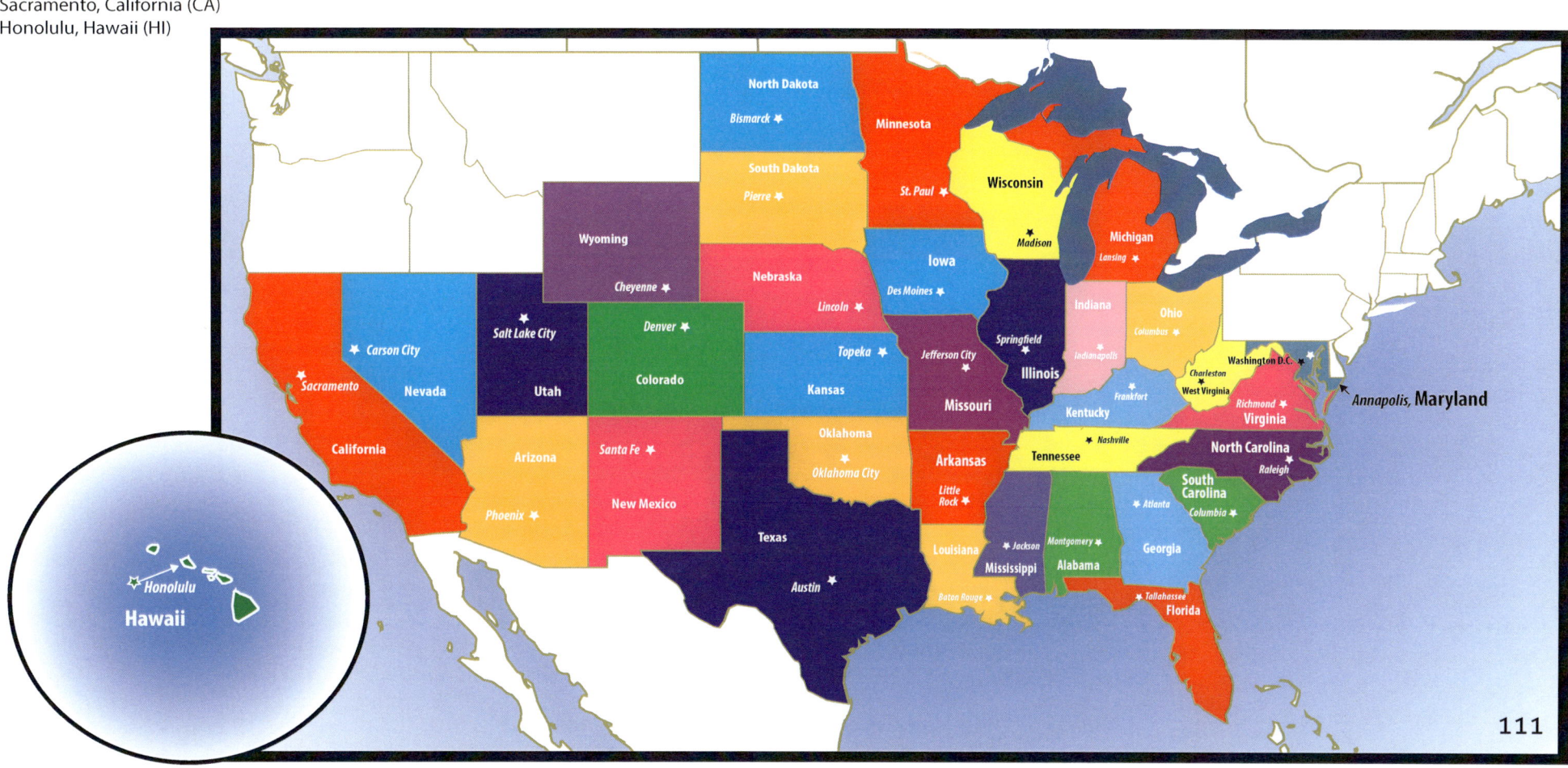

Zoom Me In!

Lesson 9

Use this sheet as a reference for this lesson's worksheets. Be sure to practice until you don't have to look!

You are learning your US States & Capitals!

This lesson you are learning:

Salt Lake City, Utah (UT)
Phoenix, Arizona (AZ)
Carson City, Nevada (NV)
Sacramento, California (CA)
Honolulu, Hawaii (HI)

Lesson 9

This Lesson's Geography:
US States and Capitals

Salt Lake City, Utah (KS)
Phoenix, Arizona (AZ)
Carson City, Nevada (NV)
Sacramento, California (CA)
Honolulu, Hawaii (HI)

Tid-Bits

Salt Lake City, Utah

Utah is located in the very center of the American West and is named after the Ute. A Native American tribe who lived in the region when Europeans first arrived. Utah is split into three main geographic zones: the Colorado Plateau, the Great Basin, and the Rocky Mountains.

Taking up about half of the state, the Colorado Plateau in Utah is dominated by breathtaking landforms, mountains, gullies, and canyons. Mesas and deserts can also be found here, as with the Great Basin. The Basin, however, is home to the unique Bonneville Salt Flats. This massive, ancient lake dried up a very long time ago and left a strange white covering of salt. This vast flat land covered in salt is ideal for racing and seeing how fast you can go! Those with the need for speed have broken many speed records here.

Wasatch Range within the Rocky Mountains, Utah. Photo: By Unknown, Public Domain

Colorado Plateau in Utah Photos: By Unknown, Public Domain

The most populated area of Utah is the Rockies; more precisely, the section of them known as the Wasatch Range. Here the capital, Salt Lake City, as well as Ogden and Provo are nestled around the Great Salt Lake. Salt Lake City is the state's economic hub, especially in the areas of finance and trade. Elsewhere, Utah has a diverse economy that also includes agriculture and mining – notably, uranium mining.

Utah's history stretches back thousands of years with various groups of Native Americans passing through the region. Like Colorado, they also had groups of Pueblo people and their cliff dwellings. In 1540, Utah was explored by the Spanish, but they did not attempt to settle because they found the conditions too harsh and the region too remote. Only in the 1830s did a significant number of people travel through the region as they migrated westward.

Beginning in 1847, a group of American Mormons settled in Salt Lake City. At this time the land was owned by Mexico. After the Mexican-American War of 1846-1848, the property was ceded to America, and the Utah territory began to expand. These first pioneers would be followed by thousands more over the next few decades.

Members of the Church of Latter-Day Saints (LDS), known as Mormons, lived in Illinois before coming to Utah. In 1844, their leader and prophet Joseph Smith was murdered. Brigham Young became the new leader and took his people westward to practice their religion in peace.

After the U.S. acquired the land from Mexico, the Mormons applied to become a state

Bonneville Salt Flats & Racing on the Salt Flats
Photos: By Unknown, Public Domain

Wagon Train on the Mormon Trail heading for Utah.
Photo By: Unknown, Public Domain

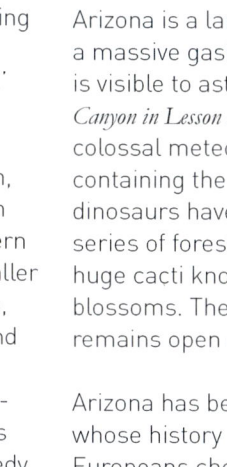

Wagon Train on the Mormon Trail heading for Utah. Photo By: Unknown, Public Domain

of the Union, calling themselves the 'State of Deseret.' This vast region encompassed modern-day Utah, Nevada, southern California, northern Arizona, and smaller parts of Colorado, Idaho, Oregon, and Wyoming. The American government thought this was a bit too greedy, and the proposal was rejected.

Instead, the U.S. created the Utah territory. Over time the Utah territory would cede land to the surrounding states and territories, becoming smaller.

Still, Utah was not granted statehood. In part, this was because of disagreements over the Mormon religion. Mormonism allowed polygamy. Polygamy is where one man could be married to more than one woman at the same time.

In 1896, after reforms to fix these issues, Utah was granted statehood after seven attempts. After admission to the Union, Utah has had a rather quiet history.

Phoenix, Arizona

Arizona is located on the border with Mexico. Nobody is sure where the name is from. A common explanation is that it comes from the O'odham (a local Native American people) word "Ali-Shonak" which means "Place of Little Spring."

Arizona is a land of broad, open plateaus and deserts. In the north is the Grand Canyon, a massive gash in the earth where the Colorado River runs through. It is so large that it is visible to astronauts on the International Space Station. *(You will learn more about the Grand Canyon in Lesson 23.)* South from the Grand Canyon is the Barringer Crater, where a colossal meteor struck the earth long ago. Nearby is the Petrified Forest National Park, containing the fossilized remains of an incredibly old forest. The remains of many dinosaurs have also been discovered in the area. Down the center of the state runs a series of forests, before giving way to the arid southern region. In the Sonoran Desert, huge cacti known as saguaro grow up to 40 feet tall and produce edible fruit from their blossoms. These Saguaro flowers bloom typically as the sun dips down at dusk and remains open all night until mid-morning the next day. Brief but beautiful.

Arizona has been home to ancient Native American groups like the Apache and Navajo, whose history is revealed in the many archaeological excavations across the state. Few Europeans chose to settle here, and the few that did were driven out by the Pueblo in 1680. Mexicans attempted to settle the region, but in 1848 the land was taken by America. In the 1870s, various settlers worked together to build canals and reservoirs to better irrigate farms. For the first time, this meant that farming was a viable resource to feed the surrounding community and beyond.

Arizona is the last of the lower 48 states to become part of the Union, achieving statehood on February 14,

LEFT: Phoenix, Arizona - By: Unknown, Public Domain
ABOVE: Barringer Crater, By: Unknown, Public Domain

Saguaro Cactus, By: Unknown, Public Domain

Petrified logs from the Petrified Forest National Park
Photo By: Unknown, Public Domain

ABOVE: Buses leaving for the Arizona Japanese Internment Camp. BELOW: Boys behind the barbwire fence in the Arizona Internment Camp. Photos by: Unknown, Public Domain

ABOVE: Arizona's Japanese Internment Camp
BELOW: Private residence, making known their bigoted viewpoint. Photos By: Unknown, Public Domain

1912. Historically, the area was called Alta California, which was part of New Spain. Then Mexico fought Spain for their independence and won in 1821. No longer was this New Spain, it was then Mexico. Then the land changed ownership once again after Mexico was defeated in the Mexican–American War. Mexico ceded much of this territory to the United States in 1848. The southernmost portion of the state was acquired in 1853 through the Gadsden Purchase.

Japanese Internment Camps

On December 7th, 1941, three years into World War II, the Japanese bombed Pearl Harbor in Hawaii. This hostile act was a declaration of war against the United States. This caused great fear that Japanese-Americans could turn against the U.S. in disloyalty. In response, the U.S. government forced Japanese-Americans to leave their homes and livelihoods to live in internment camps for the duration of the war. If they refused, they were arrested. Two of the largest, Poston and Gila River camps, were located in Arizona. About 30,000 Japanese-Americans were settled in the two camps.

The Japanese-Americans felt betrayed by being placed in the camps. Forty years later, an investigation found that the overwhelming majority of Japanese-Americans had been loyal, and there was no need for the camps. In 1988 President Reagan formally apologized and gave reparations to the surviving victims.

Shootout at the O.K. Corral

Tombstone in Arizona was a wealthy mining town thanks to the discovery of silver in 1877. With riches came opportunity for crime. The local law enforcement were three brothers named Wyatt, Morgan, and Virgil Earp. They were at odds with the Clanton-McLaury gang, outlaws who stole and murdered. They called themselves "The Cowboys."

On the morning of October 25th, 1881, there were several confrontations between the Earps and the gang. At 3 pm that day there was a showdown. Nobody knows who shot first, but when it was done, thirty seconds and thirty shots later, Billy Clanton and two McLaury brothers were killed. A friend of the Earps, Doc Holliday and two Earp brothers were wounded. More on this story, when you learn about the Gila Trail in Lesson 19.

Carson City, Nevada

Nevada's name comes from a Spanish word for 'snow-clad,' referring to the Sierra Nevada's snowy mountains found in a small portion on the west side of Nevada. Most of the Sierra Nevada is within California. These mountains cast a rain shadow over Nevada, making this state the driest in the whole country. In fact, if you were coming from these mountains into Nevada, the last thought crossing your mind would be snow! Precipitation rarely moistens the ground.

Further south lies the Mojave Desert, the driest desert in North America, which can reach temperatures upwards of 130°F. The aptly named Death Valley National Park juts into the southwest of the state from California. Here you will find the unique Joshua trees, some living to be older than the country itself. Many

Death Valley, a lone Joshua Tree
Nevada - By: Unknown, Public Domain

believe that the oldest living Joshua tree is about 1,000 years old, but the average is 500 years old. Other than ancient trees that thrive in this arid region, a few animals were made for this harsh environment. While they don't live 500 years, the kangaroo rat can survive without drinking a drop of liquid... ever. Instead, they receive hydration through the tiny bits of moisture found in the food they eat.

The Kangaroo Rat that thrives without water in Death Valley within Nevada
By: Unknown, Public Domain

Nevada's economy has traditionally focused on farming and mining. These days, tourism and gambling take center stage. The largest city in Nevada, Las Vegas, is known as the 'gambling capital of the world.' Most people live in or near the capital, Carson City.

Rock carvings and other archaeological evidence indicate Nevada was inhabited by Native American tribes long ago. Only a few Europeans arrived in the area until John C. Frémont and Kit Carson publicized it in the 1840s. The capital, Carson City is named for Kit Carson. After the Mexican-American War, this land became America's in 1848. Two years later, it became part of the Utah Territory in 1850. A handful of Mormons settled the area. Because of how remote the territory was, there was little government presence, and conflict often broke out between Mormon and non-Mormon residents. Mormons wanted the area to become incorporated into Utah territory, whereas non-Mormons wanted to join California. Most of the Mormons moved to Utah, and the state became its own territory as a compromise.

Nevada was granted statehood in 1864, despite having far less than the minimum 60,000 people required - just 7,000 in 1860. However, the discovery of silver in the

Comstock mining boom soon attracted people from across the U.S. Mining towns sprung up across the state.

Before Nevada became a state, gambling was a part of Nevada's culture. In 1864, Nevada became a state. The first appointed Governor, James Nye, pushed the state legislature to ban games of chance. He was successful, but just five years later, the laws were overturned. Gambling was legal again. Thirty-eight years later, with the feeling that they were a national joke, gambling was made illegal yet again. That was until the severe effects of the Great Depression in 1929. To raise money, Nevada decided to legalize gambling, which became a great source of wealth and today continues to draw people from all over the world. They come not only for gaming but also for the sights, including Hoover Dam and the close-by Grand Canyon. Many enjoy a myriad of shows for entertainment, including circus acts, comedians, singers, and dancers.

Area 51

The isolated nature of Nevada's land, of which a vast portion is federally owned, is set aside for U.S. Military to conduct tests and exercises in secret. The mysterious base known as Area 51 was established in 1955 in southern Nevada. Few know what goes on

Las Vegas, Nevada
By: Unknown, Public Domain

there... many theories exist. Although, many signs surrounding the area indicate the land's purpose and the government mandate for civilians to stay out. "Nellis Bombing and Gunnery Range" is a "Restricted Zone, no trespassing, no photography and use of deadly force is authorized."

Hoover Dam

In the 19th and early 20th century, Nevada's farmers needed water for their crops. Previous attempts to divert the Colorado River to water their crops had ended in disaster by accidentally creating a new lake called the Salton Sea. The farmers didn't get the water that they needed, unfortunately.

The U.S. Bureau of Reclamation hoped to solve this problem while also harnessing the

ABOVE: Aerial View of Area 51
BELOW: Signs found near Area 51 - Photos By: Unknown, Public Domain

power of the river to generate electricity. They needed to build a dam.

The coming of the Great Depression got the project moving and meant that many were unemployed and available for work. Our 31st President of the United States, Herbert Hoover, got the project started, which stimulated the economy during the depression. Hopeful people from nearby towns and cities set up a large camp near the construction site, setting their sites on being a part of this monumental project and more importantly, earn a paycheck.

In April of 1931, construction began. The working conditions were beyond dangerous, and despite the need for work, in 1931, many of the workers went on strike in protest against the fearful conditions they faced, high above the canyon, as well deep down in the tunnels being constructed with little oxygen and intense heat. On a daily basis the amount of workers ranged between 3,500 up to a maximum of 5,200. Of over 21,000 men employed on the project overall- 96 perished.

The 726-foot-high dam rose gradually from the riverbed, taking four years and five months to complete. Overall, this massive dam required 5 million barrels of cement and 45 million pounds of steel. Designed by Gordon Kaufmann, it was made to look monumen-

ABOVE: Construction of the forms that then are filled with concrete.
BELOW: Looking down at "high scalers" above the Colorado River.
Both Photos Provided by the Bureau of Reclamation, Public Domain

tal. The inside paid tribute to local Native Americans, many of whom had worked on the project. In 1935 it was completed and opened by President Roosevelt.

Sacramento, California

During the Age of Exploration, an explorer named Juan Rodríguez Cabrillo came upon the California shore. Cabrillo was an ambitious, at times ruthless Portuguese soldier who served the Spanish Empire, and he claimed California for Spain in 1542. In the early 1500s, he served in the conquest of Cuba, later he battled the Aztecs in Mexico. Eventually, Cabrillo made his fortune in Guatemala by mining gold and trading goods while participating in the slave trade. In hopes of more wealth, he set out to explore the California coast, map landmarks, and identify native villages. However, he wasn't the only to stake claim to this beautiful land.

Over 40 years later, Pedro de Unamuno sailed from the Philippines to California on an expedition. It is believed that he anchored in Morro Bay on October 18th, 1587.

Then came a soldier named Sebastián Vizcaíno from Spain in 1602, who adventured along the coast and named many places. These names include Santa Catalina Island, San Diego, Santa Barbara, and Monterey. More than 150 years later, Spain set up a mission called San Diego in Alcala during the year of 1769. Over the next 50 years, 20 more missions started along the coast. Many towns grew around these missions.

Spain lost this land after the Mexican War for Independence that lasted from 1810 until 1821.

Present-day Hoover Dam by the Bureau of Reclamation, Public Domain

During the period between the 1820s and the 1840s, Mexico and the United States argued for control of California. Mexico owned the territory at that time and would not sell it to the United States. In 1846, Californians near Sonoma rebelled against Mexican rule. The U.S. aided in their rebellion. California and part of what was once northern Mexico was briefly known as the Bear Flag

Republic. Later, after the Mexican-American War, California became part of U.S. territory.

Shortly after the area was claimed for U.S. territory, there was a gold nugget found in the river stream behind Sutter's Mill in 1848. The people who knew about the gold tried to keep it quiet, but the mill workers were not so discreet. Word got out, and not just around town. Word of gold spread like wild fire to the far reaches of the world. As it turns out, there were not only a few nuggets hiding here and there, it was the mother load! This caused a rush of settlers to the land of California in search of treasure. This period is appropriately named the "California Gold Rush,"

ABOVE: Group of 8 men digging and panning for gold in California. By: Unknown, Public Domain
BELOW: Advertisement for the Clipper Ship to take people from Boston to San Francisco.
By: Nesbit & Co, Public Domain

The flag from the time when California had claimed their independence from Mexico. Public Domain

with an estimated 300,000 people coming to California, dreaming of hitting it big! Two years later, California became the 31st state in the Union with the California Gold Rush lasting until about 1859.

Hollywood was a small community when it was first started in 1870, informally referred to as Tinseltown. Today it is a densely populated area near Los Angeles, California, with many historic studios. After the massive uprise of the film industry, the

The famous "Hollywood" sign overlooking the city. Public Domain

little community of Hollywood ultimately became world-famous.

H.J Whitley, called "Father of Hollywood," said in his diary, dated 1886, that he stood atop the big hill and looked down into the valley while on his honeymoon. A Chinese man in a wagon carrying wood approached. The man emerged from the wagon and bowed in

front of Whitley. When the Chinese man was asked what he was doing, he replied, "I holly-wood," meaning 'hauling wood.' H. J. Whitley apparently had an epiphany and thought "Hollywood" was the perfect name for his new town. His Hollywood was where movies were going to be made!

Another popular attraction in California is Disneyland Park, established on July 17th, 1955. It was the only park that was built under the supervision of the founder Walt Disney.

Where did Walt Disney come up with such an idea? To begin with, Walt Disney was a long-time animator who experienced both success and failure. The saying "practice makes perfect" was probably a characteristic that Walt Disney believed in. Years of hard work and a few significant achievements, including "Mickey and Friends," and

Walt Disney, ©Disney

the first-ever animated feature film, "Snow White," coupled with visiting

Disneyland in Anaheim, California - ©Disney

Satelite Image of the Hawaiian Islands in the Pacific Ocean - Provided by NASA, Public Domain

various amusement parks with this daughters Diane and Sharon, sparked the idea. Disneyland was opened in 1955. His vision was to provide a clean, fun, and safe environment for parents to take their children. Guests would experience rides, explore, and meet familiar characters that were so loved by the children. Disneyland was a tremendous success! Then, Walt Disney went on to enter television. He produced "Mickey Mouse Club," the "Magical World of Disney," and a unique feature film that combined live-action with animation in "Mary Poppins." This is just to name a few of his many accomplishments before his death, at 65 years old, in 1966.

Since the opening, Disneyland has welcomed over 650 million guests, giving it the largest attendance of any theme park in the world. Beyond the park, Walt Disney's legacy has created an opportunity for countless animated and television series and movies. As well, Disney provides a unique path for stardom for young singers and actors. What started in Anaheim, California, with some cartoons and a theme park idea has grown to many resorts and theme parks around the world, as well as Disney Cruises.

Beyond Disney, Hollywood, and treasure seekers, California is the third-largest state in the U.S. with millions upon millions of acres containing farmland. California has the highest amount of agricultural production. It alone produces the grapes for 90 percent of all grape juice and wine in the United States. 3.3 million tons of wine grapes are grown on over 540,000 acres each year!

Honolulu, Hawaii

A place of sheer beauty and diverse natural wonders. The state of Hawaii is an archipelago of 132 islands and islets found thousands of miles away from any mainland in the center of the Pacific Ocean. In Hawaii, the sun is hotter than anywhere else in the United States as it is closer to the equator. The islands are a whopping 2,397 miles from San Francisco and 5,293 miles away from Manila to the west. The capital of the state, Honolulu, is located on the island of Oahu.

Many of the Hawaiian Islands were formed from volcanoes; they include Maui, Molokai, Oahu, Lanai, Kauai, Niihau, Hawaii, and Kahoolawe. Each island is unique and unlike any other.

Kaua'i is lush and green with the fantastic sea cliffs of the Na Pali Coast and the Waimea Canyon, called by many the "Grand Canyon of the Pacific." On one side of the island, it is more desert-like near the canyon, the other portion of the island has more rain than most other places in the world.

Oahu has Diamond Head, the beautiful Hanauma Bay, and the world-famous North Shore that is known for its giant waves that attract surfers from around the globe.

Maui has 'Iao Valley, the House of the Sun, and the Hana Coast. The Hana Coast is a destination that many take. While getting there is dangerous, the amazing path called the "Road to Hana" is as much of a destination as the heavenly Hana Coast. In Maui, there is a site like no other atop Haleakala. People make a steep drive up, up, up to

Waimea Canyon, called by many the "Grand Canyon of the Pacific - By Amanda Predmore

Hawaii Island is believed to be the youngest of the islands. It has the Mauna Loa and Kilauea, the most prominent and most active volcanoes of all the islands. Kilauea has been the most active volcano. In January of 1983, it began to erupt. "Between then and 2016, lava flows covered about 144 square kilometers, added more than 440 acres in the Big Island's southeast, and destroyed 215 buildings," the USGS reports.

Lava from Kilauea Volcano, By: Unknown, Public Domain

Lava from Kilauea Volcano, By: Unknown, Public Domain

Home destroyed by lava from Kilauea Volcano, By: Unknown, Public Domain

Throughout the islands, Hawaiian's experience beautiful, warm, yet unpredictable weather. Here, it does not get too hot or too cold. In August, Hawaii's hottest month, it averages 81°F. It dips down to only 73°F on average in the coldest month of January.

Well, at least to the onlooking eyes above. Not to be mistaken, Kilauea quiet but still highly active, beneath the earth's surface. Only time will tell what Kilauea's next move will be.

Lava from Kilauea Volcano, By: Unknown, Public Domain

Hawaii Island, also referred to as "the Big Island," has a unique beauty that stems from the volcanic landscapes, amazing waterfalls, and the Waipio Valley. You can descend 2000 feet into the valley to horseback through taro fields, tropical rainforests, and black sand beaches that will leave you in awe.

(pictured on the bottom of the next page)

more than 10,000 feet above the sea below. Here they can take in the sunrise or sunset in a setting genuinely like no other.

Hana Coast - By: Unknown, Public Domain

The windy "road to Hana" - By: Unknown, Public Domain

Kilauea's summit itself began a continuous eruption in 2008. This activity created a lava lake that could be seen from public viewing areas inside Hawaii Volcanoes National Park.

Then, on May 4th, 2018, a magnitude 6.9 earthquake rocked the region, setting in motion events that fundamentally changed the landscape. Several fissures opened, releasing sulfur dioxide gas clouds and lava that poured through residential neighborhoods. One eruption was so explosive that it sent a plume of volcanic ash 30,000 feet into the air above. By July, lava had covered more than 12 square miles and obliterated more than 700 homes, displacing over 2,000 people. Thirty-five years this volcano erupted almost without interruption. It seems for the moment Kilauea has come to a stand-still.

Going back in time, Hawaii has a fascinating and rich history that differs significantly from the rest of the United States. There are differing views on the timeline of the first people to inhabit the island, anywhere between 124 AD and 600 AD. However, where they came from is of little debate. History tells us that long-distance navigators sporadically went to the islands from various places including, French Polynesia, Tahiti, the Tuamotus, and the Samoan Islands.

The Explorer, James Cook

The acclaimed James Cook was a British explorer, navigator, cartographer, and he served as the captain in the British Royal Navy. He drew detailed maps of places all around the world. He would make three voyages to the Pacific to which he charted the eastern coastline of Australia and visited the Hawaiian Islands. His first trip to the islands was in 1778, the first European ship to ever arrive there. Cook would visit the islands 2 separate times, then a third

LEFT: James Cook, Explorer - By: Unknown, Public Domain
HEREIN: James Cook and crew battle with locals, Hawaii.

when they had to turn back due to rough seas. Historians believe that the Hawaiians had attached religious significance to their first stay. It is said that Cook and his crew took unfair advantage of the Hawaiian's kindness with their undue "religious importance." Upon Cook's return on their second trip, one of the crewmen died, which exposed the crew as mere mortals... tensions rose. Cook and his crew thought it prudent to board their ships and set sail. However, after damage came to one of the vessels, they turned back after one week at sea. Upon their arrival, the Hawaiians greeted them with hurling stones in their direction. A battle ensued, with just a few of Cook's men surviving. Both of the ships did make it back to England, however, without their captain.

At the time of Cook's exploration of Hawaii in 1778, each island had its own chief with an overseeing Monarchy, made up of two Kings that oversaw different islands. With the maps provided by Cook's first navigation to the islands, other European explorers followed. By 1810, the Monarchy was down to just one King. King Kamehameha I, and he ruled all of the islands. This King, years earlier as a young man, was part of the group of Hawaiians that fought and killed much of Cook's crew.

The Last of Hawaii's Monarchy

As time marched on, the amount of European exploration and eventual settlement of the area grew. The Monarchy was intact, passing from son then to brother.

At just 10 years of age, Kamehameha III took to the throne. At such a young age, he was overseen by his father's favorite wife, Kaahumanu. Converted to Christianity in 1824, she was known for her wisdom and beneficent rule.

Years later, after hearing a series of

King Kamehameha III of Hawaii

121

lectures on government delivered by an American clergyman, Kamehameha III put forth several governing documents for Hawaii. These included: the Magna Carta, a Declaration of Rights on June 7th, 1839, the Edict of Toleration on June 17th, 1839, and the first constitution on October 8th, 1840. This first constitution for the island nation contained many innovations, including a representative body of legislators elected by the people and a supreme court. The first compilation of laws was published in 1842. Kamehameha also obtained diplomatic recognition of Hawaiian independence by the United States in 1842, then Great Britain and France in 1843.

Queen Liliuokalani of Hawaii

It would be more than 100 years later, in 1959, that Hawaii would become America's 50th and final state of the Union. The last Monarch of the Hawai-

Hawaiian Island of Oahu - Adobe Stock

ian Kingdom was Queen Liliuokalani. Her reign began on January 29th, 1891 and lasted until the overthrow of the Hawaiian Kingdom on January 17th, 1893. A brief time as Queen. The tide had turned.

People in Hawaii were pushing against the Monarchy, and there was a revolution. Loyalists stood beside their Queen and their way of life. Unfortunately for them, the opposition was too strong.

Those that had overthrown the Monarchy desired to become part of the United States. However, their request was denied... twice. Instead, they put in place the Republic of Hawaii with a President.

Although Hawaii was not awarded statehood, the area did become a United States territory in 1900. The government believed that having a military power in that area of the Pacific was good. Over the next several years, the United States would build military bases on the islands, including Pearl Harbor.

Pearl Harbor - On December 7th, 1941, the Japanese bombed Pearl Harbor in Hawaii off the shores of Oahu. This was an unexpected attack that led America straight into World War II.

Pearl Harbor is a U.S. naval base located on the island of Oahu, just west of Honolulu. On this fateful day in December, the Imperial Japanese Navy bombed Pearl Harbor Naval Base in a surprise attack.

The goal of Japan was to go after and sink the aircraft carriers. Next would be to drop all battleships. The attack would come in three waves with different goals.

The Japanese carriers went undetected as they had approached Pearl Harbor from the north of Oahu. In that area, no radar could detect them because of the mountains, so it was mostly a dead zone. Furthermore, that Sunday, no American surveillance planes were on the lookout.

The first wave attacked Oahu in Pearl Harbor. A Japanese pilot bombed the USS Arizona battleship, which caused it to sink in less than nine minutes, resulting in the deaths of over 1,100 men.

There were 92 U.S. ships at Pearl Harbor, 19 were sunk. 92 naval airplanes were destroyed with 31 damaged. The U.S. Army lost 96 airplanes that went down into the ocean and 128 damaged. There were 2,388 men and women killed and 1,178 wounded. The Japanese lost only 29 planes.

The attack lasted a bit less than two hours. But the consequences for both the U.S. and Japan were immeasurable.

Following the attack, Hawaii's residents and military personnel prepared themselves to be invaded by Japan. Paranoia against Japanese-American residents resulted in the police raiding the Japanese embassy. All broadcasting systems

USS Arizona is hit and going down. The bombs and subsequent explosion killed 1,177 of the 1,512 crewmen on board at the time.

An aerial view of the USS Arizona Memorial with a US Navy (USN) Tour Boat, USS Arizona Memorial Detachment, moored at the pier as visitors disembark to visit and pay their respects to the Sailors and Marines who lost their lives during the attack on Pearl Harbor on December 7, 1941.

On December 8th, 1941, President Franklin Delano Roosevelt addresses the nation:

"Mr. Vice President, Mr. Speaker, Members of the Senate, and of the House of Representatives:

Yesterday, December 7th, 1941—a date which will live in infamy—the United States of America was suddenly and deliberately attacked by naval and air forces of the Empire of Japan.

The United States was at peace with that nation and, at the solicitation of Japan, was still in conversation with its government and its emperor looking toward the maintenance of peace in the Pacific.

Indeed, one hour after Japanese air squadrons had commenced bombing in the American island of Oahu, the Japanese ambassador to the United States and his colleague delivered to our Secretary of State a formal reply to a recent American message. And while this reply stated that it seemed useless to continue the existing diplomatic negotiations, it contained no threat or hint of war or of armed attack.

President Franklin Roosevelt delivers the "Infamy" address to Congress - By: Unknown, Library of Congress

It will be recorded that the distance of Hawaii from Japan makes it obvious that the attack was deliberately planned many days or even weeks ago. During the intervening time, the Japanese government has deliberately sought to deceive the United States by false statements and expressions of hope for continued peace.

The attack yesterday on the Hawaiian islands has caused severe damage to American naval and military forces. I regret to tell you that very many American lives have been lost. In addition, American ships have been reported torpedoed on the high seas between San Francisco and Honolulu.

Yesterday, the Japanese government also launched an attack against Malaya. Last

Photo # 80-G-19948 Sailors at NAS Ford Island watch as USS Shaw explodes, 7 December 1941
By: Unknown, Library of Congress

owned by Japanese-Americans were taken by government agents, for fear that they would be communicating with Japan. Almost immediately, Japanese-Americans were rounded up and moved to internment camps, a total of 800. Martial law was declared, and Hawaii was under military control. Bomb shelters were created, and sandbags placed in front of downtown buildings. In the schools, trenches were dug with practice drills run with school children in case of bombings, and gas masks had been implemented.

Aerial view of Pearl Harbor - Library of Congress, Public Domain

always will our whole nation remember the character of the onslaught against us.

No matter how long it may take us to overcome this premeditated invasion, the American people in their righteous might will win through to absolute victory.

I believe that I interpret the will of the Congress and of the people when I assert that we will not only defend ourselves to the uttermost, but will make it very certain that this form of treachery shall never again endanger us.

Hostilities exist. There is no blinking at the fact that our people, our territory, and our interests are in grave danger.

With confidence in our armed forces, with the unbounding determination of our people, we will gain the inevitable triumph—so help us God.

I ask that the Congress declare that since the unprovoked and dastardly attack by Japan on Sunday, December

As Commander in Chief of the Army and Navy, I have directed that all measures be taken for our defense. But

Japan has, therefore, undertaken a surprise offensive extending throughout the Pacific area. The facts of yesterday and today speak for themselves. The people of the United States have already formed their opinions and well understand the implications to the very life and safety of our nation.

Last night, Japanese forces attacked Hong Kong. Last night, Japanese forces attacked Guam. Last night, Japanese forces attacked the Philippine Islands. Last night, the Japanese attacked Wake Island. And this morning, the Japanese attacked Midway Island.

U.S. Soldiers getting rescued on the underside of a sunken ship, Pearl Harbor. Library of Congress, Public Domain

7th, 1941, a state of war has existed between the United States and the Japanese empire."

One hour after his address, Congress voted. The United States declared war on Japan.

But why did Japan attack us? Japan was on the move to expand their empire. Their expansion was two-fold: firstly, they desired to acquire land that had natural resources that they needed, like oil, coal, rice, rubber, and iron. Acquiring these resources would make them self-sufficient and free from economic dependence on western powers. Secondly, they wished to create a "New Order" in East Asia, removing outside western influence. So what does Japan's expansionism have to do with the Pearl Harbor attack? The U.S. saw their expansion efforts as breaking the Kellogg-Briand Treaty of 1928, the purpose of which, was to keep peace in East Asia. At the time, Japan had trade agreements in place with the U.S. for aluminum, iron and scrap metal, and, most importantly, oil. Japan was increasing their aggression in East Asia. The U.S. responded beginning in 1938 with placing embargoes on products that had been sold to Japan. The last embargo was on oil in August 1941. This

devastated Japan's economy. No longer did they have a reliable source of oil and other vital natural resources. This gave Japan only a few months before all the supplies would run out. The Japanese generals and admirals were outraged. They made failed attempts to diplomatically negotiate with the U.S. in hopes of mending the trade relationship. In the end, the Imperial Japanese Empire retaliated, carefully planning, and executing their attack on Pearl Harbor. America, in response, declared war on Japan.

It is often said that the attack on Pearl Harbor launched the U.S. into World War II. While the declaration of war on Japan didn't put us into World War II, Germany's response did.

Termed, Adolf Hitler's "most puzzling" decision of World War II... four days after the Pearl Harbor attack, Germany declared war against the United States.

Okay, now, everyone was in World War II.

A Closer Look!
at what you have learned for the last 6 lessons!
PLUS+
This Lesson's Geography:
Helena, Montana (MT)
Boise, Idaho (ID)
Olympia, Washington (WA)
Salem, Oregon (OR)
Juneau, Alaska (AK)

Previous Learned Geography:

Listed here is the geography learned over the last 6 lessons. All lessons learned before the last 6 lessons are no longer on the map.

Salt Lake City, Utah (UT)
Phoenix, Arizona (AZ)
Carson City, Nevada (NV)
Sacramento, California (CA)
Honolulu, Hawaii (HI)
Topeka, Kansas (KS)
Oklahoma City, Oklahoma (OK)
Austin, Texas (TX)
Denver, Colorado (CO)
Santa Fe, New Mexico (NM)
St. Paul, Minnesota (MN)
Bismarck, North Dakota (ND)
Pierre, South Dakota (SD)
Cheyenne, Wyoming (WY)
Lincoln, Nebraska (NE)
Madison, Wisconsin (WI)
Springfield, Illinois (IL)
Des Moines, Iowa (IA)
Jefferson City, Missouri (MO)
Little Rock, Arkansas (AR)
Lansing, Michigan (MI)
Columbus, Ohio (OH)
Indianapolis, Indiana (IN)
Frankfort, Kentucky (KY)
Nashville, Tennessee (TN)
Atlanta, Georgia (GA)
Tallahassee, Florida (FL)
Montgomery, Alabama (AL)
Jackson, Mississippi (MS)
Baton Rouge, Louisiana (LA)

Lesson 10

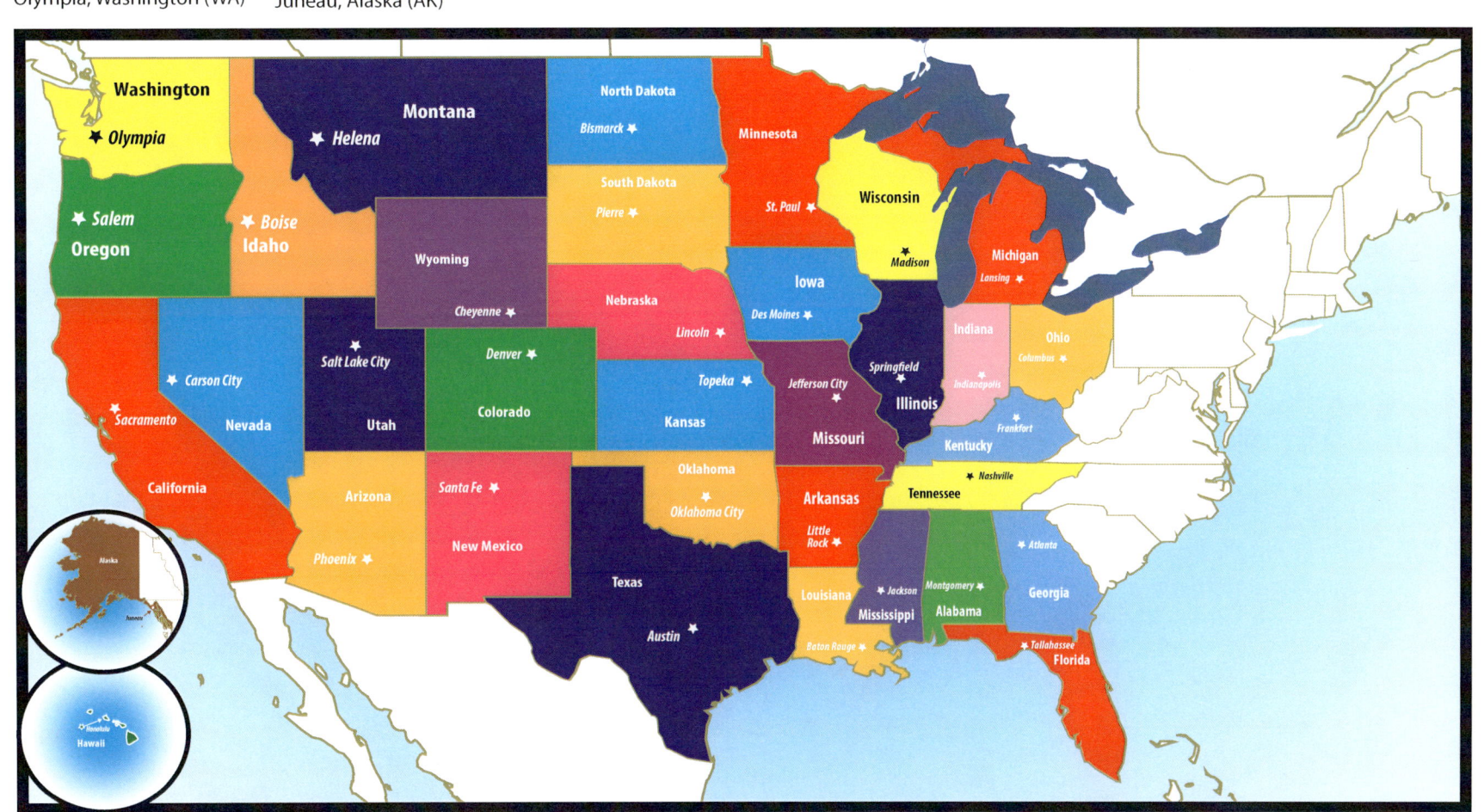

125

Lesson 10

Zoom Me In!

Use this sheet as a reference for this lesson's worksheets.
Be sure to practice until you don't have to look!

You are learning your US States & Capitals!

This lesson you are learning:

Helena, Montana (MT)
Boise, Idaho (ID)
Olympia, Washington (WA)
Salem, Oregon (OR)
Juneau, Alaska (AK)

pssst.... Alaska is GIANT! and looks like a bear

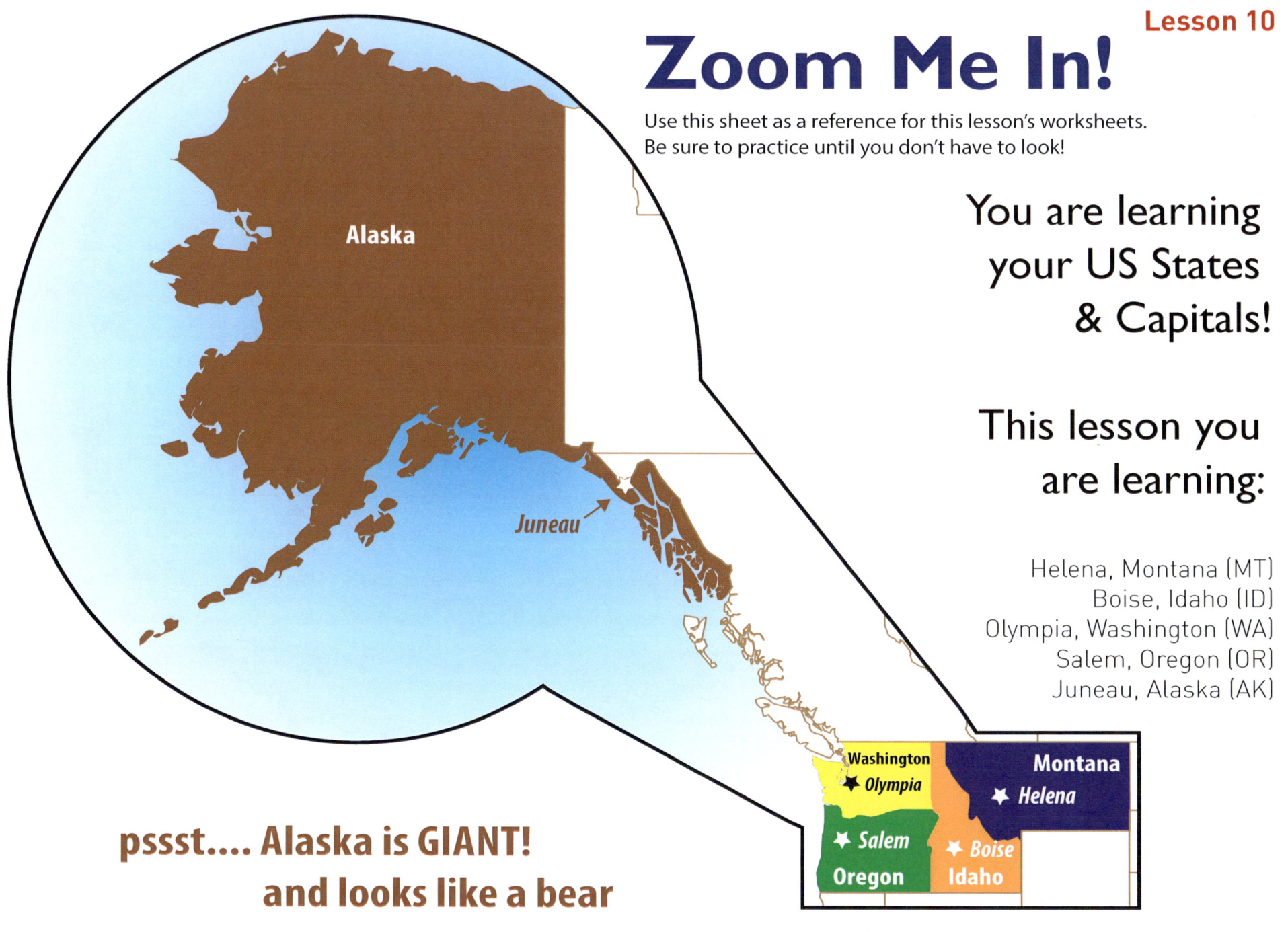

Lesson 10

This Lesson's Geography: US States and Capitals

Helena, Montana (MT)
Boise, Idaho (ID)
Olympia, Washington (WA)
Salem, Oregon (OR)
Juneau, Alaska (AK)

Tid-Bits

Helena, Montana

Montana is the fourth largest state in the Union, with one of the smallest populations in the country, only six people per square mile. Montana was named after the Spanish word Montaña, which, as you may have guessed, means mountain. Although, of all the Rocky Mountain states, Montana has the lowest mountains, with an average elevation of only 3,400 feet above sea level. In Montana, the Little Bighorn Battlefield National Monument recognizes the battle between the Sioux tribe and the United States military, which is also called "Custer's Last Stand." About 3% of Yellowstone National Park also resides in southern Montana.

American Bison, provided by National Wildlife Federation

The American Bison

Many years ago, the population of bison in the North American plains was immense. There were millions. Native Americans that lived among them, depended on the animal for their livelihood, the relationship was sacred. They only took what they needed for food, clothing, and shelter. When Americans arrived with the Manifest Destiny mindset, "move west and conquer," they ravaged this population, making it nearly extinct. The Plains culture was sadly changed forever. The near-extinction of the bison for hides was a gross abuse of power.

Completion of the western railroads split the bison into two herds, northern and southern. In 1871 the bison herd in the south was numbered around 3,000,000. In 1882 it was believed that there were about 1,000,000 buffaloes alive with at least 5,000 hunters coming after them. A war of such cruel and merciless extermination was never before witnessed. From this point forward, the bison fell away so rapidly, it was estimated that 3,000 or 4,000 were killed daily. Appeals were made to the government by the hundreds as it became evident that they were doomed. Then came 1883; thousands of hunters took

Photo from the 1870s of a pile of American bison skulls waiting to be ground for fertilizer. By: Unknown, Public Domain

to the field killing off, what was thought to be the last 10,000. By 1874 there were 3,158,780 buffaloes killed. The year following, 1875, the deed was done. The southern herd was gone from the face of the earth. Next, they went after the northern herd, which was almost swept away, just the same.

A small glimmering hope remained. Found, in captivity, a U.S. census reported 256 buffaloes, truly the last of the untold millions that covered North America during the past century.

Better late than never. On May 23rd, 1908, President Theodore Roosevelt established the National Bison Range to save the bison. Their mission was to preserve the population of the species while keeping them in partially natural conditions. Since 1908, the National Bison Range has helped recover the majestic and amazing animals' population.

Big Sky Country, Montana - Public Domain

127

Nez Percé, Native American Public Domain

Shoshone and Bannock in the south. 1805, Lewis and Clark, along with their crew of about 45 men, plus Sacagawea, her Canadian husband, and brand new baby boy, were the first European-Americans to thoroughly explore Idaho. After this, the people that visited the area were mainly fur trappers. The fur-trading company known as Hudson's Bay Company set up various forts in the 1830s that later served as stopping points along the Oregon Trail.

Where gold is found, there will also be people willing to uncover it! In 1860, a discovery of gold on Orofino Creek in Clearwater County began a gold rush. The people poured in, causing the population to sharply increase. A few years later, Congress established the Idaho Territory in 1863, which was more extensive than Texas. Eventually, the territory was split into states that included Idaho, Montana, and Wyoming.

Idaho is well known for producing more potatoes and trout than any other state in the nation. Also known as the "Gem State" for the 72 types of precious and semi-precious stones that can be found within. Some are exclusive to the area.

American Bison Herd, provided by National Wildlife Federation

Today, there are somewhere between 350,000 to a half-million bison. With a herd of purebred bison that number about 5,000 in Yellowstone National park.

The Montana Territory was made in 1864, and it went on to become 41st state in the Union in 1889. After 1890, many settlers came to claim land under the Homestead Act of 1862, which introduced farming to the region.

Boise, Idaho
The landscape here in Idaho is nothing short of amazing. Majestic mountains, peaceful lakes, and rushing rivers that bring so many to the area that seek both adventure and a slice of peace within the tranquility found among nature.

Hell's Canyon is one such place. The well-loved Snake River runs its way through, carving it deeper as it moves along. A portion of Hell's Canyon gorge is the deepest in all of North America. With a width of ten miles and a depth of 7,913 feet below the "He Devil Peak" in the Seven Devils Mountains. This canyon is deeper than the Grand Canyon

Within Idaho, known history tells us of the Nez Percé Indians in the north, the

Hell's Canyon in Idaho, Public Domain

Mountainous Idaho, Public Domain

Olympia, Washington

The state of Washington became the 42nd state on November 11, 1889. It was named in honor of the first president, George Washington. The capital is Olympia. It is known as the Evergreen State because it has so many dense forests. The Chinook tribe lived along the Columbia River, and sometimes it is called the Chinook State. They grow more apples, sweet cherries, raspberries, and pears in Washington than any other state in the U.S. Over $1.5 billion is made from apples a year in Washington. Starbucks coffee was created and headquartered in Washington.

Washington is most well-known for its natural treasures like Mount Rainier, Mount St. Helens, and the San Juan Islands within the scenic Puget Sound. Washington's north boundary is shared

Puget Sound off of Seattle/Everett area. By: Unknown, Public Domain

with the Province of British Columbia in Canada. The west side of the state borders the vast Pacific Ocean. It has incredible harbors, mountains, and wildlife. Over half of the state's population

Washington Grown Apples - By: Unknown, Public Domain

lives around Puget Sound. The Columbia River is an essential part of Washington's geography, which makes up most of the boundary between Washington and Oregon to the south. The coastal area experiences a very wet and mild climate. Whereas the eastern side of the state beyond the Cascade Mountain range has hot summers and cold winters with drier weather because of the rain shadow cast by the mountains.

Before European explorers and settlers arrived, there were two groups of native people of various tribes. The first group lived their lives on the Columbia Plateau, east of the Cascade Mountain Range. It included such tribes as the Nez Percé, Wenatchee, Yakima, and more. These Native Americans were semi-nomadic, they would move when food became scarce. The second group lived close to large bodies of water and rivers, namely Puget Sound, the Pacific Ocean, and the Columbia River. These tribes included the Chinook, Nisqually, Salish, Snohomish, and more. The Hoh River Indian Tribe lived in the northernmost Pacific coastline.

European Explorers - First came the Spanish, sailing from Mexico and Central America. They were in search of a water passage between the Atlantic and Pacific. With a stop off on the Washington coast, Spain made their claim to the land, hoping to discourage Britain and Russia from laying their own claims as they were doing in present-day Alaska. However, this did not deter the Brits. Later, in 1778, James Cook reinforced Britain's claim by sailing to Washington and trading with friendly natives for sea otter pelts. Later reports from Cook told of the abundance of fur-bearing animals. This did much to promote the abundant wealth of the Northwest. Ten years later, a man named John Meares of Britain, sailed into the Strait of Juan de Fuca, for which he named those waters after a crew member. In 1792, came George Vancouver of Britain, who explored this strait, giving names to areas and physical features as he mapped the land and waters. These included the Puget Sound, Mount Rainier, Mount Baker, and the San Juan Islands, to name a few.

Then the young United States decided to lay claim on the area. In 1792, Captain Robert Gray, a fur merchant from Boston, sailed to the Columbia River's mouth. He came into an area that would be his namesake, Grays Harbor. He staked America's claim on the west coast. Reinforcing this claim, in 1805, a group called the Corp of Discovery was on an expedition to explore the Louisiana Purchase along with the Columbia Gorge, which led them to the Northwest. The leaders of this group were Meriwether Lewis and William Clark. They explored the Columbia, wintered at Fort Clatsop before heading back to the east. Captain Robert Gray's claim was taken more seriously once the Lewis and Clark Expedition explored the area.

With fur trading on the rise and foreign competitors already in the area, John Jacob Astor from New York set up a fur depot in the coastal town of present-day Astoria, Oregon. He also sent his people northward to build Fort Okanogan, the first of its kind in Washington. The Oregon Country, which included the land of present-day Washington was claimed, and inhabited by people from England and America. Both countries agreed upon "joint occupation" in 1818. However, western expansionism with the mindset of "Manifest Destiny" was on the rise come the 1840s. Americans pressured the government to expel the Brits. In 1846, a treaty was signed, establishing a boundary at the 49th parallel. North of Washington the British went, to what is now Canada.

Amid the time of joint occupation, in 1826, logging and sawmills started being built. In 1853, the Washington Territory was established. The Oregon Trail brought a lot of settlers to Washington in the mid-1800s. Most were from the Midwest, with some immigrants coming from Europe and Canada. Settlers started going to Washington more in the 1890s when gold was found in Alaska.

The Great Seattle Fire -
On June 6, 1889, a fire started when a pot of glue burst into flames in a cabinet shop in Seattle. Over 64 acres of land were burned, and many businesses and homes. It is known as Seattle's Great Fire.

Father's Day -
Father's Day was started on June 19, 1910, by Sonora Smart Dodd in Spokane, Washington. She wanted to honor, and remember her dad, that raised her along with her brothers and sisters after her mom died. He had also fought in the Civil War. She had a lot of support from U.S. Presidents, but it did not become a national holiday until 1972.

World's Fair -
The 1962 World's Fair was held in Seattle, and the Space Needle was built just for the show. It has become an iconic symbol of the city.

Physical Features -
Washington is famous for the Cascade Mountains that hold some well known volcanoes. One-third of the state is west of the Cascades, and the rest is to the east. Seattle sits with a view of the magnificent Mount Rainier, which stands at 14,410 feet above sea level. Mount St. Helens became a famous volcano in Washington

Boeing Airplane Factory in Everett , Washington. Courtesy of Boeing

(ABOVE) By: "Scientific muralist" Ruddy Zallinger
Entitled: Great Seattle Fire - Painted in 1889
Courtesy of: Museum of History and Industry in Seattle
(LEFT) Photograph of the smoldering remains of the
Great Seattle Fire of 1889. By: Unknown, Public Domain

when in 1980, a massive eruption obliterated 200 square miles of forest, killing 57 people and thousands of animals. *(More on Helens, Rainier, and the Cascades in Lesson 13)*

Boeing and more -
The most prominent building in the world by volume is in Washington near Seattle. Inside this giant building, thousands of people make Boeing airplanes. The building is over 472 million cubic feet and is a popular destination for locals and visitors, with over 100,000 people visiting each year.

Manufacturing, agriculture, technology, and retail are essential parts of Washington's economy. They depend on companies like Boeing, Microsoft, Amazon, and the countless apple growers. The state also depends on tourism. People like to go to Washington to see nature, wildlife, water, and the cities. Farming, fishing, and wood are also important parts of the economy.

PICTURED: Downtown Seattle, Puget Sound and Mt. Rainier - Adobe Stock

Salem, Oregon

On February 14, 1859, Oregon became the 33rd state. Salem is the state capital. It is in the heart of the Northwest. Beautiful beaches that run the length from north to south along the Pacific Ocean are a popular place to visit. But watch out, the weather is hard to predict and is windy and chilly most times of the year. There is a lot of beautiful scenery and wildlife. Like Washington and northern California, it is home to the Cascade Mountains, where there is a rainforest, plateaus, mountains, deserts, and lush valleys. Mount Hood is in the Cascades, and is the tallest mountain in Oregon at 11,239 feet. Most people live west of the Cascade Mountains in the Willamette River Valley, in the cities and suburbs of Portland, Eugene, and Salem.

Before Europeans and settlers arrived, Chinook, Nez Percé, Klamath, and other Native American tribes lived.

Francis Drake, an English explorer, claimed the area for England in 1579. The Spanish and French did a little exploring in the 1600 and 1700s. In 1792, the first American explorers went to Oregon. In 1805, Lewis and Clark made it to Astoria, Oregon, where the Columbia River meets the Pacific Ocean.

Mt. Hood, Oregon's tallest mountain. By: Unknown, Public Domain

Oregon is called the Beaver State. When fur trading settlers arrived, they hunted them for their fur. Unfortunately, there was too much hunting. Soon, not enough beavers were left in the wild. Through protection plans, and controlled hunting, over time the beaver population recovered. They are called "nature's engineers" because they help keep the water from ruining the land. They are a meaningful part of Oregon's culture, history, and economy. A beaver is on the state flag and the Oregon State University is nicknamed after their mascot, the "Oregon State Beavers."

In 1830, people traveled along the Oregon Trail in an area owned by the United States and England. The first American settlement in Oregon was created in 1834. More than 12,000 people traveled from St. Louis, Missouri, all the way to Oregon. As you may remember, in 1846, the land that was owned by both the U.S. and England was split. A border between the U.S. and British territories was created at the 49th parallel. The land that was Britain's would become Canada with the signing of the British North America Act, which officially established the Dominion of Canada.

By 1847, there had been lots of attacks on settlers by local Native Americans. The local tribes were unhappy that people were taking their land and resources. The U.S. forced the tribes to move off their grounds and onto reservations.

Mount Hood is the tallest mountain in Oregon, which is a dormant volcano. The last time it erupted was in 1865. There are

City of Roses - Portland, Oregon. Oregon's largest city. By: Unknown, Public Domain

twelve glaciers on Mount Hood and serves as an incredibly popular mountain with 3 ski resorts.

Once the railroad reached Oregon in the 1880s, more and more people moved to Oregon.

Nike was founded in Beaverton, Oregon, in 1964. Their headquarters continues there today.

The Columbia River Gorge became a National Scenic Area in November 1986. The gorge is windy, very windy! Because of this, the Columbia Gorge is one of the best places to windsurf in the world.

Crater Lake - Other than beautiful beaches, Oregon is best known for Crater Lake. This almost perfectly circular lake is the deepest in the U.S. at 1,943 feet deep. The average depth is

1,500 feet. The lake resides at 6,173 feet above sea level, and it is six miles in diameter. It is part of Mount Mazama, an ancient volcano that stands 7,000 feet above sea level. It is believed that the volcano was 12,000 feet tall before a significant eruption blew the top right off! Now, it is all filled in with a lot of clear water that, on a radiantly sunny day, reflects the beautiful indigo sky brilliantly. This water is so clear, in fact, that when measured for clarity, a measurement device called a Secchi disk could be seen 134 feet down! It is also known that plants photosynthesize in the water up to a depth of 350 feet.

Crater Lake, Oregon. By: Amanda Predmore

Wizard Island is a volcanic cinder cone located at the west end of Crater Lake. If no water were around it, this cinder cone would look like a mini volcano growing up inside the crater. Only 2% of this cinder cone is peaking up from the depths below. There is one curious tree trunk named "old man of the lake." First spotted in 1896, this bobbing vertical

Top Left: Wizard Island within Crater Lake. Top Right: Aerial of Crater Lake. Both: By Unknown, Public Domain

30-foot tree trunk has become a celebrity among those that know the lake well, who spread the word to first-time visitors. It is believed that "he" has been floating for about 120 years. The "old man of the lake" spans two feet across and rises above the water's surface by just four feet. This driftwood is so well known that boat captains communicate its changing location to inform others as a safety precaution.

Thick with fir and pine forests, nature enthusiasts can explore more than 90 miles of hiking trails and may catch glimpses of a wide array of wildlife, including eagles, dear, bears, owls, grouse, and more. In the summers, the wildflowers grow in meadows. Come winter, there is always snow. A lot of snow! An average of 43 feet at park headquarters and more at the rim. The average snow depth in March is almost 10 feet. Crater Lake has one dirt road where mountain biking is allowed. The Grayback Drive provides eight miles of unpaved

Columbia River Gorge - By: Unknown, Public Domain

Brown Bear, Alaska - By: Unknown, Public Domain

(2020). It is so big; you could fit Texas in there twice! It is one-fifth the size of the lower 48 states. If you were to combine Texas, California, and Montana together, Alaska would still be bigger! The capital is Juneau. The economy depends on oil, fishing, and tourism. Alaska is filled with tremendous natural beauty. It borders Canada and has an exceptionally long Pacific

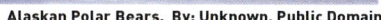
Alaskan Polar Bears. By: Unknown, Public Domain

and vehicle free roadway. Private boats or flotation devices are not allowed on Crater Lake. Only interpretive boat tours and research vessels are permitted. Crater Lake is preserved as a scenic and scientific wonder, not as a recreational lake. However, scuba diving is allowed.

Juneau, Alaska

Alaska became the 49th state on January 3, 1959. It is the largest state in size, but it ranks 48th most populated with only 710,249 Alaskans

The color filled Alaskan landscape. A slice of beauty in this vast landscape. By: Unknown, Public Domain

(LEFT) Reindeer herd in Alaska. By: Unknown, Public Domain

thrives in these harsh conditions. Off of the Alaskan coast, the incredible Wild King Salmon look for food in the Pacific Ocean for up to six years before making the ever-so mystical journey back to their spawning grounds. More caribou live in Northwestern Alaska than anywhere else. They are called reindeer and travel long distances in herds. Black bears, Grizzly bears, Kodiak bears, and Polar bears all live in Alaska, which is why it is called bear country. There is one bear for every 21 people in Alaska.

Two male moose tangle over mate. By: Unknown, Public Domain

A lone Alaskan wolf. By: Adobe Stock.

coastline. It is so far north that it reaches the Arctic Ocean and the Bering Sea. If you were to travel to Russia from Alaska, the total the distance is 3,230 miles. Here, there are many glaciers and very mild summers. As you may know, the winters are frigid. In fact, the north part of the state has a frozen tundra that never melts. The native people of Alaska are the Eskimos or Inuits, Aleuts, Tlingit, Haida, and Yuit. Most of the state land is untouched wilderness. Except for the abundant wildlife that

Photo taken after the Novarupta Volcano eruption of 1912, you can see the rooftops peaking out of the mounds of ash. By: Unknown, Public Domain

Aerial of Novarupta Volcano, Alaska. By: Unknown, Public Domain

The first to explore Alaska were the Russians in 1728. It took another twenty years before other European explorers found Alaska. Russia controlled the land from the late 1700s until the U.S. bought it in 1867 for $7.2 million. It was a very unpopular decision because people thought it was nothing but cold, uninhabitable wilderness. That is until gold was found in the 1890s.

In honor of this incredible "Great Race for Mercy," the Iditarod has been held each year since 1973. The first year 35 mushers started, but only 22 finished. It took the winner 20 days to come across the finish line. Since then, mushers are getting faster. In 2017, Mitch Seavey set the record for the fastest race at eight days, three hours, forty minutes, and thirteen seconds with his lead dogs Crisp and Pilot.

Humpback whales live off the coast, and once they are done feeding in Alaskan waters, they travel 2,400 miles to Hawaii every fall to raise their babies. Then they swim back to Alaska. Alaskan Huskies have been a part of native culture for hundreds of years. They are smaller than Siberian Huskies and can pull more than 75 pounds. They are an essential part of the Iditarod, a famous dog sled race. Dall Sheep live in the mountains. They have big curved horns that are used to charge at other males during mating season. The Muskox weighs between 400 and 800 pounds. They have long, tufted fur. The Eskimos gave the name to the animal that means "the animal with skin like a beard." Moose can weigh more than 1,300 pounds. They like to live alone, except during mating season or when they raise their babies. You are in more danger around a moose than a bear because you're more likely to meet one. There are up to ten moose attacks every year.

Fast Facts:
• In 1912, the Novarupta Volcano erupted, creating the Valley of Ten Thousand Smokes in Katmai National Park. It was the most powerful volcanic eruption in the 1900s.
• For fifteen months during World War II, two Alaskan islands were occupied by Japanese forces. • The tallest mountain in all of North America is in Alaska. Denali reaches 20,320 feet tall. Out of the 20 tallest mountains in the U.S., 17 are in Alaska.
• More than 5,000 earthquakes shake Alaska each year. In March of 1964, the biggest earthquake in North America was in Prince William Sound in Alaska. It was 9.2, which is extraordinarily strong.

Alaska is recognized for the famous Iditarod Trail Sled Dog Race. Held each March, the race goes from Anchorage to Nome, roughly 1,100 miles long. The trail was once a mail route, and it takes eight to fifteen days to finish the race. The racers are called "mushers" and they have a team of fourteen dogs. When crossing the finish line, it is required that five of those dogs must be on a towline. This means that five dogs must be pulling the sled. It is a long and dangerous race because the trail is full of steep banks, ice-covered hills, tundra, and turns. There are two trails. One is run on even-numbered years and the other on odd-numbered years. The event has the nickname "The Last Great Race on Earth." The name "Iditarod" comes from the Athabaskan word "haiditarod," meaning "far distance." In 1925, the Iditarod trail helped save children's lives. The kids were dying from a deadly disease called diphtheria, and they needed a cure. Mushers and their dogs took medicine to the kids.

(TOP & BOTTOM) 2017 Iditarod racers. By: Unknown, Public Domain

Iditarod Racers 2017
By: Unknown
Public Domain

Musher's dogs are smart and tough and come in a variety of breeds, including Siberian Huskies, Alaskan Huskies, Alaskan Malamutes, Canadian Eskimos, Chinooks, and Samoyeds.

On the first Sunday of March, the Widow's Lamp is lit in Nome. It stays lit until the last musher crosses the finish line.

Sled dogs are an essential part of a team and family. They must have the right personality for the job. They must be muscular, athletic, hardworking, friendly and have a healthy appetite. Not every sled dog is a lead dog; lead dogs are extra curious and like to be in charge. Sled dogs often get their names based on their personalities. Sometimes a team will have a theme for names based on when they were born or something the family likes. You would think the dogs get very cold, but sled dogs are bred to live in freezing temperatures. They are used to it and comfortable, but when it's too cold, they get to wear unique coats, boots, and blankets to keep them from getting frostbite.

Mushers and dogs must have a special bond. Dogs know their musher, and mushers know their dogs. They must depend on each other to make it across the finish line. Sled dogs who run the Iditarod are working dogs, but they are a part of the family. The musher loves them and takes outstanding care of them.

Traditional Igloo with sights set on the Aurora Borealis. By: Unknown, Public Domain

Northern Lights of Alaska

also called Aurora Borealis

"The Aurora is an incredible light show caused by collisions between electrically charged particles released from the sun that enter the earth's atmosphere and collide with gases such as oxygen and nitrogen. The lights are seen around the magnetic poles of the northern and southern hemispheres."

Aurora Borealis in Alaska. By: AdobeStock

135

A Closer Look!

at what you have learned for the last 6 lessons!

PLUS+

This Lesson's Geography:

White Mountains
Green Mountains
Adirondack Mountains
Allegheny Mountains

Previous Learned Geography:

Listed here is the geography learned over the last 6 lessons. All lessons learned before the last 6 lessons are no longer on the map.

Helena, Montana (MT)
Boise, Idaho (ID)

Olympia, Washington (WA)
Salem, Oregon (OR)
Juneau, Alaska (AK)
Salt Lake City, Utah (UT)
Phoenix, Arizona (AZ)
Carson City, Nevada (NV)
Sacramento, California (CA)
Honolulu, Hawaii (HI)
Topeka, Kansas (KS)
Oklahoma City, Oklahoma (OK)
Austin, Texas (TX)
Denver, Colorado (CO)
Santa Fe, New Mexico (NM)
St. Paul, Minnesota (MN)

Bismarck, North Dakota (ND)
Pierre, South Dakota (SD)
Cheyenne, Wyoming (WY)
Lincoln, Nebraska (NE)
Madison, Wisconsin (WI)
Springfield, Illinois (IL)
Des Moines, Iowa (IA)
Jefferson City, Missouri (MO)
Little Rock, Arkansas (AR)
Lansing, Michigan (MI)
Columbus, Ohio (OH)
Indianapolis, Indiana (IN)
Frankfort, Kentucky (KY)
Nashville, Tennessee (TN)

Lesson 11

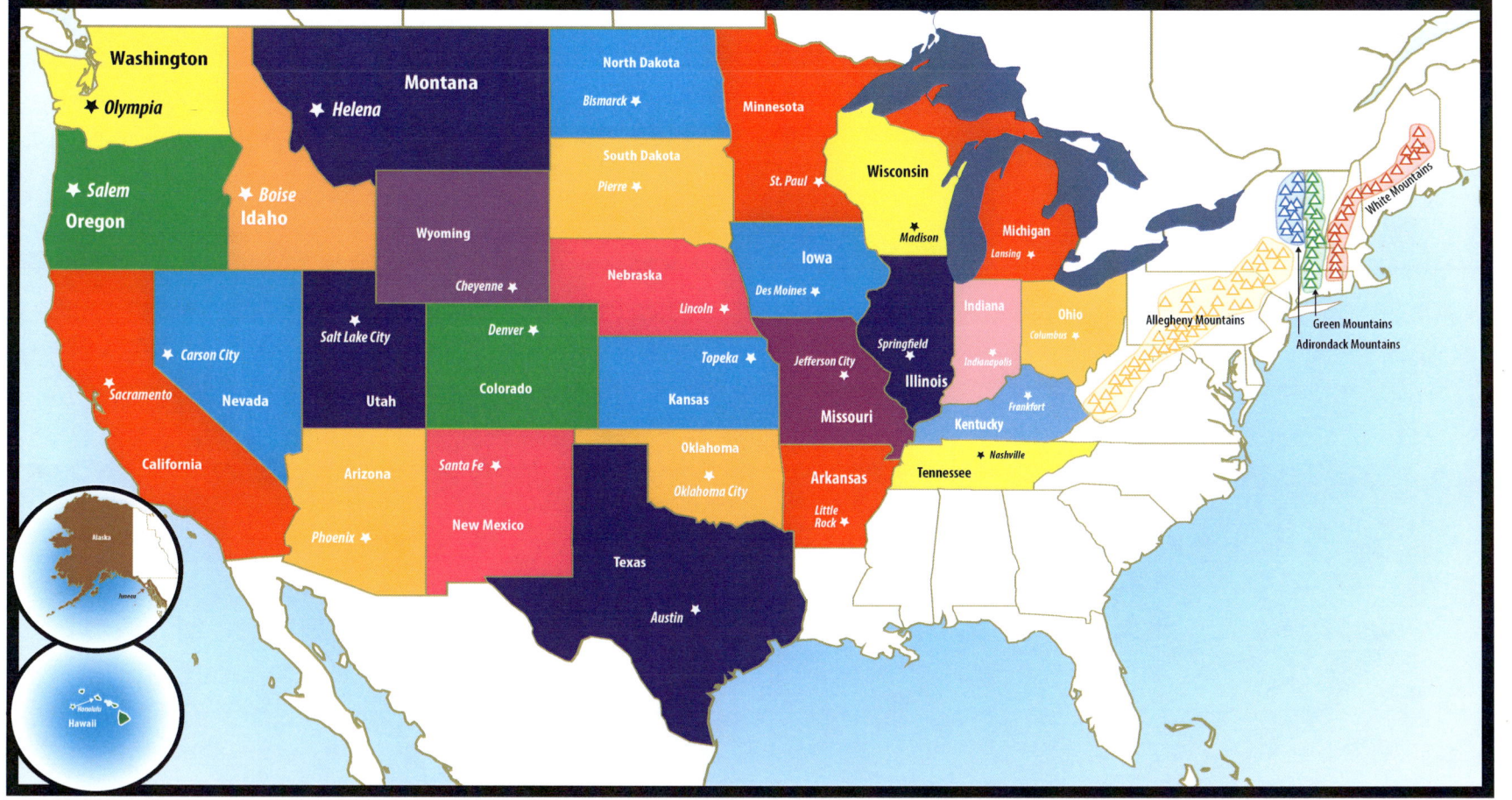

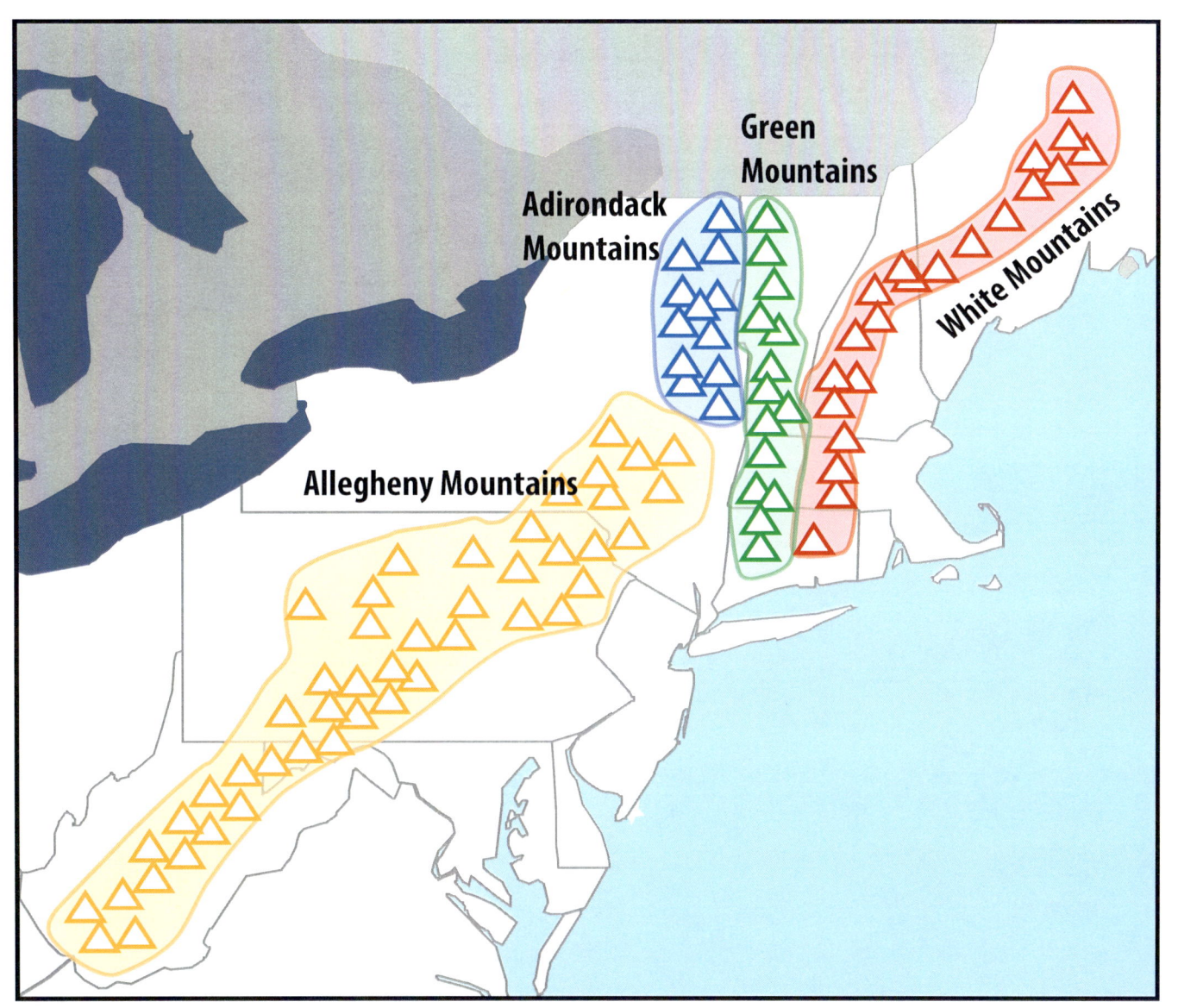

Lesson 11

Zoom Me In!

Use this sheet as a reference for this lesson's worksheets. Be sure to practice until you don't have to look!

United States of America Physical Features

Northern Appalachian Mountains:

White Mountains
Green Mountains
Adirondack Mountains
Allegheny Mountains

This Lesson's Geography:
Northern Appalachians

White Mountains
Green Mountains
Adirondack Mountains
Allegheny Mountains

Lesson 11

Tid-Bits

White Mountains

The White Mountains are a part of the northern Appalachian mountains in New England. They start in New Hampshire and stretch into Maine. The mountainous land is rugged, covered in dense forests, making it difficult to explore. There are many streams, rivers, and lakes running through them.

Europeans did not start exploring until the mid 1600s due to the challenging landscape. By then, most of New England had been settled. Once the White Mountains were explored, settlers began to move into the less desirable land. Those that did were extremely poor and had little. After the Revolutionary War, American settlers started cutting down trees in the White Mountains. Those trees were used to build homes and mills. Two types of mills were created:

those that processed logs for lumber and those that ground-up grain that local

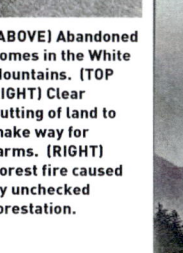

(ABOVE) Abandoned homes in the White Mountains. (TOP RIGHT) Clear Cutting of land to make way for farms. (RIGHT) Forest fire caused by unchecked forestation.

farmers grew. Where the trees used to grow, settlers built homes, farms, villages, and roads. Small communities started to grow in the mountain range. Later, many farms became abandoned when settlers moved west to land that was easier to farm, than in the mountains.

When people abandoned areas in the White Mountains, big companies bought up the land to build camps and railroads. They cut many trees down to make money off the forests. There were not any laws about logging back then, and the companies caused a lot of problems in the White Mountains with clear cutting, without replanting trees and

large forest fires burnt down the trees that were. The streams, rivers, and lakes were ruined by the significant changes made in the forests. This hurt the people in the area who needed the water for their saw and grain mills. To fix the problems that the big foresting companies created, the White Mountains were made into the White Mountain National Forest in 1918 to protect the area, making it livable once

again. Livable not only for the people and their mills but for the wildlife that calls the forest home. This move to protect the forests from massive deforestation was one good step in sustainable logging.

Today, the White Mountain National Forest is healthy and dense, with trees covering 800,000 acres, drawing many tourists each year. In fact, tourism is the main economic activity instead of logging. The railroads, shelters, mills, and houses cannot be seen any longer, for the trees have grown in their place.

Green Mountains

The Green Mountains are part of the northern Appalachian Mountain range. They stretch for 250 miles from Vermont in New

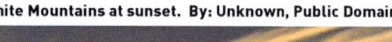

White Mountains at sunset. By: Unknown, Public Domain

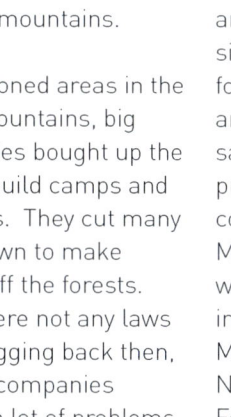

Beautiful stormy day in the Green Mountains, Vermont. By: Unknown, Public Domain

(ABOVE) Hikers hiking through the Long Trail. (RIGHT) Long Trail sign to keep explorers on track! (TOP RIGHT) Map showing how long the Long Trail is. ALL Photos, By: Unknown, Public Domain

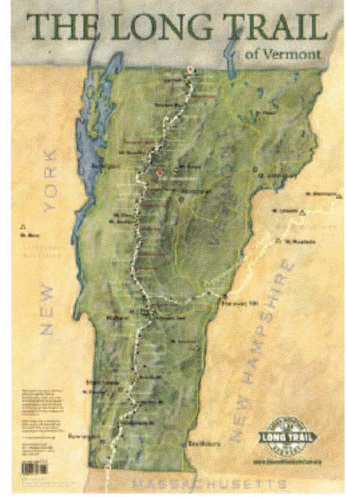

England through Massachusetts and into Connecticut. At their fullest, they are 36 miles wide. People call the part in Massachusetts and Connecticut the Berkshires, but they are still part of the Green Mountain range. Vermont's nickname is "The Green Mountain State" because of this mountain range. The name Green Mountains comes from Dr. Thomas Young, who suggested it in 1777. Dr. Young suggested the name in French: Monts Verts, which means "Green Mountains," and it is how Vermont was named!

Mount Mansfield is the tallest peak in the Green Mountains standing at 4,393 feet.

Many mountains throughout the range are more than 3,000 feet tall. Ash, northern red oak, aspen, beech, spruce, fir, sugar maple, hemlocks, and many other trees grow in the Green Mountains. Some of the hemlock trees are over 400 years old! A lot of natural minerals can be found in the Green Mountains, including talc, asbestos, verde antique marble, and more.

Vermont is a popular place to visit in the winter months because of the great skiing, snowboarding, and other winter sports to be enjoyed on the Green Mountains. In the summer people like to go mountain biking and hiking on the trails. The Long Trail is a popular footpath that goes through the Green Mountains for 273 miles. This trail is quite scenic with the forest that surrounds plus old stone walls and covered bridges. The Green Mountain National Forest was created in 1932 and includes more than 550 square miles. Today, this range of mountains is well known and loved for their beautiful scenery, hiking, and nature, making for a popular tourist destination all year long.

Adirondack Mountains

The Adirondack Mountains are known as The Adirondacks. They are part of the northern Appalachians in northeastern New York.

Before Europeans and settlers arrived, Iroquois and Algonquin tribes claimed the land. They fought over Lake George, Lake Champlain, and the water between them because it was the easiest way to travel through the Adirondacks.

Settlers started living in the Adirondacks around Lake George and Lake Champlain during the early 1700s because it was easy to thrive.

It is believed the Adirondacks were named after a Mohawk word meaning "eaters of trees." A French missionary, Joseph-François Lafitau, was the first person to use the term in 1729. He said it was a word the Mohawks used to describe Iroquois because they were terrible farmers and had to eat tree bark during the cold winters. It took more than a hundred years for the Adirondacks to be officially named in 1837.

The Adirondacks is a place where history lives. Many battles were fought there. It is also a place where medical discoveries were made, architecture was designed, industries were created, and more. Even though there are many trees in the Adirondacks, today, forest fires are rare. This was not always the case. There were two big fires in 1903 and 1908. More than a million acres of trees burned to ash. Because of these fires, New York created better ways to fight fires and keep damaging fires from happening in the first place.

The Adirondack Chair is quite famous and was

Skiing the Green Mountains in Vermont. By: Unknown, Public Domain

View of the Adirondacks in the Autumn. By: Unknown, Public Domain

The Adirondack Chair, By: Unknown, Public Domain

created in the mountains. It was first built in the early 1900s in Westport, New York, by Thomas Lee. He spent his summers at his home in the mountains, and he wanted a chair comfortable and sturdy that could sit on the hills and in the sandy soil. It took him three years to come up with the perfect design. Adirondack chairs are low to the ground with a high back, a slanted seat, and very wide armrests.

Theodore Roosevelt was Vice President to President McKinley. On September 6th, 1901, President McKinley was shot. Roosevelt traveled to be with him, but McKinley seemed to be getting better. Roosevelt took leave to hike Mount Marcy in the Adirondacks when he learned that President McKinley was actually getting worse. McKinley died eight days later. On September 14th in the middle of

River Valley in the Adirondacks. By: Unknown, Public Domain

Theodore Roosevelt, Public Domain

THE ANSLEY WILCOX RESIDENCE, DELAWARE AVENUE, BUFFALO
WHERE VICE-PRESIDENT ROOSEVELT TOOK THE OATH OF OFFICE AND BECAME PRESIDENT OF THE UNITED STATES, WITH PRESIDENT McKINLEY LYING DEAD IN THE MILBURN HOUSE A FEW BLOCKS AWAY.

the night while Roosevelt was traveling back to be with the President. Roosevelt found out he became President at North Creek train station. Taking the fastest train to Buffalo, paying his respects to Mrs. McKinley, Theodore Roosevelt was then sworn in as the 26th President of the United States.

From 1837 to 1901, Queen Victoria ruled England, and those years are known as the Victorian Era. There were many changes in the way people built houses, dressed, and did things in England. Those changes influenced America's style. Today, the Victorian Era period is evident in the Adirondacks with the preservation of history through the architecture, and the use of steamboats on Lake George. After the Civil War, Americans started to take vacations and have leisure time, which was immensely popular in Victorian England. Hunting, boating, camping, and more became exceedingly popular in the Adirondacks. This influenced luxury hotels to open for business, in turn drawing people to the area. Some people loved it so much they built houses in the Adirondacks in the Victorian style.

Allegheny Mountains

The Allegheny Mountains are a part of the Appalachian Mountain range in West Virginia. They are 400 miles long. Like many mountain ranges, people often shorten the name to just "the Alleghenies." They are beautiful, but before railroads and highways, they were all but impossible to cross. Today, those that need to head east or west through the Alleghenies use highways and railroads, making the trip a pleasure through the mountains.

The Iroquois, Delaware, Shawnee, Catawba, and other Native American tribes lived in and crossed the Alleghenies before Europeans arrived, explored, and settled the area. Native Americans created trails for hunting, trading, and warfare.

The Alleghenies served as a border between the Union and Confederate forces during the Civil War. Many battles were fought there. One of the first battles, known as the Battle of Rich Mountain, was fought over the B&O Railroad. The Union won a lot of significant territory during that battle. East of the Allegheny Mountains and southwest of Harrisburg, is a town called Gettysburg, in Pennsylvania. Here, a bloody, 3-day battle ensued on July 1st through July 3rd in 1863. Two years into the American Civil War, the Battle of Gettysburg served a crushing Southern defeat. It is generally regarded as the turning point of the war. Some speculate that this battle has been intensively analyzed and studied more than any other war conflict in U.S. history.

After a win for the Confederacy in Chancellorville, Virginia, General Robert E. Lee and his soldiers had high morale, their bravery had been increased. 71,000 strong, Lee and his men in May of 1863 went forth into the north. This mission hoped to discourage the Union more so, and possibly sway European countries to recognize the Confederacy as a sovereign nation. However, Lee overestimated his troops. The loss of human life was among the worst. Of about 93,000 Federal Union men, they experienced 23,000 casualties, of which 3,100 were killed. The Confederates had 28,000 injured, with 3,900 killed.

Months later, in November 1863, at the site of the battle, Abraham Lincoln dedicated those grounds as the National Cemetery giving his most famous words in the Gettysburg Address:

"Four score and seven years ago our fathers brought forth on this continent a new nation, conceived in Liberty, and dedicated to the proposition that all men are created equal.

Now we are engaged in a great civil war, testing whether that nation or any nation so conceived and so dedicated, can long endure. We are met on a great battle-field of that war. We have come to dedicate a portion of that field, as a final resting place for those who here gave their lives that that nation might live. It is altogether fitting and proper that we should do this.

The vast Allegheny Mountains. By: Unknown, Public Domain

THE BATTLE OF GETTYSBURG, PA JULY 3rd 1863.

Painting of Abraham Lincoln at the Gettysburg Address, Public Domain

Aerial view of the Battle of Gettysburg. Library of Congress, Public Domain

But, in a larger sense, we can not dedicate—we can not consecrate—we can not hallow—this ground. The brave men, living and dead, who struggled here, have consecrated it, far above our poor power to add or detract. The world will little note, nor long remember what we say here, but it can never forget what they did here. It is for us the living, rather, to be dedicated here to the unfinished work which they who fought here have thus far so nobly advanced. It is rather for us to be here dedicated to the great task remaining before us—that from these honored dead we take increased devotion to that cause for which they gave the last full measure of devotion—that we here highly resolve that these dead shall not have died in vain—that this nation, under God, shall have a new birth of freedom—and that government of the people, by the people, for the people, shall not perish from the earth."

Abraham Lincoln believed that his words that day would not be remembered. Thankfully, his prediction was wrong.

The day after Lincoln spoke these words at the dedication ceremony, newspapers countrywide quoted Lincoln's speech. As with any time in history, people's opinions were divided along political lines. Republican journalists praised the address as "heartfelt, believing it to be a classic piece of oratory." Whereas the Democratic side thought the speech as inadequate and inappropriate for the occasion.

Regardless of public opinion of the day, Lincoln's Gettysburg Address has endured as arguably the most-quoted, most-memorized piece of oratory in American history.

Following Lincolns' assassination in April 1865, Senator Charles Sumner of Massachusetts wrote about his words:

"That speech, uttered at the field of Gettysburg…and now sanctified by the martyrdom of its author, is a monumental act. In the modesty of his nature he said, 'the world will little note, nor long remember what we say here; but it can never forget what they did here.' He was mistaken. The world at once noted what he said and will never cease to remember it."

A Closer Look!
at what you have learned for the last 6 lessons!

PLUS+
This Lesson's Geography:
Southern Appalachian Mountains
The Great Valley
Blue Ridge Mountains
Great Smoky Mountains
Cumberland Mountains
Mt. Mitchell

Previous Learned Geography:
Listed here is the geography learned over the last 6 lessons. All lessons learned before the last 6 lessons are no longer on the map.

White Mountains
Green Mountains
Adirondack Mountains
Allegheny Mountains

Helena, Montana (MT)
Boise, Idaho (ID)
Olympia, Washington (WA)
Salem, Oregon (OR)
Juneau, Alaska (AK)
Salt Lake City, Utah (UT)
Phoenix, Arizona (AZ)
Carson City, Nevada (NV)
Sacramento, California (CA)
Honolulu, Hawaii (HI)
Topeka, Kansas (KS)
Oklahoma City, Oklahoma (OK)
Austin, Texas (TX)
Denver, Colorado (CO)

Santa Fe, New Mexico (NM)
St. Paul, Minnesota (MN)
Bismarck, North Dakota (ND)
Pierre, South Dakota (SD)
Cheyenne, Wyoming (WY)
Lincoln, Nebraska (NE)
Madison, Wisconsin (WI)
Springfield, Illinois (IL)
Des Moines, Iowa (IA)
Jefferson City, Missouri (MO)
Little Rock, Arkansas (AR)

Lesson 12

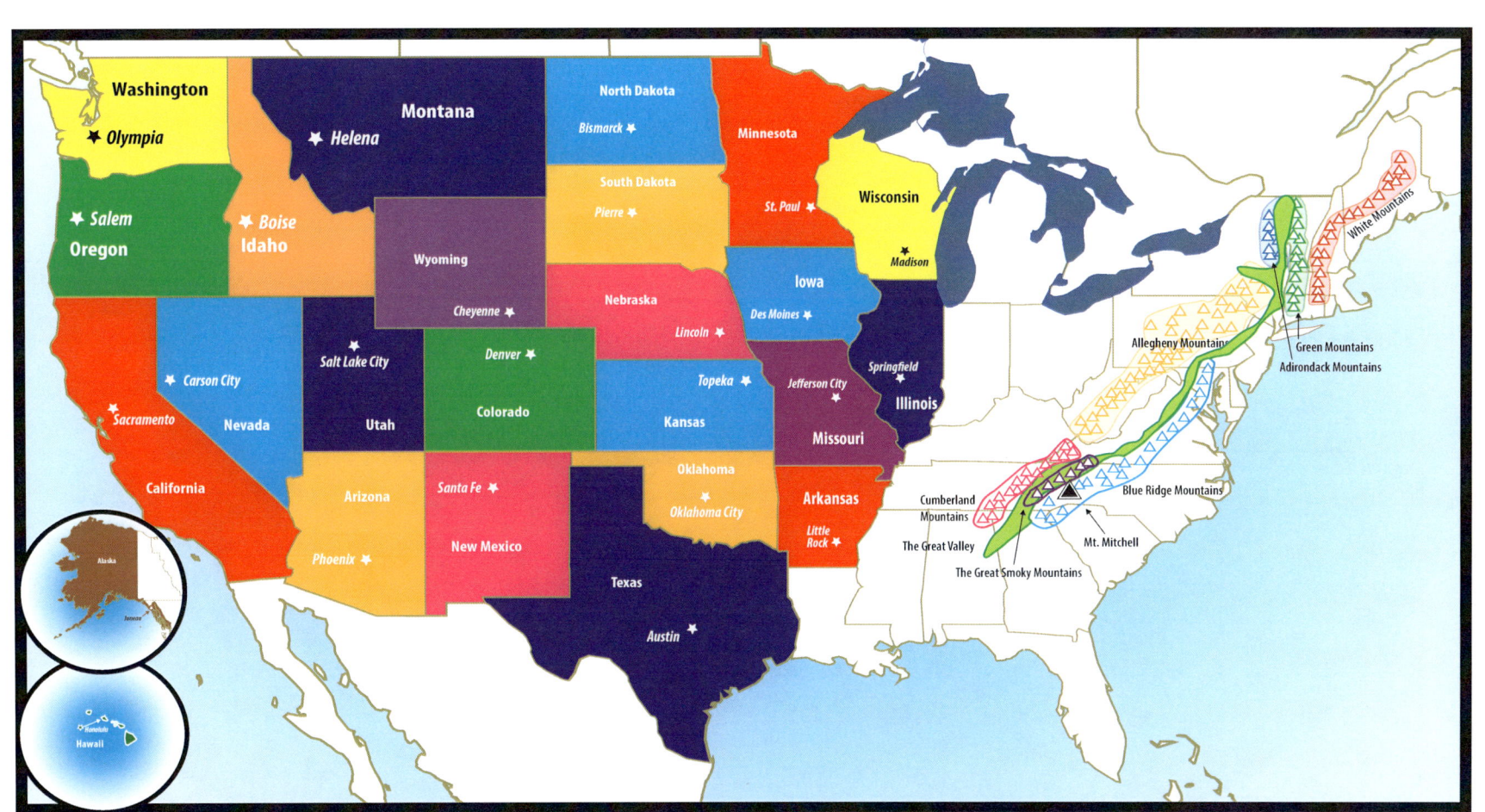

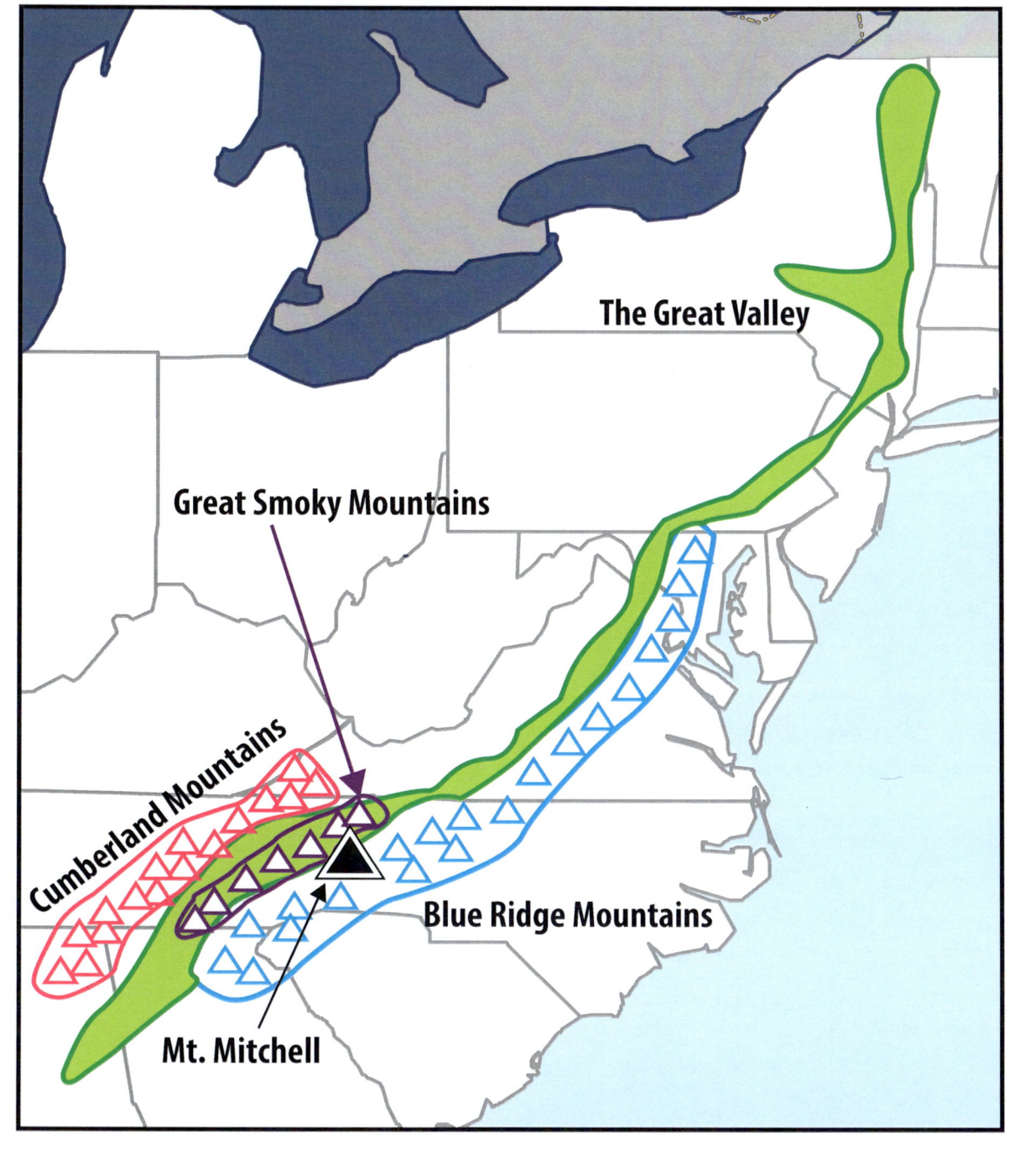

Lesson 12

Zoom Me In!

Use this sheet as a reference for this lesson's worksheets. Be sure to practice until you don't have to look!

United States of America Physical Features

Southern Appalachian Mountains:

The Great Valley
Blue Ridge Mountains
Great Smoky Mountains
Cumberland Mountains
Mt. Mitchell

This Lesson's Geography:
Southern Appalachians

The Great Valley
Blue Ridge Mountains
Great Smoky Mountains
Cumberland Mountains
Mt. Mitchell

Tid-Bits

The Great Valley is a big part of the Appalachian Mountains. It is a valley of lowlands and a vital part of North American geography. People also call it the Great Appalachian Valley or the Great Valley Region. This valley acts as a passageway for water to flow from the mountains into streams, rivers, and lakes. Like a trough or channel for the water. It stretches from Quebec to Alabama, which is over 1,200 miles long. It is so big; it goes through several regions. One of those regions is the Shenandoah Valley.

The valley was first explored and used by Native Americans before that created routes, or paths. The most prominent and most well-known route was called by many names, including the "Great Indian Warpath" and the "Seneca Trail". When Europeans arrived, they used the Great Valley to make a life for themselves and their families through trading and farming.

Americans have used the Great Valley throughout history, as the land was plentiful and easy to thrive in. Many gaps in the valley allowed people to conveniently move as they needed

The Great Appalachian Valley - By: Unknown, Public Domain

from one side to the other. Near South Mountain in southeastern Pennsylvania, a wide gap became a place for settlers to live in the 1730s. Lots of people moved there after the Native Americans signed treaties and sold the land. People called it "the best poor man's country." Then people began to move into Virginia in a region called the Shenandoah Valley. The entire area had very productive farms, and people called it the "breadbasket."

The Cumberland Gap is on the west side of the Great Valley. It was a vital route for settlers when they started moving west into Kentucky and Tennessee.

Mohawk Valley is found on the western side within the Great Valley, north of the Cumberland Gap. The Mohawk Valley became a crucial corridor for both sides during

The Great Appalachian Valley - By: Unknown, Public Domain

Lesson 12

the French and Indian War. The British utilized it strategically as a direct path to the Great Lakes giving them the ability to threaten New France head-on. Whereas to the French, the Mohawk valley provided a pathway to the Hudson Valley, which led straight to the heart of British North America.

When settlers moved west, the Mohawk Valley became a good route, especially after the Erie Canal connected New York City to the Great Lakes using the Hudson River.

During the American Civil War, people depended on the Great Valley and the Shenandoah Valley. The Blue Ridge gaps near Piedmont and north of Gettysburg were essential places during the war.

The Blue Ridge Mountains are named because they look blue from far away. This mountain range is 550 miles long.

The mountains get their blue color from the trees that release isoprene into the atmosphere. Creating a beautiful and unique haze that surrounds the moun-

Blue Ridge Mountains, By: Unknown, Public Domain

metamorphic rock is located throughout the parkway. These rocks have folds and swirls from the bands of light and dark colored minerals. "Metamorphic rocks are created from the transformation of existing rocks, in a process called metamorphism, which means 'change in form.'"
SOURCE: Wikipedia

Old Growth Forests, early 1900s - By: Unknown, Public Domain

Robert E. Lee's Army from Northern Virginia made their second invasion of the North in the Gettysburg Campaign. They crossed over the Potomac River and traveled along the Blue Ridge mountains, so that the North would not see where they were. As you recently learned, the Confederacy was defeated at the Battle of Gettysburg. It was a critical turning point in the war giving the North hope and power. This defeat for the Confederacy also meant they would never get additional support from Europe, or anywhere else.

tains. Isoprene is a colorless liquid that evaporates at average temperatures. It is made by plants, animals, and humans. It is an ingredient in natural rubber. Trees release isoprene to protect themselves and their leaves from extreme heat. Isoprene helps keep cells stable when there are drastic changes in temperature, especially when temperatures are high, above 104°F.

The Blue Ridge Parkway is a prominent part of the Blue Ridge Mountains. It is in the Southern Appalachians and is 469 miles long. The Shenandoah National Park and the Great Smoky Mountains National Park are connected by the Blue Ridge Parkway. An eye-catching

The Great Smoky Mountains are often called the "Smoky Mountains" or even "The Smokies." The area is pristine with the protection that comes with being designated a national park.

The Smokies are a part of the Blue Ridge Physiographic Province. What does that mean? Physiographic Province is a way that the U.S. groups land areas that have similar climate, underlying geology, and topography. The national park was created in 1934 and is one of the most visited in America, with over 11 million tourists each year.

A drive through the Blue Ridge Mountains, By: Unknown, Public Domain

The Great Smoky Mountains. By: Unknown, Public Domain

The Great Smokies are home to an old-growth forest of 187,000 acres. It is the biggest of its kind east of the Mississippi River. They also have the biggest black bear population in the east. Salamanders are best known for living in tropical climates. However, the Smokies have the most diverse salamander population outside of the tropics.

The Smoky Mountains get their name because there is a constant fog sitting over the mountains. Like the Blue Ridge Mountains, plants and trees release isoprene, which gives a smoky appearance.

A portion of the Cherokee Nation lived in the area when the English started exploring the Southern Appalachian Mountains in the late 1600s. The Great Smoky Mountains were in the middle of their land, but most of their villages were in the river valleys and along the base of the mountains. Conflict arose

Old Farm House at the base of the Great Smoky Mountains
By: Unknown, Public Domain

between settlers and the Cherokee people following the French and Indian War, as there was disagreement about the ownership of the land. Later, during the American Revolution the Cherokee became friends with the British. After our independence was won, Americans began battling the Cherokee people in this area and beyond.

Many Cherokees were forced to give up their land in the Smoky Mountains by 1805. In 1838, many who remained were forced off their lands to travel along the Trail of Tears to west of the Mississippi River when President Andrew Jackson passed the "Indian Removal Act." A few Cherokee people kept their property on the Qualla Boundary, which today is called the Eastern Band of Cherokee Indians.

At the base of the Great Smokies, people farmed and made their own food during the 19th century. A typical farm had 50 acres. Part of the land was used to grow food, and the other part was kept as a forest. The first settlers lived in log cabins that were sixteen feet wide by twenty feet long. As technology got better, the log cabins became bigger and fancier. When wood became easier to work with, settlers made modern homes with frames. Most farms had a barn, spring-house, smokehouse, chicken coop, and a corn crib. A spring-house kept things cold during the warm months of the year. The smokehouse cured meat. The chicken coop kept the chickens safe from predatory animals. A corn crib kept the corn dry and safe from rodents looking for a meal. Protestant Christianity was the most common religion in the area, and it was an essential part of their lives.

Daniel Boone, Frontiersman - By: Unknown, Public Domain

The Cumberland Gap is in the Cumberland Mountains. It has a meaningful place in American history. While the mountains are full of beautiful scenery, unique sandstone formations, underground caverns, and overflowing with diverse plants and animals-the mountains are dangerous to navigate because of the treacherous ridges.

Old Growth Forests, early 1900s - By: Unknown, Public Domain

Cumberland Gap. By Unknown: Public Domain

147

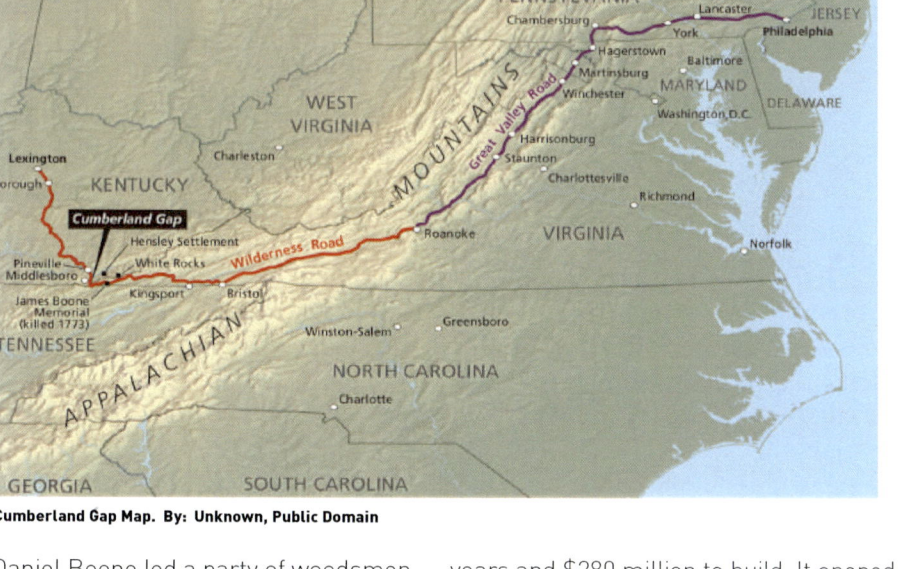

Cumberland Gap Map. By: Unknown, Public Domain

Daniel Boone led a party of woodsmen from Virginia to Kentucky in 1775. They were the first people to make known the Cumberland Gap. The Cumberland Gap became known as the safest way through. Initially utilized by the Native Americans for migration, trade, and war and eventually used by European explorers and settlers.

As settlers migrated farther and farther west, the trail changed from a path to a road. With the ease of getting through, many settled and eventually made Kentucky a state. In fact, because so many people used these trails to head west, it became known as "The Way West."

Today, people utilize the Cumberland Gap Tunnel, which is four lanes wide and 4,600 feet long. It took seventeen years and $280 million to build. It opened in 1996. It has served as a significant transportation route that people use daily.

The Cumberland Gap National Historical Park has over 20,000 acres and is 20 miles long with a width of one to four miles wide. Over 14,000 acres of the park are untouched, quiet, wilderness. Native plants and animals grow and roam free. There are over 60 rare plant species that call the park home. As for animals, you might spy a black bear or even a wild turkey! Within the park also lies historic buildings, caves, hiking trails, and guided tours. It is a great place to see a part of America's history.

Mt. Mitchell

The highest peak in the Appalachian Mountains is Mount Mitchell, that stands at 6,684 feet above sea level. It is also the highest mountain east of the Mississippi River and south of the Arctic Cordillera. The Pisgah National Forest surrounds Mount Mitchell, and Mount Mitchell State Park protects the forests, mountain, and its wildlife. It used to be called the Black Dome because it is very round. It was renamed after Elisha Mitchell, an explorer, and a professor at the University of North Carolina. He was the first person to explore the region and find out the height of Black Dome. He realized it was a hundred feet taller than Mount Washington in New Hampshire, which was thought to be the tallest mountain east of the Mississippi. Professor Elisha Mitchell fell and died in 1857 close to Black Dome at Mitchell Falls when he was verifying his previous measurements.

Illustration of Elisha Mitchell. Elisha monument photos – All By: Unknown

A Closer Look!
at what you have learned for the last 6 lessons!

PLUS+
This Lesson's Geography:
Western Mountains
Rocky Mountains Sierra Nevada
Pikes Peak Mt. Whitney
Mt. Elbert

Previous Learned Geography:

Listed here is the geography learned over the last 6 lessons. All lessons learned before the last 6 lessons are no longer on the map.

The Great Valley
Blue Ridge Mountains
Great Smoky Mountains
Cumberland Mountains
Mt. Mitchell
White Mountains
Green Mountains
Adirondack Mountains
Allegheny Mountains
Helena, Montana (MT)
Boise, Idaho (ID)
Olympia, Washington (WA)
Salem, Oregon (OR)
Juneau, Alaska (AK)
Salt Lake City, Utah (UT)
Phoenix, Arizona (AZ)
Carson City, Nevada (NV)
Sacramento, California (CA)
Honolulu, Hawaii (HI)
Topeka, Kansas (KS)
Oklahoma City, Oklahoma (OK)
Austin, Texas (TX)
Denver, Colorado (CO)
Santa Fe, New Mexico (NM)
St. Paul, Minnesota (MN)
Bismarck, North Dakota (ND)
Pierre, South Dakota (SD)
Cheyenne, Wyoming (WY)
Lincoln, Nebraska (NE)

Lesson 13

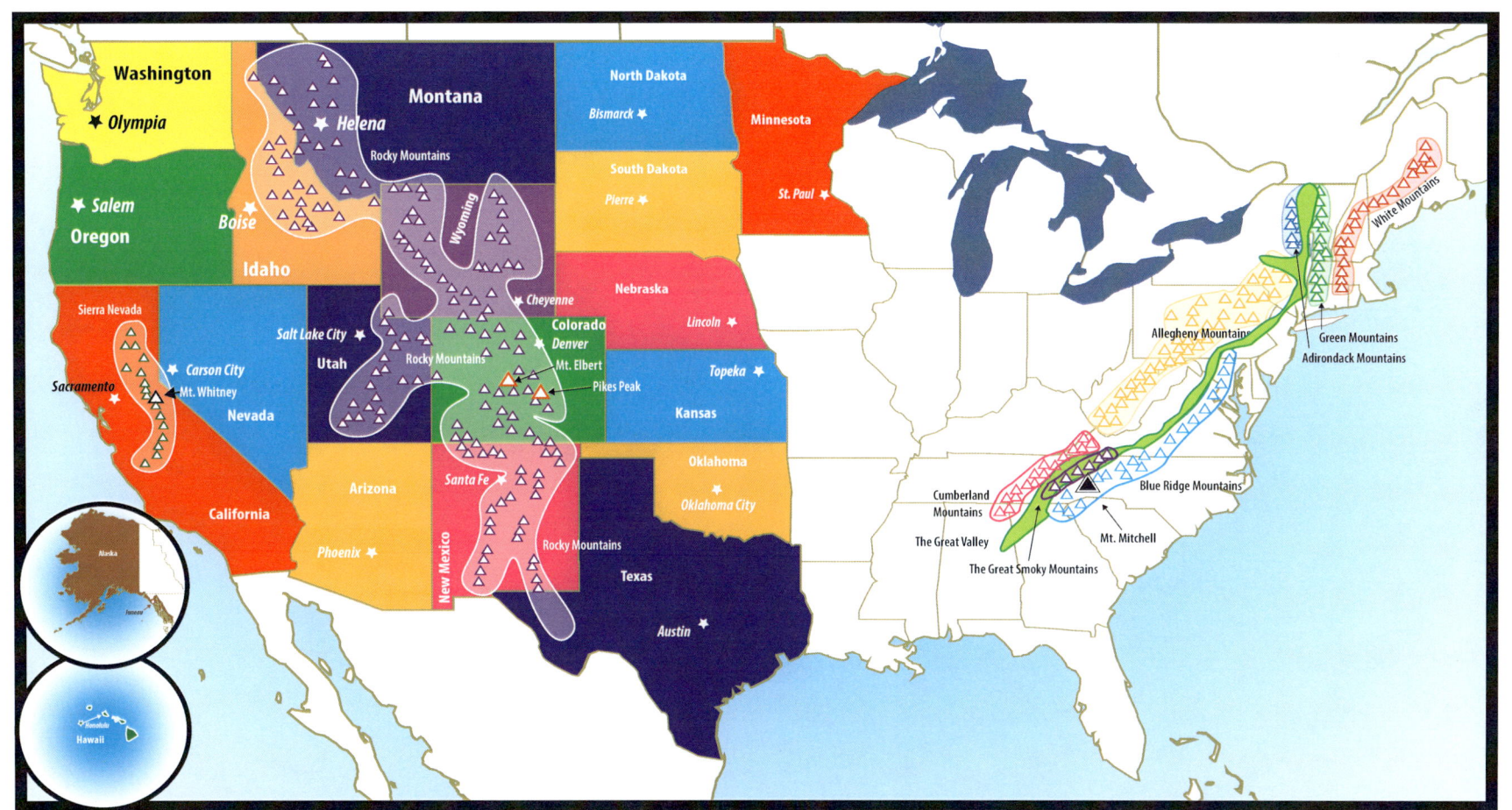

149

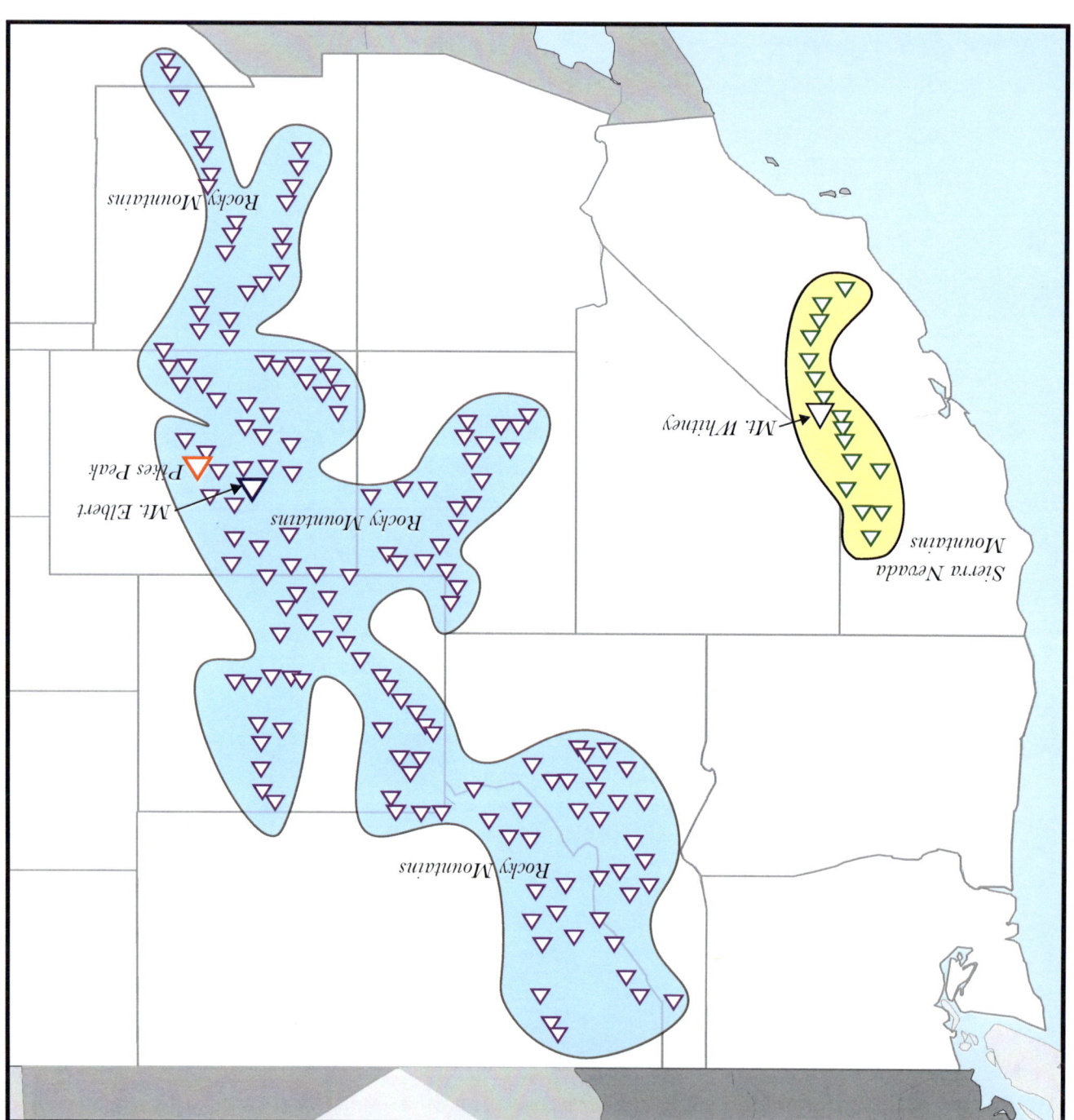

Zoom Me In!

Use this sheet as a reference for this lesson's worksheets. Be sure to practice until you don't have to look!

United States of America Physical Features

Western Mountains

- ~~~ Rocky Mountains
- ▽ Pikes Peak
- ▽ Mt. Elbert
- ~~~ Sierra Nevadas
- ▽ Mt. Whitney

Lesson 13

This Lesson's Geography:
Western Mountains

Rocky Mountains
Pikes Peak
Mt. Elbert
Sierra Nevada
Mt. Whitney

Lesson 13

Tid-Bits

Coyote, Rocky Mountains

Male Big Horn Lamb, Rocky Mountains

Big Horn Lamb, Rocky Mountains

The Rocky Mountains

People often call The Rocky Mountains, simply "The Rockies." They are the most extensive mountain range in North America and the second-longest in the world. Only the Andes in South America are longer. The Rockies are 3,000 miles long and go from Canada to Montana and into New Mexico.

The Continental Divide marks the high point in North America where water flows west to the Pacific or east to the Atlantic. Although to note, the Continental Divide found in the United States runs east to the Mississippi River that then flows into the Gulf of Mexico through the Mississippi Delta on the south side of Louisiana. The Continental Divide within the United States and Canada is in the Rockies. However, in Canada all waters flow east to the Atlantic.

Rocky Mountains

The Rockies have lots of forests filled with trees of all kinds, including spruce, pine, oak, fir, juniper, and more. Among these trees are grizzly bears, black bears, bighorn sheep, badgers, coyotes, white-tailed deer, elk, wolves, and more, live high and low in the Rockies.

Ecology and climate change a lot in the Rockies because there are so many different elevations. Ecology is a branch of biology, and it studies the relationship between animals and the place they live. An animal's habitat is made up of lots of things. The higher the elevation, the colder the weather is. Latitude is also relevant to climate. Latitude lines are invisible lines that go around the world in an east-west direction. The equator is

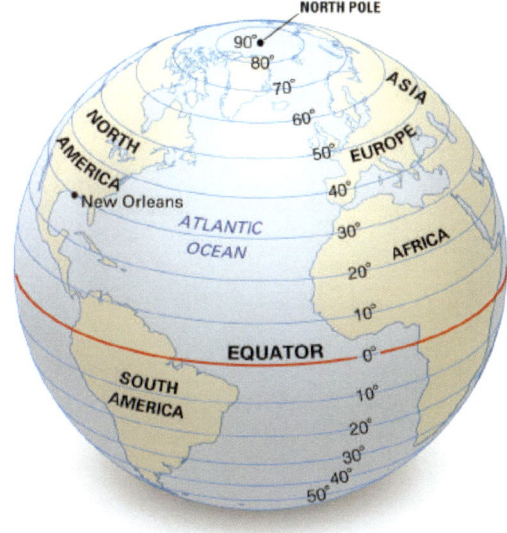

151

Cliff Palace in Mesa Verde National Park is in the Rockies and was home to the Pueblo people.

The Rocky Mountains can be anywhere from 70 to 300 miles wide. They are very tall. Mount Elbert in Colorado is the tallest mountain in all of the Rockies, including the Canadian Rockies. Mt. Elbert stands at an impressive 14,440 feet above sea level. The top 30 tallest mountains in the Rockies are in Colorado. Out of 100 of the highest peaks, 78 are in Colorado.

The Rockies also have several smaller mountain ranges. The Big Horn Mountains, the Front Range, the Wasatch Mountains, and the Bitterroot Range are all part of the Rocky Mountains. National parks protect several parts of the Rockies. Yellowstone National Park, Rocky Mountain National Park, Glacier National Park, and Grand Teton National Park help preserve the land and animals in these areas. These National Parks are also popular places for visitors that go fishing, hunting, biking, camping, hiking, mountaineering, skiing, and snowboarding.

a latitude line, marking the center of the earth and the point closest to the sun. The closer the latitude is to the equator, the hotter the climate. The farther the latitude is from the equator, the colder it gets. The two points that are farthest from the equator are the north and south poles. The northern Rockies are in Canada. The southern Rockies are in New Mexico. So the Rockies are colder in the north than in the south.

Mesa Verde National Park is in the Rockies and was home to the Pueblo people. They left behind their homes made long ago that we can now admire and learn from. The park is 52,485 acres big, and the National Park status was put in place by President Theodore Roosevelt and Congress in 1906. The name means "green table" in Spanish. It is one of the most important archaeological sites in the United States. More than 600 Native American cliff dwellings and the famous Cliff Palace are just a portion of the 5,000 archaeological sites protected by Mesa Verde National Park. Archaeologists believe it is the biggest and most significant cliff dwelling in North America. The Pueblo people survived by hunting, gathering, and farming. Important crops for them were corn, beans, and squash. Archaeologists believe the first cliff dwellings were built around 650 AD. In 1100 AD, the cliff dwellings started getting bigger and more detailed. Puebloes left the area and moved to Arizona and New Mexico because of prolonged droughts.

Pikes Peak is a famous mountain in the Rockies. It is the highest peak on the southern Front Range and stands at 14,115 feet above sea level. It is in Pike National Forest and is twelve miles west of Colorado Springs, Colorado.

Pikes Peak hasn't always been called that. It has been called by many names. Some names were Sun Mountain, Sitting Big, Great Peak, Long Mountain, El Capitan, Pike's Peak, Grand Peak, and James Peak.

People refer to Pikes Peak as a fourteener, which means its peak is over 14,000 feet above sea level. The U.S. has 96 fourteeners. They are all west of the Mississippi River. Alaska has 29 of the fourteeners, but Colorado has the most with 53.

Pikes Peak is made out of Pikes Peak granite, which is pink in color. It gets its pink color from the potassium feldspar, which is a mineral.

The Spanish were the first Europeans to visit Pikes Peak in the 1700s. Americans didn't see the mountain until 1806 when Zebulon Pike took an exploration team. They tried to climb to the top of Pikes Peak but weren't able to. Zebulon Pike wrote in his journal:

Pikes Peak Granite. By: Unknown, Public Domain

"Here we found the snow middle deep; no sign of beast or bird inhabiting this region. The thermometer, which stood at 9° above 0 at the foot of the mountain, here fell to 4° below 0. The summit of the Grand Peak, which was entirely bare of vegetation and covered with snow, now appeared at the distance of 15 or 16 miles from us, and as high again as

Zebulon Montgomery Pike was an American brigadier general and explorer for whom Pikes Peak in Colorado was named. By: Unknown, Public Domain

what we had ascended, and would have taken a whole day's march to have arrived at its base, when I believed no human being could have ascended to its pinnacle. This with the condition of my soldiers who had only light overalls on, and no stockings, and every way ill provided to endure the inclemency of the region; the bad prospect of killing anything to subsist on, with the further detention of two or three days, which it must occasion, determined us to return."

Fourteen years later, in 1820, Edwin James and two explorers scaled the peak to its summit. They were the first European-American team to make it to the top. Edwin James had recently graduated from Middlebury College in Vermont. He wasn't supposed to go on the trip, but the botanist, who was supposed to go, died. It took Edwin James and his team two days to climb Pikes Peak. He was the first person to document Colorado's state flower: the blue columbine.

In present-day Denver, gold was found in 1958. Newspapers called the area Pike's Peak and created the slogan "Pike's Peak or Bust" for those who went to Colorado for the gold. There was not a lot of gold in the Pikes Peak area, but nearby. However, the towering mountain made it easy for people to see as they traveled to Denver. Then again, in 1893, gold was found southwest of Pikes Peak. The people that headed there were a part of the last big gold rush in the lower 48 states.

Edwin P. James, a 19th-century American botanist, geologist, and medical practitioner, was an important figure in the early exploration of the American West. James was also known for his time spent creating relationships with Native Americans in the United States, and also aiding African Americans to escape slavery.

Pikes Peak inspired Katharine Lee Bates to write "America the Beautiful" in 1893. She had a heart for adventure and had summited the mighty mountain. When she came to the top, she found herself in utter awe. She could barely believe the beauty before her. Two years later, she published the song in The Congregationalist. Today, there is a plaque at the top of Pikes Peak with the words to her song.

It used to be very arduous to get to the top of Pikes

Buffalo Bill Cody (LEFT) earned his nickname by hunting and killing over 4,000 buffalo, and his status as an Old West legend was cemented with his traveling Wild West show. Seen here with "Pikes Peak or Bust" slogan. Others photographed are unknown. Photo by: Unknown, Public Domain

America the Beautiful plaque at the top of Pikes Peak. By: Unknown, Public Domain

Pikes Peak inspired Katharine Lee Bates to write "America the Beautiful" in 1893.

Peak. Today, the ascent is not so troublesome. Pikes Peak Highway is nineteen miles long from bottom to top. There is a switchback road with lots of sharp hairpin-turns, making it dangerous to drive at high speeds. People call them "The W's" because of the shape they make in the side of the mountain. The highway became famous because of a car race that happens each year. The competition is called Pikes Peak International Hill Climb. There is also a race for bicycles called USA Cycling Hill Climb National Championships.

Pikes Peak International Hill Climb - Auto Race. By: Unknown, Public Domain

Pikes Peak Highway. By Unknown, Public Domain

If you want to get to the top the old-fashioned way, you can take Barr Trail to the top on the east side of the mountain. People can hike or bike up and down the trail.

Pikes Peak is over 14,000 feet high, which means life is a little different at that altitude. Water boils at 186°F instead of 212°F at sea level. There is 40% less oxygen at the top of Pikes

Pikes Peak - By Unknown, Public Domain

Peak than at sea level, which means people breathe faster. Some people get altitude sickness because of the difference in elevation. Pikes Peak is so high it has a polar climate, which means it can snow any time of the year. At times, thunderstorms can bring winds that blow over 100 miles an hour!

Mount Elbert is the tallest peak in the Rocky Mountains. It is also the tallest point in Colorado. It is a fourteener that

reaches 14,440 into the sky. The only mountain taller than Mount Elbert is Mount Whitney in the Sierra Nevada. Mount Elbert is in the San Isabel National Forest in the Sawatch Range of the Rockies. It is twelve miles outside Leadville, Colorado.

Samuel Hitt Elbert was Governor of the Colorado Territory from 1873 to 1874. People respected him as his leadership proved to be an essential ingredient to the success of a treaty made in 1873. This treaty helped the U.S. gain three million acres of land

Samuel Hitt Elbert*

for mining and railroading from the Ute tribe. Mount Elbert was named after Samuel Elbert.

In 1874, Henry W. Stuckle was the first person to make it to the top. There are different levels of difficulty in mountaineering and climbing. The easiest and most popular are Class 1 and Class 2. Mount Elbert is a gentle giant because it is a manageable mountain to climb with Class 1 and Class 2 paths.

Mount Elbert is easy to spot from Leadville, Colorado, with its snow-capped peak. The elevation is so high that the weather can change quickly. During warm summer afternoons, thunderstorms can roll over Mount Elbert quickly, causing snow and hail.

Mt. Elbert, Aerial View*

Mt. Elbert

Pika, Mt. Elbert - By: David Kingham

Elk, Mt. Elbert*

The beautiful "Wallcreeper, Mt. Elbert."*

Five routes lead to the top of the highest mountain of the Rockies. The most popular and easiest is the Northeast Ridge, which does not require special mountaineering skills. People have climbed on foot, on horse, and on bike. During the hunting season, many people hunt on the mountain. The most significant danger when climbing to the top is altitude sickness, which can be life-threatening. Altitude sickness makes it hard to breathe. It can also paralyze, making it impossible to move, and can lead to death. If someday you want to climb to the top of the mountain and return the same day, you will have to get an early start! The best time to hit the trail is around 6 a.m. Otherwise, you could be caught in an afternoon thunderstorm.

Black Bear, Mt. Elbert*

Mule Deer, Mt. Elbert*

Initially, people thought Mount Elbert was 14,433 feet tall, but they found it was actually 14,440 feet tall. After the Great Depression, people were really upset about the height of Mount Elbert and its neighbor, Mount Massive. The two mountains are only twelve feet different in height. People chose sides. Mount Massive's supporters put piles of rocks on the top to make it taller, but Mount Elbert's supporters knocked down the rock piles. Eventually, people stopped fighting and accepted that Mount Elbert is taller than Mount Massive.

The mountain is home to a lot of different kinds of animals. Black bears, bighorn sheep, pikas, pocket gophers, turkey, elk, mule deer, grouse, marmots, and many birds call it home all year round. Grizzly bears used to live on Mount Elbert, but they were extirpated or removed.

The Sierra Nevada mountain range runs between central California and the Great Basin. Most of the mountain range is in California. Still, the Carson Range within the Sierra Nevada is in the state of Nevada. The range is 400 miles long and 70 miles wide. The name "Sierra Nevada" is a Spanish phrase meaning "snowy mountain range."

Aerial View of the Sierra Nevada*

Within the Sierra Nevada grows a famous tree named General Sherman. The General is one of the biggest trees in the world. It is in the Sequoia and Kings Canyon National Park, where there are giant Sequoias. General Sherman is 275 feet tall and 36 feet around at the bottom. Many trees get smaller as they grow taller, but not Sequoias. General Sherman is about 17.5 feet around, sixty feet above the ground.

Lake Tahoe is on the border of California and Nevada, within the Sierra Nevada mountains. This lake is found at 6,225 feet above sea level. It is 191 square miles, making it the largest clear freshwater alpine lake in North America, and the second deepest behind Crater Lake in Oregon.

Within the Sierra Nevada is the unique Mount Whitney. At 14,505 feet above sea level, Whitney is the tallest mountain in the lower 48 states of America.

Yosemite Valley in the Sierra Nevada is a famous and popular place to visit because it is filled with amazing natural features. With big, beautiful waterfalls and lakes, green meadows and granite domes, it is no wonder that John Muir, the famed conservationist, wrote this:

"The far-famed valley came suddenly into view throughout almost its whole extent: the noble walls, sculptured into endless variety of domes and gables, spires and battlements and plain mural precipices, all a-tremble with the thunder tones of the falling water. The level bottom seemed to be dressed like a garden, sunny meadows here and there and groves of pine and oak, the river of Mercy sweeping in majesty through the midst of them and flashing back the sunbeams."

There are three national parks, two national monuments, and twenty wilderness areas in the Sierra Nevada.

Lightning show in the Sierra Nevada*

thunderstorms during the monsoon season, which can leave an inch of rain very quickly. The lightning during these storms has started wildfires. The winters are just barely cold enough to have a heavy snowpack. This snowpack is how California gets most of its water. The water also helps create electricity.

Reservoirs were built in the Sierra Nevada canyons during the 1900s to collect the water that melts from the snow-pack. Aqueducts were also built to take that water throughout California for people to use on farms, cities, and suburbs. *(You will learn more about California and its water supply coming through the Delta in Lesson 16 under the San Francisco Bay)*

The west slope of the Sierra Nevada welcomes the clouds and rain that come from the mighty Pacific Ocean. However, this side of the mountains are a bit selfish and do not share the life-giving rain with the other side of

Yosemite Valley in the Sierra Nevada*

Yosemite, Devils Postpile National Monument, Sequoia and Kings Canyon National Park are some of the most famous.

The Sierra Nevada has a mild climate. Warm air blows in from the Pacific Ocean on the western slopes. The winds carry moisture to keep the land wet in the summer and snowy in the winter. The eastern slopes are dry and have less than 25 inches of rain and snow a year. However, on occasion in the summer, there are

the mountains that face east. This is because of a phenomenon described as a "rain shadow" that is cast by the high mountains within the range. This rain shadow has a tremendous effect on the climate and ecology of the Central Basin. Nevada is the driest state in the U.S. because of the Sierra Nevada's rain shadow.

Many animals thrive in the Sierra Nevada, including black bears and grizzly bears, badgers and bobcats, northern flying squirrels, and golden beavers. Mountain sheep live in the southern part of the Sierra Nevada.

James W. Marshall found gold on January 24th, 1848 while working at Sutter's Mill outside of Coloma, California, in the Sierra Nevada's western foothills. He was building a lumber mill along the American River when something shining brightly caught his eye. Looking closer, something in the river was reflecting the sun's light within the riverbed. With his curiosity piqued, he reached down and picked up a shiny gold nugget.

Lake Tahoe, in the Sierra Nevada.*

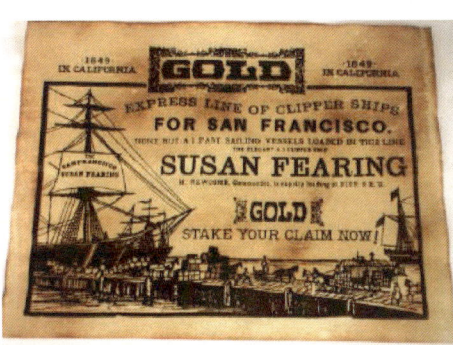
Gold Diggers, California Gold Rush*

Less than three months later, Samuel Brannan, a newspaper publisher in San Francisco, confirmed the rumors when he held a gold vial in the street and shouted, "Gold! Gold! Gold from the American River!" By August of 1848, the New York Herald reported on the gold discovered in California all the way across the country. President James Polk spoke to Congress on December 5th, 1848, about the gold. Immigrants started rushing to California's gold country from around the world. These people were known as "forty-niners." They lived in tents, wood shanties, E-deck cabins from ships, and anything else they could find. Whenever and wherever someone found gold, miners would show up and set up camp by the hundreds to look for treasure. From all over the world, 300,000 miners, merchants, and immigrants settled in California by 1855.

Advertisement for the Clipper Ship Express Line to the San Francisco Bay for the California Gold Rush

Tourism is the most important economy for the Sierra Nevada. National parks and Lake Tahoe bring the most visitors, who travel to see the beauty of the region.

Mount Whitney

At 14,505 feet tall, Mount Whitney is the tallest peak in the lower 48 states. Sequoia National Park is on the west slope of the mountain. To reach the top of Mount Whitney, one would have to take the John Muir Trail starting in Happy Isles, Yosemite Valley, 212 miles away. Mt. Whitney is partially dome-shaped, but there are jagged ridges on the sides. It has an alpine climate and ecology, but it is above the tree-line, which means very few plants grow at the top. One such plant that does thrive in these conditions is the sky pilot. This is a cushion

Mt. Whitney*

The John Muir trail to Mt. Whitney*

Smithsonian Institution Shelter*

*Photos are by: Unknown, Public Domain

(LEFT) The pollinator attracting Sky Pilot, found up on Mt. Whitney.*

(WITHIN) The pollinator Apollo butterfly.*

plant growing close to the ground that blooms beautiful lavender flowers from June to August each year. This flower has a pungent urine smell that attracts pollinators. With few creatures living close to the peak, the ones that do are continually on the move. The Apollo, a tiny butterfly and a pollinator that likes the sky pilot flowers, as well as the Gray-crowned rosy finch, can be found near the top of Mount Whitney.

Lone Pine is a small town fifteen miles away from the base of Mount Whitney. The citizens of this town financed the first trail to the top. Gustave Marsh oversaw the design and the engineering of the pathway. It opened on July 22nd, 1904. On July 26th, 1904, Byrd Surby was the first person to die on Mount Whitney. Byrd Surby was an employee of the U.S. Bureau of Fisheries. He took a break from hiking the trail to eat his lunch when he was suddenly hit and killed by lightning. Gustave Marsh started designing a stone hut to protect others from lightning strikes at the peak. The hut was finished in 1909 and became the Smithsonian Institution Shelter.

After World War II, people tried to rename the mountain after Winston Churchill, but it did not work. The mountain is still called Mount Whitney today.

Gray-crowned rosy finch*

A hike up, Mt. Whitney*

A Closer Look!
at what you have learned in the last 6 lessons!

PLUS+
This Lesson's Geography:
Northwest Mountains
Cascade Mountains
Mt. Rainier
Mt. St. Helens
Denali

Previous Learned Geography:

Listed here is the geography learned over the last 6 lessons. All lessons learned before the last 6 lessons are no longer on the map.

Rocky Mountains
Pikes Peak
Mt. Elbert
Sierra Nevada
Mt. Whitney
The Great Valley
Blue Ridge Mountains
Great Smoky Mountains
Cumberland Mountains
Mt. Mitchell
White Mountains
Green Mountains
Adirondack Mountains
Allegheny Mountains
Helena, Montana (MT)

Boise, Idaho (ID)
Olympia, Washington (WA)
Salem, Oregon (OR)
Juneau, Alaska (AK)
Salt Lake City, Utah (UT)
Phoenix, Arizona (AZ)
Carson City, Nevada (NV)
Sacramento, California (CA)
Honolulu, Hawaii (HI)
Topeka, Kansas (KS)
Oklahoma City, Oklahoma (OK)
Austin, Texas (TX)
Denver, Colorado (CO)
Santa Fe, New Mexico (NM)

Lesson 14

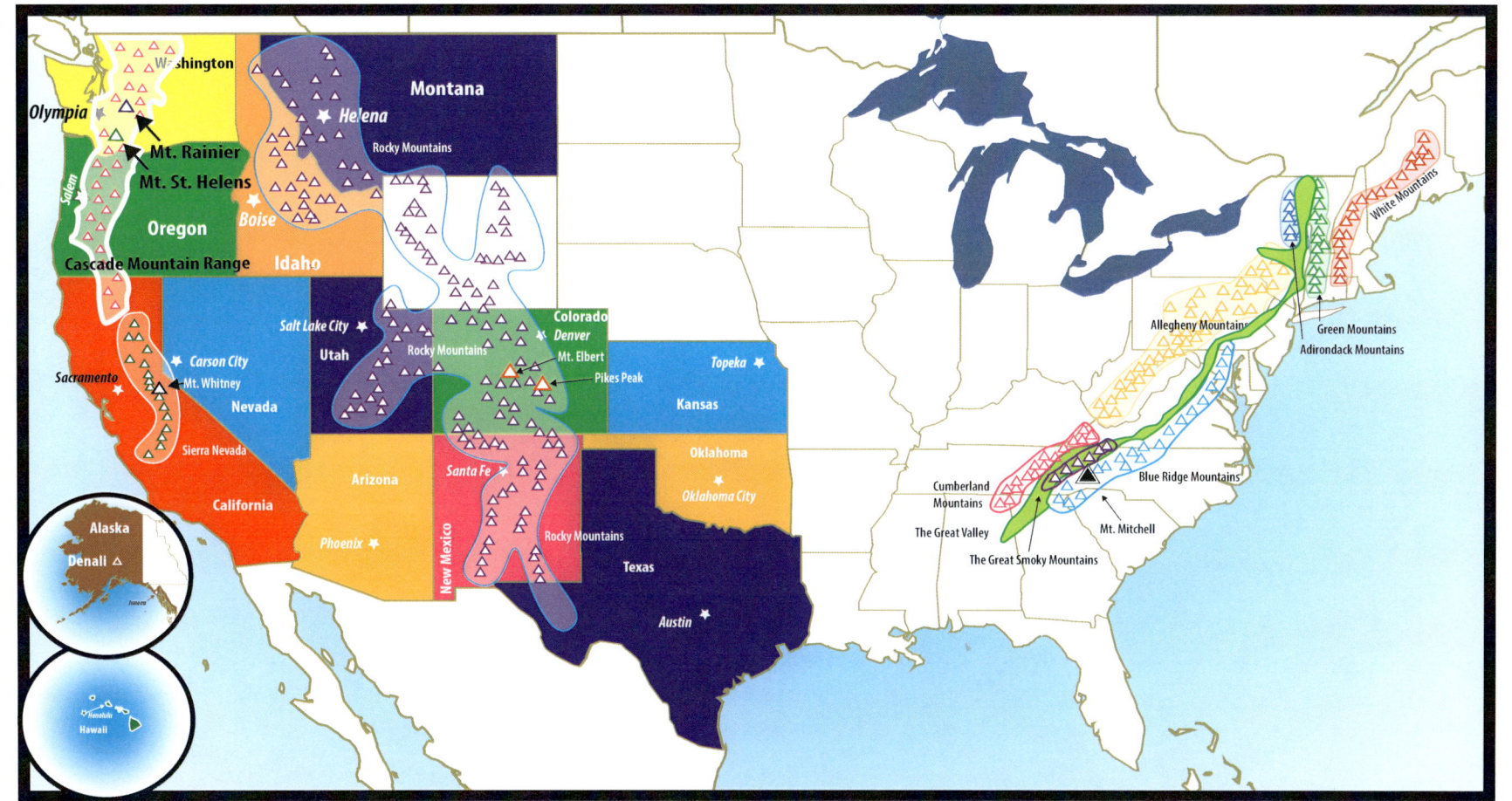

Lesson 14

Zoom Me In!

Use this sheet as a reference for this lesson's worksheets. Be sure to practice until you don't have to look!

United States of America Physical Features

Northwest Mountains

△ **Cascade Mountains**

△ **Mt. Rainier**

△ **Mt. St. Helens**

△ **Denali**

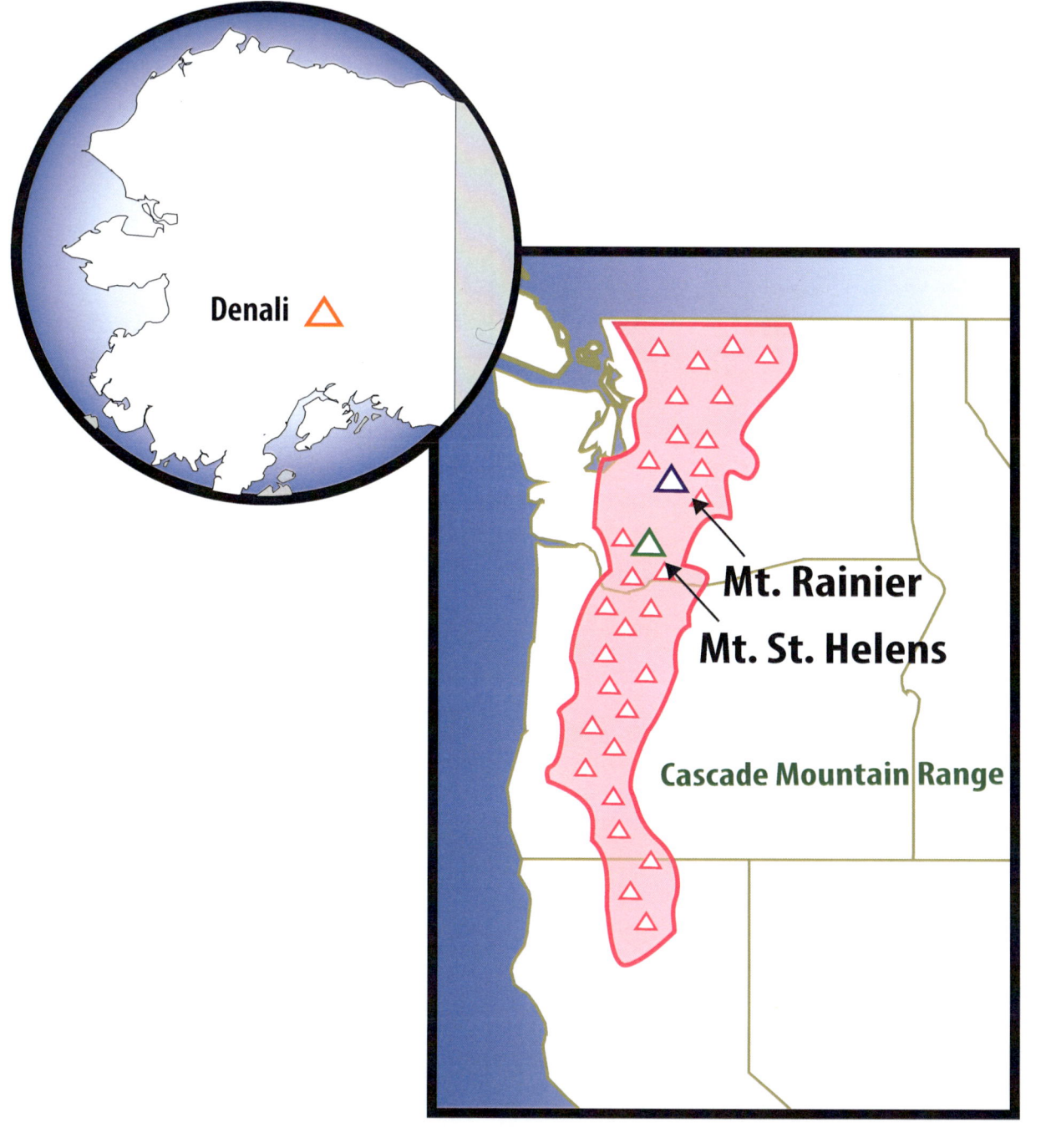

Denali △

Mt. Rainier

Mt. St. Helens

Cascade Mountain Range

This Lesson's Geography:
Western Mountains

Cascade Mountains
Mt. Rainier
Mt. Saint Helens
Denali

Map showing the "Ring of Fire"

Tid-Bits

Lesson 14

The Cascade Range, also known as the Cascades, is a prominent mountain range, found in the west of North America. This range spans from southern British Columbia in Canada, southward through Washington, Oregon, and into northern California. Although, this range is called the Canadian Cascades north of the U.S. border.

The Cascades have both non-volcanic mountains as well as volcanoes. The North Cascades are non-volcanic, while the High Cascades, found in Washington and Oregon, have a few exciting volcanoes. They are called the "High Cascades" because of their high elevations. Of which, Mount Rainer, the highest peak of all, stands at an impressive 14,411 feet.

The Cascades make up a portion of the "Ring of Fire." The Ring of Fire is a great ring of volcanoes in and around the Pacific Ocean. Every eruption in the lower 48 states over the last 200 years is from the Cascade volcanoes. The two most recent include Lassen peak in northern California, that caught everyone off guard with a series of explosions that began in 1914, concluding in 1921. All this, with what was thought to be a dormant volcano. Then, there was the massive eruption of Mt. St. Helens in 1981, which you will learn about in this lesson.

The High Cascades stand twice as large as their neighboring mountains. In fact, these mountains stand out massively, visible from more than 100 miles away on days without clouds. Mt. Rainier can clearly be seen from downtown Seattle, Washington – the distance between the two is 107 miles.

The precipitation on the west side of the mountains is considerable with annual snow amounts measuring

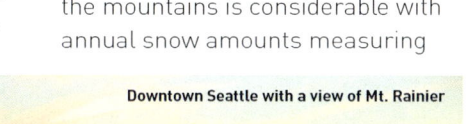

Downtown Seattle with a view of Mt. Rainier

more than 1,000 inches. Mount Baker in Washington has a record for accumulating 1,140 inches of snow in 1998. That equals 95 feet of snow. In previous years, Mount Rainer held the record at Paradise in 1978.

The east side of the range is a different story. Annual rainfall is as low as 9 inches in the foothills due to the rain shadow effect. As you learned in Lesson 13, Nevada is the driest state in the U.S. due to the rain shadow caused by the Sierra Nevada mountains. Rain shadows are caused by mountain ranges that block clouds coming in from the ocean. The ocean side of the mountains get most of the precipitation while the other side stays relatively dry.

For further information on rain shadows, here is a link to a brief educational program put together by Central Washington University that teaches about the Rain Shadow in the Northwest and around the world.
https://bit.ly/RainShadow3

The astoundingly beautiful Columbia Gorge waterway splits the states of Washington and Oregon, where the Cascade Range has a break in the continuity.

161

British Navigator George Vancouver

Lewis & Clark Expedition Painting, By: Unknown, Public Domain

The Columbia River Gorge that separates the Cascades and serves as a border between Washington and Oregon

Many myths have been created by the Native tribes that reside in the area. In one such legend, Mount St. Helens is said to be a beautiful maiden that Hood and Adams fought over. In addition, the tribes had multiple names for the High Cascades and their smaller peaks, such as Kulshan for Mount Baker and Louwa-la-Clough (which means "smoking mountain") for Mount St. Helens.

A Pacific Northwest Coast Tribe

In 1792, George Vancouver, a British navigator, explored Puget Sound and named each high mountain after various English people. For instance, Mount Baker was named for his third lieutenant, Joseph Baker, and Mount Rainier was named after Admiral Peter Rainier.

Likewise, in 1792, he termed Mount Hood after Lord Samuel Hood, an admiral of the Royal Navy. Mount St. Helens was named after Lord St. Helens, Vancouver's friend, who conducted a survey of the area in the late 1800s. Vancouver never actually named the range itself, only a portion of the peaks that laid there. They referred to it as the "eastern snowy range." Spanish explorers that explored the range before Vancouver called it Sierra Nevada, or "snowy mountains."

In 1805, the Lewis and Clark Expedition went through the Cascades. They were the first non-indigenous people to view Mount Adams. Even so, they thought it was Mount St. Helens. They later called Mount St. Helens, Mount Rainer. They did name one mountain as they spotted the snowy pinnacle, "Jefferson," after their friend and President. In their journals, they referred to the Cascades as the "Western Mountains." However, later, the name that came to be, was taken from their documented observations.

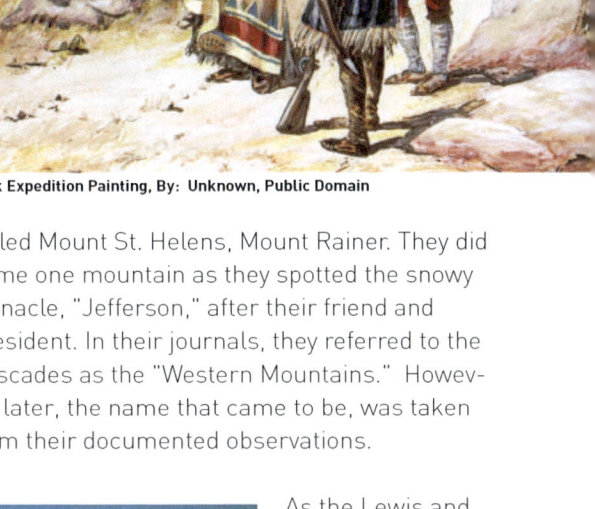

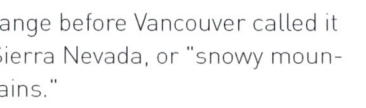

Cascade Mountain Range, the Three Sisters in Sisters, Oregon.

As the Lewis and Clark expedition went forth, they had to face a tremendous battle. The rapids located in the Columbia River Gorge. They referred to the "rapids" as "cascades." High mountains loomed over the rapids making this path seemingly impassable. Clark described the Cascades as having a "Great Shute" extending about one half mile, where the Columbia was 450 feet wide and dropped about twenty feet over both large and small rocks, "water passing with great velocity foaming & boiling in a most horrible manner."

They were brave men, for even after they saw that the local Indians did not cross in that area, they decided that they could get the canoes across by ropes

Fort Vancouver, Hudson's Bay Company

and a temporary log "road." While they, and their canoes were beat up a little, they made it.

The mountains surrounding were termed "mountains by the cascades," for the water that cascaded fiercely down the river. That is the name that stuck, the Cascades. Today, these rapids that were so intimidating, are submerged beneath the Bonneville Reservoir created by the Bonneville Dam.

The settlement and exploration of the Cascades greatly increased when the Hudson's Bay Company was established at Fort Vancouver. The company was a popular trading post, used by many trappers that were exploring the area, looking for beavers, and other furry animals.

The first land path for United States settlers through the Cascade Range was Barlow Road, established in 1845. The route offered an

End of the Oregon Trail

Upper Cascades' Black Bear

overland link for the Oregon Trail. Before this establishment, settlers would battle through the Columbia River's rapids to advance through the area. The road leaves Hood River and goes along the side of Mount Hood in an area now called Government Camp. Then continues until the trails end in present-day Oregon City. Somewhere along the trail, it turned into a toll trail costing each wagon $5.

Soil conditions for farming are generally good, especially downwind of volcanoes. This is because volcanic rocks are often rich in potassium bearing minerals such as orthoclase, that decay quickly. This gives richness to the soil that plants need to grow strong. On the snow-capped mountains, such as Mt. Hood and Mt. Bachelor in Oregon, the storage of water in the form of snow and ice is essential for many reasons. Firstly, the mountains are used as ski resorts that stimulate the local economy. In late winter, much of that water flows into reservoirs to be captured for its potential energy harnessed by hydroelectric generators. Then, the water is used to

Bonneville Dam and Wheat Crop

Upper Cascade's Wolf Pack

Oregon Cascade's Beaver

Elk in the Mt. Rainier area

irrigate crops. All good... good for our economy, good for drinking, good for having electricity, good for food.

Lastly, the wildlife that calls the Cascades home... Black bears, coyotes, bobcats, cougars, beavers, deer, elk, moose, mountain goats, and a few wolf packs that are returning from Canada, all live in the Cascades. Fewer than 50 grizzly bears reside in the Canadian Cascades and Washington.

Mt. Rainier

This active stratovolcano resides within Mount Rainier National Park. It stands 14,411 feet tall, making it the highest mountain in Washington state. It also makes it the highest in the Cascade Range in the Pacific Northwest.

By the way, a stratovolcano, which could also be called a composite volcano, is a cone-shaped volcano built up by many layers of solidified lava, pumice, tephra, and ash. Stratovolcanoes are steep and topped with a crater called a summit. Some stratovolcanoes have collapsed summit craters that are named calderas. Stratovolcanoes can have both explosive and effusive eruptions. The lava that leaves stratovolcanoes has a high

viscosity, meaning that the liquid is very thick. Because of this, the lava does not go far.

Scientists believe that Mount Rainier has not produced a significant eruption in the past 500 years. This makes Rainier potentially the most dangerous volcano in the Cascade Range because of its great height, frequent earthquakes, active hydrothermal system, and extensive glacier mantle.

Let us break that down a bit...

An earthquake is where the earth violently shakes due to movement in the earth's crust or volcanic action. Sometimes the ground breaks apart when this happens.

A Hydrothermal System, simply put, is the movement, or rather, circulation of incredibly hot water within the earth's crust. Since we cannot see through the ground, how do we know that there is an active hydrothermal system? Well, in the case of Mt. Rainier, fumaroles have been located. A fumarole is an opening in the

planet's crust that emits steam filled with gases. Such gases would be carbon dioxide, sulfur dioxide, hydrogen chloride, and hydrogen sulfide. This gas-filled steam forms when superheated water boils, resulting in pressure that builds up until it pushes a hole out of the earth's crust and escapes. On Mt. Rainier, fumarolic activity is widespread. The gases that escape have been captured and studied by many different scientists since the 1980s.

In case you do not know what a glacier is, it is a slow-moving river of ice formed by the accumulation of snow compacted over time. Glaciers are found on mountains or near the north or south poles.

Now, why is Mt. Rainier so dangerous due to extensive glacier mantle? Mount Rainier is currently listed as one of the 16 volcanoes with the highest likelihood of causing significant loss of life and property. The devastation would

be more tremendous if it were to erupt as powerfully as Mount St. Helens did. This is because of the massive amounts of glacial ice on the volcano compared to Mount St. Helens. Mount Rainier has 26 glaciers containing more than five times as much snow and ice as all the other Cascade volcanoes combined. If only a small part of this glacial ice melted by volcanic activity, the amount of water rushing down would trigger enormous amounts of debris and mudflow to the surrounding valleys. Also, the area surrounding Mt. Rainier is vastly more populated. It is estimated that about 80,000 people and their homes are at risk of being within the debris and mudflow hazard zone. Lastly, the simple fact that Mt Rainier is a much bigger volcano, almost twice the size of St. Helens.

Glaciers are among the most visually outstanding, always changing features of Mount Rainier. They serve as an essential source of streamflow for several rivers, including some that provide water for hydroelectric power and irrigation. Glaciers flow under the influence of gravity sliding over rock. Glacier movement is faster near the surface and along the centerline. During

Fumarole, by Unknown, Public Domain

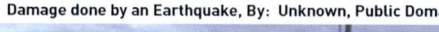

Damage done by an Earthquake, By: Unknown, Public Domain

Glacier By: Unknown, Public Domain

May 1970, the Nisqually Glacier up on Mt. Rainier, was measured moving as fast as 29 inches per day. Glaciers move more quickly in the summer than in the winter. This is due to meltwater at the bottom of the glacier.

The summit is topped by 2 volcanic craters. Each is 1,000 feet in diameter, and they overlap. The only reason you

Pictured at the two overlapping craters at Mt. Rainier's summit, the thermal heat from the volcano does not allow for snow and ice to stick. By: Unknown, Public Domain

can see the crater's rims, is that thermal heat from the volcano does not allow for snow and ice to stick, it is just too warm! The summit has made the world's largest volcanic glacier cave system within the ice-filled craters. Inside, there are approximately 2 miles of passages. There is also a tiny crater lake that is around 130'x30' feet in size and about 16 feet deep. This crater lake is the highest in North America with a surface elevation of about 14,203 feet. It is found in the lower portion of the west crater, under more than 100 feet of ice, and only accessible through the ice caves.

Although not many take a dip in this lake!

Mount Rainier was first known by local natives that spoke Salishan as "Talol," "Tacoma," or "Tahoma." As mentioned, the current name was given by George Vancouver, who named it in honor of his friend, Admiral Peter Rainier. The map of the Lewis and Clark expedition of 1804–1806 refers to it as Mt. Regniere.

In 1890, the United States Board on Geographic Names announced that the mountain would be called Rainier. Even so, there were protests against the name "Mt. Rainier," from those that wished to call it Mt. Tacoma. Congress was still thinking about changing the name even in 1924. Though it is evident that the Mt. Rainier stuck!

Well... Sort of...

Leading up to the Super Bowl in 2014, the mountain's name was temporarily changed from Rainier to Mount Seattle Seahawks. This was after Colorado renamed the 53 fourteeners after the 53 members of the Denver Broncos.

Seahawks fan and Mt. Rainier Climber holds up the 12th man flag. By Unknown, Public Domain

After the 2015 name change to the tallest mountain in North America, which was called Mount McKinley and now is Denali, the debate over Mount Rainier's name intensified. So, who knows, maybe someday it won't be called Mt. Rainier!

Typically, about five earthquakes are recorded each month near the summit. Then, shallow earthquake swarms occur over two or three days, about 13,000 feet below the summit. The swarms happen from time to time, believed to be caused by the circulation of hot fluids underneath the mountain. Scientists think that hot springs and steam vents within Mount Rainier National Park are generated by such fluids. Seismic swarms, which are many shallow earthquakes, are standard features in volcanoes, and are rarely associated with eruptive activity.

River valleys and many other areas around the mountain were once the home of indigenous tribes. They hunted in the mountain's forests and meadows. These tribes include the Nisqually Indian Tribe, the Puyallup Tribe of Indians, the Muckleshoot Indian Tribe, the Cowlitz Indian Tribe, the Confederated Tribes, the Bands, the Yakama Nation, and more.

The summit has made the world's largest volcanic glacier cave system within the ice-filled craters. Inside, that are approximately 2 miles of passages. Up there also is a tiny crater lake that is around 130 by 30 feet in size and about 16 feet deep. All three photos: By Unknown, Public Domain

John Muir, By Unknown, Public Domain   Quote from John Muir at the base of Mount Rainier, By: Unknown, Public Domain

"...the most luxuriant and the most extravagantly beautiful of all the alpine gardens I ever beheld in all my mountain-top wanderings."
–John Muir, conservationist, 1889

A man named John Muir ventured up the mountain in 1888. He said that the view was beautiful, but most beauty could be found below without the danger of climbing. He strongly advised the protection of the mountain, and in 1893, the area became the Pacific Forest Reserve. Its mission was to preserve and protect the timber, watersheds, and other physical and economic resources. Then, railroads and businesses encouraged the concept of a national park to increase tourism, public entertainment, and natural resources protection. President William McKinley made Mount Rainier National Park on March 2nd, 1899. It was America's fifth national

A Pacific Northwest Coastal Tribal member. By: Unknown, Public Domain

park, and Congress made the park for the "benefit and enjoyment of the people."

Mount Rainier is a tough climb because of its massive glaciers. In fact, these glaciers are the biggest in the United States, south of Alaska. Usually, climbers can get to the summit within two or three days, the success rate being a mere 50%. Typically, the climbers' physical

conditioning and the weather remain the most common reasons for failure. Many attempts each year, anywhere from 8,000 to 13,000, show up to make it to the top.

Those that do not have the need for such elevation, like to hike, backcountry ski, take photos, and camp in and around this great mountain.

(Top Right and Left) A hiking party make their way towards Mt. Rainier's summit. A dangerous climb. Both photos, by: Unknown. Public Domain

Mount St. Helens is a stratovolcano located in southwestern Washington State within the Cascade Range. It is just 112 miles south of Mt. Rainier. Mount St. Helens is well known for its massive ash explosions and pyroclastic flow.

The May 18, 1980 eruption of Mt. St. Helens. By: Unknown, Public Domain

Mt. Saint Helens pyroclastic flow, By: Unknown, Public Domain

Well, you probably know what ash is, but what is pyroclastic flow?

Pyroclastic flow is a quick moving current of volcanic matter and hot gas that moves away from the volcano. The heated gases can reach up to 1,830°F. That's extremely hot. Pyroclastic flow can speed up or slow down depending on the density of the current, the gradient of the slope, and the volcanic output rate. The flow can speed downhill from 62 miles per hour, all the way to 430 miles per hour. Destruction is unavoidable.

Here at Mount Saint Helens, that destruction occurred on May 18th, 1980. Mount St. Helens erupted on that day, causing a massive pyroclastic avalanche, and killing 57 people.

Here is that story... Seismic activity at Mount St. Helens began on March 16th. A tremor measuring 4.2 on the Richter scale was recorded just four days later. Then on March 23rd and 24th, there were 174 different recorded tremors. The first eruption occurred on March 27th. A wide 250-foot gash split open on top of the mountain with ash blasting 10,000 feet into the air. Ash that spewed from the volcano made it all the way to Spokane, Washington, 300 miles away! The eruption created a lightning show, static electricity was in the air. This got everyone's attention.

Hazard watch was issued by authorities for a 50-mile radius around the mountain. The National Guard set up roadblocks to prevent access and many residents evacuated, except one. Eighty-four-year-old Harry Truman, was one resident who refused to move.

Harry Truman, the one resident determined to stay in his home. By: Unknown, Public Domain

Throughout April, scientists watched a bulge on the north side of Mount St. Helens grow larger and larger. Finally, on May 18th at 8:32 a.m., an abrupt 5.1-magnitude earthquake with a simultaneous eruption jolted the mountain. The north side pulsated and roared. Ash, rock, gas, and glacial ice blasted out laterally 650 miles per hour with pyroclastic flow crashing down the mountainside at 100 mph. Almost instantly, fourteen miles of the Toutle River was buried up to 150 feet deep in debris. Superheated partially molten rock flowed for miles destroying everything in its path.

This 24-megaton explosion devastated 230 square miles around the mountain. Geologist Mr. Dave Johnston

was out that morning observing the mountain. He was the closest to the volcano when it erupted. His last words on that fateful morning were "Vancouver, Vancouver, this is it!"

The hot air alone scorched and burned millions of trees.

Before Mt. St. Helens blew

The hot air alone scorched and burned millions of trees. When the glacier upon the mountain melted, it caused a massive mudslide that wiped out homes and dammed up rivers throughout the area. The plume of ash continued to flow out of the volcano for nine hours, eventually reaching 12 to 16 miles above sea level. The plume of ash

moved eastward at an average speed of 60 miles per hour, reaching Idaho by noon. Ash from the eruption was found the following morning collected atop cars and roofs as far as the cities of Minneapolis, Minnesota, and Edmonton in Alberta, Canada. Locally, the falling ash clogged carburetors, leaving thousands of motorists stranded. Fifty-seven people died overall from suffoca-

Geologist, Mr. Dave Johnston. Photo of him observing the mountain. By: Unknown, Public Domain

Street sign taken down in the eruption, buried in volcanic ash. By: Unknown, Public Domain

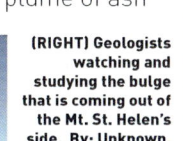

The dust has settled, all that remains is charred earth and a mountain that lost 1,300 feet in a matter of seconds. By: Unknown, Public Domain

(RIGHT) Geologists watching and studying the bulge that is coming out of the Mt. St. Helen's side. By: Unknown, Public Domain

Photo taken during the May 18, 1980 eruption of Mt. St. Helens. By: Unknown, Public Domain

tion, burns, or other injuries. Of those killed, 27 were never found, including that stubborn Harry Truman.

When the ash cleared, the top of Mount Saint Helens could be seen... well, the mountain at least. The top was no longer there; it had been completely destroyed. Mount St. Helens lost 1,300 feet in a matter of seconds.

Today, analysis of current activity at Mount St. Helens indicates that the volcano remains active and shows signs of long-term uplift and impending earthquakes. However, there are no signs that a significant eruption will happen anytime soon. Between 2004 to 2008, there were dome-building eruptions at Mount St. Helens. When this happened, the magma pushed through to the top. When magma bubbled up and out of the volcano, the new lava cooled, resulting in a new dome. One notable dome-building event happened on March 8th, 2005, when a 36,000-foot plume of steam and ash emerged that was seen from Seattle. This relatively minor eruption was accompanied by a 2.5 magnitude earthquake. Other exciting phenomena were witnessed, including a lava spine nicknamed the "whaleback." The "whaleback" had long shafts of cooled, solidified magma that was formed from pressurized magma deep within the volcano. The "whaleback" was fragile and broke down soon after it formed.

Scientists continue to monitor the growing volcano and earthquake activity. They believe that the magma down deep in Mount St. Helens has been slowly re-pressurizing since 2008. Re-pressurization is likely caused by the arrival of a small amount of new magma 2.5 to 5 miles beneath the surface.

As scientists continue to study Mt. St. Helens, they take measurements not only related to ground deformation and seismic activity, but they are also trying to learn about the volcano deep down below. They do this by taking two different types of measurements. Firstly, they measure the types and amounts of volcanic gases being released. The other is based on the strength of the volcanoe's gravity field. These types of measurements are thought to show the amount and depth of the magma below. The information collected at Mount St. Helens helps other scientists understand behaviors at other volcanoes, improving their ability to predict when the "big one" will happen.

Two years following the massive eruption, Mt. St. Helens and the area surrounding the volcano became a protected area with the Mount Saint Helens National Volcanic Monument. Here there is a center that offers recreational and learning opportunities. Visitors can view the crater, lava dome, pumice plain, and the effects of the landslide. They will also see the life and beauty that has come back into the area.

Denali, previously known as Mount McKinley, has a summit elevation of 20,310 feet above sea level, making this mountain the

A backside angle of the lateral explosion. May 18, 1980. By: Unknown, Public Domain

Ash covered everything and to avoid breathing it in, everyone wore masks. By: Unknown, Public Domain

Farmer showing the destruction of his land from the tremendous amount of ash. By: Unknown, Public Domain

The new dome. By: USGS, Public Domain

Small dome building eruption. By: USGS, Public Domain

Small dome building eruption. By: USGS, Public Domain

The "Whaleback" from the dome building activity. By: USGS, Public Domain

tallest in all of North America. In the world, Denali is the third tallest mountain behind Aconcagua in South America, and Mount Everest in Asia. Denali is in Alaska within a grouping of mountains called the Alaskan Range. This monumental mountain is a popular attraction and treasure of the Denali National Park and Preserve. The mountain has two peaks. The southern summit of the mountain is larger than the northern. The upper part of the

Top Ridge of Denali, Public Domain

mountain is covered in glaciers and snow all year long.

The indigenous people group that have made their home around the mountain are called the Koyukon. They gave the mountain its name, calling it Denali, or "the high one." In 1896, the mountain was renamed "Mount McKinley" by a gold prospector in favor of the then-presidential candidate, William McKinley. From that time in 1917 until 2015, the mountain was recognized as Mount McKinley. In August of 2015, the name was changed back to Denali.

Many have attempted to climb the mountain, beginning with James Wickersham in 1903. James was unsuccessful in his adventure, but it prompted more adventurers to attempt the challenge. Finally, in 1913 climbers Harry Karstens, Walter Harper, Hudson Stuck, and Robert Tatum were the first to make it all the way to the top!

Two meteorological weather stations were built in 1990 and 2002, located in two different areas with elevations of 18,733 feet and 19,000 feet. These weather

stations transmit data for climbers and for scientific study.

Temperatures in this part of the world are frigid, and atop of Denali, those temperatures never reach above freezing. In fact, in the winter of 2003, it was recorded to be -74.4°F. This, combined with a wind chill of 18.4 MPH, resulted in overall temperature of -184.4°F. Even in the summer, temperatures dip as low as -22.9°F, then add the windchill, it brings it down to -59.2°F. Up there, there is no getting away from the cold!

Koyukon man, Public Domain

Denali in Alaska - Adobe Stock

A Closer Look!
at what you have learned in the last 6 lessons!

PLUS+
This Lesson's Geography:
The Great Lakes

Huron
Ontario
Michigan
Erie
Superior

Together the first letter of each lake creates an acronym that spells HOMES!

Previous Learned Geography:

Listed here is the geography learned over the last 6 lessons. All lessons learned before the last 6 lessons are no longer on the map.

- Cascade Mountains
- Mt. Rainier
- Mt. St. Helens
- Denali
- Rocky Mountains
- Pikes Peak
- Mt. Elbert
- Sierra Nevada
- Mt. Whitney
- The Great Valley
- Blue Ridge Mountains
- Great Smoky Mountains
- Cumberland Mountains
- Mt. Mitchell
- White Mountains
- Green Mountains
- Adirondack Mountains
- Allegheny Mountains
- Helena, Montana (MT)
- Boise, Idaho (ID)
- Olympia, Washington (WA)
- Salem, Oregon (OR)
- Juneau, Alaska (AK)
- Salt Lake City, Utah (UT)
- Phoenix, Arizona (AZ)
- Carson City, Nevada (NV)
- Sacramento, California (CA)
- Honolulu, Hawaii (HI)

Lesson 15

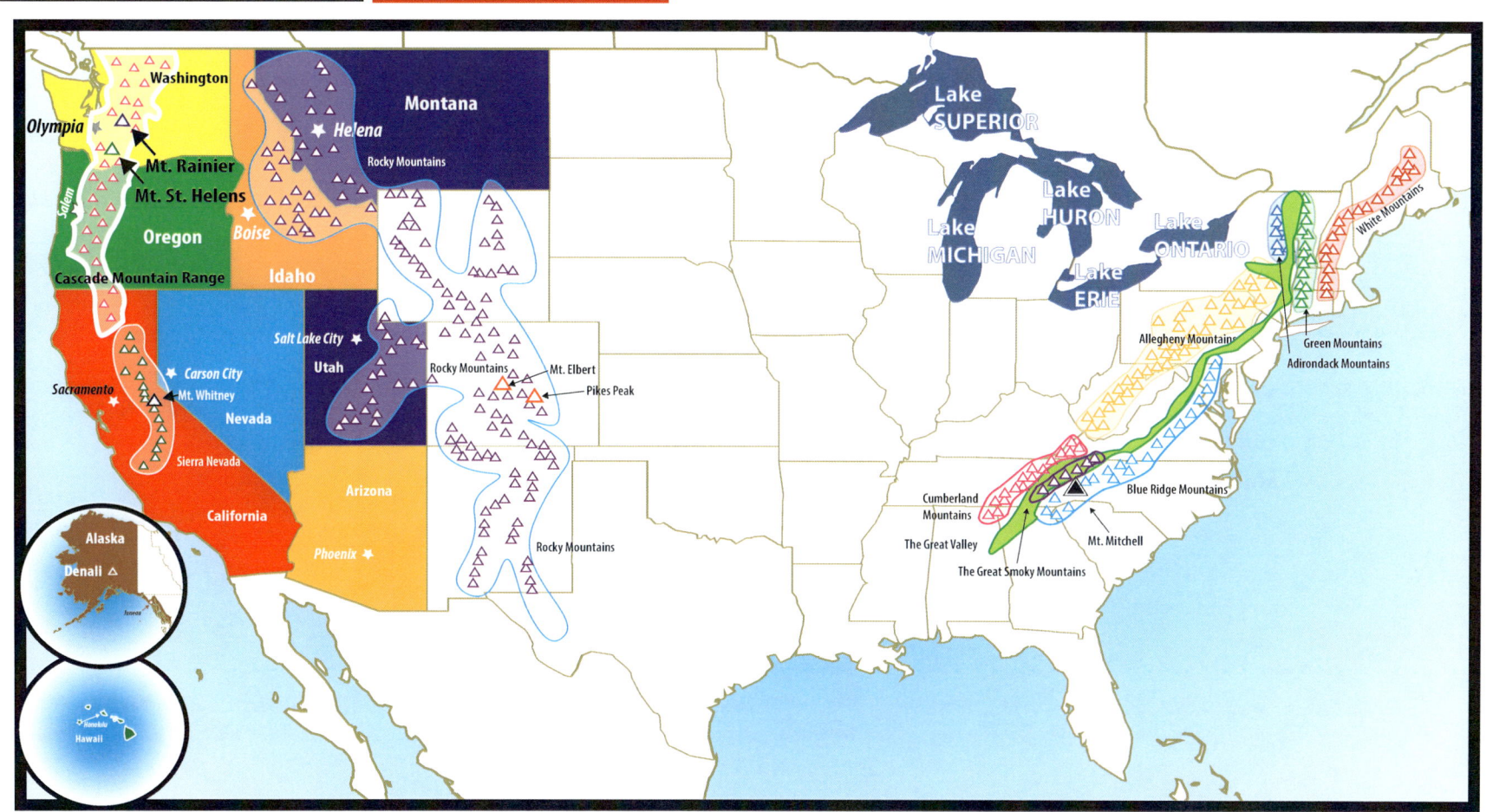

Lesson 15

Zoom Me In!

Use this sheet as a reference for this lesson's worksheets. Be sure to practice until you don't have to look!

United States of America Physical Features

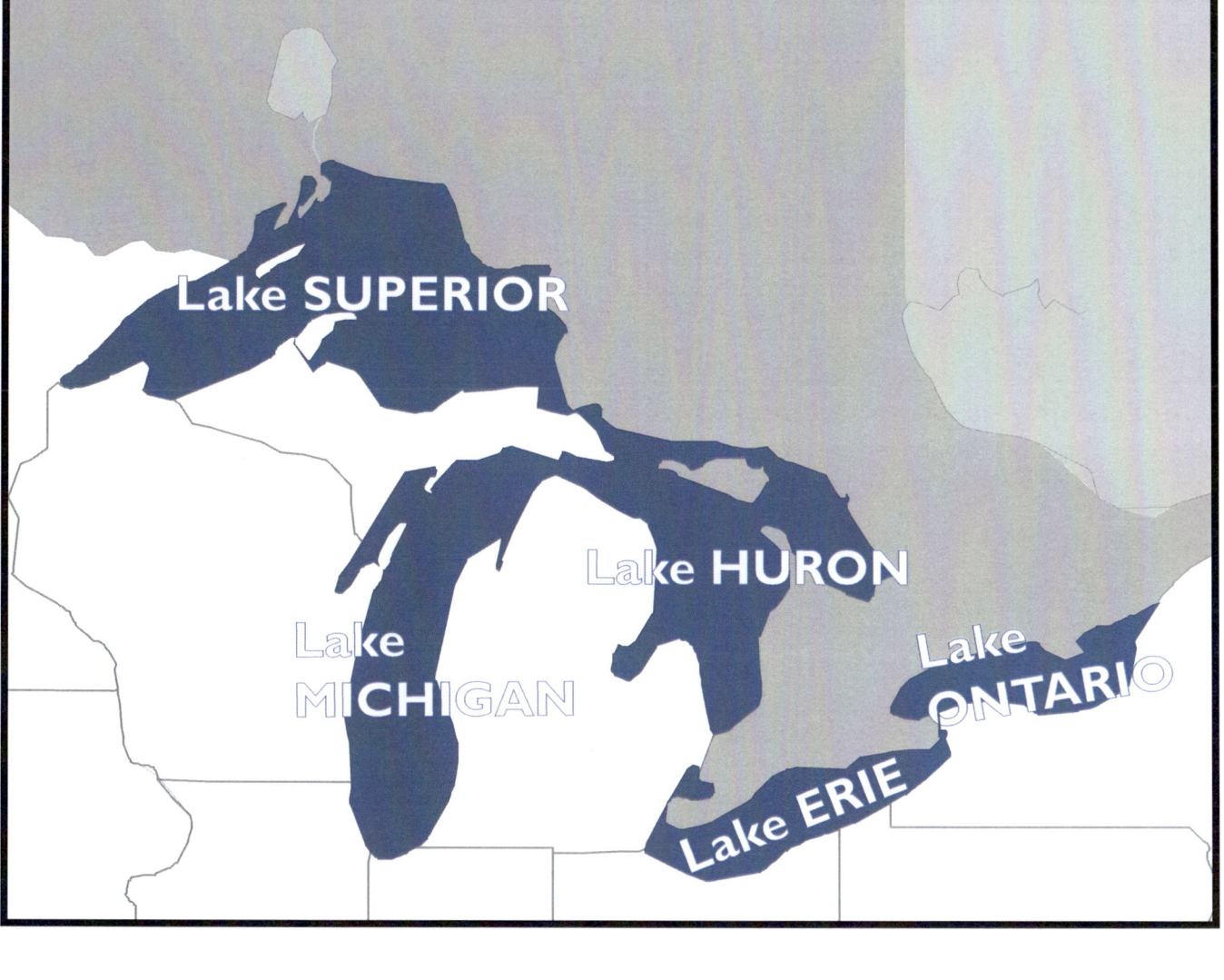

*This may help!

Try using this acronym for the Great Lakes!

HOMES

The Great Lakes

Lake **H**uron

Lake **O**ntario

Lake **M**ichigan

Lake **E**rie

Lake **S**uperior

This Lesson's Geography:
The Great Lakes

Lake Huron
Lake Ontario
Lake Michigan
Lake Erie
Lake Superior

Tid-Bits

The Great Lakes are national treasures for the United States and Canada, and is one of North America's most recognizable and loved features. The names of these massive interconnected lakes are Lake Huron, Lake Ontario, Lake Michigan, Lake Erie, and Lake Superior. Together they cover about 94,850 square miles of land, making up the largest connected area of freshwater on Earth. In fact, the size of the Great Lakes exceeds the breadth of the entire United Kingdom.

(LEFT) Satelite image of **The Great Lakes plus Hudson Bay**, By: **NASA**, Public Domain.
(RIGHT) Satelite image of **The Great Lakes, Lake Ontario** on the right in the foreground, **Lake Erie** to the left with **Lake Huron** in the background. By: **NASA**, Public Domain

Lake Huron, By: **Unknown**, Public Domain

Although to note, there is a lake in Russia that is larger by volume. Meaning it has more water, this lake is called Lake Baikal.

The only lake that is entirely within the boundary of the United States is Lake Michigan. All the others span the border between Canada and the United States. As

Lesson 15

denoted in the name, Lake Superior is the largest and deepest of

Lake Ontario, By: **Unknown**, Public Domain

all the Great Lakes. On the other hand, Lake Ontario is the smallest, while Lake Erie is the shallowest. Lake Huron has the longest shoreline of all the lakes.

The Great Lakes affect the climate of the surrounding land. They absorb a lot of heat in the summer. In the winter, they release heat into the air. As a result, the ground closest to the lakes are cooler in the

173

Lake Huron, By: Unknown, Public Domain

Lake Erie, By: Unknown, Public Domain

summer months and have warmer winters. Even so, large portions of the lakes freeze during the winter.

The Great Lakes are essential to the economy of not only the U.S. and Canada, but also many countries around the world. Major U.S. cities that benefit directly by the lakes include Milwaukee in Wisconsin, Chicago in Illinois, Cleveland in Ohio, and Detroit in Michigan. In Canada, one of the cities that benefits directly from the Great Lakes is Toronto, which resides in the province of Ontario. From Canada and the U.S., ships carry essential exports to the rest of the world. They include iron ore, coal, grain, and manufactured goods. Once ships reach the vast Atlantic, those goods are delivered to ports all over the world. As well, the U.S. and Canada receive goods from other countries, that are delivered through ports found along the Great Lakes. These are called imports.

Fishing was once an important industry in the lakes. However, pollution and other factors led to its collapse. Today only some commercial fishing takes place. Mostly, people enjoy fishing as a sport. The lakes are a popular recreation destination not only for power-boating and sailing but also for the many beaches that stretch along the shores.

Lake Huron, By: Unknown, Public Domain

Accidents involving ships in the seas and oceans across the planet have been happening ever since the boat was invented. Icebergs, storms, and many other reasons have left thousands of shipwrecks lying along the seabed. Although, it is not just the oceans and seas where vessels meet their doom. Some freshwater lakes have swallowed a significant number of ships that now rest at the bottom of their waters, forever. The Great Lakes of North America is one such interconnected lake.

Lake Michigan, By: Unknown, Public Domain

Sand Dunes by Lake Michigan, By: Unknown, Public Domain

The Great Lakes Shipwreck Museum states: "The lakes have caused the sinking of around 6,000 ships and the death of 30,000 people." Although, historian Mark Thompson, author of "Graveyard of the Lakes," has estimated that there are more like 25,000 shipwrecks at the bottom of these lakes.

Traversing through these waters is not easy, and many ships have become lost in the swirling depths. The Great Lakes have sea-like features with rolling waves, strong currents, and profound depth. They promise an uncertain time for sailors when crossing through the region.

Lake Superior, By: Unknown, Public Domain

The Great Lakes region has stunning vistas, beautiful waters, imports and exports, and water for cities. Plus, you can gaze at the Northern Lights' unique colors in certain areas during the spring and autumn seasons.

Lake Superior, By: Unknown, Public Domain

One of thousands of shipwrecks at the bottom of the Great Lakes. This one is at the bottom of Lake Huron. By: Unknown, Public Domain

Lake Erie, By: Unknown, Public Domain

Lake Superior, By: Unknown, Public Domain

Lake Ontario, By: Unknown, Public Domain

A Closer Look!
at what you have learned in the last 6 lessons!

Lesson 16

PLUS+
This Lesson's Geography:
Bays & Sounds

Chesapeake Bay
Hudson Bay (Canada)
San Francisco Bay

Puget Sound
Pamlico Sound

Previous Learned Geography:

Listed here is the geography learned over the last 6 lessons. All lessons learned before the last 6 lessons are no longer on the map.

Lake Huron
Lake Ontario
Lake Michigan
Lake Erie
Lake Superior
Cascade Mountains
Mt. Rainier
Mt. St. Helens
Denali
Rocky Mountains
Pikes Peak
Mt. Elbert
Sierra Nevada
Mt. Whitney

The Great Valley
Blue Ridge Mountains
Great Smoky Mountains
Cumberland Mountains
Mt. Mitchell
White Mountains
Green Mountains
Adirondack Mountains
Allegheny Mountains
Helena, Montana (MT)
Boise, Idaho (ID)
Olympia, Washington (WA)
Salem, Oregon (OR)
Juneau, Alaska (AK)

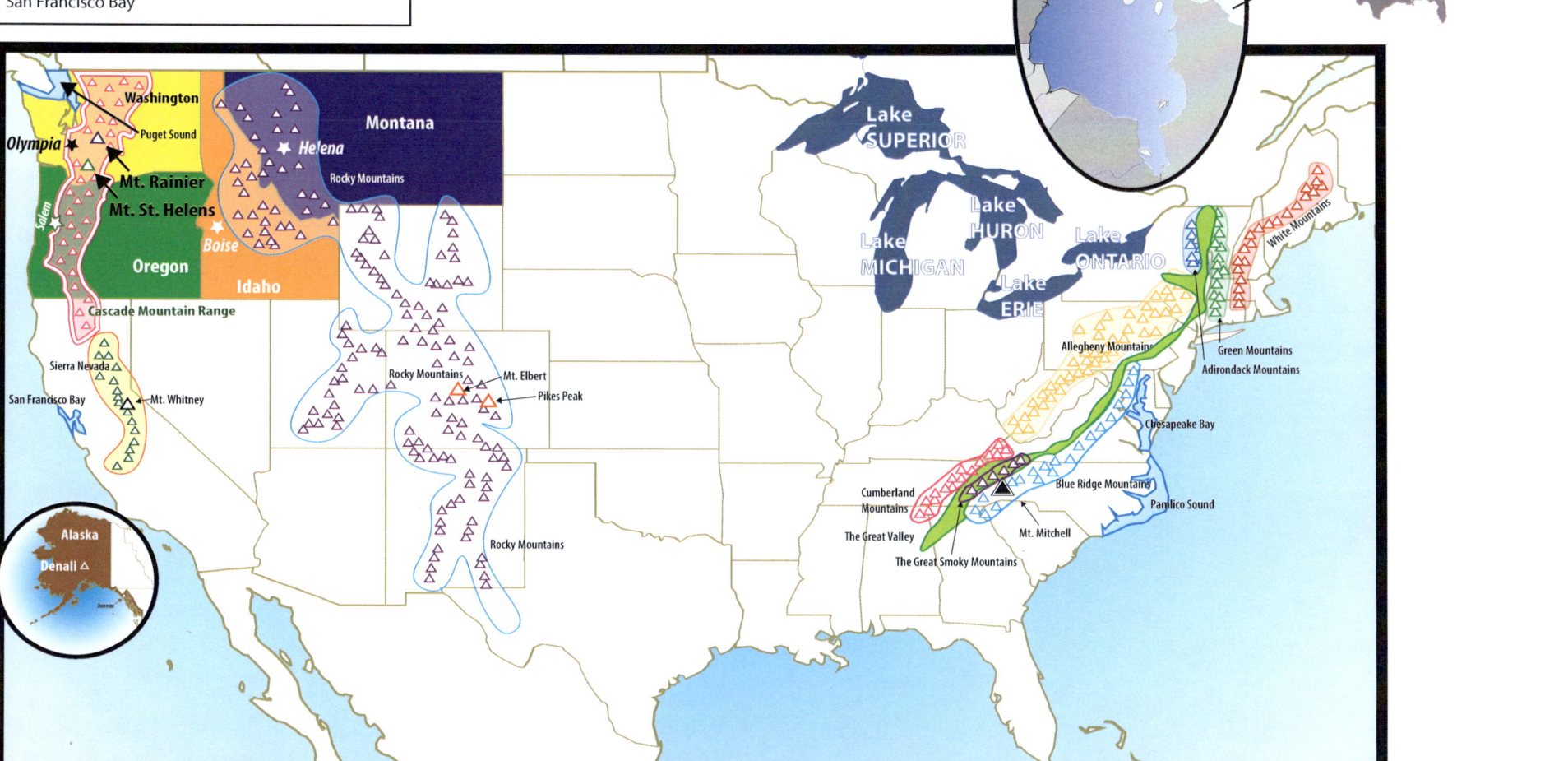

Hudson Bay in Canada

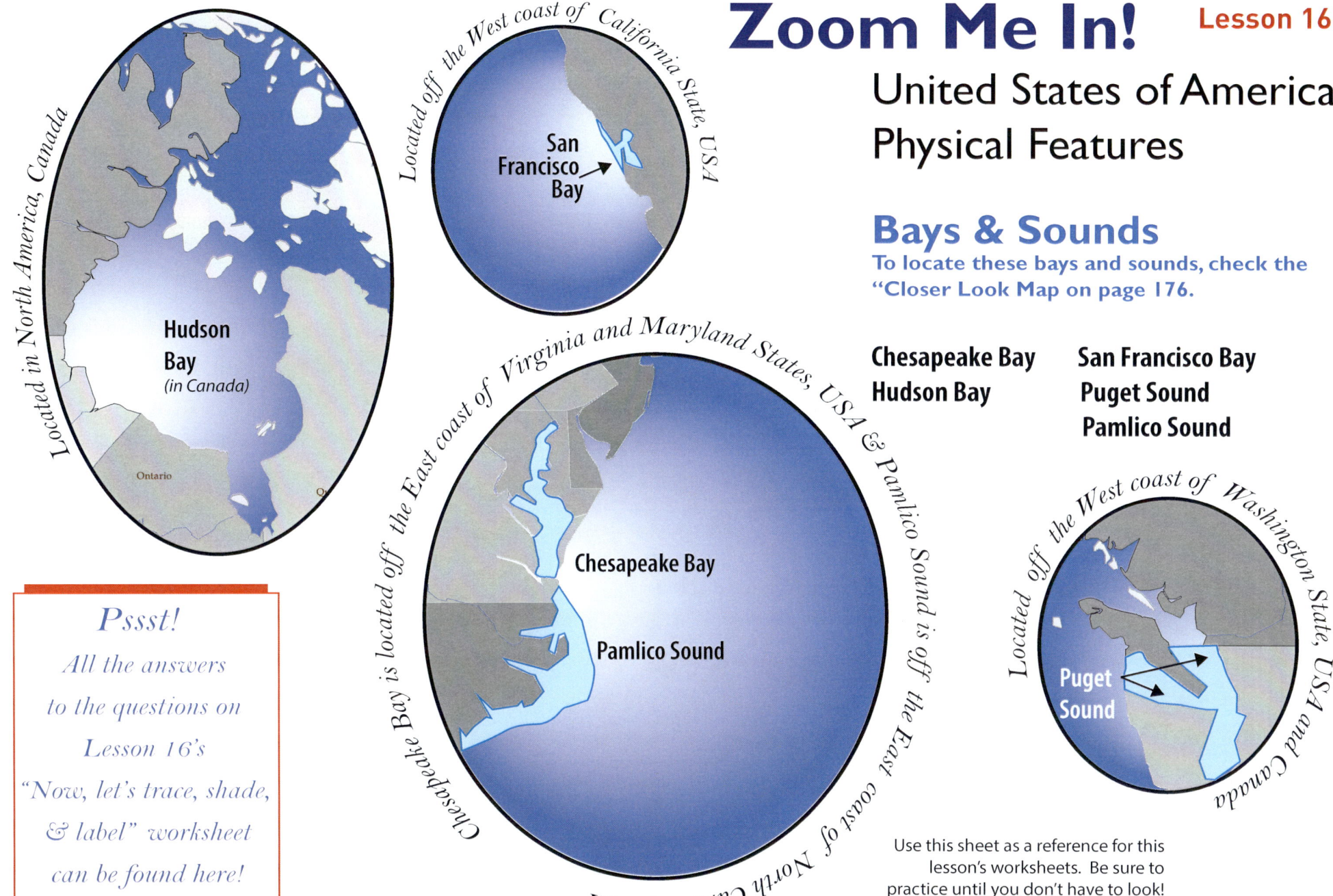

This Lesson's Geography:
Bays & Sounds

Chesapeake Bay
Hudson Bay (in Canada)
San Francisco Bay
Puget Sound
Pamlico Sound

Tid-Bits

The Chesapeake Bay is known for its beauty and bounty, and for being the largest estuary in the United States, bordering Virginia, and Maryland. An estuary means there is a body of water with at least one river flowing into it and connecting to the ocean. With this connection, the freshwater from the river and the saltwater from the ocean mix. This makes the water saltier than freshwater and less salty than the ocean. When this happens, the water is referred

Chesapeake Bay Watershed. By: Unknown, Public Domain

Aerial of the Chesapeake Bay. By: Unknown, Public Domain

Lesson 16

build because it goes over the water and under the water. It made it much easier for people to go where they needed to go while allowing sea-going vessels to pass over the bridge. It is known as "One of the Seven Engineering Wonders of the Modern World."

to as brackish water. The Chesapeake Bay has brackish water with over 150 streams and rivers flowing in. All those rivers go to the Chesapeake Bay from six different states! Water from New York, Pennsylvania, Maryland, West Virginia, Virginia, Delaware, and Washington, D.C., goes to the ocean through the Chesapeake Bay.

The Chesapeake Bay is an essential part of the ecology and economy of Maryland and Virginia. Over 2,700 types of plants and animals depend on and live off the Chesapeake Bay area. 500 million pounds of seafood is fished out of the Chesapeake Bay every year. It is 200 miles long, and the width changes from three miles wide to 30 miles wide. Most of the bay is 21 feet deep, but it is 174 feet deep at its deepest. Three billion gallons of water go into the bay every day from just the Susquehanna River.

There are two big bridges. One is in Maryland. It goes from Kent Island to Sandy Point, and it is called the Chesapeake Bay Bridge, nicknamed "Bay Bridge." It is 4.3 miles long and is a dual-span bridge - dual means two! The first span opened in 1952, and it was the world's longest over-water steel bridge. The second span came in 1973. Then there is the Chesapeake Bay Bridge-Tunnel in Virginia that opened in 1964 and goes from Virginia Beach to Cape Charles. This bridge was hard to

(TOP) Osprey (BOTTOM) The Blue Heron and the famous Blue crab. With permission by: Chesapeake Bay Foundation

During the Revolutionary War, the French defeated the British Royal Navy in a naval battle called "Battle of the Chesapeake" on the Chesapeake Bay. The French and Americans were allies.

Aerial of the Chesapeake Bay Bridge-Tunnel. By: Unknown, Public Domain

Chesapeake Bay Bridge "Bay Bridge." By: Unknown, Public Domain

When the Brits lost, General George Washington was able to lead the Americans on to more victories, with the ultimate victory of becoming a sovereign nation.

Hudson Bay

Once upon a time, it went by Hudson's Bay, but it was shortened somewhere in history. The Hudson Bay is a massive body of saltwater in America's neighbor, Canada! The bay has over 470,000 square miles of surface area. NASA's satellite images shown here illustrate just how big it is. It would cover almost half of the United States! There are so many rivers from all over Canada flowing into Hudson Bay. Water from Alberta, Ontario, Quebec, Manitoba, Nunavut, Alberta, and Saskatchewan flow in. Even American rivers from North Dakota, South Dakota, Minnesota, and Montana make their way into the Hudson. There is only one larger bay in all world. The Bay of Bengal is bigger and much, much deeper. The Hudson Bay has an average depth of only 330 feet, but the average for the Bay of Bengal is 8,500 feet deep! That's a big difference.

Paintings of General George Washington and the Battle of Chesapeake during the American Revolutionary War. By: Unknown, Public Domain

Discovered during the Age of Exploration, navigators sailed long distances attempting to find alternate routes for trade, specifically another route to Cathay and the Indies. As they sailed west, they found the Hudson Bay in the late 1400s.

English explorers and colonists named Hudson Bay, after Sir Henry Hudson. He began to explore the bay beginning August 2, 1610 on his ship called Discovery. This British explorer and colonist started his fourth journey in 1611 when he sailed around Greenland and into the bay. He mapped much of the eastern shoreline, and as he made is way south it became winter and his ship slowed to a stop, stuck in the ice. He and his crew had no choice but to winter on the shore of James Bay, the southern tip of Hudson's Bay. When spring came, the ship became free of its icy prison. The crew boarded, ready to head home. Henry Hudson, did not. He was determined to continue with their mission to explore and map the entire bay. Instead

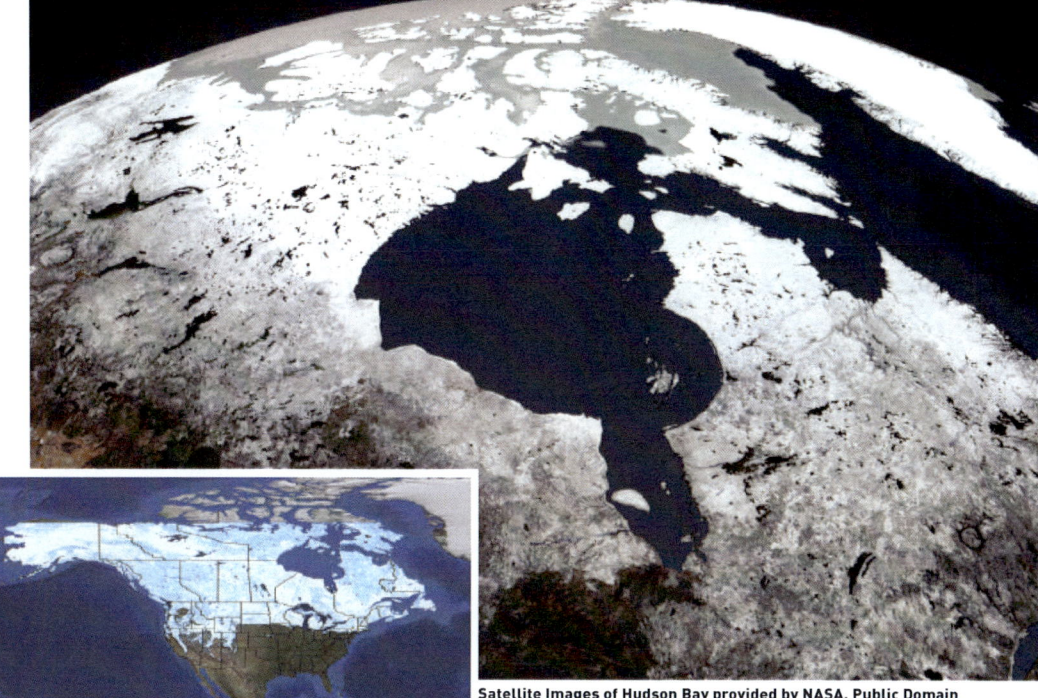
Satellite Images of Hudson Bay provided by NASA, Public Domain

of listening to Hudson, most of the crew declared, "MUTINY!" Leaving him and a couple crew members on a small boat. Their fate, unknown. Another explorer, Sir Thomas Button,

Sir Henry Hudson, Public Domain

179

tried to find Henry Hudson and a new way to India in May 1612. Sir Button didn't find him, and no one knows what happened to him, and probably never will.

Nonsuch, a British trading ship meaning "unequaled," sailed to the Hudson Bay in 1668 to trade for the first time. They brought beaver furs. The Hudson's Bay Company was born. They built a lot of forts and trading posts close to the major rivers all over the region and beyond. This made it easy for them to explore the land and for the native people to bring their furs to the British for trading. Some of the trading posts continue to be used until the 1900s.

The land that serves as the watershed for Hudson's Bay was taken over by Hudson's Bay company. This vast land

Museum recreation of the Nonsuch ship. Public Domain

was named Rupert's Land. The size of this land coupled with their trading posts and forts, gave them a trade monopoly. A monopoly is when a person or enterprise is the only supplier of a service or a product - in this case,

HUDSON BAY POST FORT McMURRAY - 1911-

Public Domain

A fort of Hudson's Bay Company

furs. France did not like this. They tried to take it from Britain until 1713 when a treaty was signed. Over 150 years later, that monopoly ended in 1869. Hudson's Bay Company sold Rupert's Land, under pressure from the British government, to Canada for $1.5 million. This was two years after Canada gained their independence from Britain in the British North America Act of 1867. While the company does not trade in furs any longer, it is still in business more than 350 years later in Canada as a department store.

Hudson's Bay Company Storefront

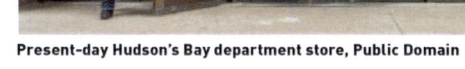

Hudson's Bay Company Land called Rupert's Land

The San Francisco Bay is an incredibly famous estuary in Northern California. The big cities of San Jose, San Francisco, and Oakland are collectively known as the San Francisco Bay area. About 40% of California's freshwater travels from the rivers into the Pacific Ocean through the San Francisco Bay.

trapped in the icy Hudson Bay, Public Domain

Present-day Hudson's Bay department store, Public Domain

How does the water make it from the source in the Sierra Nevada to the Pacific? Here is one route!

Melt-water from the Sierra Nevada mountains travels through streams to the Sacramento River and San Joaquin River. The rivers flow into the Suisun Bay to the Carquinez Strait and into the Napa River. The Napa River flows into the San Pablo Bay, and the San Pablo Bay flows into the San Francisco Bay. All of that water flows from the San Francisco Bay, through the Golden Gate Strait and into the ocean. Although they are all different water bodies, the system is called the San Francisco Bay and the Bay-Delta.

Salmon in the Bay-Delta, Public Domain

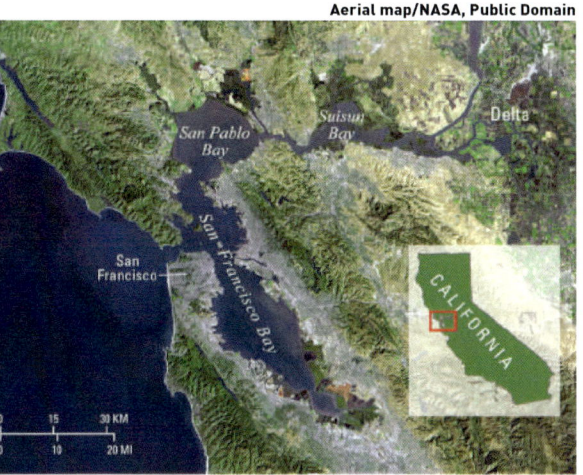

Aerial map/NASA, Public Domain

Almost half of all the water runoff and snow-melt in California are drained through just five rivers. The largest rivers are the San Joaquin and the Sacramento. Just like the ocean, the Bay-Delta has two high tides and two low tides every day!

When failed gold miners started farming, the Delta began to change. It had been a big marsh, but the farmers drained the swamp to live off the land in the 1800s. The government wanted the farmers to drain the marsh, so laws were passed. It was easy to grow things from the fertile peat soil once levees were built to keep the water from destroying the farms. By the 1930s, the Delta was no longer a marsh. This is what the Delta looks like from above today. There are more than 1,100 miles of water running through excellent farmland and natural areas.

Sandhill Crane in the Bay-Delta, Public Domain

Like the Chesapeake Bay and Hudson Bay, the Delta is an estuary. Collectively, the San Francisco Bay, San Pablo Bay, and Suisun Bay are part of the Delta, making these connected bodies of water, the largest estuary on the Pacific coast. Here, more than 750 plants and animals thrive. Every year, millions of birds land in the Delta during their migration. Sandhill cranes spend Autumn and Winter here. Many locals make their living fishing off the Delta. In fact, 80% of California's fish live or swim through the Delta. Notable fish include the Chinook salmon, striped bass, and sturgeon.

LEFT: Map of the Bay Delta. BELOW: Aerial of the Bay Delta.
ABOVE: Farmer reclamation of marshlands that would become the Bay-Delta. All: Public Domain

The San Francisco Bay has five big islands. First on our list is Angel Island, which is likened to Ellis Island in New York. When immigrants entered the United States on the Pacific Coast, they would check in at Angel Island. Many of the immigrants were from Asia. You can still visit the island today by boat, for it has become a National Park. Next is Alcatraz Island. This island is famous for being a tough federal prison, that was thought to be inescapable with a location in the center of the bay. While it no longer serves as a prison, it is a popular place for

Angel Island, Public Domain

Treasure Island

Yerba Buena Island, Public Domain

Alcatraz Island, Public Domain

Alameda Island, Public Domain

tourists to visit. Yerba Buena Island is very hilly. A tunnel goes through the island to connect it to San Francisco Bridge and Oakland Bay Bridge. Treasure Island is a flat man-made island built between 1937 and 1938 for the Golden Gate International Exposition of 1939. The largest island is Alameda, but it wasn't always an island. It was created as a way to get big ships in and out of the Port of Oakland. So, people dug it out and made a waterway in 1901. Today it is home to the city of Alameda.

The California Gold Rush brought lots of people to the San Francisco Bay between 1848 and 1855. All those people turned the bay into a vital port and shipping center for the United States. Many that parked their boats in the bay and went searching for gold, never returned. For whatever reason they abandoned the boats in the harbor. Because no one wanted them anymore, the boats were turned into houses in San Francisco.

The Golden Gate Bridge is one of the most famous bridges in all the world. It is a suspension bridge over the place where the San Francisco Bay meets the Pacific Ocean. It connects San Francisco to Marin County. Joseph Straus designed the Golden Gate Bridge in 1917, but it didn't open until 1937. When it opened, it was the longest and tallest suspension

Joseph Straus, designer
of the Golden Gate Bridge, Public Domain

ABOVE: Ships abandoned in the San Francisco Bay. BELOW; Illustration depicting how the abandoned ships were utilized in housing development.

HIGH AND DRY.

LEFT: Construction workers high up the Golden Gate Bridge. BELOW: Present-day Golden Gate Bridge at sunset. BOTH: Public Domain

The hilly San Juan Islands in the Puget Sound in Washington State, Adobe Stock

bridge in the world. It is 476 feet tall and 4,200 feet long. For its beauty, it is the most photographed bridge. It is one of the wonders of the modern world.

The Puget Sound is on the coast of Washington in an area called the Pacific Northwest. It is an inlet of the Pacific Ocean and a part of the Salish Sea. It is part of a complex estuary system, connecting to the ocean through the Strait of Juan de Fuca, Deception Pass, and Swinomish Channel. It has an average depth of 450 feet. In spots it can reach up to 930 feet deep. The San Juan Islands are a large group of islands in the Puget Sound. It is 100 miles long from Whidbey Island to Olympia. The Puget Sound is the third largest estuary in the United States behind the Chesapeake Bay and the San Francisco Bay.

The Salish Sea was named in 2009 by the United States Board on Geographic Names. It is a way to talk about the entire area that includes the Puget Sound, the Strait of Juan de Fuca, the Strait of Georgia, the Bellingham Bay, and the San Juan Islands. People often say "the Puget Sound area" to talk about the land surrounding the water. That includes Seattle, Tacoma, Olympia, and Everett.

Puget Sound was named in 1792 by George Vancouver, the same explorer that named many mountains in the Cascade Mountain Range. The Puget sound was named after a lieutenant on the exploration: Peter Puget. Fort Nisqually was the first European settlement in the area; it was created by the Hudson's Bay Company in 1833. Americans on the Oregon Trail made their first settlement in Tumwater, in 1845. This early settlement was created in part by George Washington Bush, an African and Irish settler. Because he was of mixed race, he was not allowed to live in the Oregon Territory. However, at the time, the governing body in the Oregon Territory did not enforce the rules north of the Columbia River. So, George Washington Bush left the Oregon Trail with five families to settle in Tumwater, Washington, in the Puget Sound area. Washington became a territory separate from the Oregon Territory in 1853. Thirty-three years later, the Puget Sound area was a destination for the Northern Pacific railroad, allowing people to easily travel from one side of the country to the other.

Washington State with the San Juan Island Archipelago highlighted. Freeworldmaps.net

Washington State Ferries run between the bigger islands in the Puget Sound and the mainland. Every year, over 24 million people use ferries. It's the biggest ferry service in America. Many people love going to the Puget Sound with its unending places to explore! It is one of the most popular tourist attractions in Washington. Whale watching, kayaking, visiting the quaint towns in the San Juans are just a few of the many activities people do here in the area. Notably, the San Juan Island named Lime Kiln Point State Park is a prime whale-watching site.

Washington State Ferry - Public Domain

At high tide, the San Juan archipelago comprises over 400 islands and rocks, of which 128 are named. Most of the San Juan Islands are hilly, with Orcas Island having the tallest hill of all, called Mount Constitution. The islands also have fertile land for growing. The 478 miles of beaches found on the islands are sandy and rocky. The harbors can be deep or shallow with calm waters and even reefs. Commonly located along the shores, the Madrona trees grow twisty and orange. On the islands are forests of evergreens and pine trees.

Seattle gets a lot of rain every year, but the San Juan Islands get a lot less rain because the Olympic Mountains make a rain shadow. As you have learned, any area within a rain shadow has way less rainfall.

The Pamlico Sound stretches 80 miles long and 15 to 20 miles wide along North Carolina's Atlantic coast. It is the largest lagoon on the eastern shore. A lagoon is a shallow body of water connected to a bigger body of water, but separated by a barrier of either islands or reefs.

Pamlico Sound, Albemarle Sound, Croatan Sound, Bogue Sound, Currituck Sound, and Roanoke Sound make up the Albemarle-Pamli-

Puget Sound with the San Juan Islands, Adobe Stock

Whale watching at Lime Kiln Point State Park, Mt. Baker in the background. Public Domain

Kayaking in the Puget Sound. Public Domain

Mt. Rainier as seen from Tumwater, Washington outside of Olympia in the Puget Sound region. Public Domain

Aerial of the Pamlico Sound featuring the Outer Banks. Public Domain

Wildlife of all sorts found in Pamlico Sound. ALL: Public Domain

co Sound System, a complicated network of lagoon estuaries covering more than 3,000 square miles. The Outer Banks is a long sandy island that is a barrier between the Pamlico Sound and the Atlantic Ocean.

Giovanni da Verrazzano was an Italian explorer. In 1524, he thought he had found the Pacific Ocean. What he actually found was the Pamlico Sound instead. He thought the Outer Banks was the land between the Atlantic and the Pacific oceans. Can you imagine the United States only being 20 miles wide?

In the 1940s and 1950s, the United States Atomic Energy Commis-

sion thought about using the area between Cape Hatteras and Cape Fear on the Outer Banks to test atomic bombs. Luckily, they found somewhere else because 37 years later, in 1987, the United States government made Albemarle-Pamlico Sound an "estuary of national significance." People from all over the country and the world go to the Outer Banks of Pamlico Sound to vacation because it is a great place for water sports, fishing, boating, kayaking, sailing, parasailing, and so much more. Tourism made over $1.3 billion in the Pamlico Sound. 90% of North Carolina's commercial fishing is done in the Pamlico Sound, and is worth over $100 million every year.

The Outer Banks is essential for wildlife. The Pea Island National Wildlife Refuge, Swanquarter National Wildlife Refuge, and many other wildlife preserves are in the Outer Banks. Wild horses have lived in the Outer Banks for hundreds of years. Waterfowl use the banks of Pamlico Sound as a nesting site. Dolphins and sea turtles swim in the sound. Seals can be seen swimming from the shores. Sometimes, although more rare, whales, orcas, and sharks can be found in the waters. It is a place for all kinds of animals to live in.

Giovanni da Verrazzano, Italian Explorer

Water sports of all kinds in Pamlico Sound. ALL: Public Domain

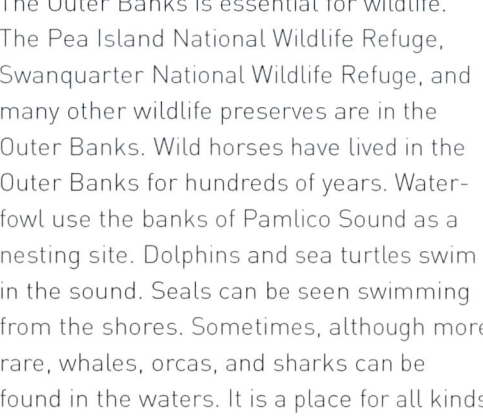

A Closer Look!

at what you have learned in the last 6 lessons!

PLUS+

This Lesson's Geography:
Eastern Rivers

St. Lawrence River
Ohio River
Mississippi River

Missouri River
Arkansas River

Previous Learned Geography:

Listed here is the geography learned over the last 6 lessons. All lessons learned before the last 6 lessons are no longer on the map.

Chesapeake Bay
Hudson Bay (Canada)
San Francisco Bay
Puget Sound
Pamlico Sound
Lake Huron
Lake Ontario
Lake Michigan
Lake Erie
Lake Superior
Cascade Mountains
Mt. Rainier
Mt. St. Helens
Denali

Rocky Mountains
Pikes Peak
Mt. Elbert
Sierra Nevada
Mt. Whitney
The Great Valley
Blue Ridge Mountains
Great Smoky Mountains
Cumberland Mountains
Mt. Mitchell
White Mountains
Green Mountains
Adirondack Mountains
Allegheny Mountains

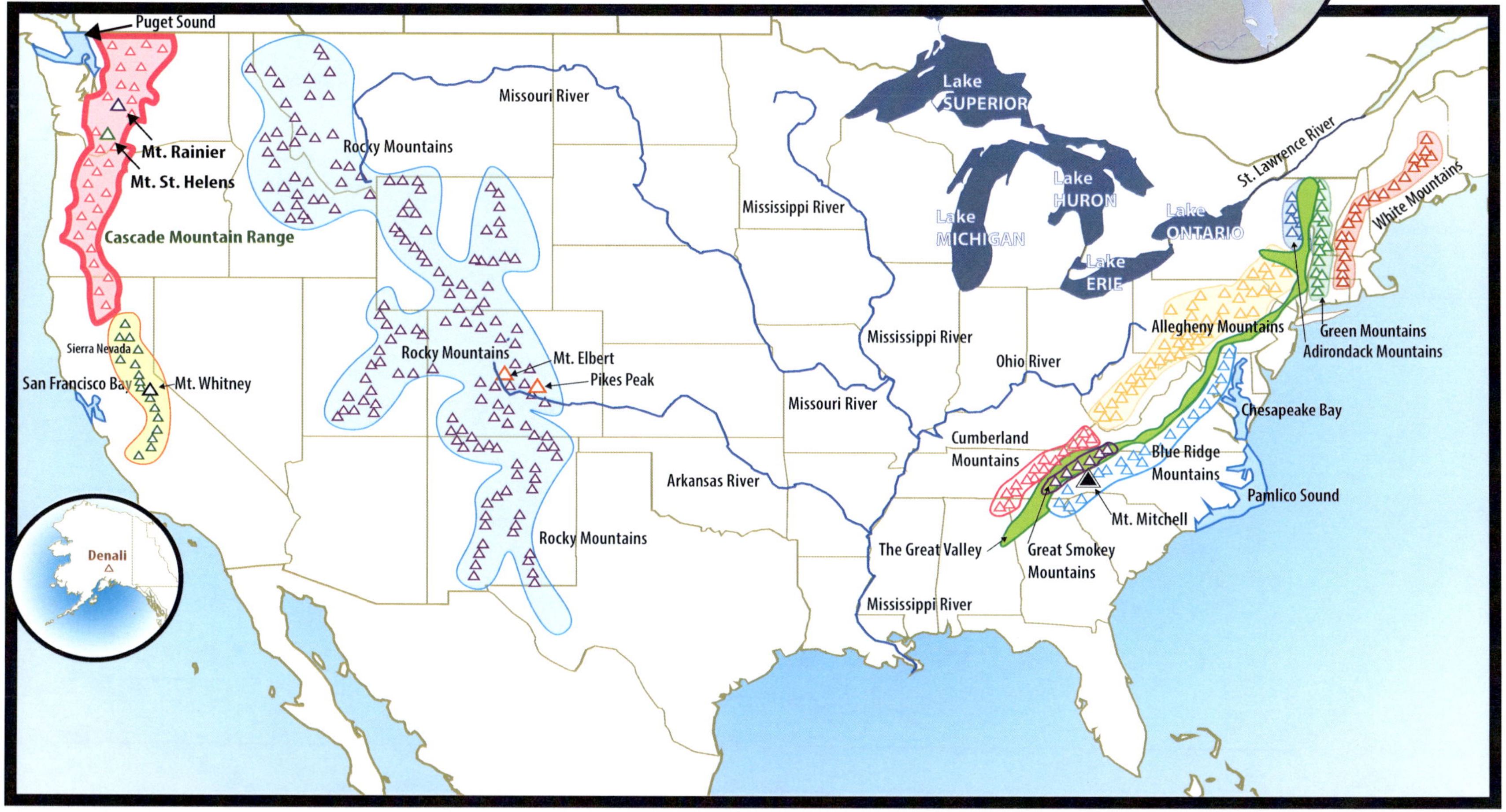

Lesson 17

Hudson Bay in Canada

Zoom Me In!

Use this sheet as a reference for this lesson's worksheets. Be sure to practice until you don't have to look!

United States of America Physical Features

Rivers (East)

St. Lawrence River
Ohio River
Mississippi River
Missouri River
Arkansas River

Lesson 17

This Lesson's Geography:
Eastern Rivers

St. Lawrence River
Ohio River
Mississippi River
Missouri River
Arkansas River

Tid-Bits

The Saint Lawrence River is a vital waterway that begins at the east end of Lake Ontario flowing towards the Atlantic Ocean.

Lesson 17

Aerial of the St. Lawrence River, Public Domain

ABOVE & BELOW: A lock along the St. Lawrence Seaway, Public Domain

This river is part of an extensive seaway system called the St. Lawrence Seaway. The entire seaway system is about 2,340 miles long. In the city of Duluth, Minnesota, at the seaport of Lake Superior, is the beginning of the Saint Lawrence Seaway. As mentioned, it eventually meets up with the St. Lawrence River on the east outlet of Lake Ontario. The St. Lawrence River flows for 740 miles to the Gulf of Saint Lawrence, then to the Cabot Strait and into to the Atlantic ocean.

This seaway allows ships to travel to the industrial and farming areas surrounding the Great Lakes leading out to the Atlantic Ocean and beyond. So, why is this river and the connected seaway something to learn about? Just another river, that is connected to another stream, to another, and on and on. Well, what do people use waterways for? Since ancient times, waterways have been the life source for communities, and today is no exception. As you are going to learn, rivers are used to transport necessary resources that contribute to a healthy economy, not only for farming, but also for industry. In the case of the St. Lawrence River and the seaway, it provides a navigable waterway for these resources for the United States and Canada.

The St. Lawrence Seaway is, in part, a man created system. It contains both natural waterways such as rivers and lakes. It also has waterways that are man-made, including locks, canals, and dams.

Locks are created where two areas of a waterway are at two different levels. When a boat passes from one level to the next, they are closed into an area called a lock, within,

St. Lawrence River (circled) is part of the St. Lawrence Seaway, represented by the entire map.

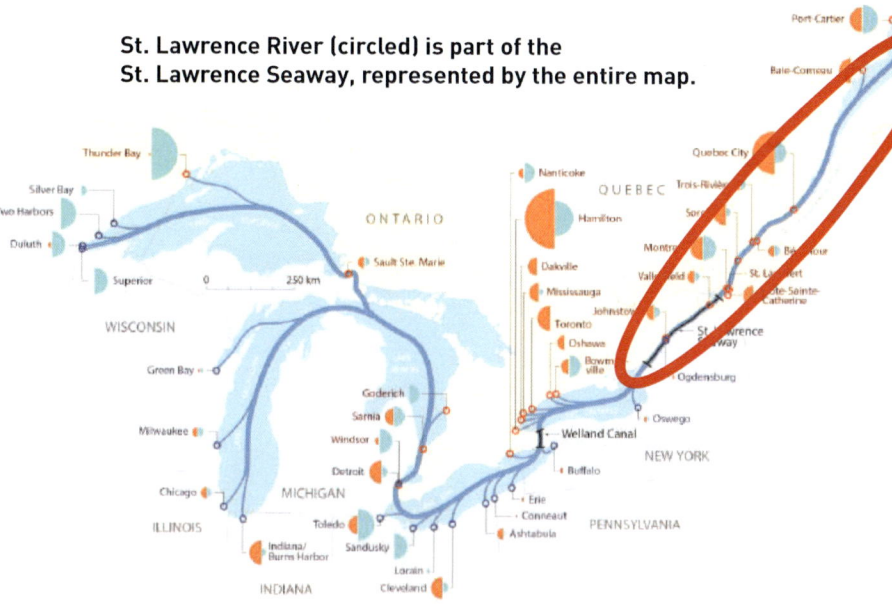

St. Lawrence River, view from Canada. Public Domain

dam is built to hold back water, the water needs to go somewhere!

The area the water is rerouted to is called a reservoir. These waters within reservoirs can be used to harness electricity. The water is also routed through canals for various purposes, as you have learned. Although some dams serve to produce electricity, many are to help protect land downriver from flooding and to use the regulated water to hydrate farms during dry spells.

Illustration representing the six tribes of the Iroquois League of Nations. Public Domain

water levels rise or fall. This brings the water level even with the water where the boat is passing through to.

Canals are waterway channels built to reroute water from a river or stream for various reasons, including the ability to allow boats to navigate by dams and rapids. Canals are also utilized for routing water for irrigation to food grown on farms and purification for us to use. Because of the different uses of canals, they can look different based on what purpose they are serving.

Dams are barriers constructed across rivers, keeping the water held back. While there are quite a few different designs out there, they serve similar purposes. Once the

These locks and canals are managed by both the Canadian government and the United States. Together these two governing bodies advertise the seaway as part of "Highway H₂O."

The construction of this seaway system began in 1954. In addition to building canals, locks, and dams, workers deepened many waterways. The seaway opened to ships in 1959.

The Ohio River has exciting tales to tell from history. Although, let's begin by learning how the river begins and where it leads to!

To begin with, in the southwest corner of Pennsylvania is a city called Pittsburgh. Within are two river tributaries, called Allegheny and Monongahela. Where these tributaries come together creates the start of the Ohio River flowing northwest out of Pennsylvania. Then, abruptly turns southwest to join the Mississippi River in Illinois, 981 miles from its beginning.

Canal going by farmland. Public Domain

The state's name Ohio, came from this vital river and means "Good River." The name came from the Seneca Indians that once were among the six tribes of the Iroquois League of Nations, occupying New York, Pennsylvania, and Ohio. Others along the Ohio River Valley were mound builders.

The confluence of the Allegheny River (top river) and the Monongahela River (right river) that begins the Ohio River. Adobe Stock

Angel Mounds close to Evansville, Indiana. Public Domain

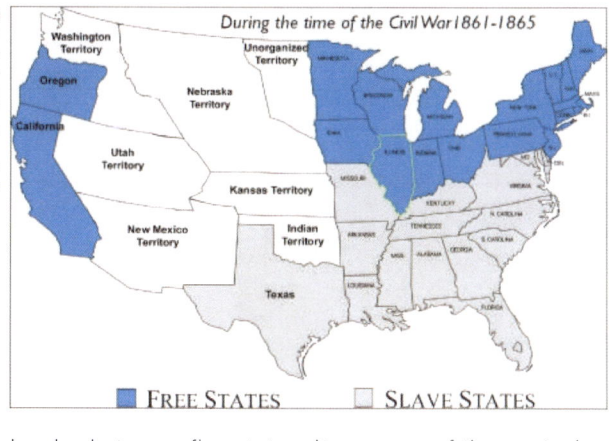

RIGHT: Map showing free states and slave states during the time of the American Civil War. Public Domain

During the time of the Civil War 1861–1865

■ FREE STATES   □ SLAVE STATES

RIGHT: African American slaves in the cotton fields in the Deep South. Public Domain, Library of Congress

Before European colonization, the Mississippian culture built numerous regional chiefdoms and major earthwork mounds in the Ohio River Valley. These include the Angel Mounds close to Evansville, Indiana. The mound builders included the Osage, Omaha, Ponca, and Kaw tribes that lived in the Ohio River Valley. The pressure from the Iroquois League of Nations promoted the migration of the mound builders west of the Mississippi River in the 1800s to the area now known as Missouri, Arkansas, and Oklahoma.

In the late 1700s, the Ohio River served as the southern boundary of the Northwest Territory before providing the border between five states. It was one of the central passages for pioneers during the westward expansion in the realization of Manifest Destiny.

Shortly before the American Civil War began, this river served as part of the separation between the free states and slave states. The saying "sold down the river" started as the cry of upper south slaves. They were carried down the Ohio and Mississippi rivers to be delivered to plantations that grew cotton and sugarcane in the Deep South.

Before and during the Civil War, the Ohio River was called the "River Jordan"

by slaves crossing it to escape their bondage and find freedom in the North via the Underground Railroad. Depending on where they were coming from, they might have passed through the "River Jordan" a few times in their dangerous journey. It is estimated that many slaves, in the thousands possibly, found freedom for themselves across the Ohio River.

LEFT: Cover art for a published work by Anthony Gene Carey. BELOW: Illustration depicting an auction selling slaves. BOTH: Public Domain

States and Territories of the United States of America August 7 1789 to April 2 1790
Public Domain

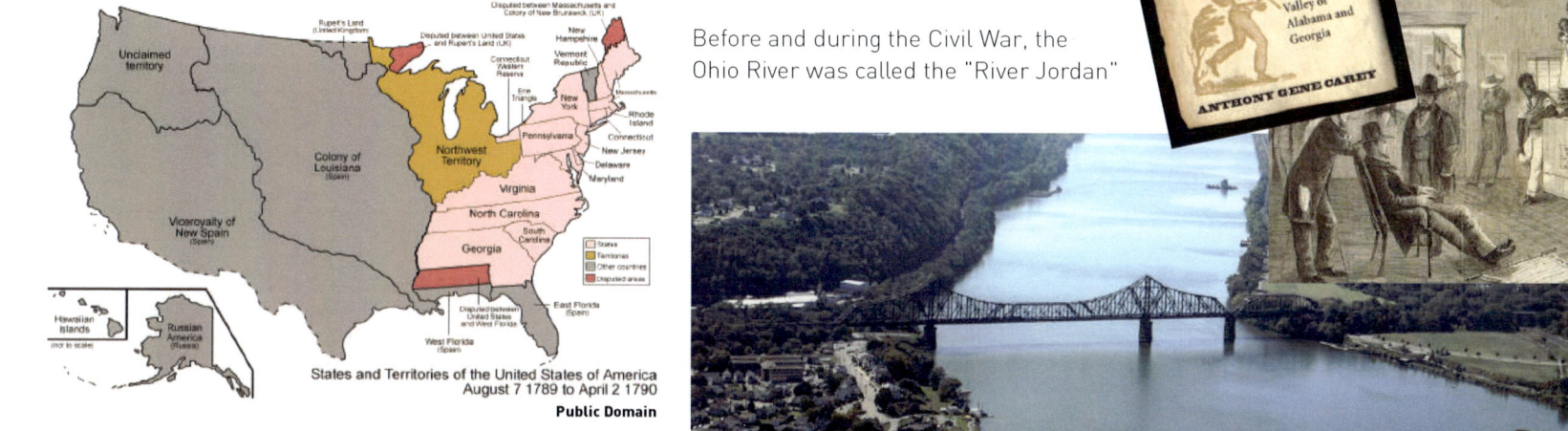

LEFT: Aerial of the Ohio River. Public Domain

Painted depiction of the French & Indian War. Public Domain

Falls of the Ohio. Public Domain

Going back in time, more than a century before the Civil War, and before the United States had formed, from 1754 to 1763, the Ohio River Valley was the center of great conflict. France and Great Britain went to war with each other in what is now called the French and Indian War. You would think that by the name of this war that the French were fighting Indians, but this wasn't the case. Indians fought as allies alongside the French against Britain, although some tribes sided with Britain. This war sparked a worldwide conflict known as the Seven Years War, which was fought on four continents and the Philippines. The height of the conflict was between 1756 to 1763. Before the battle began, both France and Great Britain controlled territories in North America. Britain had the 13 colonies that would eventually become the United States. France had what was referred to as New France, the area east of the Appalachians, around the Great Lakes into what is now eastern Canada. Both countries desired to control fertile Ohio River Valley for all of its resources and were willing to fight for it. Even though France got help from its Native American allies, Britain won the war. Their victory gave Britain control over most of the colonies in North America. That is, for a while, until the American Revolutionary War. This was when America declared its independence from Britain and fought to become a sovereign nation.

Before becoming President, Thomas Jefferson, in his Notes on the State of Virginia published in 1781–82, wrote:

Territories claimed in 1750 by the British, French, Spanish, and Russian. Public Domain

"The Ohio is the most beautiful river on earth. It's current gentle, waters clear, and bosom smooth and unbroken by rocks and rapids, a single instance only excepted."

This exception that he spoke of is still the exception today. The lower Ohio River is interrupted by rapids known as the "Falls of the Ohio," where water level drops 26 feet over 2 miles making this portion of the river unnavigable for boats. However, in the early twentieth century, McAlpine Locks and Dam was built, creating a shipping canal that bypassed the rapids. With this detour created, commercial navigation from the Ohio River in Pennsylvania to the Mississippi River is smooth sailing.

Later, during most of the 19th century and especially between 1829 to 1870, U.S. Westward Expansion utilized the Ohio River for a convenient way to travel from western Pennsylvania. Look at your map. What choices did pioneers have for travel along these rivers to make a new life for themselves in the west?

Painted depiction of Westward Expansion. Public Domain

Westward Expansion of the U.S., 1829-1870

▲ Port cities • Other cities

Purple indicates states as of 1803. Areas that became states or territories between 1803 and 1860 are shown in other colors.

Provided By: Rand McNally

Pioneers heading west. Public Domain

devious efforts along the Ohio River as well as the Mississippi River. They chose places where protection from law enforcement was absent. One such man by the name of Samuel Mason operated a gang out of Cave-In-Rock, Illinois. He would stop travelers on their way down the river, steal their goods, destroy their boats or sell them, and sometimes even kill their victims.

Today, the Ohio River is a source of drinking water for over three million people in large cities, including Pittsburgh, Pennsylvania; Cincinnati, Ohio; and Louisville, Kentucky. These cities also use the river just as generations and civilizations before, to transport products such as coal, oil, steel, and many manufactured goods.

Well, after reaching the Ohio River's mouth, settlers had a choice to go north or south on the Mississippi River. If they went north they could stop at St. Louis, Missouri and take various over land trails west, such as the Oregon Trail. Or, maybe they wished to continue on the Missouri River. They also had a choice to stay in St. Louis or continue northward up the Mississippi.

During this time of western pioneer movement, there were river pirates! These pirates concentrated their

The Mississippi River shares some of its history with the Ohio River, but is distinctly unique. Firstly, the Mississippi is North America's longest river. Native Americans get credit for the Mississippi name, which means "Father of Waters." Intimate knowledge of the great river translated into incredibly vibrant writings of Mark Twain. As Twain learned to pilot steamboats on the Mississippi, he wrote about his initial perspective in this poetic excerpt from the essay "Two Ways of Seeing a River" from the book "Life on the Mississippi [James R. Osgood and Company, 1883].

"Now when I had mastered the language of this water and had come to know every trifling feature that bordered the great river as familiarly as I knew the letters of the alphabet, I had made a valuable acquisition.

The hideout for Samuel Mason and his gang of river pirates. Public Domain

I still keep in mind a certain wonderful sunset which I witnessed when steamboating was new to me. A broad expanse of the river was turned to blood; in the middle distance the red hue brightened into gold, through which a solitary log came floating, black and conspicuous; in one place a long, slanting mark lay sparkling upon the water; in another the surface was broken by boiling, tumbling rings, that were as many-tinted as an opal; where the ruddy flush was faintest, was a smooth spot that was covered with graceful circles and radiating lines, ever so

The source of the Mississippi River. Public Domain

Mark Twain, Public Domain

delicately traced; the shore on our left was densely wooded, and the sombre shadow that fell from this forest was broken in one place by a long, ruffled trail that shone like silver; and high above the forest wall a clean-stemmed dead tree waved a single leafy bough that glowed like a flame in the unobstructed splendor that was flowing from the sun.

There were graceful curves, reflected images, woody heights, soft distances; and over the whole scene, far and near, the dissolving lights drifted steadily, enriching it, every passing moment, with new marvels of coloring.

I stood like one bewitched. I drank it in, in a speechless rapture. The world was new to me, and I had never seen anything like this at home."

Like Twain, many have been in awe of the Mississippi River that begins its long journey at Lake Itasca in northern Minnesota. Then, flowing south for 2,350 miles to the Mississippi Delta that empties into the Gulf of Mexico in southern Louisiana.

The Mississippi River is home to millions of birds, including ducks, geese, and swans that glide along the Mississippi during spring and autumn migrations. The pathway taken is called the Mississippi Flyway. Common fish in the river include walleye, catfish, and carp.

As with all major rivers in the world, the Mississippi has a long history of trade. Today, it continues as one of the busiest commercial water routes in the world. Products transported along the river include coal, oil, steel, iron, and grain shipped from many Midwestern farms.

As you may remember from the French and Indian War, the French lost. Before the war concluded, in 1762, France ceded its Louisiana

LEFT: Swans and ducks. CENTER: Swan. RIGHT: Geese. ALL: Public Domain BELOW: Steamboat on the Mississippi River, Adobe Stock

Historical map showing the Louisiana Purchase of 1803, the Florida Purchase of 1819, and the territories of the United States and Spain. Newspaper clipping, from: Unknown. Public Domain

St. Louis was the point from which President Thomas Jefferson sent Lewis & Clark to explore the new Louisiana Territory, and beyond, in May of 1804. Two years later, when the explorers returned in September of 1806, the city became the "Gateway to the West" for mountain men, adventurers, and settlers that took part in a movement called U.S. Western Expansion. A monument commonly referred to as the same name, "Gateway to the West," was built and dedicated to the American people to symbolize this critical piece of U.S. history. It is the centerpiece of Gateway Arch National Park and has become an internationally recognized symbol of St. Louis.

The Missouri River runs brown, that is until more recently. The Missouri River carried vast amounts of soil through the entirety of its course, giving it the nickname the "Big Muddy." However, today, dams trap much of the dirt in the upper part of the river allowing the lower part of the river to be far cleaner.

As with all rivers you learned about today, the Missouri serves as a busy shipping lane. Tugboats move cargo on barges between the mouth that connects to the Mississippi, all the way to Sioux City, Iowa.

Territory to Spain in return for help in the fight. The Mississippi River was the east boundary for this territory. Later in 1800, Spain and France signed a secret agreement to exchange the Louisiana Territory for territories in Tuscany. Then in 1803, France sold the region to the United States. This is referred to as the Louisiana Purchase that made this territory and beyond part of the United States.

The Missouri River is the
longest tributary of the Mississippi River and the second-longest river in North America at 2,315 miles long. It is formed by the coming together of the Jefferson, Madison, and Gallatin rivers in the Rocky Mountains about 4,000 feet above sea level at Brower's Spring. It flows initially northward then southeasterly until it meets the Mississippi River just north of Saint Louis, Missouri.

Painted depiction of Lewis and Clark on their Corp of Discovery expedition. By: Unknown, Public Domain

"Gateway to the West" monument within the Gateway Arch National Park, Public Domain

Grain Barge passing through Jefferson City, Missouri. Public Domain

While the Arkansas River is smaller than most rivers you have learned about today, it does serve as an important tributary of the Mississippi River. Its source comes from the Rocky Mountains in Colorado flowing 1,469 miles east and southeast, going through Colorado, Kansas, Oklahoma, and Arkansas.

Once, in 1859, gold was discovered in Leadville, Colorado, near the river's source, which brought thousands of people seeking to strike it rich. Unfortunately, the quickly recovered placer gold, which can be panned out of the river, was depleted rapidly.

In the early nineteenth century, a portion of the Arkansas River formed part of the border between the United States and Spanish occupied Mexico. Mexico pushed Spain out of Texas, and Texas was part of Mexico's land for a time.

Leadville, Colorado Gold Rush in the Arkansas River. A man panning for gold. Public Domain

Then, in 1836, Texas became its own country until it was decided to cede its autonomy as a self-governed state and became part of the Union in 1845. Sixteen years later, Texas seceded from the Union and joined the Confederacy along with ten other states and fought in the Civil War.

During the American Civil War, both the Confederate and the Union tried to prevent the other from using the Arkansas River and its tributaries to move forces and supplies.

As the war drew to a close, with the North winning over the South, Federal troops arrived in Texas to restore order on June 19, 1865.

Arkansas River, Public Domain

Union Major General Gordon Granger and 2,000 Union soldiers arrived on Galveston Island to take possession of the state and enforce the new freedoms of former slaves. The Texas holiday Juneteenth commemorates this date.

Confederate soldiers from Texas. Public Domain

Since the 1800s, a portion of the river in central Colorado is known for its exceptional trout and fly fishing. Other than fishing, the Arkansas River is enjoyed by many locals and tourists alike for rafting the rapids, lazily floating down, and enjoying the scenery while vacationing on houseboats and camping.

Union Major General Gordon Granger, Public Domain

A Closer Look!

at what you have learned in the last 6 lessons!

PLUS+

This Lesson's Geography:
Western Rivers, Plus a Lake

Colorado River
Red River
Rio Grande River

Columbia River
Great Salt Lake

Previous Learned Geography:

Listed here is the geography learned over the last 6 lessons. All lessons learned before the last 6 lessons are no longer on the map.

St. Lawrence River
Ohio River
Mississippi River
Missouri River
Arkansas River
Chesapeake Bay
Hudson Bay (Canada)
San Francisco Bay
Puget Sound
Pamlico Sound
Lake Huron
Lake Ontario
Lake Michigan
Lake Erie
Lake Superior

Cascade Mountains
Mt. Rainier
Mt. St. Helens
Denali
Rocky Mountains
Pikes Peak
Mt. Elbert
Sierra Nevada
Mt. Whitney
The Great Valley
Blue Ridge Mountains
Great Smoky Mountains
Cumberland Mountains
Mt. Mitchell

Lesson 18

Hudson Bay in Canada

Map Labels

Puget Sound
Mt. Rainier
Mt. St. Helens
Columbia River
Cascade Mountain Range
Great Salt Lake
Sierra Nevada
San Francisco Bay
Mt. Whitney
Denali
Rocky Mountains
Missouri River
Mississippi River
Lake SUPERIOR
Lake HURON
Lake MICHIGAN
Lake ERIE
Lake ONTARIO
St. Lawrence River
Mt. Elbert
Pikes Peak
Rocky Mountains
Ohio River
Missouri River
Cumberland Mountains
Blue Ridge Mountains
Mt. Mitchell
Chesapeake Bay
Pamlico Sound
Arkansas River
Colorado River
Red River
Rocky Mountains
The Great Valley
Great Smokey Mountains
Mississippi River
Rio Grande River

Zoom Me In!

Use this sheet as a reference for this lesson's worksheets. Be sure to practice until you don't have to look!

Lesson 18

United States of America Physical Features

Western Rivers Plus a Lake

Colorado River
Red River
Rio Grande River
Columbia River
Great Salt Lake

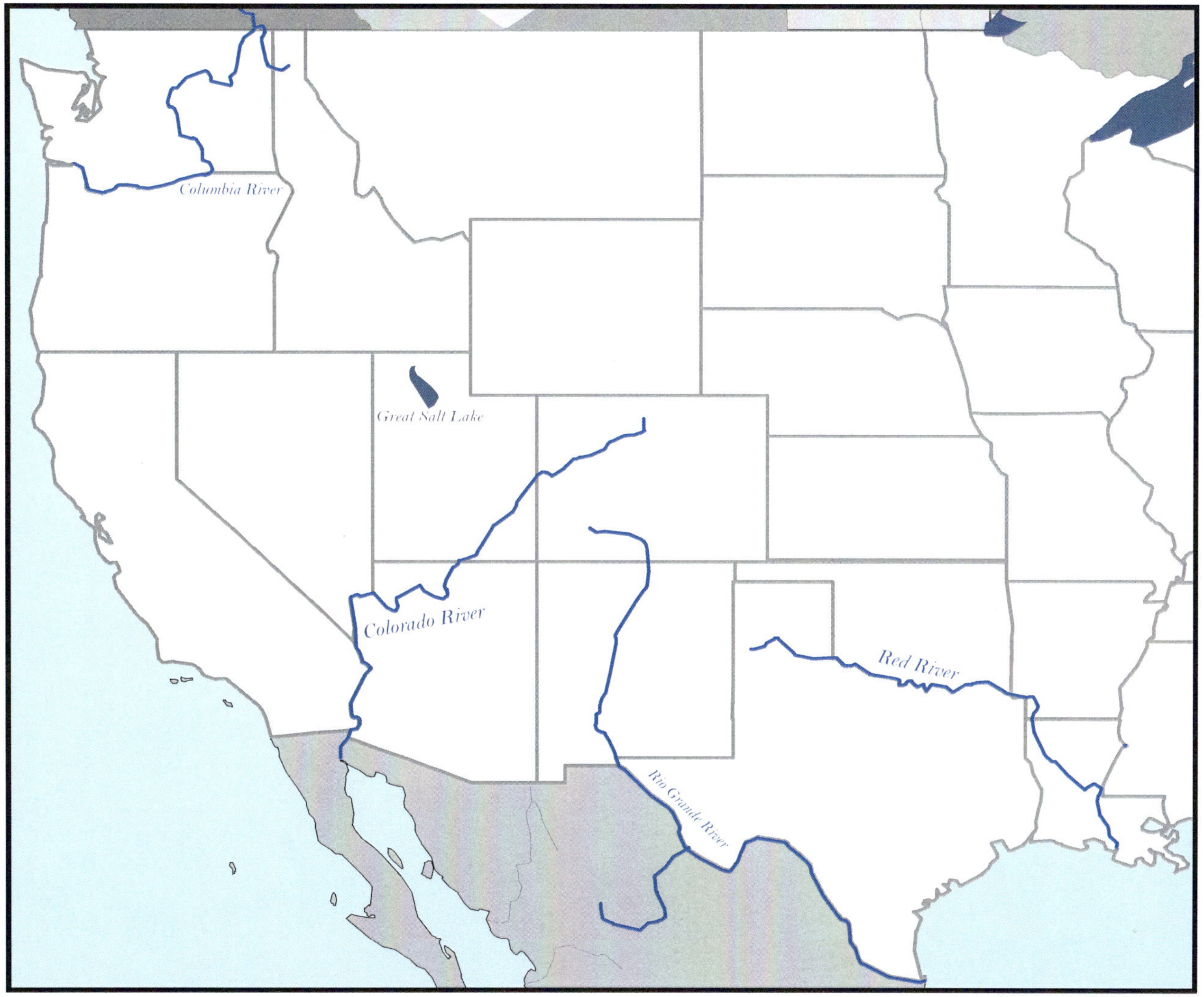

197

This Lesson's Geography:
Western Rivers, Plus a Lake

Colorado River
Red River
Rio Grande River
Columbia River
Great Salt Lake

Tid-Bits

Lesson 18

Aerial of the Colorado River – Adobe Stock

Map shows the watershed, or drainage basin, of the Colorado River. Provided by USGS

The Colorado River runs from the southwest of Colorado, between the Rocky Mountains and then on into Mexico. The mouth of the river opens into the Gulf of California, a part of the Pacific Ocean. Most notably, the Colorado River runs through the Grand Canyon in Arizona.

Starting as a chain of little streams in northern Colorado, much of its 1,450 miles, is a narrow passage that runs through deserts before it meets the ocean. However, by the time it reaches the Gulf of California, virtually most of the water has been utilized by people within the Colorado Basin. Several dams are located along the

river, including the Hoover Dam, built to harvest electricity and maintain control of water levels to avoid flooding . Dams along the river are utilized to capture water in a reservoir to irrigate farms and provide water for over 40 million people. One of the largest reservoir lakes in the world, Lake Mead, was created by Hoover Dam.

A drainage basin, which can also be called a watershed, is land that collects precipitation and then drains off into a common outlet. Outlets include rivers and streams, bays, and lakes. Rain, snow, sleet, or hail can be attributed to precipitation. Water will always travel downhill, wherever it's located. The force of gravity means water will take the most direct path, collecting at the lowest point. This "lowest point" is

called runoff. Runoff will ultimately form minor streams over time, then connecting to other streams further along until the streams come together, creating a river. Some water seeps into the ground, forming groundwater. People and animals also utilize groundwater for everyday use. Most of the water that doesn't evaporate in the sun, or soak down into the ground, flows until it reaches sea level. Typically, at sea level, there is an ocean that

The Hoover Dam on the Colorado River, straddling the border of Arizona and Nevada. Adobe Stock

Colorado River, Public Domain

Fishing on the Colorado River, Public Domain

Horseshoe Bend featuring the Colorado River - Public Domain

Aerial of the Southern Red River, Public Domain

Aerial of the Southern Red River, Public Domain

receives the water. Sometimes, at sea level, there is a lake that collects the water.

Many animals live along and in the Colorado River, including these freshwater fish: trout, Walleye, Yellow Perch, Bass, and Bluegill fish. Other than fishermen, bears love catching fish in the river as well. Elk and Moose are a couple of animals that live here too. As for plants, the Cottonwood trees, columbine flowers, and prickly pear cacti, all grow near the water.

The Red River, also called the Red River of the South, served as part of the U.S.–Mexico border until Texas became U.S. territory after the signing of the Treaty of Guadalupe Hidalgo.

The Red River has the second-largest river basin within the southern Great Plains and measures 1,360 miles, making it one of the largest rivers in the country. Its drainage basin is a vast area of approximately 93,000 square miles. This means that an area of 93,000 square miles surrounding the river has water that flows downward, draining into the Red River.

Interestingly, the Red River is a saltwater river! It is thought that the saltiness is caused by an ancient inland sea that covered certain areas from which the runoff flows. As time went by, that body of water evaporated, leaving salt deposits of sodium chloride.

The name of this river came from the color of its watershed, a murky brown with a reddish tone. It rises in the east of New Mexico, traveling across Texas and Louisiana. Before the 1900s, and before flood control systems, a segment of the river joined the Mississippi River via Old River. Today, the river connects to Atchafalaya River, then into Atchafalaya Bay, finally flowing into the Gulf of Mexico.

President Thomas Jefferson, sanctioned an expedition in 1806, allowing for exploration of the Red River. This venture was intended to explore, map, and research this new land recently acquired through the Louisiana Purchase.

During the American Civil War, the Red River was utilized by a Union General to transport troops, supplies, and ammunition in a campaign called the Red River Campaign.

At that time, President Abraham Lincoln had authorized a crusade against Shreveport, Louisiana. Shreveport was a major

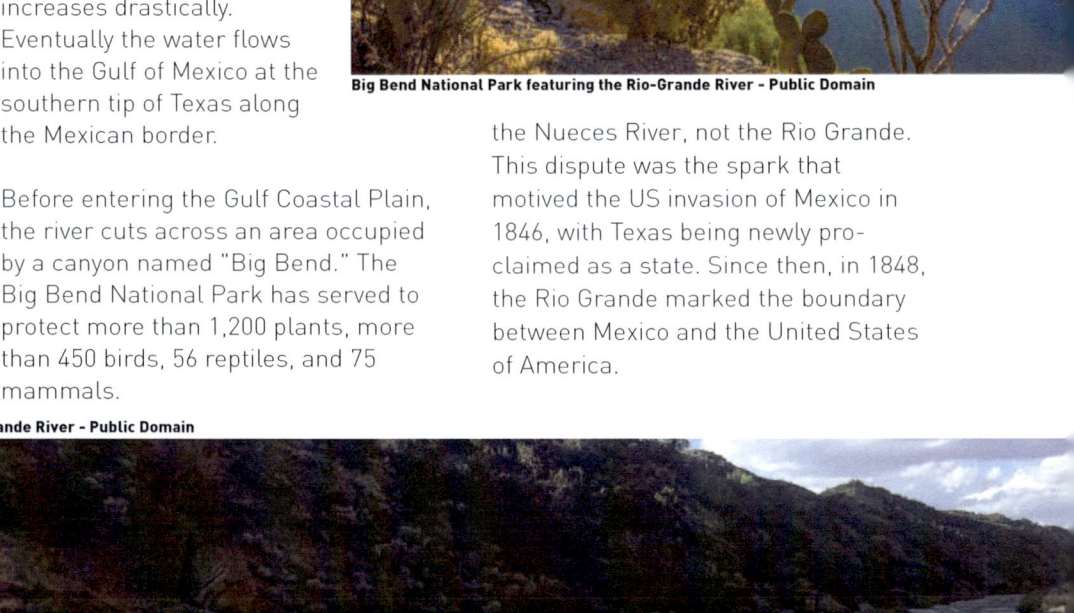

Illustration of the Red River Campaign of the Civil War - Public Domain

supply depot and a gateway to Texas. The goal of the campaign was to secure the area along the Red River to Shreveport, and then execute several objectives. First, they wanted to prevent an alliance with the French in Mexico. Securing the area would mean that they would have the ability to deny southern supplies to Confederate forces. Lastly, they needed to secure vast quantities of Louisiana and Texas cotton for northern mills.

The Confederate Army knew about the campaign and was waiting for them. Union troops did not see this coming and were ill-prepared. This confrontation between the north and the south is referred to as the battle of Mansfield. The fight went for 12 days from May 10th until May 22nd in 1864. It is considered by some to have been the most humiliating defeat of the entire war. The Union forces of 12,000 had

700 men killed or wounded and 1,500 taken prisoner; 20 Union artillery pieces and 200 wagons were captured. Almost 1,000 horses and mules were lost. The Confederate army of 8,800 had 1,000 killed or wounded. In the end, the Union Army retreated, and the Confederate Amy victorious—even with fewer men fighting and fewer men killed. After this loss, the campaign was abandoned.

The Rio Grande is a crucial
landmark in the southwest United States and northern Mexico. Its name comes from the Spanish term: "Big River," though it is recognized as Rio Bravo by Mexican citizens. The Rio Grande measures approximately 1,885 miles, though the river changes course from time to time, which alters the river's length.

The beginning of the river starts as snowmelt in the Rockies within south-central Colorado. It begins the journey downward in frigid temperatures. However, this climate soon changes drastically from cold to hot from a frigid environment filled with pine and juniper trees to an arid environment characterized by mesquite, creosote bush, cactus, and many other desert plants. The journey of the Rio Grande is south-bound. As the snowmelt follows gravity's pull coupled with getting closer to the equator, the temperature increases drastically. Eventually the water flows into the Gulf of Mexico at the southern tip of Texas along the Mexican border.

Before entering the Gulf Coastal Plain, the river cuts across an area occupied by a canyon named "Big Bend." The Big Bend National Park has served to protect more than 1,200 plants, more than 450 birds, 56 reptiles, and 75 mammals.

In the late-1830s and early-1840s, the river was a source of debate. Mexico and the Republic of Texas disagreed on the border between the two countries. Mexico drew the border at

Big Bend National Park featuring the Rio-Grande River - Public Domain

the Nueces River, not the Rio Grande. This dispute was the spark that motived the US invasion of Mexico in 1846, with Texas being newly proclaimed as a state. Since then, in 1848, the Rio Grande marked the boundary between Mexico and the United States of America.

Rio-Grande River - Public Domain

Columbia River - Amanda Predmore

Bonneville Dam on the Columbia River - By: BPA, Public Domain

Salmon Ladder at the Bonneville Dam on the Columbia River - By: BPA, Public Domain

There are 14 dams along the Columbia, producing up to 45% of the hydroelectric power in the United States. That makes this river incredibly important.

The Columbia River has many tributaries, of which the Snake River is the largest. The drainage basin extends into seven U.S. states and a Canadian province. It is estimated to be the size of France! By volume, it is the fourth largest river in the nation. It holds the title for the most enormous flow of any North American river entering the Pacific.

Regarded as highly significant to the region's cultural and economic progress throughout known history, the river and its tributaries have been used for transportation for hundreds, if not, thousands of years, linking many indigenous groups.

Columbia River - Amanda Predmore

The Columbia River is by far the largest in the Pacific Northwest region of North America. The river flows in both Canada and in the United States. Its source is the Columbia Lake, which is 2,690 feet above sea level, located in British Columbia, Canada. The river flows southerly into Washington, then switches direction and heads west, forming much of the boundary between Washington and Oregon. At 1,243 miles, it makes its way boldly into the Pacific Ocean.

Multiple dams have been installed along the Columbia, giving it the nickname the "Electric River." These dams produce hydroelectric power, which is a renewable energy source. Hydroelectric power is created with the build-up of pressure from water that moves from the reservoir to a turbine inside the dam. That force spins the turbine. The spinning turbine causes the generator to turn, producing electricity sent out to near and far, for us to use in our everyday lives.

The river system hosts many species of anadromous fish. This type of fish migrates between freshwater and saltwater. These fish, particularly the salmon, have served as a core food source for the Native Americans that lived along the Columbia and its tributaries.

Native Americans had inhabited the Columbia Riverbanks long before Europeans began to explore and settle the area. When European explorers first saw the river in 1775, further exploration by Spain, Britain, and the U.S. led to all three countries laying claim to the Pacific Northwest. One such campaign to reinforce the United States' claim was the Lewis and Clark Expedition. It is commonly stated that the purpose of this expedition was to travel through the Louisiana Purchase and explore this vast land. However, Thomas Jefferson had this in mind before the turn of the century. One year into his Presidency, he began actively organizing the expedition in 1802 and early 1803.

include the entire land west to the Columbia River and the Pacific coast, which Jefferson wanted his expedition to explore and reinforce their prior claim to the territory.

Jefferson turned to Congress for funding under the pretense that the expedition was to explore the newly purchased Louisiana territory.

Painting depicting the Corps of Discovery being led by Lewis and Clark. Public Domain

During this time, rumor had it that an old enemy was willing to sell. This welcome yet unexpected news was that Napoléon of France was ready to market the Louisiana land to the United States. In response, Jefferson jumped at this opportunity and made the deal. Overnight the United States had doubled in size. However, the Louisiana Purchase did not

Thomas Jefferson and William Clark depicted in this painting, planning the expedition to the west, before France sold the Louisiana territory to the United States. By Unknown, Public Domain

Napoleon Bonaparte of the French Empire. Public Domain

While Jefferson was incredibly curious about the western land, the animals, the topography, and the natives, there was an underlying plan within this expedition. He desired to stake claim to land in the northwest. There were European countries that had already made their claims. To his lasting credit, Jefferson knew that unless our young nation attained Louisiana, and joined the race to claim the Pacific coast, the U.S. may never expand beyond the Mississippi. The Louis and Clark Expedition was created to this end. To find a way west, explore and document, build positive relationships with the natives, and enforce the United States' claims.

After the expedition, the way west was made known, trails established, and what began as a trickle of a few brave people eventually turned into a steady stream heading west.

The Great Salt Lake is unable to decide how large or If you are unfamiliar with the word, endorheic, you're probably curious about what it means. It is after all what makes this lake unique. The word endorheic is an Ancient

ALL 3 Photos LEFT on page: Northwest Pacific Indian Tribes fishing along the Columbia River at Celilo Falls

Greek word that means "to flow within." Endorheic lakes tend to be found in deserts, do not have much inflow of water, and depends mainly on rainfall. Many lakes have this much in common that are not endorheic... the difference that makes the Great Salt Lake and other endorheic lakes special, is that they don't have any outflow of water. The water is held captive!

The Great Salt Lake has a major river tributary named Bear River, in addition, the lake does receive precipitation, but only about 5 inches a year. Any loss of water is either by evaporation or seeping into the ground. When this happens, the water leaves behind a mineral that makes this lake salty. The Great Salt Lake, is saltier than the ocean. You may be familiar with another couple of endorheic lakes. The Caspian Sea and the Dead Sea.

Because of the saltiness of these types of lakes, the water is never used for human consumption and few living creatures can survive within and around the lake.

As mentioned, when water loss occurs, the lake shrinks. Some endorheic lakes have disappeared altogether leaving behind salt pans, such as the Great Salt Lake Desert. *(You will learn more about the Great Salt Lake Desert in Lesson 22)*

Due to the Great Salt Lake's warm waters, "lake-effect snowfalls" are a frequent phenomenon in the surrounding area. When cold winds blow across the lake, followed by the passage of a cold front, the temperature difference between the warm lake and the cold air forms clouds that lead to snow. This occurrence only happens with large lakes and is not typical of much smaller lakes. When this happens, excessive amounts of snow drifts gently to the ground.

TOP, LEFT, CENTER, BOTTOM: Great Salt Lake photos from different angles around and above the lake. Public Domain

RIGHT: Photo of community located near the Great Salt Lake showing the "Lake-snow-effect." Public Domain

A Closer Look!
at what you have learned in the last 6 lessons!

PLUS+
This Lesson's Geography:
Historic Trails

Cumberland Road
Santa Fe Trail
Mormon Trail

Gila Trail
Old Spanish Trail

California Trail
Oregon Trail

Previous Learned Geography:

Listed here is the geography learned over the last 6 lessons. All lessons learned before the last 6 lessons are no longer on the map.

Colorado River
Red River
Rio Grande River
Columbia River
Great Salt Lake
St. Lawrence River
Ohio River
Mississippi River
Missouri River
Arkansas River
Chesapeake Bay
Hudson Bay (Canada)
San Francisco Bay
Puget Sound
Pamlico Sound

Lake Huron
Lake Ontario
Lake Michigan
Lake Erie
Lake Superior
Cascade Mountains
Mt. Rainier
Mt. St. Helens
Denali
Rocky Mountains
Pikes Peak
Mt. Elbert
Sierra Nevada
Mt. Whitney

Lesson 19

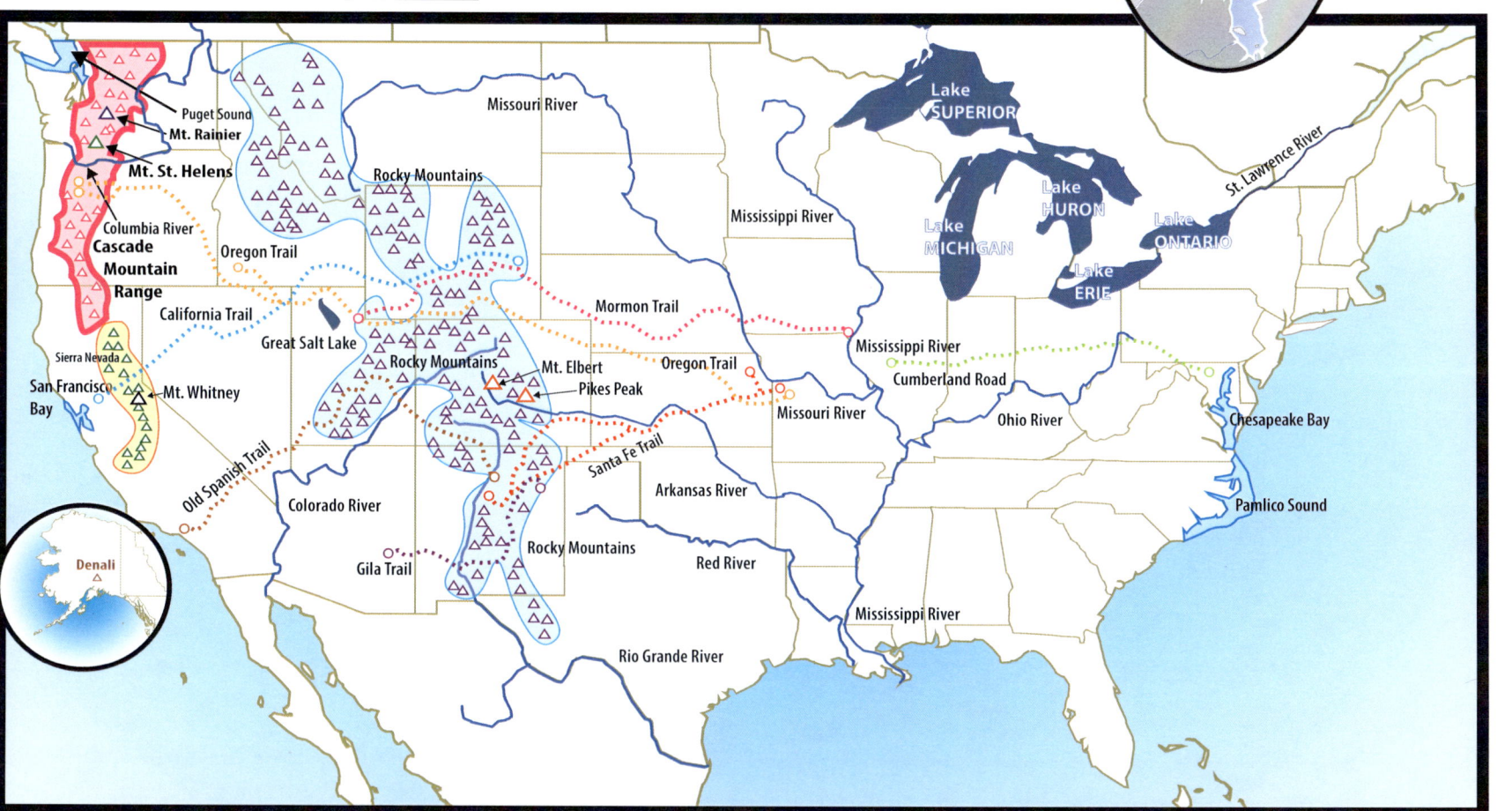

Zoom Me In!

Use this sheet as a reference for this lesson's worksheets. Be sure to practice until you don't have to look!

United States of America Physical Features

Historic Trails

Lesson 19

Cumberland Road
Santa Fe Trail
Mormon Trail
Gila Trail
Old Spanish Trail
California Trail
Oregon Trail

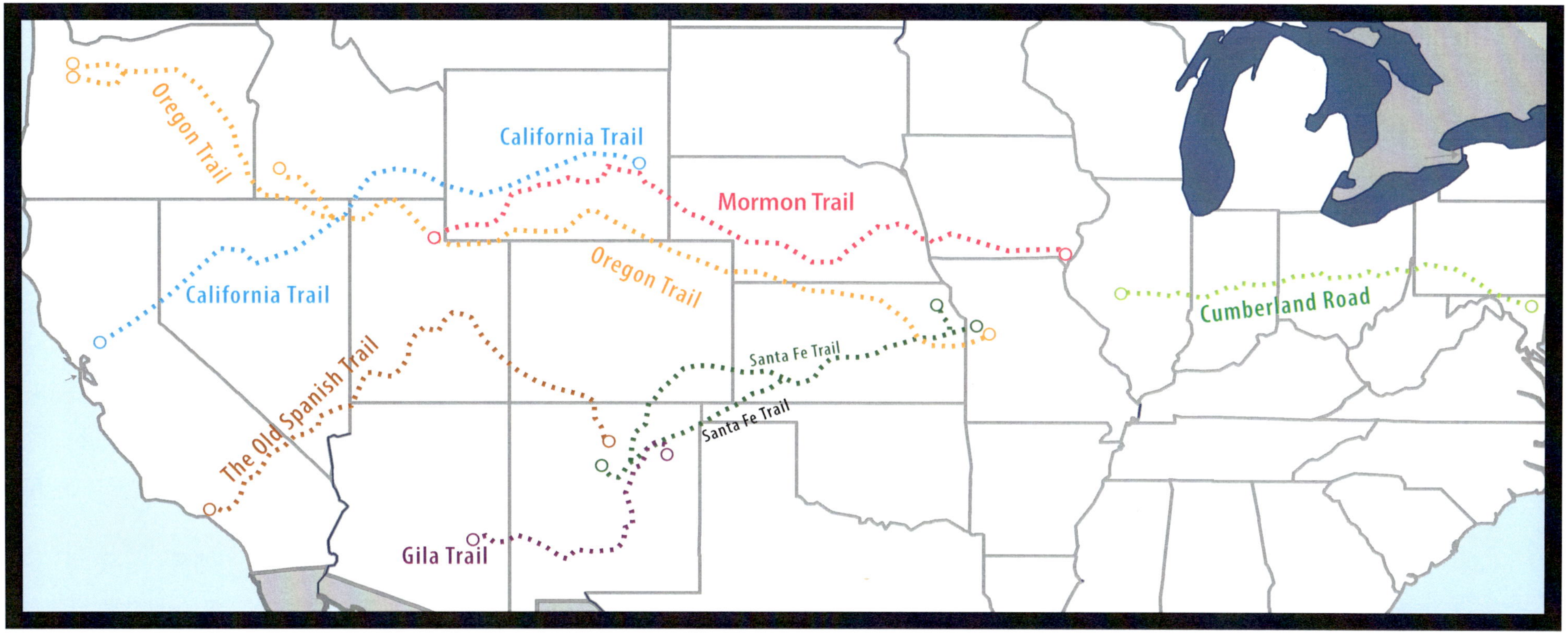

205

This Lesson's Geography:
Historic Trails

Cumberland Road
Santa Fe Trail
The Mormon Trail
Gila Trail
Old Spanish Trail
California Trail
Oregon Trail

Tid-Bits

Cumberland Road

When James Madison was the 4th American President, the country was already looking to the west. Ohio became a new state, and it was an attractive place for people to move to that desired new farmland. Until the Cumberland Road was built, there was no easy way for people to travel to the west. Initially, there were various roads and paths that Indians and military used that were not linked together. The plan was to take these older roads, combine, and

BELOW: Casselman Bridge along Cumberland Road, deemed the first highway. Public Domain

ABOVE & RIGHT: Public monuments for the "Braddock's Road" which turned into the Cumberland Road and the "National Road" which was historically called the Cumberland Road. Public Domain

lengthen to create a more extensive path that went from Maryland all the way to Ohio, then to Illinois, 620 miles in all.

Businessmen realized that connecting one part of America to another would help the country grow. They depended on new transportation systems to make that happen. This great accomplishment helped people to believe in the concept of Manifest Destiny for the United States.

Every road has a beginning, historically speaking, that is. For the Cumberland Road, that beginning was the Braddock Road, which had been opened by the Ohio Company in 1751. The Ohio Company was run by the French. It was based on fur trading with the native Indians before the French and

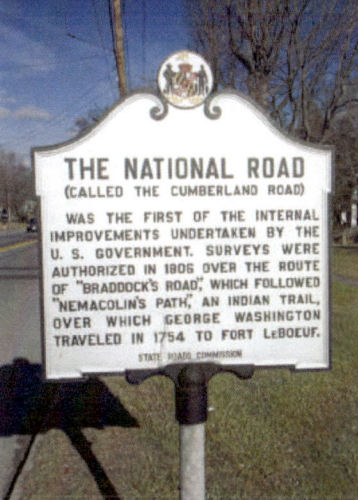

Indian War. The Braddock Road went from the upper Potomac River all the way to where the Ohio River begins, which is at the confluence of the Allegheny and Monongahela Rivers. The Cumberland Road mostly aligned with this older footpath until Uniontown, Pennsylvania.

While this was the start of the Cumberland Road, the need to connect the east to the west persisted. For twenty-six years, from 1811 until 1837, construction created a road that reached all

Lesson 19

the way to Illinois. From there, some travelers would hop onto the Missouri River to continue their journey west.

Initially, people marked the path with granite stone to show its beginning until a monument was built in 2012 to show the historical starting point.

Santa Fe Trail

Native Americans had used parts of this trail since the 1500s. Then, Spanish settlers in the 1700s used the Santa Fe Trail to travel across the southwest of North America. In the 1800s, the Santa Fe Trail was one of the longest and most important trade routes in America. It has been called America's first highway connecting the little town of Independence, Missouri, to Santa Fe, New Mexico.

The historical Santa Fe Trail that shows where the wagon wheels trod. Public Domain

Painting of the Santa Fe Trail. Public Domain

The trail was not just used as a trade route, it served as an essential part of westward expansion. Although along its path, travelers would experience a dangerous country, including possible confrontations with Comanche Indians. Once settlers made it all the way through the Santa Fe Trail, they could connect to various other trails to continue west to California.

During this time, the Santa Fe Trail was in Mexico's land, until the Mexican-American War. The American Army used this trail route to invade New Mexico in 1846. With the signing of the Treaty of Guadalupe Hidalgo, this land along the Santa Fe Trail became American land.

Wealthy businessmen realized they could build a railroad track that followed the Santa Fe Trail to connect western markets to economic opportunities in the east. For example, they could send cattle by train to Chicago and transport coal from Colorado to the eastern coast.

In 1862, Congress passed the Pacific Railroad Act that encouraged land purchase for the building of railroads westbound. Wherever the railroad went, there also towns and businesses grew up. This successful profit-driven venture spurred the railroad companies to continue building westward, eventually reaching the Pacific, up and down the coastline.

The Mormon Trail was the route that members of the Church of Jesus Christ of Latter-day Saints, commonly called Mormons, used to travel from Nauvoo, Illinois to Salt Lake City, Utah. Today it's known as the Mormon Pioneer National Historic Trail, part of the U.S. National Trails System.

Brigham Young, Mormon leader during the time of migration to Utah. Public Domain

The Sana Fe Trail, provided by the "Keepers of the Santa Fe Trail.

Brigham Young and his followers arrived in 1847. The Mormons came to Utah when they were driven out of Illinois from religious persecution. Along the way of the trail to Salt Lake City, they established settlements that provided food and housing for later travelers. It made traveling simpler and safer for newcomers because they did not have to worry about food and lodging.

Pioneers traversing the Mormon Trail. Public Domain

After the initial group was settled, the next task was to organize additional trips for Mormons to make it to present-day Utah. Each year during the Mormon Migration, people were organized into "companies." Each company bearing the name of its leader and subdivided into groups of 10 and 50. They traveled the trail split up by the vanguard company.

Present-Day Mormon Pioneer National Historic Trail. Public Domain

The vanguard company was a large group of approximately 150 men and slaves, a few women, and children. The group was split into 14 vanguards assigned to accompany each Mormon Migration company. A portion of the group carried

The Gila Trail, also known as the Butterfield Stage Trail, was the main southern route for immigrants coming into California. It connected with the Santa Fe Trail in New Mexico and the nearby Old Spanish Trail that makes it all the way to California. It seemed a safer trail because it did not have mountain passes or snowstorms. The settlers did have to deal with dry desert regions, hot weather, and lack of water. Cattle and sheep herds were driven along this route, as well as the Butterfield Overland Stage, who delivered mail from 1858 until 1861.

TOP LEFT: Painting entitled "Zion in Her Heart." By: Clark Kelley Price. TOP RIGHT: Monument for the Mormon Trail. BOTTOM LEFT: Illustration depicting the Mormon emigration. ALL: Public Domain

Present-day Gila Trail, Public Domain

surplus supplies, while the other served as militia and night guard.

By 1849, many Mormons who remained in Iowa or Missouri were poor. Unable to afford the costs of wagons, oxen, and supplies necessary for the trip. To assist those, a revolving fund was established called the Perpetual Emigration Fund. By 1852, those who wished to emigrate had done so.

They wanted to establish a town in the Great Basin area crossing Iowa. When they stopped in Iowa, they led the most extensive group into Salt Lake Valley. Salt Lake Valley was outside the boundaries of the United States. Here they could create their own community with their own laws and regulations. Mormons continued to use this trail until the First Transcontinental Railroad was completed in 1869.

This was desert land. As such, the trail followed the rivers through to Arizona. Fur trappers traveled along the path during the 1820s. The Forty-niners came to Arizona on the trail, then skipped on over to the Old Spanish Trail on their way to strike it big in the California Gold Rush!

After the Civil War, cattle crossed the Gila, and ranches began being established. Along the Gila Trail, in present-day New Mexico, was a town named Shakespeare. Colonel Boyle from St. Louis, Missouri, staked many claims under the name of Shakespeare Mining Company, effectively renaming the town of Ralston to Shakespeare. Here, they mined for silver! Today, it is a ghost town.

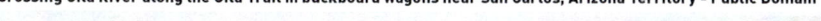

Crossing Gila River along the Gila Trail in buckboard wagons near San Carlos, Arizona Territory - Public Domain

The Gila Trail made its way through Arizona and was a place full of peril. Back then, the law was not fully established. Without that accountability and enforcement, this area of the country was known as the wild west. Gangs of violent men intimated, ruled, robbed, and killed.

The most famous event along the Gila Trail happened in the last old frontier town of Tombstone, Arizona. The gunfight at the O.K. Corral occurred on October 26th, 1881.

Members of America's first organized crime gang, referred to themselves as the "Cowboys." On this fateful day, a couple of Cowboys had an argument with Wyatt, Virgil, and Morgan Earp. This argument ended with two of the Cowboys getting hit with guns across their faces. Their Cowboy intimidation tactics did not work on the Earp brothers. Wyatt knew a fight was coming and quickly deputized his brothers so that he would have backup in case things got ugly. Later that same day, the Cowboys gathered, sending threats out. Tensions rose, and the Earp brothers

Tombstones of those killed at the O.K. Corral. Public Domain

moved in along with the help from Wyatt's friend Doc Holliday. Twenty-four seconds and thirty shots later, Billy Clanton, Tom, and Frank McLaury were shot and killed. The Cowboys retaliated soon after by maiming Morgan Earp and killing his brother Virgil. After this, history tells us of Wyatt's response in the "Earp Vendetta Ride." This "Ride" was a deadly search by a federal posse led by Deputy U.S. Marshall Wyatt Earp.

Their target, all Cowboys.
On September 16th, 1881, thirty days before the gunfight at the O.K. Corral, the local paper called "The Tombstone Epitaph" wrote about the "Cow-boy Nuisance" in Arizona:

"It has come to pass in this county that life and personal property are unsafe; even in the town of Tombstone it seems as if one of the leading industries is to be destroyed. There is not a teamster to-day who is not in fear and dread of the cow-boys, or so-styled "rustlers" depriving him of his hard earnings... How must such men feel to be robbed by a band of thieves and cutthroats, who take pride in announcing to the public that they are "rustlers!" Where is the teamsters protection? Can you find any officers who will follow, arrest and recover your property? If you can, I would like to see him... These chaps seem to have no difficulty in evading the law, while others, not inclined to work, daily join the band and they are increasing fast in numbers. Our town is filled with spies watching every move of the officers and imparting their information to their comrades... Men who come to examine different mines outside of town, when they learn how the cow-boys stand fellows up, do not wish to run such risks; they quietly take the road they came and get into civilization as soon as possible."

Today, with a population of more than 1,800 (2018) the historic town of Tombstone has a crime rate 2.2 times smaller than the U.S. average. It seems that over time things have improved!

The town sees many visitors from all over wanting to hear the stories and see the places where the legendary Earp brothers, and Doc Holiday, took their stand against those corrupt cowboys.

The Old Spanish Trail was used for trading and transporting goods from New Mexico to Los Angeles. California-bred horses

TOP: The town of Tombstone, Arizona that is found along the Gila Trail. This is the site of the gunfight between the "Cowboys" and the Earp brothers and Doc Holliday. Public Domain. **BOTTOM:** The Tombstone graveyard. Adobe Stock.

Present-day "Old Spanish Trail" Public Domain

inevitable." While the use of many trails was for western expansion, this trail was a combination of other trails used by Spanish explorers, and trappers. Above all it was a well-traveled trade route between Los Angeles and Santa Fe. People traded animal flesh, material goods, contraband, and Indian slaves. Sheep and high-quality woolen goods were sold for a supply of horses raised on California's ranches.

the California side. Jedediah Smith was the first mountain man to cross the mountains from Nevada to California. His trail became known as the California Trail.

The swift Humboldt River was an essential part of the long, challenging trail. By providing life-giving water and grass, both the travelers and their livestock fared well. The Humboldt River also served as a dividing point where the Oregon Trail and the California trail meet. Some continued along the California Trail, and some desired to go north, taking the Oregon Trail. Likewise, those traveling along the Oregon Trail who wanted to head south would hop onto the California Trail. One group of settlers missed the junction and found themselves at the Great Salt Lake of Utah. From there, they went west and found the Humboldt River, and got back on track!

You have learned a bit about the California Gold Rush, here are some additional tid-bits!

ABOVE & BELOW:
Monuments erected along
the Old Spanish Trail.
Public Domain

and mules were valuable and easily traded as well. This overland route was challenging because it crossed remote deserts and mountains of Mexico's far northern frontier, which is now part of the United States.

You have learned about the doctrine of Manifest Destiny, the belief that it was the destiny for American citizens to move west, which was both "justified and

Along the Old Spanish Trail in 1769, came Franciscan priests who established 21 California missions. They were built along the coastline and ministered to caravans traveling up from Mexico. In fact, the El Camino Real (translated "The Royal Road) connected all the missions in California and emerged as a major wagon route.

Because of the Old Spanish Trail, Santa Fe became the center of overland continental trade with Mexico.

The California Trail
covered the western half of the North American continent. Fur trappers and mountain men were responsible for finding paths through the Sierra Nevada Mountains to get from the desert side to

Old Spanish Trail. Public Domain

Monument sign marking the
California Trail. Public Domain

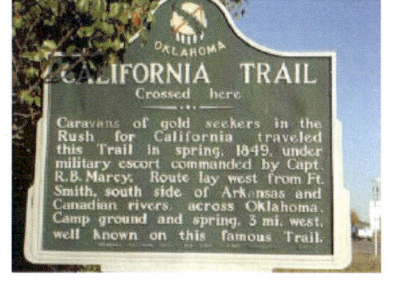

In 1848, newspapers in the east were advertising and publishing articles about California's Gold Rush. There were three ways to get to California. The longest way was by ship from Boston or New York sailing down to South America around the horn and traveling north to San Francisco, which took 6-8 months.

A second way that was quicker, was a combination of land and sea. Travelers would take a ship from Boston or New York, and disembark in Panama. Then, cross the Isthmus of Panama to hop on a boat, and head north to San Francisco Bay. This was said to only take 2 months. However, this route had some issues. It was a high possibility that gold-seekers would encounter hostile Indians and dangerous mosquitoes that caused illness. If they reached the west coast of Panama, they had to wait for a ship going north to take them to San Francisco. People discovered that many of the boats were already full of passengers. They would have to wait possibly several more months to catch a ride.

The third way to get to the goldfields was by going overland. People would buy wagons, supplies, mules, or oxen and use the Santa Fe, Oregon, Old Spanish Trail, and the California Trail to make it there. Depending on where one was traveling from would determine the length. Most people made it, but there was one unlucky group, the Donner Party. They listened to some bad advice to try and short cut the route. This landed them in terrain that was difficult to survive. Eventually, after making it through the desert, they found themselves at the foot of the Sierra Nevada before Winter was to set in. During a night's rest on the mountain, they awoke to several feet of snow. They and their Indian guide could not locate the trail, they were stranded without hope. Many died of starvation and hypothermia.

Abandoned wagon on the California Trail. Public Domain

Those who chose overland routes needed to prepare correctly for the journey ahead. Firstly, a pioneer with his sights set on heading west was to sell their farm or business and begin putting together an "outfit." Most had no idea what they would be facing on the trails. So, they would turn to books, pamphlets, and guides that gave detailed trail information on how to survive the trek, and how to pack for it.

A pioneer's typical outfit, for a family of 3-6 people, usually consisted of one or two small, sturdy farm wagons. They would bring 6-10 head of oxen with the chains and yokes to attach them to their wagons.

Traveling rough terrain meant that the wagons

Illustration of a wagon train continuing on their journey on the California Trail at night. Public Domain

211

California Trail Pioneers. Public Domain

had to be small and light. These smaller wagons could be easily pulled by 4 to 6 mules, oxen, or horses. However, more animals were brought, in case any of the animals would stray off, die, or be stolen during the trip. This was often the case.

Packing food for the trip needed to be compact, lightweight, and could not go bad. Many brought dried fruit and vegetables to provide some variety and Vitamin C to prevent scurvy. The

A glance at the inside of a typical covered wagon, all packed up and ready to go. Public Domain

recommended food to take per adult for a 4 to 6 month trip was 150 pounds of flour, 20 pounds of cornmeal, 50 pounds of bacon, 40 pounds of sugar, 10 pounds of coffee, 15 pounds of dried fruit, 5 pounds of salt, half a pound of baking soda, 2 pounds of tea, 5 pounds of rice, and 15 pounds of beans. Condiments like: mustard, cinnamon, nutmeg, vinegar, pepper, and other spices were usually included. Ex-trappers, ex-army soldiers, and Indians often used pemmican made by pounding jerky until it was a coarse meal. To prepare, they would pour rendered fat and sometimes pulverized dried berries over it—this was very light-weight and could keep for months. This food source provided much needed energy. Meat filled barrels were also brought by many. Some took along cows and goats for milk, chickens for eggs and dinners. Also, food like pickles, canned butter, cheese, or pickled eggs were brought by some.

Back then, canned goods were expensive, and food preservation was primitive. Besides, canned goods were also heavy. Therefore, bringing this type of food was not popular.

The typical cost of enough food for four people for six months was about $150. The

A modern photo of an old covered wagon. Public Domain

cost of other supplies, like livestock and wagons, could easily double this cost. In the 1800s, $150.00 represented about 150 days' worth of work or half a year's typical salary. Many poor were excluded from traveling unless they were able to get a job herding animals, guarding livestock, or driving a wagon. The required amount of food lessened if beef cattle, calves, or sheep were taken along for a walking food supply. Before the 1870s, vast herds of buffalo in Nebraska

A relic of the past, an old wooden wagon wheel. Public Domain

or buy Moccasins and buffalo robes from Indians encountered on the way. A thin fold-up mattress, blankets, pillows, ground covers were used for sleeping on the ground at night. About 25 to 30 pounds of soap was recommended for bathing and washing clothes. A washboard and tub were also usually included to aid in washing clothes.

TOP & BOTTOM RIGHT: Families of pioneers traveling through the California Trail. BOTTOM LEFT: A reconstructed wagon resembling what a new wagon would have looked like in the pioneering days. Public Domain

Unless you were a small child, pregnant or injured, travelers never rode in the wagons. It was too dusty, too rough of a ride, and most importantly, it was too hard on the livestock. Most walked nearly all the way.

Travelers also brought books, Bibles, trail guides, writing quills, ink, and paper to keep a diary or write a letter.

As the pioneers traveled, they would need to find grazing fields for their animals, protect themselves from hostile Indians, and carry extra supplies to fix wagons, care for animals, and family. This route usually took 5-6 months to accomplish if everything went smoothly. Scurvy and Cholera were common illnesses. Along the way items were often abandoned to lighten the load for the animals especially when climbing mountains or crossing the desert. Even today you can find discarded items along that trail. Most people made the trip successfully.

The Oregon Trail

The trails you have learned about have similarities in how they began and what they were used for. Many trails were initially created by the indigenous people and the Spanish. Trails were blazed for trade, exploration for claiming the land for various governments, mapping the vast spaces, and study for purposes of different types of sciences. All, was the case with the Oregon Trail.

What was known as Oregon Country, was claimed by many countries. Included were Great Britain, France, Russia, and Spain. Later, the U.S. joined the effort to check out the land to see if we could claim it, and settle.

As you have learned, President Thomas Jefferson sent Lewis and Clark for exploration. In 1804 they set out and mapped their journey going west. Before their adventure, there were fur trading companies that explored, traded, and set up trade posts that were for those traveling to and from the west. Over decades, a combined effort of mountain men, missionaries, and companies like John Jacob Astor's Pacific Fur Company, paved the way for what was to become the Oregon Trail.

In 1839, a small group of 18 brave men descended from Illinois to begin a colony in Oregon country on behalf of the United States of America. They wanted to make it a territory. These men were some of the first pioneers to travel the Oregon Trail. They were led by Thomas J. Farnham. Together, they carried along with them a large flag with their motto, "Oregon or the Grave." They called themselves the "Oregon Dragoons." The group split up near Bent's Fort, and Farnham was removed as their leader. Only 9 of the members reached Oregon.

provided fresh meat and jerky for the trip. In general, wild game and fish could not be depended on, but it was a welcome change in a boring diet when found. Travelers could hunt antelope, buffalo, trout, deer, and occasionally sage hens, elk, bear, duck, geese, and salmon along the trail. Many travelers went via Salt Lake City, Utah, and the Salt Lake Cutoff to get repairs, fresh or additional supplies, fresh vegetables, and new livestock.

Nearly all brought at two changes of clothes with extra wool jackets and hats, and multiple pairs of boots—two to three pairs often wore out on a trip. Along the trail, pioneers would trade

Illustration depicting the Oregon Trail and the dangerous trials faced along the way. Public Domain

Illustration of Samuel K. Barlow, Public Domain.

A sign along the route that he and Philip Foster created for the last portion of the Oregon Trail. Public Domain

Monument along the Old Oregon Trail (before Barlow Road) to Robert Newell, Joseph Meek and others that helped pave the way and lead many west. Public Domain

In 1840, two men named Robert Newell and Joseph Meek, along with their families, arrived in Walla Walla in Oregon Country with 3 wagons. They were the first to reach the Columbia River over land.

In 1843 the "Great Migration," as history calls it, had anywhere from 700-1,000 emigrants that traveled to Oregon Country. Their guide was a former U.S. Army Captain and fur trader, John Gantt. He charged a dollar per person for the trip to Fort Hall along the Snake River in present-day Idaho. Fort Hall was run by Hudson's Bay Company. Upon their arrival, they were advised to abandon their wagons and move forward on their pack animals. The new leader, Marcus Whitman, disagreed, and the pioneers went forth as they had. The trip went as expected, until it didn't.

Photograph of the "Great Migration" of the Oregon Trail. Public Domain

The first significant obstacle they faced was in the Blue Mountains of Oregon Country. Here they had to clear cut a trail through dense forests. After this, their next hurdle would divide them.

As they arrived to The Dalles, they came upon the raging Columbia River that could not to be crossed. Before them, they believed there was only one option. The Lolo Trail would be used to herd the animals through to get by Mt. Hood, this trail was too rough for the wagons. By faith, they would take their wagons apart, protect what they could, and send it all down the Columbia, hoping to be reunited with their possessions once again. How many people herded animals and how many people rafted down with the wagons and supplies is unknown. What is known is that a man by the name of Samuel K. Barlow didn't like the idea of this path. He believed there was another way, a better way around Mt. Hood that would take them into the Willamette Valley, their ultimate destination.

Of about 100 wagons, 70 took the first option. 30 wagons decided to trust their new leader. Samuel K. Barlow knew there was a better way.

"God never made a mountain that had no place to go over it or around it," he proclaimed.

The 30-wagon caravan went forth, separating from the rest. First, the

Painting of the "Great Migration" of the Oregon Trail. Public Domain

pioneers went south of The Dalles, turned southwest at Tygh Valley, then west forging an overland trail up and over Mt. Hood, at an elevation of 4,155 feet. This trail forged would become known to all as Barlow Road. Barlow joined up with Philip Foster, and the two men led the formation of this important passage through the wilderness in the spring of 1846, with only hand axes and saws.

Barlow Road was the first to be built over the Cascade Range. It also ended up being the final leg of the Oregon Trail, which ends in present-day Oregon City. This last portion of this iconic trail was the most arduous section of all, not only to pass through, but for the men who built it.

TOP LEFT: Wagon train along the Oregon Trail. MIDDLE TOP: Family at rest along the Oregon Trail. MIDDLE CENTER: At night, or when threatened during the day, the wagons would stop moving. The drivers then would line up all the carriages in a circle. This was a way of protecting the settlers from attack. They would keep their cattle and other animals within the circle. TOP RIGHT: A sole pioneer with his wagon on the Oregon Trail. BOTTOM LEFT: The museum found at the end of the Oregon Trail in Oregon City, Oregon. MIDDLE BOTTOM: Old time photo of Oregon City which was where the Oregon Trail, ended. BOTTOM RIGHT: A sign for weary travelers needing direction. ALL: Public Domain

A Closer Look!

at what you have learned in the last 6 lessons!

PLUS+

This Lesson's Geography:

Historic Canals

Erie Canal
Pennsylvania Canal
Chesapeake & Ohio Canal

Ohio & Erie Canal
Miami & Erie Canal

Previous Learned Geography:

Listed here is the geography learned over the last 6 lessons. All lessons learned before the last 6 lessons are no longer on the map.

Cumberland Road
Santa Fe Trail
Mormon Trail
Gila Trail
Old Spanish Trail
California Trail
Oregon Trail
Colorado River
Red River
Rio Grande River
Columbia River
Great Salt Lake
St. Lawrence River
Ohio River
Mississippi River
Missouri River

Arkansas River
Chesapeake Bay
Hudson Bay (Canada)
San Francisco Bay
Puget Sound
Pamlico Sound
Lake Huron
Lake Ontario
Lake Michigan
Lake Erie
Lake Superior
Cascade Mountains
Mt. Rainier
Mt. St. Helens
Denali

Lesson 20

Hudson Bay in Canada

Zoom Me In!

Use this sheet as a reference for this lesson's worksheets. Be sure to practice until you don't have to look!

United States of America Physical Features

Historic Canals
Erie Canal
Pennsylvania Canal
Chesapeake & Ohio Canal
Ohio & Erie Canal
Miami & Erie Canal

Lesson 20

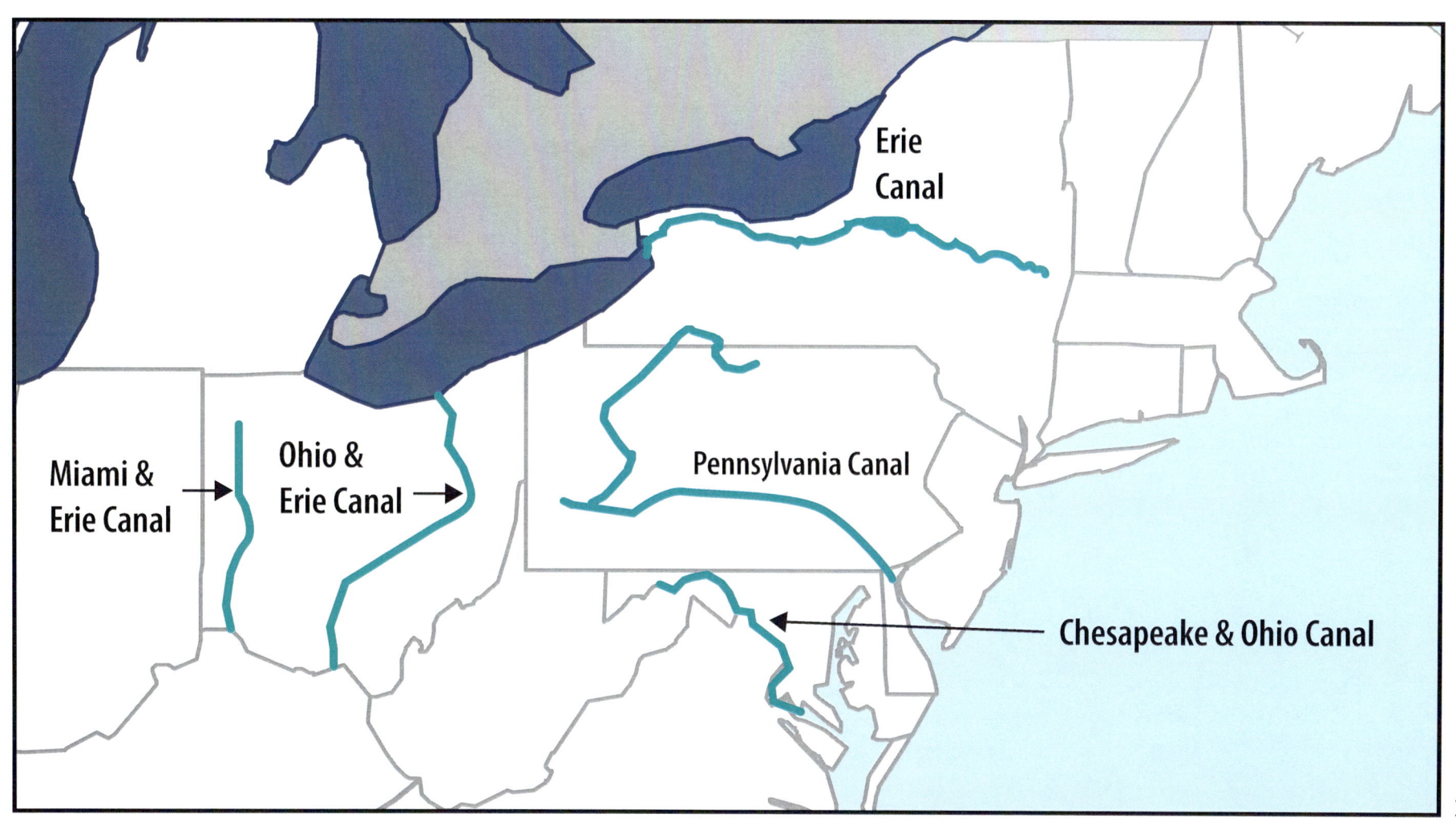

217

This Lesson's Geography:
Historic Canals

Erie Canal
Pennsylvania Canal
Chesapeake-Ohio Canal
Ohio-Erie Canal
Miami-Erie Canal

Tid-Bits

In learning about these four historic canals, you will discover they have common purposes. First, it provided a way to get products to far away customers. Canal shipping was less expensive, which lowered costs for trade, increasing profit for businesses. This allowed America to depend less on European imports and more heavily rely on its own resources. For long distance travel, canals replaced wagons, for travel by boat. The Allegheny Portage Railroad and Public Works system, combined with the canals, increased trade speed. What once took 23 days to travel from Philadelphia to Pittsburgh, then only took 4 days. These historic canals were a giant step in building the nation's economy and influencing western expansion. Now that we understand what the canals have in common, let's learn about what makes them unique!

The Erie Canal

In 1807, a flour merchant named Jesse Halle tried to sell his flour to cities along the eastern coast. He went flat broke in the process. While sitting in the debtor's prison, he wrote a set of letters. Within, he detailed his thoughts about a canal system that would get his product to market faster. It would cover 400 miles from Buffalo, New York, on the eastern shore of Lake Erie to Albany, New York, on the Hudson River. His ideas were smart, and they got the attention of New York politicians. Mayor Dewitt Clinton believed that the canal

Present-day Erie Canal, Public Domain

would be a significant economic success for his city.

The Erie Canal ended up being 363 miles long and connected the Great Lakes with New York City via the Hudson River. It was considered a complex and challenging venture when it was designed, but that did not stop the project. When built, the canal provided a direct route from New York City to the Midwest. Hereafter, all the states inland now had a way to move their goods back-and-forth quickly and inexpensively.

Lesson 20

When it was designed, as mentioned, it was thought to be a tough project... and it was. Throughout the construction of the canal, many of Clinton's associates criticized the project calling it "Clinton's Folly" or "Clinton's Ditch." The reason, was that the construction of the canal through the Appalachian Mountains proved to be difficult and dangerous. It took canal laborers eight years to finish the canal. They used animal power, axes, and blasting powder to get through the massive rock. With about 50,000 workers, approximately 1,000 were killed on the job. The deaths came from diseases within swampy terrain, careless use of gunpowder while blasting, drowning, and many canal collapses that buried workers under tons of rock.

The original Erie Canal was a major engineering feat. West Point Academy in New York had the only engineering program in North America. This project provided for the education of a new generation of American engineers and builders to come forward. Engineers invented new equipment to uproot trees and stumps, and they also invented cement that hardened underwater!

Erie Canal, mid 1900s - Public Domain

Erie Canal Towpath, whereas the horses are towing this barge. Public Domain

The Erie Canal opened in October of 1825. The first group of boats sailed from Buffalo to New York City in just 10 days, which was record time.

With New York City becoming the great gateway to all the abundant resources inland, it soon became the nation's economic center, and the first port of entry for immigrants from Europe. Between 1820 and 1850, New York City's population grew four times over. The canal also provided an economic boost to the whole country. Businesses now could ship their products for a tenth of what it cost before the Erie Canal was built. This canal helped New York City become the commercial capital that it is today.

Manufactured goods like furniture, clothing, and food could be shipped to the inland frontier. Farmers now had the ability to send their crops of corn and wheat to the east coast markets. And poor, indebted Jesse Halle, hopefully lived to see the day that he could send his flour east.

The Erie Canal also started the idea of tourism. Vacationers, including Europeans, such as Charles Dickens, visited the canal on different excursions from New York City to Niagara Falls.

The Erie Canal covered the homelands of several groups of Indians. The state and federal policies wanted to remove the Indians from their land. They sent the Indians to isolated parts of New York and other states. Some were sent out west to parts of the Louisiana territory.

TOP RIGHT: Construction of an Erie Canal Lock. **MIDDLE RIGHT:** Digging out the area where the canal was being built. **BELOW:** Historical illustration of the Erie Canal. **ALL:** Public Domain

By 1918, the Erie Canal was made twice as wide and twice as deep, so more ship traffic could sail. When the Saint Lawrence Seaway was built in 1959, that waterway replaced the Erie Canal.

In 2000, Congress made the Erie Canal a National Heritage Corridor to preserve the state's historic canal, and the communities that cropped up along the way.

The Pennsylvania Canal

The canal era began in 1797 within Pennsylvania. The first canal built was to carry riverboats along the Susquehanna River around Conewago Falls. Then, the great Erie Canal was built, giving New York a competitive advantage over Pennsylvania. Well, that just would not do! New York state would not be the only to move people and materials to and from the country's interior. Pennsylvania moved quickly to begin a statewide project building canals for hundreds of miles.

The "Pennsylvania Canal" is better termed the "Pennsylvania Canal System" for the "system" is made up of not only canals, but also dams, locks, towpaths, aqueducts, viaducts, and railroad. The Pennsylvania Canal, as found on your maps, is a small representation of the entire system. What's more important to understand about the Pennsylvania Canal System, is why it was created, what it did for Pennsylvania, how it was used for the Underground Railroad, and finally, why it is no longer used.

Pennsylvania Canal system

Map by W.H.Shank, P.E.

Public Domain

The Pennsylvania Canal System was built to move bulky goods and connect Philadelphia to Pittsburgh. More importantly, this system would move people and products to new growth markets in the developing Northwest Territory via the Ohio River. This created a marketplace that could compete with New York.

Many canal systems were already in place. Privately paid for by industry that needed to move their products to other parts of the state. Then the "Pennsylvania Main Line Canal" connected all of the private canals. This allowed movement of people and goods much farther than the smaller unconnected canals. This integration was foundational to Pennsylvania becoming an industrial powerhouse. It allowed people to travel from Pennsylvania to Pittsburgh in three and a half days. Naturally, this increased tourism as well.

As a crowning achievement, the Pennsylvania Canal system erected the Allegheny Portage Railroad topping 2,100 feet in elevation. As the name denotes, this railroad ascended and descended the Allegheny Mountains. Then, to continue the journey, passengers and cargo would transfer to a wheeled flat car, which had halved canal boats placed on them to continue on the waterway canal system.

It was a really big deal! The Pennsylvania Canal System was an engineering marvel of its time.

North Branch of the Pennsylvania Canal System, near Shickshinny. Public Domain

An unexpected result of the Pennsylvania Canal was the rise of the Underground Railroad. Slaves traveled from the south to the north to get to Canada. The Pennsylvania Canal, was one escape path. Some freedom seekers traveled the canal by boat at night with "agents" of the Underground Railroad, guiding the way. One slave, Jacob Green, escaped from his master in the south and traveled as a paying customer on the Allegheny Portage Railroad.

Jacob Green was one of the famous cases of a slave using the canal system to escape. He escaped from a farm in present-day West Virginia. Then he returned and stole a horse from the same farm and fled again. On a third visit to the area from which he had escaped, he rescued five slaves from a nearby farm. Upon his arrival in Pennsylvania, he was accused of stealing the horse and being a runaway slave. Which, as we know, he was guilty of.

Allegheny Portage Railroad, National Historic Site. Public Domain

Early train transporting people for tourism, Public Domain

burg to get to the canal system. He was utterly committed to abolition and frequently risked his life and freedom to assist others. He described himself as a "violent abolitionist."

Like Sam Williams, James Heslop was also an abolitionist and an agent of the Underground Railroad. He was a white man that did not struggle with freedom. Still, he was committed to helping African-Americans make their way to freedom. Because of this, his house was frequently searched by slave hunters. In his zeal to help slaves escape, he had several secret hiding places in his home to temporarily keep them safe while he hid them. One was an old abandoned mine, and another was a cellar underneath his stable. He never lost one slave.

While the canals offered a route to move people and goods, it did not provide great speed. Railroads with locomotives powerful enough to haul heavy loads of grain, coal, and other essential products, were the fastest way to get the job done! While the canals' usefulness was brief, lasting only about 50 years, this giant technological advancement brought us forward. For Pennsylvania, it made the state one of the most important industrial states in the nation.

**President John Quincy Adams
Public Domain**

Jacob Green had made it to the "free state" of Pennsylvania. However, according to the Fugitive Slave Act of 1850, by law, if he were guilty of being an escaped slave, Pennsylvania authorities would need to send him back.

He was almost arrested but escaped through the back door of a friend's barbershop, never to be seen again. It was assumed that Green finally made it to Canada as a free man. He used the Pennsylvania Canal as part of his escape route.

Who was this barbershop friend of Jacob Green's? None other than Samuel Williams. An African-American man, born and raised in Pennsylvania. He dedicated his life as an extraordinary abolitionist, who worked to free slaves. An abolitionist is a person who is entirely against slavery. He was an African-American that became an "agent" for the Underground Railroad. He helped people travel across Pennsylvania through Hollidays-

The Chesapeake-Ohio Canal

On July 4th, 1828, President John Quincy Adams began the opening ceremonies for the construction of the Chesapeake-Ohio Canal. In the 19th and early 20th century, this canal provided jobs and opportunities for people from the Potomac River Valley in Washington, D.C., to the mountains of western Maryland.

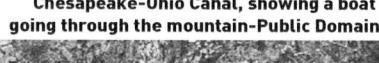
Chesapeake-Ohio Canal, showing a boat going through the mountain-Public Domain

Today, what remains of this canal provides a place to enjoy nature and recreation but, most importantly, tells the story of the important role it had in American history. Stories about transportation, the Civil War, industry, and commerce that influenced America's growth.

Initially, George Washington tried to improve this swampy area by constructing canals, but it was never completed.

Later, a company was formed called the C & O Canal Company. They raised over $3 million from private and

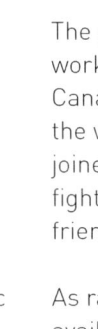

Public Domain

Towpath along the Ohio-Erie Canal. Public Domain

public investors, including the federal government, as well as the states of Maryland and Virginia. They all hoped the waterway would bring trade and, therefore, jobs. The canal was finished in 1815 at the cost of $11 million.

Boats began to appear on the canal after the first short section was completed. As sections opened, more and more trade moved along the canal. In fact, trade was so busy that more than 500 boats were operating on the canal at the same time. Coal was one of the most essential products to be shipped. The Chesapeake-Ohio Canal was intended to go all the way to the Ohio River,

but it never made it that far.

The Chesapeake-Ohio Canal ran alongside the Potomac River. During the Civil War, this canal was a dividing line between the Union and the Confederacy. The canal was essential to both sides.

The Union forces protected the canal, using it for transportation purposes, moving troops and war supplies. At the same time, the Confederates tried to damage both the canal and the boat traffic. It became the battleground for many raids and fights.

The people who worked at the C & O Canal were divided by the war. Boatmen joined both sides, fighting against former friends and neighbors.

As railroads became available, canal traffic began to decline. This, along with a significant economic depression and floods, resulted in financial distress. The government sold the entire canal for 2 million dollars to the National Park Service.

In 1961, President Eisenhower proclaimed the canal a national monument. In 1971, Congress declared the C & O Canal a national historical park, saving its historical features for everyone to enjoy. Today visitors can examine the locks and take rides on canal boats, bike, or walk along much of the 185-mile canal trail.

The Ohio-Erie Canal

In the early 1800s, most of the United States was still wilderness settled by Indian nations. Many European settlers came west to places like the Cuyahoga Valley, Ohio, looking for productive farmland. Once they raised their crops, they had only their local community to sell their goods to. Ohio's location was isolated, and it was difficult to get goods back-and-forth to the east coast.

George Washington and Thomas Jefferson talked about solving this problem in the 1780s when

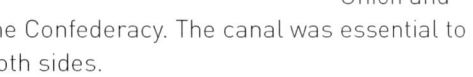

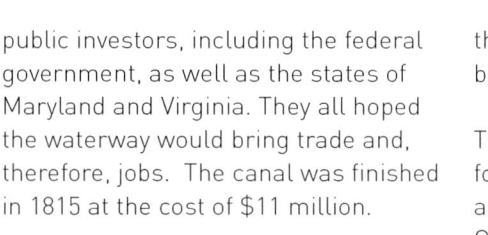

Historic illustration of one of many battles fought on the Chesapeake and Ohio Canal during the Civil War. Public Domain

19th century image of a canal boat being brought along on a towpath along the Ohio and Erie Canal in greater Akron area. Public Domain

TOP LEFT, MIDDLE, & RIGHT: The Great Flood of 1913 in Ohio that wrecked the Ohio-Erie Canal. Public Domain

that land became America's after the French and Indian War. However, the United States was a young nation with undeveloped resources for tackling such an endeavor. In the east, the economy depended on imports from Europe. The west had no way to export over the Appalachian Mountains. The first steps toward uniting a country geographically divided began in 1817, with the Erie Canal construction. Pennsylvania was in the midst of creating their network of canals, and Ohio knew it would benefit them also. In 1822, the state legislature passed a resolution to survey the land. The Ohio-Erie Canal would link the great Ohio River to Lake Erie. Construction began in 1825, finishing in 1832. By connecting Ohio to New York and into New Orleans in the south, it helped Westward Expansion tremendously. The national market economy and a booming industrial market were created.

Little towns and villages popped up along the path of the canal. They attracted many new businesses, because suddenly transportation was available.

Property values along the canal increased, and the canal provided the nation with mobility. By 1850, Ohio was the third most populated state in the country. Americans were able to buy and sell goods with each other, relying on their own resources rather than turning to Europe. This canal system, along with others that you have learned about in this lesson, helped our young country become an essential player in the world economy.

The canal held water that changed in elevation. This required locks to be built to raise and lower the barges and canal boats. This process of raising and lowering the boats in the locks took time. The happy consequence, was that people would depart from their boats looking for various goods and services. Cities flourished at these lock locations with people needing grocery stores, inns, blacksmith shops, and much more.

The Ohio-Erie Canal stayed in existence until the great flood of 1913. It was the second deadliest flood in the United States, and it brought an end to the Ohio-Erie Canal. The massive amount of rain swept over the state for five days and dropped several weeks-worth of rain in under a week. The entire state flooded; the locks gave way. The dams broke as if they had been hit by dynamite, releasing walls of water from the reservoirs. The water crushed gate after gate of the locks as it rushed into the towns along the canal. After the devastation, they rebuilt the towns. The canal, however, had extensive damage. It was decided not to restore it to its former functionality. The repairs were just too much money. The Ohio-Erie Canal was never used for transportation again.

Today, however, the waterway is a major recreational route. All year-round people visit the Ohio-Erie Canalway National Heritage Area, a national park.

A photo before the Great Flood of 1913. Public Domain

The Miami and Erie Canal was one of Ohio's most important canals during the mid-nineteenth century.

During the late 1810s, Governor Thomas Worthington and Governor Ethan Allen Brown both supported internal improvements, especially canals. Both men

Ohio-Erie Canal towpath trail in downtown Akron. BOTH By Bruce Ford, courtesy of Summit Metro

223

Old time photo of the Miami and Erie Canal. Public Domain

grants to the United States. Many of Ohio's communities today, including Akron, began as towns for the canal workers.

Once completed, the canal faced numerous difficulties. Flooding could do severe damage to the locks, walls, and towpaths, requiring extensive repairs. Especially in northern Ohio when cold weather would cause the canals to freeze. Usually, canals in the northern half of the state were drained dry from November to April. In southern Ohio, canals generally stayed open the entire year.

The difficulties Ohioans faced with the canals paled in comparison to the advantages. Most importantly, the cost to ship goods to and from the east coast declined tremendously, from $125 per ton, to $25 per ton of goods.

Most canals remained in operation in Ohio until the late 1800s. By the 1850s, canals were losing business to the railroads. Railroads had several advantages over the canals, making them much more popular. While railroads cost more to ship people and goods, they could deliver them way quicker than the canals. As well, railroads were not limited by a water source. These advantages put the canals out of business.

believed that Ohioans needed quick and easy access to the Ohio River and Lake Erie, if they were to profit financially. Farmers and business owners would be able to transport their products quickly and cheaply with canals rather than roads. Canals would also open new markets for Ohio goods. Both this canal and the Ohio and Erie Canal were commissioned to be built at the same time.

Canal construction went quickly, but not easily. At the peak of development, there were more than four thousand workers. These workers were em-

ployed by various private business-es that had bid on different portions of the canal. Once the trench for the canal was dug, they laid down sandstone lined with wood. Locks were made exclusively from wood. The submerged wood swelled, creating a waterproof barrier. Workers generally earned thirty cents per day, plus room and board. A typical day began at sunrise and did not end until sunset. While thirty cents per day seems a poor wage in today's money, it was good money back then especially for Irish immi-

Present-day photo of the Miami and Erie Canal. Public Domain

A Closer Look!
at what you have learned in the last 6 lessons!

PLUS+
This Lesson's Geography:
Native American Regions
- Eastern Woodlands
- Plains
- Plateau
- Northwest Coast
- California
- Great Basin
- Southwest

Previous Learned Geography:

Listed here is the geography learned over the last 6 lessons. All lessons learned before the last 6 lessons are no longer on the map.

- Erie Canal
- Pennsylvania Canal
- Chesapeake & Ohio Canal
- Ohio & Erie Canal
- Miami & Erie Canal
- Cumberland Road
- Santa Fe Trail
- Mormon Trail
- Gila Trail
- Old Spanish Trail
- California Trail
- Oregon Trail
- Colorado River
- Red River
- Rio Grande River
- Columbia River
- Great Salt Lake
- St. Lawrence River
- Ohio River
- Mississippi River
- Missouri River
- Arkansas River
- Chesapeake Bay
- Hudson Bay (Canada)
- San Francisco Bay
- Puget Sound
- Pamlico Sound
- Lake Huron
- Lake Ontario
- Lake Michigan
- Lake Erie
- Lake Superior

Lesson 21

NORTHWEST
COAST
TERRITORY

United States of America Physical Features

Zoom Me In! Lesson 21

Use this sheet as a reference for this lesson's worksheets. Be sure to practice until you don't have to look!

Native American Regions

Eastern Woodlands **California**
Plains **Great Basin**
Plateau **Southwest**
Northwest Coast

NORTHWEST
COAST
TERRITORY

PLATEAU
TERRITORY

EASTERN
WOODLANDS
(Northeast)

PLAINS TERRITORY

GREAT BASIN
TERRITORY

CALIFORNIA
TERRITORY

EASTERN WOODLANDS
(Southeast)

SOUTHWEST
TERRITORY

This Lesson's Geography:
Native American Regions

Eastern Woodlands (NE)
Eastern Woodlands (SE)
Plains
Plateau
Northwest Coast
California
Great Basin
Southwest

Tid-Bits
Eastern Woodlands
Northeast Native Americans

Lesson 21

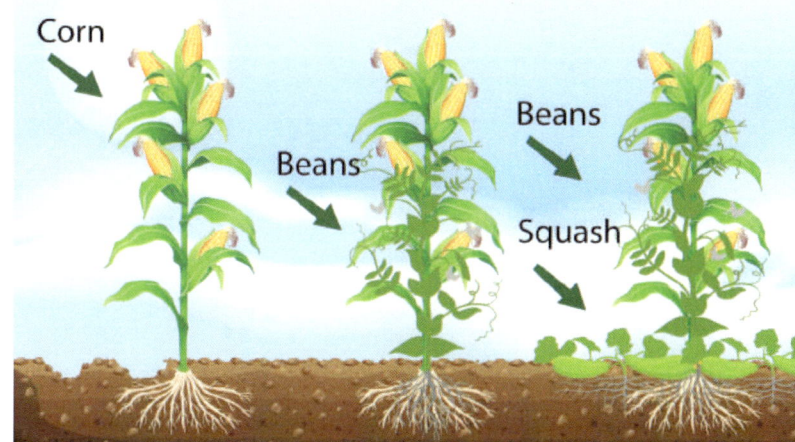
Illustration depicting the "Three Sisters" - Public Domain

Painting of Iroquois Indians. Public Domain

The Algonquian, Iroquois, and Sioux were the dominant tribes of the northern portion of the Eastern Woodlands. These were also the three main Native languages spoken by the northeast tribes. There were many tribes in the northeast, and smaller tribal groups included the Pequot, Menominee, Piasa Bird, Oneida Kickapoo, Huron, Wampanoag, Hiawatha, Abenaki, and Mohican, but there were many, many more.

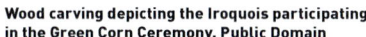
Wood carving depicting the Iroquois participating in the Green Corn Ceremony. Public Domain

There were many different climates and regions in the northeast, including forests and rivers, oceans, meadows, wetlands, and more. Tribes in the northeast were farmers, gatherers, and hunters. They ate deer, fish, birds, maize (corn), nuts, beans, squash, seeds, berries, roots, and more. They even ate maple syrup! The "Three Sisters" are corn, beans, and squash. The Three Sisters were a very important food grouping for these Native Americans because together, these plants were easy to grow, nutritional, and kept for long periods of time.

The Eastern Woodland people of the northeast had a special way of planting these three. Small flat-top soil mounds were created for each crop. Each crop was circular, about a foot high, and 20 inches in diameter. First, they would plant many maize seeds close together in the center. Those tribes nearest the Atlantic Ocean would use rotten fish or eels buried along with the maize seeds for fertilizer. They would patiently wait for the maize to grow to 6 inches tall. Then came the beans and squash seeds that are planted around the maize. They would alternate between the two kinds of seeds. The three plants benefited from each other. The maize provided a structure for the beans to climb. The beans provided nitrogen to the soil that the other plants needed. The squash spreads along the ground, blocking the sunlight. This prevented weeds! The squash leaves also acted as a "living mulch," creating a micro-climate retaining moisture in the soil. The squash's prickly hairs on the vine discouraged pests from eating the beans and corn. Together these vegetables contain complex carbohydrates, essential fatty acids, and all nine essential amino acids, a very healthy diet indeed! Maybe you could try planting a little mound of the "Three Sisters!"

Tribes of the Northeast were surrounded by forested areas, so wood was an essential part of their lives and culture. They used wood to build their homes, make tools, and utensils. They would carve out their dishes and spoons from wood as well. When someone was invited to a feast or meal, they would say, "Come, and bring your bowl and spoon."

Hand carved wooden bowl - Public Domain

Algonquian tribal members - Public Domain

Native American tools for everyday use and hunting - Public Domain

Little Sioux Girl - Public Domain

Depending on people's gender and age, they had different jobs in their family and society. Older people took care of the children and taught them. Women were in charge of taking care of their babies, cooking, making tools, making clothes, fishing, farming, and gathering. Men held council, went to war, hunted, fished, and built houses. Each tribe was divided into different clans or social groups. These clans united people and allowed them to live together and help one another survive. Each clan was known by an animal, like a bear, heron, or hawk.

Sioux Women - Public Domain

Most Northeast Native Americans made decisions as a community. They would talk about a problem, and as a group, they would decide what to do. They had leaders, but none of the leaders made a decision for the entire group. To make a decision, people would have to make convincing arguments for their ideas. Persuasion was a very important skill. Leaders had to be very

ABOVE: Longhouse-Public Domain BELOW: Wigwam - ALL: Public Domain

persuasive and give amazing speeches to impress others and make their idea seem better than everyone else's.

Different tribes lived in different kinds of buildings. Wigwams and longhouses were the most common ways people lived in the northeast.

Wigwams were circles. They were held up by poles and had dome roofs. In the middle of a wigwam, there was a fire pit. When lit, smoke would go up and out of a hole in the ceiling. The fire was for heating and cooking. Depending on what materials were available is what the wigwams were built out of. Most were constructed out of bark, plants, woven leaves, and anything else that could be found. Two or three generations of a family lived in one wigwam together.

Longhouses were long rectangles with an arched roof and two doors—one door on each end. In the middle of the longhouse, there were many hearths for fires to cook over and heat the longhouse. The longer the longhouse, the more fires it had. Most longhouses had five fires. People could walk and live on either side of the hearths. Most longhouses were 22 feet wide and 40 feet long. Some of the biggest families had longhouses as long as 400 feet. Several generations of one family would live in a longhouse.

Eastern Woodlands
Southeast Native Americans

The Chickasaw, Seminole, Creek, Cherokee, Choctaw, Natchez, Yuchi, Pascagoula, Caddo, and more made up the Native American tribes of the Eastern Woodlands in the southeast. It is a diverse region made up of sub-tropical areas, grasslands, forests, floodplains, rolling hills, rivers, mountains, and more. The tribes had to survive hot summers, but the winters were mild. This attracted more Native Americans to this area because they didn't have to endure the cold, harsh climate of the north. The land was very diverse, and so were the people, but they had much in common.

The southeast

Cherokee Mother and Baby - Public Domain

Cherokee Indians - Public Domain

Cherokee Woman - Public Domain

region had wild game, and the soil was good for farming in most areas. Different varieties of corn were the most critical food. Out of which they made different types of food products including hominy and corn flour. The tribes also grew beans and squash. Just as in the northeast, the "Three Sisters" were also utilized in the same way. Although their diet went a bit beyond with wild greens, like spinach, which was easy to find. They also grew grapes, plums, walnut trees, potatoes, acorns, berries, and more. They hunted animals like deer, bison, elk, beavers, squirrels, rabbits, and bear. Where they could, tribes would fish.

Women were in charge of providing food for her family by farming, gathering wild food, cooking and preserving food as well. Men's responsibilities included trading, hunting, and going to war. With these duties, men were away much of the time. When they were available, they would build houses as needed, help clear the fields, and harvest in the fall. Older people took care of the children and taught them. They also made baskets, pottery, clothes, and other things the community needed. No matter the station, everyone helped in making ceremonial objects.

Painting of Indian Bird hunt. By Unknown - Public Domain

Modern photo of unknown ceremony of the Nanticoke Indians - Public Domain

229

Tribes in the southeast believed in a connection between people and nature. They deemed the world a spiritual place. Animals, plants, and other natural objects were sacred. Animals had souls, and hunters would only hunt what they needed because they did not want to anger the souls of the animals. Plants were seen as friendly. Corn was so important to the tribes, that almost every tribe had a Green Corn Ceremony.

The southeast tribes wanted to make sure children understood good behavior by rewarding the children when they did good things. When boys killed their first deer, they were celebrated in the same way girls were, when they made their first basket. Bad behavior was often met with jokes and teasing. Boys could play and have fun, but girls were kept indoors, being taught how to do things around the house.

Villages and towns were the common way to live. Most villages were small, but some had as many as 1,000 people. There were two kinds of villages. Some had community buildings for storing food and other goods. While others had community buildings for cooking. In the middle of the village was a ceremonial building for religious ceremonies or community gatherings.

Most of the settlements were semi-permanent. They were near good soil and a waterway like a lake or a river. Most houses were rectangular with thatched roofs and open sides to let the breeze keep the people cool.

Plains Native Americans

Tribes living in the plains lived in vast grasslands. There was lots of space to roam. Life was harder for the Plains tribes because their food was less plentiful and harder to find. Fewer people lived in the Plains region because of this. Those that did had very similar ways of living. The Plains Native American tribes included: Blackfoot, Arapaho, Assiniboine, Mandan, Cheyenne, Comanche, Crow, Gros Ventre, Kiowa, Lakota, Lipan, Apache, Cree, Ojibwe, Sarsi, Stoney, and Tonkawa. The Comanche and

the Lakota were the most powerful tribes in the region.

People living close to the Missouri and Mississippi rivers had more plentiful food and water. Plains Native Americans depend-

Hunting Buffalo in the Plains. By: Alfred Jacob Miller

Illustration of a Plains Indian – Public Domain

Mandan girls gathering berries. By: Edward S. Curtis, c. 1908, Library of Congress, Public Domain

ed on growing maize (corn), beans, squash, and sunflowers. They also hunted elk, buffalo, small game, fish, birds, and anything else they could find. Maize was an essential part of the Plains people's diets. It could be eaten raw, dried as a whole kernel to be saved for the winter time, or be ground into cornmeal. Corn was easy to grow in the region, and still grows there today. They would plant their crops in the spring, hunt during the summer, and harvest in the fall.

Horses were a significant part of life for the Plains people. However, horses were not native to North America. In 1541, Spain brought them for trade. Before horses, Indians depended on dogs to carry things, but they couldn't go very far. When horses arrived, the Plains Indians were able to travel farther and hunt better. Horses gave them access to different animals, food, and land. Life became more manageable.

Younger people were expected to treat older people with respect, but joking around and teasing were important parts of the culture. Joking was a way to have fun. It was also a way of making sure younger people knew the right way to act. Everyone joked, and if a person did not, they did not have a good reputation in the tribe.

Chickasaw Native American Girls

Comanche Native Americans - Public Domain

An Omaha Hunter, Engraving by: C.A. Powell Public Domain

Stoney Native American Mother and Child. Public Domain

Blackfoot Native American Woman By Edward S. Curtis -Public Domain

Tribes were groups of families, so people were surrounded by their extended family. Plains children were raised by their grandparents, siblings, aunts, uncles, and other family members. Children were socialized at a young age and learned through play. Girls were given dolls to take care of, because they would take care of children when they were older. Boys were given toy bows and arrows to practice shooting, and gain strength as they grew to be hunters.

People on the plains often lived in tepees when they were hunting or looking for food. Tepees were easy to pick up and move because they were made from buffalo skin and three or four poles. Two or three generations could live in one. Within, a fire would burn in the center to keep it warm and give off light. The tepees were decorated with artwork representing the family

Cheyenne mother and baby-Public Domain

Lakota Native American By Edward S. Curtis -Public Domain

4 Arapaho Native American Women in front of a tepee on the plains. Public Domain

Lakota Oglala War Party. By: Edward S. Curtis, Public Domain

history. During the winter months, Plains people lived in earth lodges. They were much bigger than tepees, but like the tepees, they were circular. At the door, people often had a knocker made out of deer hooves to jangle.

The Plains people had a seasonal cycle that determined where they lived. They lived in an earth lodge during the winter to protect themselves from deadly storms. In the spring, they planted crops to grow. In the summer, the hunters would leave the tribe with their tepee to forage wild food, and hunt for animals. In the fall, they would return to their crops to harvest. Later in the fall, before winter came, they would hunt once again, and preserve the food for the winter. When winter came, they moved back into their earth lodges.

Plateau Native Americans - Tribe Unknown - Public Domain

Columbia Plateau Native Americans on horses in 1908 By: Benjamin Gifford-Public Domain

Plateau Native Americans

Salish, Shuswap, Kalispel, Okanagan, Sinkaietk, Wenatchee, Ntlakapamux, Sahaptin, Nez Percé, Kutenai, Walla Walla, Modoc, Yakama, Klamath, and more made up the tribes of the Plateau Native Americans. They lived in an area of extremes. In the winter, the temperatures could be freezing, down to –30 °F. In the summer, the humidity could be high, with temperatures reaching into the 100s °F. The earth is covered in grassland, steppe, and wooded areas.

Plateau tribes were hunters and gatherers, relying on wild food to survive. They hunted deer, elk, caribou, bear, and birds with short spears, as well as bows and arrows. In the winter, they tracked animals through snow and forests. They fished with spears, nets, and traps to catch eels, trout, salmon, and other fish. They would gather wild carrots, parsnips, berries, nuts, onions, and bitterroot.

The famous Chief Joseph of the Nez Perce Tribal Nation

Plateau Indians - Painting - Public Domain

Plateau North Americans

Walla-Walla Nez Perce-Public Domain

Trade was essential for tribal culture. They traded with each other but also with tribes from the Northwest Coast, the Great Basin, and Great Plains regions. Products and goods from the Plateau tribes could be found as far away as California and Alaska because the trade routes and relationships had been well established for generations. Trading allowed the Plateau tribes to survive during difficult times. It also helped them make friends and communicate with people from far away.

When boys turned a certain age, they went on a vision quest. A vision quest meant that the boy would spend time on a mountaintop, where he would not eat anything for days. While he was on the mountaintop, he hoped he would be able to communicate with a spirit guardian. When he returned to his village after his vision quest, he was a man.

Tribes made decisions together. No one person made a decision for the tribe. The "chiefs" were leaders, but they did not make decisions. Their perspective lent knowledge for the tribe to make decisions. All tribes depended on their chiefs and families to keep the peace, maintain traditions, and pass down customs. Chiefs were given respect because of their wisdom and bravery. Some tribes had women in places of authority and respect.

During the winter, people in the Plateau region lived in permanent villages. They had semi-permanent camps scattered throughout their region, that were close to plentiful hunting and gathering areas. Once horses arrived in America during the mid 1500s, Plateau tribes became more nomadic because they could travel farther and faster to hunt buffalo. Villages were as small as a hundred people or as a big as a thousand. During difficult times, tribes would come together and help one another in their villages. These villages were close to rivers and lakes, which gave them a bountiful place to fish during the winter months.

There were two kinds of houses for Plateau tribes. Semi-subterranean houses were made by digging a circle several feet into the ground. They could be as wide as 40 feet. The roof was a cone of wood and bark. The smoke hole in the roof was also the door that people would go in and out of. People would have to walk on the roof and climb down a ladder to get into the house. Surface houses were built by leaning posts together and then covering them with mats or canvas. These houses became more popular as time went by. They were similar to tepees, but less mobile.

Northwest Coast Native Americans

The Tillamook, Chinook, Tlingit, Hupa, Coos, Tsimshian, Kwakiutl, Haida, Bella Coola, Salish, and other tribes lived in the Northwest Coast region of the United States. These tribes lived along the Pacific coast and had access to the ocean, fjords, rivers, and waterways. So much of their way of life had to do with water resources. The area has many mountains and dense forests, making their environment abundant in wildlife and varied in climate.

Northwest Coast Native Americans with their art-Public Domain

These tribes lived off the land like other Native American tribes. Still, they

Northwest Coast Native American Men and their Canoes-Public Domain-circa 1906

Public Domain

Northwest Coast Native Americans fishing on the Cililo Falls on the Columbia river

A group attending a Potlatch pose for a photo. Public Domain

focused primarily on fishing and gathering. Some of the fish they would eat included: herring, salmon, smelt, cod, mollusks, and gray whales. Some fished from the shores, and others built canoes to make fishing on lakes and in the ocean easier.

The region had lots of food to eat, and they did not have to work hard to survive. They often had more food than needed, which allowed the tribes to have more people and complex societies. There was a hierarchy of families within the tribes. Some families were considered more important than others. This importance was passed down from parents to children. These families would have control over specific resources that other people or tribes needed, making them powerful.

A potlatch, which is a showy feast, was a big deal to the Northwest Coast tribal culture. Held only by the most wealthy and influential families in the tribes. At a potlatch, the family would give away food and other gifts to show how much wealth and power they had. These feasts held ceremonial and governmental importance.

Northwest Coast Native American Wood Carved Art Public Domain

Art was a meaningful part of the Northwest Coastal tribal culture. A lot of their art was created from carving wood. They would make beautiful carvings out of red cedar, redwoods, and other large hardwood trees. They used sharkskin to sand the wood, so it was smooth to the touch. Some of the things they would carve were used for ceremonies, and others were for transportation, like canoes and paddles. Other art was pragmatic and included items used for hunting or eating. As well as the most recognizable totem-pole.

During the summer, people worked very hard to hunt and gather all the food they would need to eat during the cold winter months. The tribe would send small groups of people to different areas to gather food and resources. During the summer months, they would live in small homesteads on beaches or riverbanks. When winter came, they would all go back to their village. The villages had large permanent houses where people lived, worked, and made art.

The Northwest Coast Native American Totem-pole-Public Domain

These houses were all rectangular with floors, plank walls, and plank roofs. Some were very large. In the middle, there would be a large fire pit where cooking and entertaining would occur. The houses could quickly be taken apart and transported on canoes if the tribe had to move somewhere else. Some tribes would have a clubhouse and a sweat lodge for the entire tribe to use and gather in.

California Native Americans

Many tribes make up California Native Americans. Karok, Maidu, Cahuilleno, Mojave, Yokuts, Pomo, Paiute, Modoc, and many more. A diverse group of peoples and cultures peacefully lived on the land.

Recreation of Northwest Coast Native American Home-Public Domain

The California Native Americans enjoyed plentiful food, a pleasant climate, and healthy land. Many tribes depended on foraging for nuts. Acorns were a staple of many tribes. They would use bows and arrows, throwing sticks, snares, traps, and more to catch their food. Hunting and fishing was how they provided meat for their people.

California Native American man from the Hupa tribe
By: Edward S. Curtis, Library of Congress, Public Domain

California Native American Shaman-Public Domain

Men and women had their jobs. Men were often the hunters. Women and children were the gatherers, and they used nets and baskets to collect their food. Women sometimes hunted small game like rabbits and mice, using traps.

Shamans were religious people within the tribes. There were two principal religions for the California Native Americans: Kuksu and Toloache. They had a lot of economic, political, and social power because people listened to, and respected them. Each tribe had at least one shaman, and some had many more. Both men and women could be shamans. Many people went to them to be healed physically and mentally. They were seen as healers, advisers, artists, and poets.

Marriages were often arranged by tribes and families. When the couple married, the wife went to live with her husband's family to learn the ways of his people. The husband's family gave his new wife's family goods. People who

California Native American Village-Public Domain

could have children were responsible for providing food for the community. The older generation took care of the babies and little kids. The children were taught and looked after by grandmas, grandpas, aunts, and uncles.

Life was different in the California Native American Territory than it was in other tribal regions. They experienced peaceful lives without the threat of war. This allowed their focus to be fruitful in other areas of life. Art was a part of their lives, as was storytelling. Their storytelling was a beautiful way to pass the time, and remember their history. People also sang songs. Most songs were short, but some songs could last many days, because they told very long stories. Their focus was also on their civil structure. Many formed tribelets, which was a small segment of the tribe that governed itself. Most tribelets would live together, and establish a permanent village to live in all year round.

People lived in all sorts of houses. Some were permanent, and others were temporary. Their homes were perfect for the area they lived in. In northern California, people built homes made out of wood. In southern California, people made houses out of thatched palm. In the desert, people made homes out of brush. Around Sacramento, people lived in houses dug into the earth. All over the California area, people made earthen houses out of the mud. Houses came in all sizes and were made from lots of different materials from their environment. Some were small dwellings, not much bigger than a tiny bedroom or a big closet. Other's lived in houses resembling apartments. Several

California Native American Art on Tepee-Public Domain

Engraving image of a group of California Native Americans. Public Domain

Summer huts of California Indians.
Engraved Image-Public Domain

California Native American artful jugs-Public Domain

TOP LEFT:
Engraving of California Native Americans canoing.
MIDDLE LEFT:
Engraving of California Native Americans Hunting.
BOTTOM LEFT:
Engraving of California Native American Fishing with a spear. **ALL: Public Domain**

Painting of Comanche Indians, Public Domain

Navajo Weaver, By: Edward S. Curtis
Library of Congress, Public domain

Paiute Indian Men-Public Domain

families had their own space to live in, but the buildings were attached.

Great Basin Native Americans

Great Basin Native American tribes included the Comanche, Navajo, Hopi, Bannock, Shoshone, Paiute, Washoe, Ute, Numa, Mono, Shoshone-Bannock, Gosiute, and others. They lived in an area with mountains, deserts, basins, and a few plateaus. The weather could be very cold and scorching hot, depending on the area. It was not an easy place to live, but many tribes made their home in the Great Basin.

Rare set of Comanche arrowheads excavated from the Bear Creek Comanche campground active in the 1800's. The site occupied some mile of frontage along the cold spring fed waters of Bear Creek. Arrowheads were excavated in the 1970s by John Pruett of Liberty Hill, Texas.
Public Domain

Navajo on horseback in the Canyon de Chelly
By: Edward S. Curtis, Library of Congress, Public Domain

To survive, these tribes had great hunters and gatherers. They depended on bows and arrows, knives, spears, nets, harpoons, hooks, and traps to catch rabbits, antelope, buffalo, waterfowl, deer, mountain sheep, elk, birds, and fish. If the tribe had access to rivers and lakes, they did a lot of fishing. Although the tribes hunted and fished, 70% of their food was grown. They depended on plants, roots, seeds, and nuts to survive. The area was not great for farming, so most of their food grew wild.

When Europeans arrived, they brought with them horses. Some Great Basin tribes decided to use horses, while others did not. Tribes that did, lived in the northern and eastern parts of the Great Basin region. These tribes began using tepees and living more nomadic lives. They also started hunting bison like the Plains tribes. Great Basin tribes that did not use horses continued to live the way they always had.

Tribes in the Great Basin area were small. Having a small group allowed them to move quickly and often so they would not run out of food. Tribes did not stay together. They would only come together for a few days for special occasions. Some of these occasions were in the spring for rabbit drives, hunts, and when fish were plentiful. Come, autumn, together, they would gather to forage for piñon nuts while they were in season. These small tribes did not have large governing bodies or politics like other tribes. They were busy hunting and gathering food to eat.

Comanche Chief, By: Quanah Parker-Library of Congress, Public Domain

Marriage traditions depended on the tribe. When a couple got married, they would have choices about who they lived with. Sometimes the wife would live with her husband's family. Sometimes the husband would live with the wife's family. A married couple would often live on their own, when they had a baby. Decisions like this were many times based on food supply. In their culture, it was easy for a married couple to get divorced if the marriage was unhappy. People liked being married because it meant there was less work for one person to do. So even if a person got divorced, they would get married again soon to someone else.

Great Basin tribes had a harder life than in other regions because the food was hard to find and hunt. Many villages were not permanent because the land couldn't support people for more than a few days at a time. Come winter, however, they stayed in one place because it was too cold to move. Tribes used two kinds of shelters. In the summer, they lived in a semicircle made out of the brush to keep the wind away. In the winter, they lived in homes with domed roofs made out of brush, grass, or mats.

Three Comanche Native American Men-Public Domain

Southwest Native Americans

Apache, Pueblos, Navajo, Hopi, Hualapai, Yuman, Pima, Mojave, Tohono O'odham, Tiwa, Jicarilla Apache, Maricopa, and more, were the tribes of the Southwest. It was a very populated area that is made up of plains, plateaus, canyons, mesas, basins, and steep escarpments, which is like a cliff. The region has very little rain and many droughts - which means little to no water. Even though it has a dry climate, the land grows many plants that survive desert conditions. The region is plentiful, and the Southwest tribes knew how to live off the land.

Two Apache Indian Women at Campfire. By: Edward S. Curtis-Library of Congress, Public Domain

Southwest Native American Buffalo Hunt Painting-Public Domain

Lakota Sioux War Dance-Public Domain

They were hunters and gatherers. Their diet was made up mostly of plants and small game. They would gather piñon-juniper, cottonwood, yucca, cactus, creosote bush, mesquite, sycamore trees, and more. They hunted rabbits, coyotes, bobcats, mule deer, fish, waterfowl, reptiles, rattlesnakes, and small mammals. Southwest tribes also farmed, which was essential to provide more food than what they could hunt for or gather in the wild. They grew maize (corn), beans, squash, cotton, beans, wheat, melons, apricots, peaches, and more. They also raised turkeys, dogs, sheep, and donkeys. When they had access to water, they would fish!

Many Southwest tribes were matrilineal, which means kinship or family. This is where men married into a woman's family. In contrast, in western cultures, women marry into men's families, and those cultures are called patrilineal. Some Southwest tribes were bilineal, which means kinship was recognized by both the father and the mother.

Babies were an essential part of families in the tribe. They were loved very much and taken care of with warmth. Southwest tribes did not want to upset children and allowed them to get away with many things. Even as tiny babies, they were included in meals, family circles, and meetings.
The Pueblo people did not have tribes. Instead, they had moieties. Each moiety was in charge of governing themselves.

For tribes that did not move around, they lived in permanent houses called adobes. An adobe is made out of clay and straw baked into a hard brick. These homes were several stories tall. Each home was for one family, and they were connected with other adobe homes. Other Southwest tribes lived in earthen houses, where the ground was dug down into, enforced with a wood frame and packed in with dirt. The roofs were often dome-shaped, with some made out of thatch. These houses helped keep people protected from the desert heat and winds. Regardless of what type of home they lived in, with their vast trade network, their homes were filled with beautiful art from Mexico.

Navajo Grandmother and grandchild - Public Domain

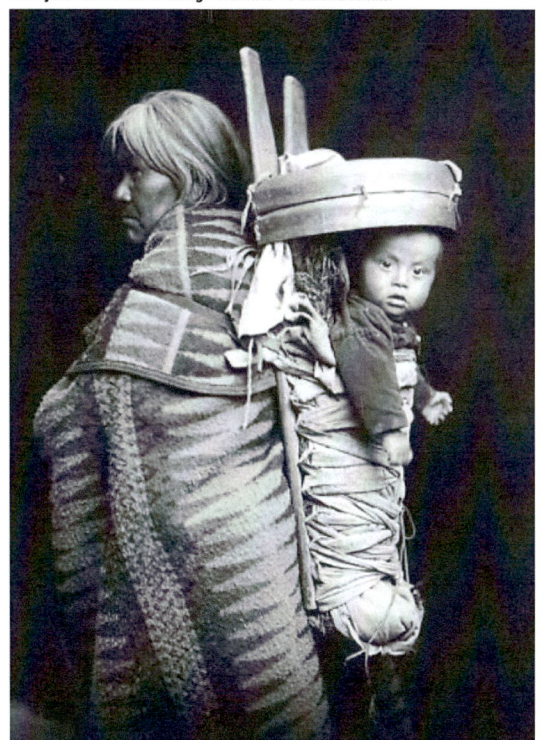

Navajo Yebichai (Yei Bi Chei) dancers. Edward S. Curtis. USA, 1909. The Welcome Collection, London-Public Domain

Rock Village Cave Ancient Arizona Pueblo Ruins-Anasazi, By: Unknown, Public Domain

A Closer Look!

at what you have learned in the last 6 lessons!

Lesson 22

PLUS+
This Lesson's Geography:
Deserts

Mojave Desert   **Painted Desert**
Sonoran Desert   **Great Salt Lake Desert**
Colorado Desert

Previous Learned Geography:

Listed here is the geography learned over the last 6 lessons. All lessons learned before the last 6 lessons are no longer on the map.

Eastern Woodlands	Miami & Erie Canal	Great Salt Lake
Plains	Cumberland Road	St. Lawrence River
Plateau	Santa Fe Trail	Ohio River
Northwest Coast	Mormon Trail	Mississippi River
California	Gila Trail	Missouri River
Great Basin	Old Spanish Trail	Arkansas River
Southwest	California Trail	Chesapeake Bay
Erie Canal	Oregon Trail	Hudson Bay (Canada)
Pennsylvania Canal	Colorado River	San Francisco Bay
Chesapeake & Ohio Canal	Red River	Puget Sound
Ohio & Erie Canal	Rio Grande River	Pamlico Sound
	Columbia River	

Hudson Bay in Canada

NORTHWEST COAST TERRITORY

PLATEAU TERRITORY

Puget Sound

Missouri River

PLAINS TERRITORY

Oregon Trail

Columbia River

GREAT BASIN TERRITORY

CALIFORNIA TERRITORY

Great Salt Lake Desert

Great Salt Lake

Mississippi River

Mormon Trail

EASTERN WOODLANDS (Northeast)

St. Lawrence River

Erie Canal

San Francisco Bay

California Trail

Colorado River

Painted Desert

Mississippi River

Miami & Erie Canal

Ohio & Erie Canal

Pennsylvania Canal

Old Spanish Trail

Mojave Desert

Santa Fe Trail

Oregon Trail

Cumberland Road

Ohio River

Chesapeake & Ohio Canal

Chesapeake Bay

Colorado Desert

Sonoran Desert

Gila Trail

SOUTHWEST TERRITORY

Arkansas River

Red River

EASTERN WOODLANDS (Southeast)

Pamlico Sound

Rio Grande River

Mississippi River

NORTHWEST COAST TERRITORY

Zoom Me In! Lesson 22

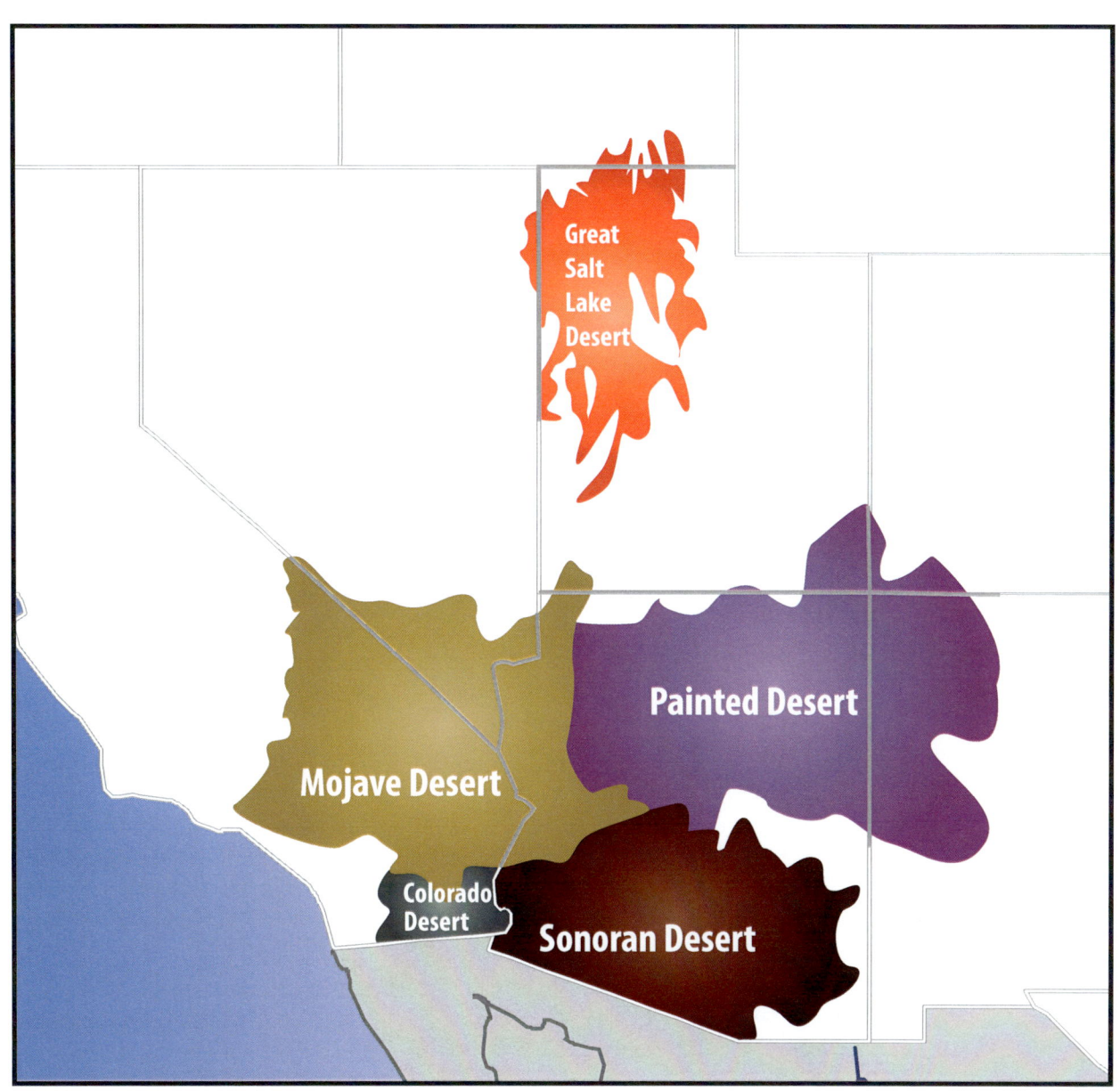

United States of America Physical Features

Use this sheet as a reference for this lesson's worksheets. Be sure to practice until you don't have to look!

Deserts
Mojave Desert
Sonoran Desert
Colorado Desert
Painted Desert
Great Salt Lake Desert

This Lesson's Geography:

Deserts

Mojave Desert
Sonoran Desert
Colorado Desert
Painted Desert
Great Salt Lake Desert

Tid-Bits

Types of Deserts

When you think of a desert, what image comes to mind? Sandy? Rocky? Icy? What kind of temperatures are in a desert? Hot? Warm? Chilly? Freezing? Is it a windy place? Does it have animals or plants? Do you think you would like to live in a desert?

The word desert comes from the Latin word dēsertum, which means 'an abandoned place.' Varying estimates conclude that deserts cover 20-33% of the Earth's surface. Not all deserts are the same. However, a broad definition of a desert, is a barren landscape where little precipitation falls and, consequently, living conditions are hostile for plant and animal life.

There are two types of deserts, hot and cold. Although there are subcategories within these two types of deserts. We will keep it simple for this lesson. However, feel free to dig deeper to discover what different hot and cold deserts there are in our world!

Orange flowering Barrel cacti, found in the Mojave Desert. Public Domain

Lesson 22

HOT DESERTS

During the daytime, hot deserts, often reach above 100°F in the summer. At night, the temperature drops sharply. The Sahara, which you may have learned about, is the world's largest hot desert, and in southern Africa, there is the Kalahari. In this lesson, you will be learning about the hot deserts found in the southwestern United States. Most hot deserts are in a region called the tropics. The tropics are within two latitude lines referred to as the Tropic of Cancer and the Tropic of Capricorn. Between these lines in the center lies the equator. The tropics are the closest to the sun, making the tropics the hottest area on Earth.

COLD DESERTS

Cold deserts are outside of the tropics, farther from the equator than hot deserts. They are quite dry and have few to no plants because it is so cold and dry. A cold desert covers much of Antarctica. The Gobi in central Asia is another cold desert. In the United States, we have the Painted Desert and the Great Salt Lake Desert.

Now that we have learned what types of desserts there are, let's learn about these deserts in the United States.

Joshua Tree set against the sun going down on the Mojave Desert as seen from the Eastland Ranch. Public Domain

Desert Tortoise, Public Domain
Greater Road Runner - Public Domain
Great Basin Collared Lizard, Public Domain
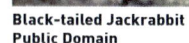
Burrowing Owl, Public Domain

Black-tailed Jackrabbit
Public Domain

The Mojave Desert

Our first desert that we are learning about is the Mojave Desert, located in the southwest. The Native American Mojave tribe lived on the natural vegetation of the area, like prickly pears and agave blooms. They hunted deer and sheep, living close to the Colorado River for fishing and a reliable source of water.

Painting: Jedediah Smith leading the way through the Mojave Dessert, Public Domain

Explorers came to the desert beginning in 1776. Jedediah Smith was the first mountain man to cross the Rocky Mountains, and travel through the Mojave on his way to California, during the gold rush era. Many people followed his route, as they made their way west to mine for gold. Some, however, struck it rich along the way! That's right, in the Mojave, silver was found. This silver mine was named the Bonanza King Mine. In the 1940s, Kaiser Steel Company came to the Mojave, taking more than 2,000,000 tons of iron ore. It was used to build the Liberty Ships for World War II.

Many people have come to the desert, but not all were there to exploit the land. In the 1930s, naturalist Mary Beal hiked in the Providence Mountains identifying and recording different species of plants and wildlife.

This desert biome is rich with wildlife that survives the extreme conditions. In fact, some are only found in the Mojave. These include the Greater Road Runner, the Great Basin Collared Lizard, the Red-spotted Toad, the Desert Tortoise, the Kit Fox, the Burrowing Owl, and the Black-tailed Jackrabbit.

The Sonoran Desert is one of the most tropical deserts in North America, located in Arizona. It has a vast variety of cacti, trees, and flowers, making this desert full of beauty. It receives 3-15 inches of rain each year, mostly falling during the monsoon season, from July to September. The hottest and driest part of this desert is near the lower Colorado River.

Kit Fox, Public Domain

Saguaro Cactus
Public Domain

Barrel Cactus, Public Domain

Horned Sidewinder Rattlesnake, Public Domain

Horned Sidewinder Rattlesnake, Public Domain

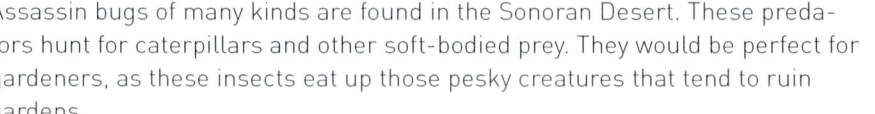

Opuntia Cactus, Public Domain

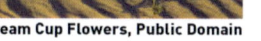

Cream Cup Flowers, Public Domain

The plant life of the Sonoran Desert is the most varied of all North American deserts. It has the tall pole-like Saguaro Cactus, the Barrel Cactus, Organ-pipe Cactus, Cholla, Yucca, Century Plants, and the Palo Verde Tree. Thorn forests also occur in the southern part of this desert. Animal life here is varied and includes the Desert Bighorn sheep, Mule deer, Collared Peccaries, mountain lions, gray foxes, coyotes, and a myriad of snakes, including the fast and venomous horned sidewinder rattlesnake. This snake can travel up to 18 miles per hour! The predators of the desert have an abundant food source, finding rabbits and rodents of all kinds. Birds include roadrunners, Gila woodpeckers, Gambel's quail, a variety of owls and hawks can be spotted if you are lucky!

What about bugs? The Sonoran Desert teems with all sorts of interesting creepy crawling creatures. Here are two that you may never have heard about before now.

Assassin bugs of many kinds are found in the Sonoran Desert. These predators hunt for caterpillars and other soft-bodied prey. They would be perfect for gardeners, as these insects eat up those pesky creatures that tend to ruin gardens.

This common species uses an interesting technique for capturing their food: the tibiae on their front legs is coated with sticky glue, which helps hold their prey while their sharp beak delivers salivary poison. If handled carelessly, these bugs can deliver a painful bite.

Scale insects *(pictured on the following page)* are among the most peculiar insects, as they don't look much like insects at all. In fact, they don't appear to be alive. These bugs are immobile, concealed beneath a blanket of fine white threads made of wax. These wax threads look more like little balls of cotton. The wax offers protection from the sun and possibly predators.

These bugs lead a lazy life drawing sap from their host plant. When the eggs first hatch they give rise to minute legged versions called crawlers that get swept from plant to plant in the breeze. Once they settle down onto a host plant, their legs are rarely ever used again.

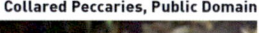

Collared Peccaries, Public Domain

Assassin Bug, Public Domain

TOP LEFT TWO: Scale Bugs. **LEFT:** Cats-Claw. **RIGHT:** Mealy
By: By Obsidian Soul - Own work

Agricultural Area in the Colorado Desert, Public Domain

The Colorado Desert, Public Domain

Coachella Valley Golf, Public Domain

Agriculture in the Sonoran Desert, Public Domain

Usually, when we think of a desert, we do not think of a place where people live and thrive. However, within the desert are two valleys, the Imperial Valley, and the Coachella Valley. These valleys receive irrigation from the Salton Sea. This irrigation brought into the desert has produced many agricultural areas, which brought people. The population of this desert began to grow significantly in the last decades of the 20th century. It has become an attractive retirement and resort spot.

The Colorado Desert is part of the Sonoran Desert and holds much in common. It sits between the Coachella and Imperial Valleys.

A trendy resort called Palm Springs is in the Colorado Desert. The Hoover Dam, built-in 1935, and the All-American Canal in 1940 allowed this region to become popular.

This land is considered a desert because of the lack of rainfall. However, water from the Colorado River keeps it well irrigated. There are 3,000 miles of irrigation canals throughout the region. People plant fields that grow alfalfa, cotton, and sugar beets. Large floodlights are installed in the fields, so that when the days are scorching hot, the field hands can work at night. Truck crops and livestock are numerous.

Truck crops are the name of large scale vegetable crops that are grown to ship to faraway markets. This is made possible through the use of railroads and large refrigerated trucks. Other important crops include cabbage, tomatoes, onions, radishes, celery, strawberries, melons, lettuce, and broccoli.

This canal brings the Colorado River into the Colorado Desert for irrigation and for use by the population. Public Domain

Palm Spring, a resort town in the Colorado Desert, Public Domain

Aerial The Painted Desert, Public Domain

The Painted Desert

One example of a cold desert is the Painted Desert in Arizona. It is named for its landscape of varied and brilliant colors.

This desert is 93,000 acres with colorful rocks ranging from deep lavender to vibrant reds, oranges, and pinks. It is in northern Arizona and stretches from the Grand Canyon National Park eastward to the Petrified Forest National Park.

A large part of it lies within the Navajo Nation. It was named by a Spanish explorer, Francisco Coronado in 1540. He was searching for the Seven Cities of Gold. A mythical place thought to be real in the 16th century, and believed to be in Pueblo country—the Pueblos came before the Navajo's migrated to the area.

Much of the Painted Desert and the Petrified Forest National Park is protected as a national wilderness area. Cars and motorcycles are not allowed in the park, but nature enthusiasts enjoy easy hikes into the beautiful hills.

Owing to the rain shadow of the Mogollon Rim, this desert has a cold desert climate. Although the summers are hot and dry, the winters are very cold and virtually snow-free. The rainfall is limited to 10 inches a year. The most significant amount of rain occurred on a single day in 1991, with 2 inches.

The Painted Desert, like many others in low latitudes, has a monsoon season. At the beginning of the summer, the southwest heats up

Lightning Storm within the Painted Desert, Public Domain

Vista view of the Painted Desert, Public Domain

Vista view of the Painted Desert, Public Domain

Bonneville Salt Flats in the Great Salt Lake Desert, Public Domain

more quickly than the water bodies around it. The difference between the heat of the land and the cold water causes winds in the region to shift direction. This results in the monsoon season that brings summer clouds with moisture. The winds blow from the south, drawing the moisture-rich air from the Gulf of Mexico, the Gulf of California, over the Painted Desert and other parts of Arizona. The summer monsoon season usually has heavy rain and frequent thunderstorms. However, it still only comes out to about 10 inches of rainfall each year.

This desert is composed of stratified layers of siltstone, mudstone, and shale. These rock layers contain abundant iron and manganese compounds, which is why the colors are so bright and beautiful. Thin limestone layers and volcanic flows top the mesas. Characteristics of this land are referred to as "Badlands." The term came when explorers decided the area was bad land to travel through. Despite these "Badlands" being challenging to traverse, the landscape has unusual beauty within its mountains, hills, and gorges.

Wind and water continue to change the face of the landscape, exposing layers of color. Fossilized plants and animals are found in this region, as well as dinosaur tracks, and even some evidence of ancient Native American culture.

The Great Salt Lake Desert is an immense, dry lake in northern Utah. It is known for its white salt deposits and the area called the Bonneville Salt Flats. Named after Captain B.L.E. Bonneville, who led expeditions in the 1830s to explore this ancient basin.

It is one of the most unusual natural features in Utah, stretching over 30,000 acres. It is located near the Utah-Nevada border. The salt flats were formed when an ancient endorheic lake dried up. The lake was huge and filled much of the basin. Since it did not have an outlet, it eventually evaporated leaving behind a thick layer of salt.

The Great Salt Lake is a remnant of the dry Lake Bonneville. The flats include micro-environments, and in some spots, the soil is so salty nothing will grow. Other places that are not as salty, do have different kinds of plants and animals.

Some speculate that Lake Bonneville was the size of Lake Michigan of the Great Lakes. It is thought that the lake covered at least 1/3 of present-day Utah. One can see different levels of the receding lake etched into the mountains that surround the salt flats.

The first recorded crossing of the desert occurred in 1824, when mountain men came to explore the region. Some travelers thought this was a shortcut to the California gold fields. Such

Dinosaur tracks in the Painted Desert, Public Domain

was the case with the Donner-Reed party, that followed tragic advice.   In this desert, many of their oxen died, and wagons were abandoned. As you may remember, the delay in their trip left them in the Sierra Nevada Mountains during the harsh winter, few survived.

In 1910, a permanent crossing of the Bonneville Salt Flats was finished when the Southern Pacific Railroad connected Salt Lake City and San Francisco.

The Great Salt Lake Desert is an excellent example of a cold desert climate. Its elevation is 4,000 feet above sea level, which makes temperatures cooler. Because of the high altitude, temperatures drop quickly after sunset. Summer nights are cool. Winter highs are generally just above freezing in the daytime. When the sun goes down on a winter night, this desert is bitterly cold, with temperatures well below freezing.

Utah Salt Flats Racing Association hosts annual races on the Bonneville Salt Flats. The World of Speed is one of the coolest, speed-driven races in the United States. It is held for four days in mid-September, and one can see some of the fastest racing vehicles anywhere. The salt flats provide the best conditions for setting land speed records.

A Closer Look!
at what you have learned in the last 6 lessons!

Lesson 23

PLUS+
This Lesson's Geography:
Remarkable Features

- Grand Canyon
- Black Hills
- Ozark Highlands
- Okefenokee Swamp
- Olympic Rainforests
- Niagara Falls

Previous Learned Geography:

Listed here is the geography learned over the last 6 lessons plus this lesson's new geography. All lessons learned before the last 6 lessons are no longer on the map below.

- Mojave Desert
- Sonoran Desert
- Colorado Desert
- Painted Desert
- Great Salt Lake Desert
- Eastern Woodlands
- Plains
- Plateau
- Northwest Coast
- California
- Great Basin
- Southwest
- Erie Canal
- Pennsylvania Canal
- Chesapeake & Ohio Canal
- Ohio & Erie Canal
- Miami & Erie Canal
- Cumberland Road
- Santa Fe Trail
- Mormon Trail
- Gila Trail
- Old Spanish Trail
- California Trail
- Oregon Trail
- Colorado River
- Red River
- Rio Grande River
- Columbia River
- Great Salt Lake
- St. Lawrence River
- Ohio River
- Mississippi River
- Missouri River
- Arkansas River

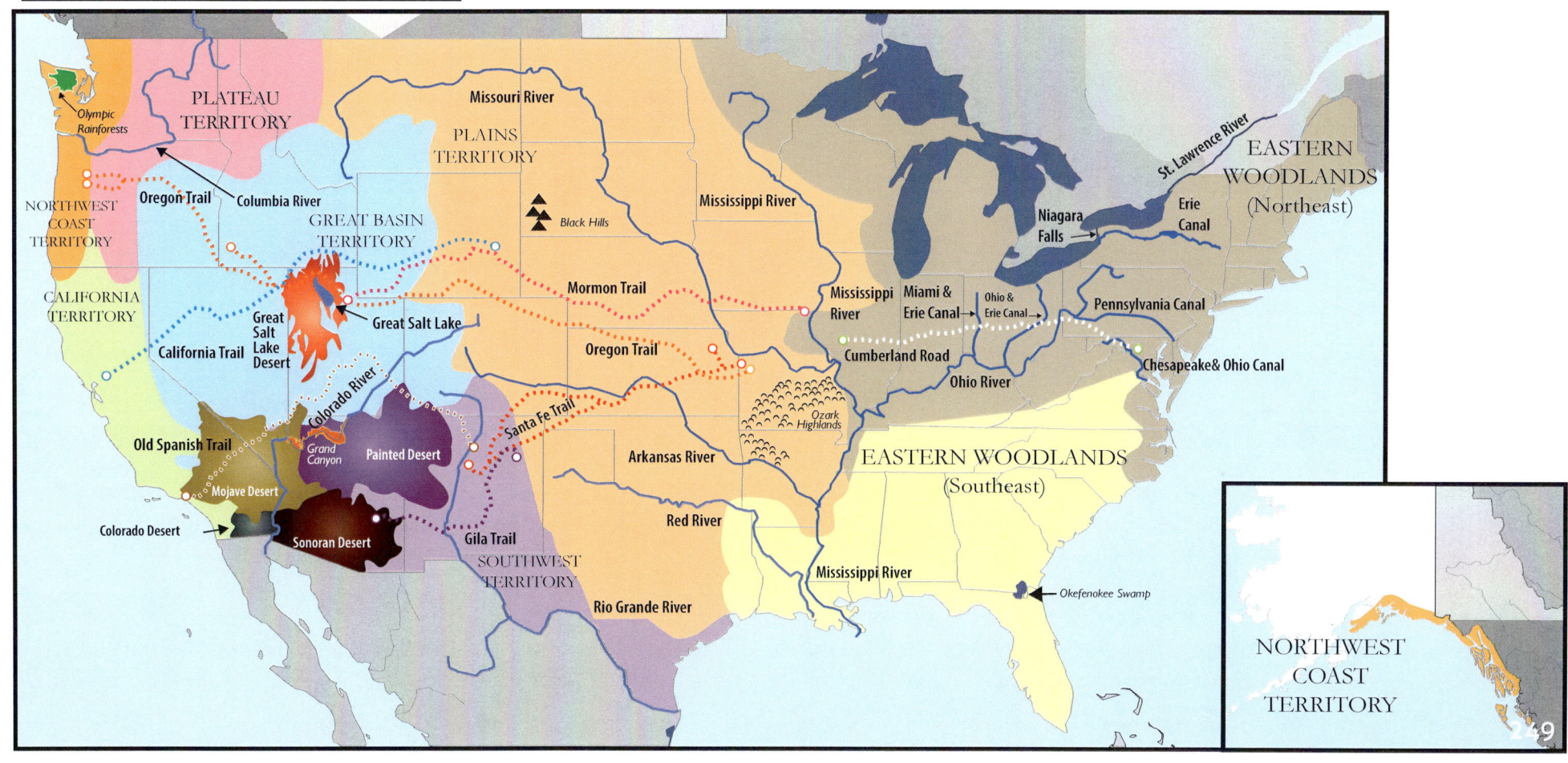

249

Zoom Me In! Lesson 23

United States of America Physical Features

Use this sheet as a reference for this lesson's worksheets. Be sure to practice until you don't have to look!

Remarkable Features

Grand Canyon

Black Hills

Ozark Highlands

Okefenokee Swamp

Olympic Rainforests

Niagara Falls

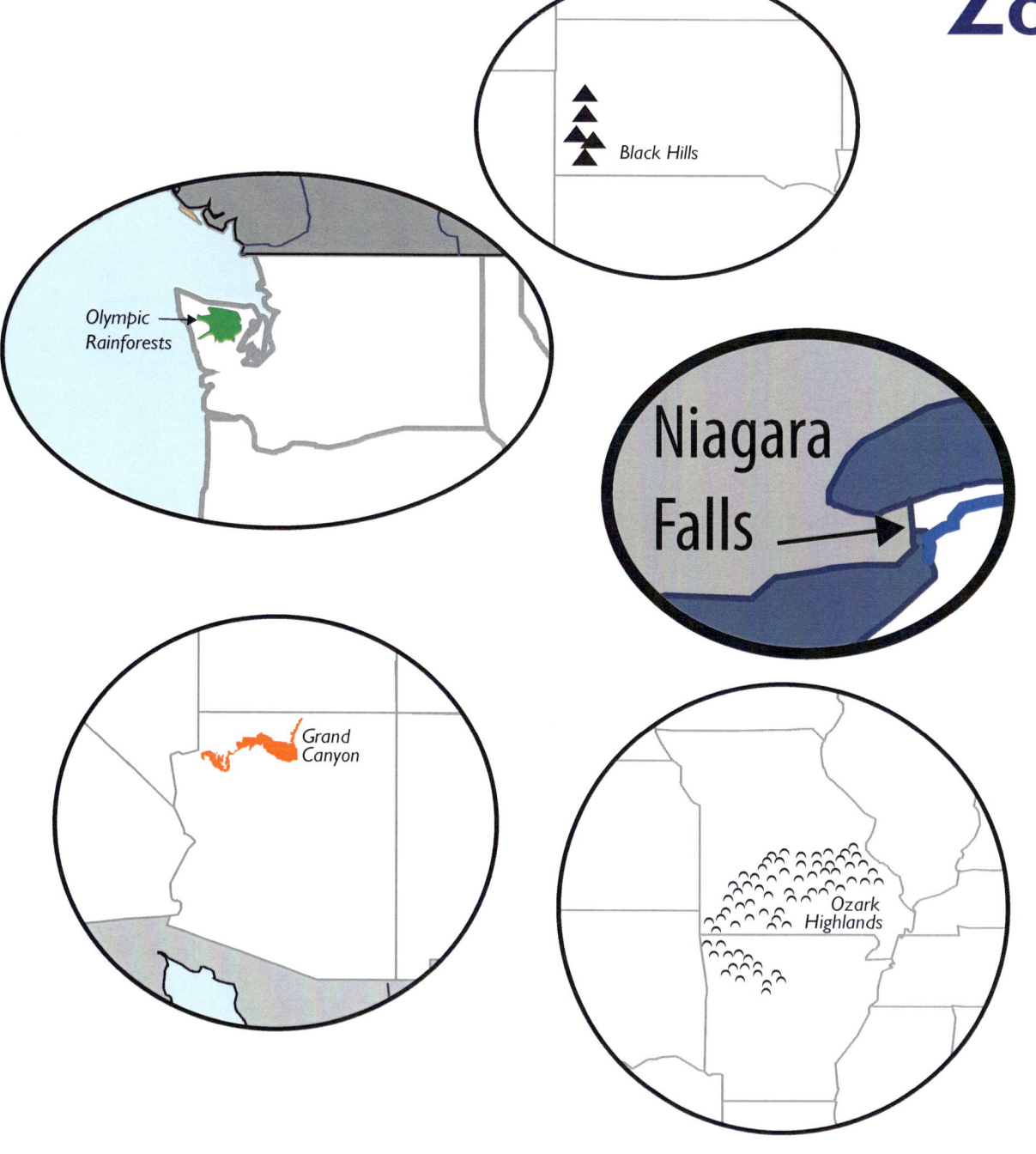

Black Hills

Olympic Rainforests

Niagara Falls

Grand Canyon

Ozark Highlands

Okefenokee Swamp

Lesson 23

This Lesson's Geography:
Remarkable Features

- Grand Canyon
- Black Hills
- Ozark Highlands
- Okefenokee Swamp
- Niagara Falls

Grand Canyon, By: Amanda Predmore

Tid-Bits

The Grand Canyon is one of the most visited attractions in the world and is recognizable globally. There is nothing quite like it in all the world. It is located in northwestern Arizona near Flagstaff. Technically, it is a hole in the ground, but it is an incredible hole in the ground. It is beautiful to look at and fascinating to study. It gives a geologic look into the history of the land. It is breathtaking, leaving the visitor in awe. It also causes a lot of debate as to what stories the land holds.

The Grand Canyon is more than 250 miles long and anywhere from four to eighteen miles wide. It is more than a mile deep in the Colorado Plateau. At the base of the Grand Canyon, winds the long Colorado River.

There are layers upon layers of rock, which sometimes is called "strata". The strata can be grouped into four parts. At the bottom, there are several kinds of granite. The second group is the Grand Canyon Supergroup, a sequence of various types of sedimentary rock that is layered at about a 45-degree angle. The third group has nine layers of horizontal walls. The fourth is at the top. It is made of gravel, lake sediment, landslide deposits, and lava flow. Throughout

Grand Canyon, Adobe Stock

the rocky walls of the Grand Canyon, fossils of all kinds are trapped at all elevations. Including various marine animal and plant fossils.

There are several theories as to how the Grand Canyon came to be created. It is hotly debated by scientists and thinkers of all kinds. Evolutionists, young-earth creationists, and old-earth creationists have a lot to say on the subject.

Those that believe in evolution, like studying the Grand Canyon because they believe the canyon gives evidence for evolution and the history of the Earth. This viewpoint lends itself to the hypothesis that the Earth is billions upon billions of years old. As it relates to the Grand Canyon, evolutionists believe that the Colorado River slowly carved away the strata, creating the canyon, along with other factors dealing with plate tectonics and movement of the continents.

Others base their studies in the Grand Canyon, looking for evidence to support Biblical events related to a catastrophic flood and the history associated with Noah and the Ark. This viewpoint lends itself

ABOVE & BELOW: Grand Canyon, By: Skywalk, Public Domain

to a young-earth model, where it is believed that the Earth is somewhere between 6,000 to 10,000 years old. As it relates to the Grand Canyon, a young-earth viewpoint believes that the Grand Canyon was formed quickly. The young-earth scientist believes that the rocks within the Grand Canyon are the perfect place to test the Genesis account of Earth's history. One such account, in Genesis 7:11, states that all the springs of the great deep burst forth, and the floodgates of the heavens were opened. The young-earth view is that if this happened, the Earth's surface would have been severely scoured at the beginning of the flood, leaving an unconformity in its wake. They believe that this unconformity has been found in the Grand Canyon and at the base of most fossil-filled rock around the world. In Genesis, 7:19 the text says that the waters rose greatly on the Earth, covering all of the mountains by about 15 cubits (22.5 feet). The young-earth viewpoint believes that the marine layers found in the top portion of the Grand Canyon, and on top of mountains on all continents, point to a worldwide flood.

Spanish explorers were the first Europeans to see the Grand Canyon in the 1540s. In 1858, the American explorer and botanist, Joseph Christmas Ives, mapped and explored the Grand Canyon and

Grand Canyon West Rim with the Colorado River running through. Public Domain

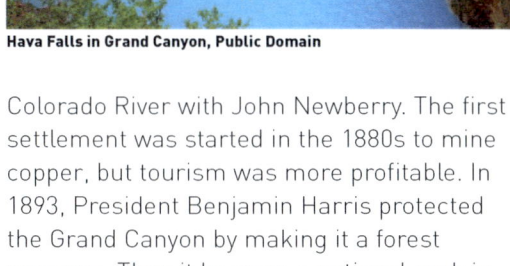

ABOVE: Down in the Grand Canyon, Public Domain

Hava Falls in Grand Canyon, Public Domain

Colorado River with John Newberry. The first settlement was started in the 1880s to mine copper, but tourism was more profitable. In 1893, President Benjamin Harris protected the Grand Canyon by making it a forest preserve. Then it became a national park in 1919.

More than five million people visit the Grand Canyon every year. Archaeologists have studied the Grand Canyon for information about people from the past. They have found ruins and artifacts in caves of the canyon. Some artifacts have been shaped like bighorn sheep and deer, which makes archaeologists think the people who lived there were hunters. Pueblo people of the Paiute, Navajo, Zuni, and Hopi tribes lived in and near the Grand Canyon. Today, the Havasupai call the canyon their ancestral home because they had lived there for many generations before America was established. As America developed and spread west, the Havasupai lost much of their land to the national park. In 1975, the Havasupai were able to take a lot of their land back and make money through tourism. The Havasupai tribe recently built the Skywalk, which reaches out over the canyon with a glass floor so people can straight down!

The Black Hills

The Arikara tribe lived in the Black Hills within present-day southwest South Dakota. The Cheyenne, Kiowa, Pawnee, and Crow tribes followed them. The Lakota, or Sioux, came in the 1700s from Minnesota and took over the land. The other tribes had to move west.

There is not much written history about the Black Hills because there is no record until the Sioux took over the land from the Arikara. The Lakota called the area Paha Sápa, which means Black Mountains. Today, we call the area the Black Hills.

François and Louis de La Vérendrye traveled near the Black Hills in 1743. They were the first people to document the area in the name of France. During the 1780s, the Lakota had more power in the Dakota area. Between 1817 and 1857, many fur trappers and traders had relationships with the Native Americans, creating a successful Fur Trade Era.

In 1857, people started moving to eastern South Dakota more, and more. Homesteads, settlements, and railroads were constructed. The Black Hills maintained a reputation for being a wild "Indian

View of the Skywalk that juts out above the Grand Canyon. Provided By: Skywalk

Chief Flying Hawk of the Oglala Dakota, cousin of Crazy Horse. He fought in many battles with the U.S. including the Great Sioux War of 1876, Battle of the Little Big Horn in 1876, and the Wounded Knee Massacre in 1890. He went on to chronicle the Lakota history and educate through the public schools through to about 1930.
Image by: Unknown, Public Domain

Sylvan Lake within the Black Hills, Public Domain

Country." White settlers continued to move further and further into Lakota land. The U.S. tried to take more land, but they were defeated by the Lakota in the 1860s. The U.S. and the Lakota signed the Fort Laramie Treaty of 1868, to make peace between the two nations. The treaty established the Great Sioux Reservation, with the agreement that the U.S. would not settle the area "forever." The Sioux and Cheyenne tribes also claimed their right to the land because it was sacred for their people.

There had always been rumors of gold in the Dakota area. When General Custer found gold, it was no longer a rumor. This sparked a massive migration of people into French Creek within the Black Hills.

The Black Hills were filled with thousands of miners in search of gold. Deadwood, Central City, and Lead City

became essential towns. Later, Hill City and Custer City were built in the Southern Hills. Railroads followed. The gold mines produced four million dollars every year after 1880.

Black Hills Gold Miners, Public Domain

The silver mines produced three million dollars every year.

With miners trespassing on Sioux land, in 1876, the Great Sioux War started. This was the last major Indian war fought in the Great Plains. The Lakota defeated General Custer and his troops at the Battle of Little Bighorn. The U.S. defeated the Lakota, Cheyenne, and Arapaho in 1876 and claimed the Black Hills. The Lakota continued to deny U.S. governing and continually tried to reclaim their land by filing lawsuits.

In the case of United States v. Sioux Nations of Indians, on July 23rd, 1980, the Supreme Court said the Black Hills were taken illegally from the Sioux Nation. The U.S. was told to give the Lakota $106

An example of a gold nugget, Public Domain

million in return for the land. The Lakota did not take the money because they wanted their land back. They believe if they accepted the settlement, the U.S. government was justified in taking the Black Hills. Today, (2020) the money is in a bank account and worth over $1.2 billion.

Black Hills War Path, Unknown Artist, Public Domain

Black Elk Peak in the Black Hills, Public Domain

Beaver Lake in the autumn, Ozark Mountains in Arkansas. By: Gregory Ballos

ABOVE: Beauty found in the Ozark Mountains. Public Domain

The Ozark Mountains are also called the Ozarks, Ozark Plateau, and the Ozark Highlands. Located in the south-central United States, spanning the length from St. Louis, Missouri, to the Arkansas River. The mountains cover over 50,000 square miles and run next to the Ouachita Mountains in Arkansas.

The Ozarks are covered by forests and plateaus. These mountains are the only large mountainous regions between the Appalachians and the Rockies. It has many high peaks over 2,000 feet tall. Among the higher peaks, there are three plateaus: The Boston, Springfield, and Salem plateaus, have defining features with underground streams and springs, sinkholes, and caves. In fact, in Missouri, there are well over 6,000 documented caves, mostly found in the Ozarks.

The Ozark Highlands Trail is 218 miles long in northwest Arkansas, and goes through some of the most scenic and wild parts of the Ozarks. Hurricane Creek Wilderness Area, White Rock Mountain, Hare Mountain, Marinoni Scenic Area, and other spots are along this trail.

People love going to the Ozarks for many reasons, the outdoors are one of the biggest draws. The area is full of outdoor beauty, including lakes, rivers, forests, and more. The hills and twisty roads bring motorcyclists and bicyclists from all over the country. The clean air and bountiful waters attract fishers, boaters, and water sports fans. For canoers and kayakers, the Ozarks are a perfect setting with tranquil rivers and fast rapids.

Ozark Mountains at sunrise in Missouri, Public Domain

BELOW & RIGHT: Hurricane Creek in the Ozarks, Public Domain

With miles and miles of forests, hikers, campers, and adventurers love to explore. People like to hike Pedestal Rocks Loop, the Lost Valley Trail, Hemmed in Hollow, and so many other amazing trails. There are historic sites and caves to explore, and climbing the sandstone rocks.

Nestled in the mountains, there are pretty towns full of history, antique shops, and folk music festivals. Eureka Springs is famous for its Victorian architecture.

The Okefenokee Swamp

The "land of trembling earth," as this place was called by the Seminole Indians. The Okefenokee Swamp is the largest swampland in North America, covering about 700 square miles. This swamp has a fascinating ecosystem. An ecosystem is a community of animals that interact with each other all in one environment.

The most significant parts of this habitat are the Cypress swamps, winding waterways, and floating peat mats. In the Okefenokee, there are both wet and dry prairies covered in shrubs and scattered with Black Gum and Bay trees throughout. A famous path called the Trail Ridge, forms the eastern border of the swamp. There are at least 400 species of mammals, over 200 varieties of birds, and more than 60 different types of reptiles.

RIGHT: Sunrise in the Okefenokee Swamp LEFT: Subtropical forest in the Okefenokee Swamp. BOTH: Provided by: Taylor Coleman

TOP LEFT & CENTER: Canoes ride through the Okefenokee Swamp, Provided by: Taylor Coleman

Logging operations began in 1910, lasting 25 years. Thousands of Cypress, Pine, and Red Bay trees were removed from the swamp. In 1937, United States President Franklin D. Roosevelt, established the Okefenokee National Wildlife Refuge, to protect it from logging and over-development. The refuge covers 80% of the swamp. The safety of the swamp ecosystem is better ensured, as there are no roads within. Those that wish to explore, travel through in canoes.

Eastern Indigo Snake. By Ltshears - Own work, CC BY-SA 3.0

BELOW: Rainbow snake, By Charles Baker - Own work, CC BY-SA 4.0

Because of the subtropical climate, rainfall is about 50 inches a year. Most of the water comes from 1,400 square miles of upland watershed. The Okefenokee waters are shallow, averaging 2 feet deep. However, in some places the depths can go all the way to 10 feet down.

The swamp has an awesome variety of creatures and a mixture of plant species in a highly diverse environment. Grasses, ferns, and bushes live in the dryer areas. Water lilies, Pickerelweed, and Yellow-eyed grass, are found in sites with more water.

Peat moss mats found throughout the wetter areas of the swamp serve as a rich growing foundation for some kinds of shrubs and trees. These floating mats are called tree islands.

Cougar within the Okefenokee Swamp, By: Unknown, Public Domain

Venus Flytrap that is about to get a meal of a Muscoid fly. By Beatriz Moisset - Own work, CC BY-SA 4.0

The Okefenokee Swamp environment plays host to some carnivorous plants that attract, capture, and digest insects. Some plants capture insects with a glue-like substance on their leaves. Others have air-filled traps that snap shut when an insect touches its hair-trigger.

Almost all species of wading birds and waterfowl can be seen in the Okefenokee Swamp during different seasons. White ibises, Blue herons, and Wood storks are common in the area. Blue-winged teals and other ducks visit in the winter. Bitterns can be seen during the summer. Many species of birds pass through this swamp on their migratory paths from warmer to colder regions, and back again. Wood ducks and Sand Hill cranes live in the swamp all year round. The birds bring the Okefenokee Swamp alive with a thousand voices playing unique melodies. The eyes take in a display of wondrous proportion as these creatures carry on with their determined path.

Red Bellied Turtle of the Okefenokee Swamp, Public Domain

Great Egret of the Okefenokee Swamp, Public Domain

Otter of the Okefenokee Swamp, Okefenokee National Wildlife Refuge, Public Domain

The large mammals in the swamp include black bears, white-tailed deer, and bobcats. Smaller animals are Grey foxes, possums, and raccoons. The water mammals are otters, minx, and beavers. There are two kinds of rabbits in the swamp, the cottontail that lives on higher ground and the marsh rabbit that lives in wetter lands.

Because of the wetland habitat, the Okefenokee Swamp is ideal for egg-laying amphibians. There are approximately 36 different kinds, including the Barking tree frog, Ornate Chorus frog, Dwarf Siren, and the Slimy salamander.

Reptiles make up the most diverse group of vertebrates. Within, there are five kinds of venomous snakes that slither their way through the swampland.

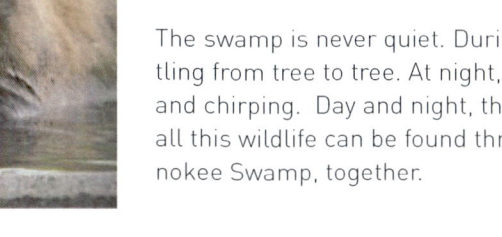

Black bear in the Okefenokee Swamp National Wildlife Refuge, Public Domain

The Indigo snake is the largest and least likely to be seen. The scales of the rainbow snake are as colorful as any tropical bird. Cottonmouths, and rattlesnakes, are the biggest group of poisonous snakes in the swamp.

The most common lizards are blue-tailed skinks and green anoles. Mud turtles, snappers, soft-shells, and basking cooters can be seen in the mud just under the water's surface.

The American Alligator in the Okefenokee National Wildlife Refuge, Public Domain

There is one reptile that dominates all. Can you guess what lives in this murky swamp?

If by chance, you guessed this quick, scaly, four-legged, commanding American alligator, that strikes fear in almost everyone and everything, then you would be right! These American alligators are the most talkative of all alligators. They begin making noise before they have even hatched out of their eggs. When baby alligators, called hatchlings, are ready to meet the world, they make high-pitched whining noises. When they are all grown up, American alligators bellow and roar at each other so loudly, that they can be heard up to 165 yards away. The calls of these alligator's day and night, the females' motherly protective behavior, their sheer size of between 8-11 feet, give these reptiles a reputation of dominance unmatched by any other wildlife in the swamp.

The swamp is never quiet. During the day, birds can be heard trilling and whistling from tree to tree. At night, the frogs and toads bring on a chorus of croaking and chirping. Day and night, the alligator bellows, and roars. And even though all this wildlife can be found throughout the south, they all appear in the Okefenokee Swamp, together.

The Olympic Rainforests

What exactly makes a rainforest? Rain, rain and more rain - twelve to fourteen feet of rain per year!

The temperate rainforest is a biome with a

Trail through the National Olympic Rainforest Park, Public Domain

canopy of trees that shuts out at least 70% of the sky. It is mainly made up of species of trees that do not need fire to regenerate. They regenerate under shade and in natural openings in the canopy from seedlings. The temperate rainforest biome is within what is referred to as mid-latitude. Mid-Latitude is below or above the tropic zone that you have learned about. The Pacific Northwest has rainforests that extend from Oregon all the way up to Alaska. About 1,200 miles. The Olympic Rainforest is found in Washington state. Other areas of the world within the mid-latitude, also have temperate rainforests.

There are four temperate rainforests, collectively called the Olympic Rainforests. Within are the Hoh Rainforest, Quinault Rainforest, Queets Rainforest, and Bogachiel Rainforest.

Washington State's Olympic Rainforest is unique. Beautiful coastlines, steep craggy mountain peaks, and misty valleys. Untamed and dotted with tide pools and sea stacks. One can take a peaceful walk along the shoreline, catching a glimpse of a passing whale. One of the nation's most massive Sitka spruce trees is in this park, standing at an impressive 191 feet, among other giants.

This park has a temperate climate, which means mild temperatures, that never go to extremes. The Olympic Rainforest rarely drops below freezing or goes above 80°F. This encourages an incredibly unique ecosystem. You can find mosses, ferns, Douglas fir, red alders, Western hemlocks, and Sitka spruce in temperate rainforests. There are also epiphytes, which are plants growing on other plants, like mistletoe, Cat-tail moss, and licorice ferns.

Nurse logs are another part of a rainforest. When trees fall because of age or storm, they become homes for other life. Small mammals and insects make homes in the dead trees, and seeds grow on the bark.

Within the Olympic National Park, the Hoh Rain Forest has trails for hikers of different abilities. A hiker can find moss and ferns covering the forest floor, as well as towering pines, Bigleaf maples, and Vine maples that provide a dense canopy of green overhead.

The Quinault Rain Forest is the rainforest with the most massive Sitka spruce tree mentioned earlier that is more than 1,000 years old, 191 feet tall, with a 96-foot spread of branches. In the Quinault, there are several beautiful waterfalls, as well as a Bigleaf maple grove.

The Queets Rain Forest has Sitka spruce that is in the shadow of the great Western Hemlock. The Western Hemlock can grow to 312-feet high, with a trunk 23-feet around. The cool, moist conditions found under the canopy of old-growth forests allow lettuce lichen to grow, which is the favorite food of deer, elk, and other animals.

The Bogachiel Rain Forest has hanging mosses, old-growth cedar, and spruce trees. The wetlands create a wonderland habitat for ferns to flourish.

Olympic National Park, By: Adam Jewell

Old Growth Western Hemlock, Public Domain

Hoh River Trail through the Hoh Rainforest, By: Amanda Predmore

Olympic National Park, By: Adam Jewell

The Kalaloch Cedar in the Olympic National Park, By: Amanda Predmore

Olympic National Park, By: Adam Jewell

Niagara Falls

One of the most impressive natural sites in North America is the Niagara Falls. This landmark consists of a series of waterfalls on the Niagara River. Canada and the United States share Niagara Falls as it straddles the border. The people who lived near these waters were the Iroquois Nation, who named Niagara, meaning "thunder of waters."

Every minute, thousands of tons of water pour over the Niagara Falls. Some of that water, however, is redirected into giant tunnels before it can continue on. These tunnels carry the water to electric power plants. The water turns the turbine, which turns a generator. The generator creates electricity that is routed to thousands of homes and businesses on both sides of the border.

Niagara Falls has become a famous tourist attraction. Millions of people visit each year. One of the attractions to Niagara Falls was a boat named "Maid of the Mist." Visitors that rode the boat were issued a raincoat and a hat to keep them dry. As they neared the falls, the roar

Henri Rechatin, famed tightrope walker from France, shown here above Niagara Falls. Public Domain

Niagara Falls sky view showing both the U.S. and Canadian public viewing areas. Public Domain

Niagara Falls, AdobeStock

of the water was awesome, the site, even more so, and they could feel the mist.

Many daredevils have tried to do fantastic and death-defying-stunts over the falls, to get famous. There is quite a list of people that tried different things, and here is a list of just a few who survived.

In 1859, Jean François Gravelet-Blondin was known as the "Great Blondin." He walked a tight rope across the Niagara Falls multiple times. He pushed a wheelbarrow, rode on a bicycle, and

Henri Rechatin, famed tightrope walker from France, shown here above Niagara Falls, which he performed several times. Public Domain

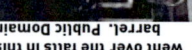

Annie Edison Taylor who went over the falls in this barrel. Public Domain

Niagara Falls sky view. Public Domain

even walked across with his hands and legs bound in chains. 25,000 people would come to watch him.

In 1867, a young Italian named Maria Spelterina was the first and only woman to cross the falls by tight rope. She wore woven baskets instead of shoes, covering her head with a paper bag for dramatic effect.

There were many more that didn't survive. Therefore, after 1896, the New York Niagara Parks Commission refused to issue permits for stunts. Although, they would issue a permit once in a generation, to limit fatalities. However, they did give permission a bit more often than this.

All but one of the remaining feats were done illegally. Some that made it, said "it was a small price to pay to be immortalized in the history books!"

In October of 1901, an older woman named Annie Edison Taylor went over the falls in a barrel. She thought she would get famous and make a lot of money. While she did survive the fall, she did not get much money, nor fame. She worked as a street vendor for 20 years in Niagara selling her story, before she died penniless.

In 1989, Peter DeBernardi and Geoffrey Petkovich were the first duo to go over the falls together, and they survived.

In 1995, Steven Trotter and Lori Martin were the first man and women to make it over the falls together in one barrel.

Then, in 2012, high-wire artist Nik Wallenda made a historic crossing after receiving special permission from both the U.S. and Canadian governments. He then went on to cross the Grand Canyon in 2013, which was televised live by the Discovery Channel to 183 countries. Well... that is it for this generation! What about your generation, who will be next?

The Canadian view of the Niagara Falls. Public Domain

Annie Edison Taylor who went over the falls in this barrel. Public Domain

Aerial view of the Niagara Falls and the "Maid of the Mist" boat tour. Public Domain

Aerial view of the Niagara Falls. Public Domain

Ground view of the Niagara Falls, Public Domain

A Closer Look!

at what you have learned in the last 6 lessons!

Lesson 24

PLUS+
This Lesson's Geography:
Remarkable Features

Mississippi River Delta   **Gulf of Mexico**
Mammoth Cave   **Death Valley**
San Andreas Fault

Previous Learned Geography:

Listed here is the geography learned over the last 6 lessons plus this lesson's new geography. All lessons learned before the last 6 lessons are no longer on the map below.

Grand Canyon	Eastern Woodlands	Cumberland Road
Black Hills	Plains	Santa Fe Trail
Ozark Highlands	Plateau	Mormon Trail
Okefenokee Swamp	Northwest Coast	Gila Trail
Olympic Rainforests	California	Old Spanish Trail
Niagara Falls	Great Basin	California Trail
Mojave Desert	Southwest	Oregon Trail
Sonoran Desert	Erie Canal	Colorado River
Colorado Desert	Pennsylvania Canal	Red River
Painted Desert	Chesapeake & Ohio Canal	Rio Grande River
Great Salt Lake Desert	Ohio & Erie Canal	Columbia River
	Miami & Erie Canal	Great Salt Lake

Map

- PLATEAU TERRITORY
- PLAINS TERRITORY
- Olympic Rainforests
- NORTHWEST COAST TERRITORY
- Oregon Trail
- Columbia River
- GREAT BASIN TERRITORY
- Black Hills
- EASTERN WOODLANDS (Northeast)
- Niagara Falls
- Erie Canal
- CALIFORNIA TERRITORY
- Mormon Trail
- Great Salt Lake
- Miami & Erie Canal
- Ohio & Erie Canal
- Pennsylvania Canal
- California Trail
- Great Salt Lake Desert
- Oregon Trail
- Cumberland Road
- Chesapeake & Ohio Canal
- San Andreas Fault
- Death Valley
- Colorado River
- Grand Canyon
- Painted Desert
- Santa Fe Trail
- Ozark Highlands
- Mammoth Cave
- Old Spanish Trail
- Mojave Desert
- Gila Trail
- Sonoran Desert
- SOUTHWEST TERRITORY
- Red River
- EASTERN WOODLANDS (Southeast)
- Colorado Desert
- Rio Grande River
- Mississippi Delta
- Okefenokee Swamp
- **Gulf of Mexico**

NORTHWEST COAST TERRITORY

Zoom Me In!

Lesson 24

Use this sheet as a reference for this lesson's worksheets.
Be sure to practice until you don't have to look!

United States of America Physical Features

Remarkable Features

Mississippi River Delta
Mammoth Cave
San Andreas Fault
Gulf of Mexico
Death Valley

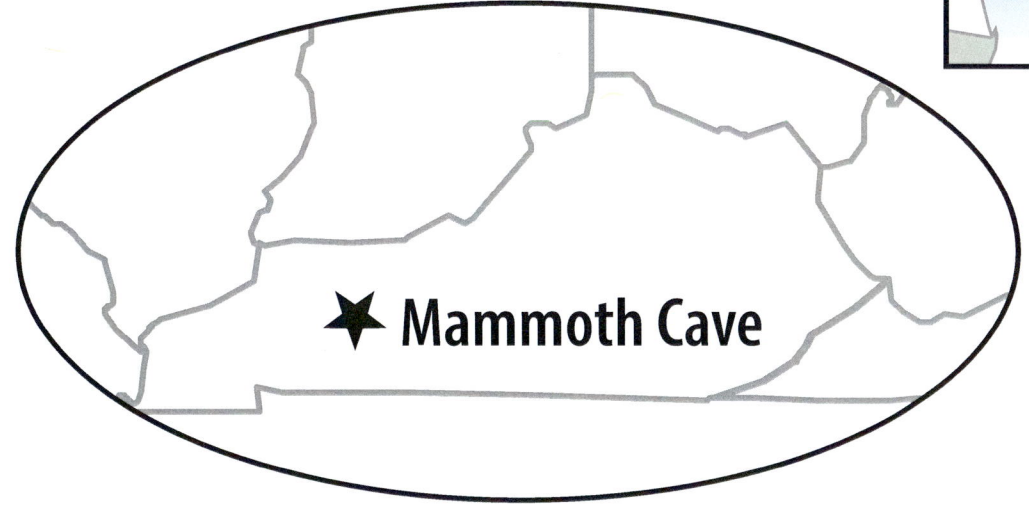

263

This Lesson's Geography:

Remarkable Features

Mississippi River Delta
Mammoth Cave
San Andreas Fault
Gulf of Mexico
Death Valley

Tid-Bits

The Mississippi River Delta
is the end of the road for the longest river in North America. After traveling 2,348 miles and carrying tremendous amounts of sediment, sand, and gravel, the Mississippi River fans out into several smaller streams until the water reaches the Gulf of Mexico. This portion of the river is called The Mississippi River Delta.

It is called a delta because the shape is like the Greek Delta alphabet symbol, which is a triangle. Naturally, deltas are at its lowest elevation, sea level, when the river meets the sea.

ABOVE & BELOW: Mississippi River Delta, NASA Satelite Imagery, Public Domain

Lesson 24

The Mississippi River Delta was discovered while the explorer René-Robert Cavelier, Sieur de La Salle was claiming the territory of Louisiana for France, in the late 1600s. The French built a fort in that area to assist and manage ships passing through on the Mississippi River. They made a village in the marshes of the Delta, which was constantly threatened by hurricanes. Ships traveling in the area had to deal with shifting conditions of tides, currents, and mudflats.

In 1803, the United States purchased Louisiana from Napoleon of France. The delta's soil was incredibly fertile, which made for bountiful crops. Once harvested, these crops needed to be shipped to other parts of the United States. Thus, the port at the delta became important for the local and national economy. The main crops were sugarcane, cotton, and a flower called Indigo. The Indigo flower was processed for its brilliant blue dye, used to color cloth.

The importance of trade in Mississippi became even more popular after the Civil War. This demand led to the transformation of the delta swampland, building levees.

With the amount of rich sediments carried down the river to the delta, Louisiana's land continues to be added to. People built homes and used the area for farmland. The river also created natural levees depositing sediment in different regions, making the delta's composition, a consistently changing land.

Mississippi River Delta Ground View. Public Domain

Mississippi Delta Soy Bean Crop. Public Domain

The path of Hurricane Katrina, By: Supportstorm & NASA. Public Domain

Hurricane Katrina in the Gulf of Mexico
By: NASA, Public Domain

People trapped by rising waters, New Orleans, By: NOAA

A natural delta always changes because of the cycles of the river. The natural cycles of the Mississippi River Delta have been constrained by building levees for flood control. Much of the land that people live on there is below sea level.

On August 29th, 2005, after days of closely watching satellite imagery, and submitting evacuation orders, Hurricane Katrina hit the delta. Right above the delta is the state of Mississippi and Louisiana. These two states were fully devastated by the hurricane. Category 5 winds, topping out at 175 miles per hour, caused 23 levees to fail. By the time it reached landfall, the hurricane was a Category 3, with 127 mph winds.

When the levees failed, the ocean rushed in, covering the land below sea level. New Orleans was wrecked. It was the most significant engineering disaster in U.S. history, with 80% of New Orleans flooded. The damage a city experiences with suddenly being overwhelmed by the ocean was horrific. 1,833 dead, the majority caused by drowning. Estimated losses of $161 billion. The path of the hurricane more directly went through Mississippi, the death toll was 238, 67 missing and an estimated loss of $125 billion. The levee failure in the delta was the direct cause of the high number of deaths in Louisiana.

Hurricane Katrina was so powerful that she did not entirely dissipate until reaching the state of Ohio.

Hurricanes, known as tropical cyclones, are wind fields generated by warm rising air and cold falling air, with a center called the "Eye." A hurricane can be as long as 600 miles across and have internal winds spiraling upwards of 75 to 200 mph. A hurricane usually lasts more than a week. It moves slowly at 10 to 20 miles per hour across the ocean, gathering heat and energy through contact with the warm ocean water.

In terms of direct effects, Hurricane Katrina destroyed all forms of communication possible as line breaks caused the Internet to be inoperable. Broadcasting and publishing became central to distribute

Rescue Helicopter bringing stranded people to safety New Orleans (AP)

People attempting to get to safety from the rising waters, New Orleans, By: NOAA

Inside the eye of Hurricane Katrina viewed from a Lockheed WP-3D Orion Hurricane Hunter. Public Domain, Provided by NOAA

The "Eye" of Hurricane Katrina

Aerial image of boats brought into the Gulf of Mexico shoreline of Alabama, which was also heavily affected by Hurricane Katrina. By: NOAA

Containers sit among debris from Hurricane Katrina in Gulfport, Mississippi (AP Photo/David J. Phillip)

ABOVE: A flooded neighborhood in New Orleans. By: Jocelyn Augustino/FEMA, Public Domain.

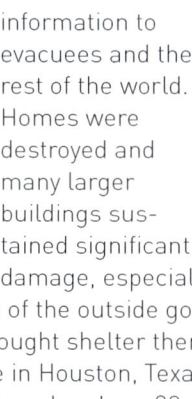

ABOVE: People are stranded on a roof due to floodwaters from Hurricane Katrina on August 30th, 2005 in New Orleans, Louisiana. (AFP/Getty Images) LEFT: Floodwaters from Hurricane Katrina pour through a levee along Inner Harbor Navigational Canal near downtown New Orleans on Aug. 30, 2005, a day after Katrina passed through the city. (AP Photo/Vincent Laforet)

BELOW: An aerial view of damage caused by Hurricane Katrina the day after the hurricane hit New Orleans, Louisiana, August 30, 2005. By: Jocelyn Augustino/FEMA)

Coast guard on the lookout for survivors to rescue from the flood waters. By: Coast Guard, Public Domain.

In this Aug. 31, 2005 picture, a walk through the destruction in her childhood neighborhood in Long Beach, Mississippi after Hurricane Katrina ravaged the area. By: Rob Carr

information to evacuees and the rest of the world. Homes were destroyed and many larger buildings sustained significant damage, especially the Superdome, where two sections of the outside got peeled off by the wind. Those who sought shelter there had to be moved into the Astrodome in Houston, Texas. In Mississippi, Long Beach was flattened under a 32 foot tide, 90% of the buildings along the shoreline in Biloxi-Gulfport were wiped out.

Countrywide, those displaced from their homes were welcomed as guests in homes willing to help. Approximately 200,000 people needed places to stay. Extensive facilities like the Astrodome housed 16,000 people. As time has passed, many moved out of the area forever. Many stayed and rebuilt. There are monuments throughout the city. In Louisiana's Gentilly neighborhood, a patch of grass with a wooden kiosk tells the story of the catastrophe.

"This place is a memorial to the trauma of the Flood." Near this memorial, a section of concrete levee gave way that fateful August morning in 2005, sending the floodwaters of Hurricane Katrina crashing into the neighborhood. The monument is a reminder of the suffering, and as the memorial declares, *"a symbol of the residents' resilience and determination to return home."*

Mammoth Cave, Historic Entrance - Public Domain

Mammoth Cave

When you think of a cave named Mammoth Cave - what images come to mind? Did Woolly Mammoths once roam the area where this cave is found with ancient drawings of this animal? Or, is the opening of this cave really, really big? What do you think the name says about this national treasure?

Let's find out!

Mammoth Cave National Park is in the center of Kentucky. It is called Mammoth because of the extensively large, or you could say "mammoth" cave system. There are more than 360 miles of passages that have been mapped. There are even more passages that exist that have not been mapped! Can you think of a place that is 360 miles away? Is that a far-off place? How long would it take to drive there? For this cave, the name fits! Mammoth Cave is the largest known in the whole world.

Mammoth Cave stairwell up the Mammoth Dome Public Domain

Life abounds in and around this tranquil cave. 130 types of animals live in the cave, most are nocturnal. Bats, spiders, and eyeless cavefish thrive in this underground environment. If you do not know what nocturnal means, it is defined as "at night or nighttime." In this case, the animals are awake and active during the night, and sleep during the day. In the cave, it is very dark. In fact, after entering, and then making your first turn, it is pitch black. So, the animals that live within, have eyes that can see in the dark, or have heightened senses that allow them to flourish in this environment. If you were to explore this cave, you would need to bring a reliable flashlight, and maybe a backup! Unless you can see in the dark?

Life in the cave includes some of the most diverse species in the world. Types of animals within include a wide variety of amphibians, crustaceans like the Kentucky Cave shrimp, eyeless fish without pigment, insects like the Cave cricket, and mammals such as the Indiana bats. Outside the cave, throughout the National Park, frogs, reptiles, raccoons, and whitetail deer are also found abundantly. There are almost 53,000 acres to explore and at least 70 miles of winding trails that are open to hikers and horseback riders. One path goes past springs, sinkholes, and the "wild cave." Within the "wild cave," there is an extreme crawling cave tour offered that goes for five miles. This tour is extremely physically demanding and is for experienced hikers.

It is believed that people roamed this land thousands of years ago. Remains of mummies that were buried within, have been discovered. Explorers have also found that the cave floor is covered with gourds, muscle shells, cane torches, slippers, and other exciting items. More than likely, this cave was used as a shelter for the Native Americans that lived there.

In the 1700s, the Mammoth Cave was purchased and changed owners many, many times. In 1838, the cave was sold to Franklin Gorin, who intended to make money by giving tours. One of his famous

Mammoth Cave Tour, Public Domain

Mammoth Cave earlier explorers, Public Domain

Travertine Formation within the Mammoth Cave

The San Andreas Fault

What is an earthquake? Have you ever experienced an earthquake, if so, what was it like? If not, what do you think it would be like?

If you do not know what an earthquake is, or why it happens, here is a simplified definition. An earthquake is what happens when two giant blocks of the earth, that are pushing against each other, suddenly slip past one another. The surface where they slip is called the fault or the fault plane, and it is usually below the earth's surface.

slaves, Stephen Bishop, drew up maps of the cave system, and gave the names to many of the features within. Strange and inspiring stories were written about the adventures of people exploring throughout.

Some Kentuckians found an interest in this cave, and decided to convert the entire region into a National Park. The problem was that many people called this land their home, and didn't want to leave. Thousands of people were forcibly removed from their homes through "Eminent Domain." This is where the United States government can take private property from people and convert it to public use. Although, the 5th Amendment of the U.S. Constitution provides that the government can only exercise this power, if they provide just compensation to the property owners. Regardless of payment, some people that live in Kentucky have long memories, and are still unhappy about that.

In this 53,000-acre park, there are many exciting things to see and do. People can hike Green Bluffs River Trail that crosses the River Styx, as well as the Heritage Trail to see the sunset. They can look at the old railroad engines on display for train enthusiasts. These engines were a vital part of the caves, and the park's rich history. They can go river rafting and go fishing along the Mammoth National Park Green River.

Because of the 400-mile labyrinth of geological wonders inside the cave, droves of people go there each year. Although the cave is the main highlight of the visit, some people find the stories and legends just as exciting.

The fault you are learning about today is called the San Andreas Fault. Which, unlike most, can be easily seen. This fault is the sliding boundary between the Pacific Plate

Illustration of the world's tectonic plates and the hypothesis behind how they move against each other. Public Domain

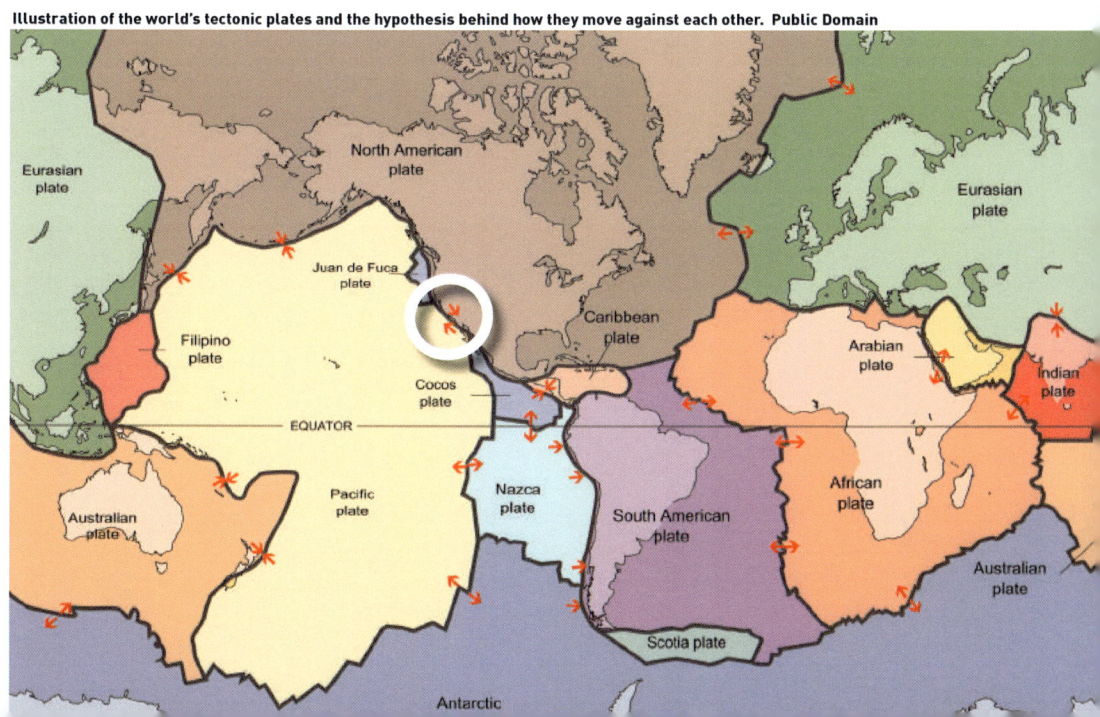

ALL: Aerial photos of the San Andreas Fault. Public Domain

and the North American Plate. When we say "plate," we are not talking about dishes. We are talking about those giant blocks of the earth, that seismologists refer to as "tectonic plates." The San Andreas Fault is a crevice in the ground that separates the North American Plate from the Pacific Plate. On the west side of the San Andreas Fault is the Pacific Plate, whereas, the east side is the North American Plate.

The North America Plate covers almost all the continent of North America, part of northeastern Asia, and covering all of Greenland. On the North American continent, along the San Andreas Fault, begins the Pacific Plate that goes way past Hawaii, including a portion of New Zealand and almost making it to Japan.

These two giant pieces of the earth are puzzled together, and in some spots, they grind side by side. In other places, the plates push directly into each other creating valleys and mountains. The San Andreas Fault is what is referred to as a "right moving strike-slip fault." This means that the two plates do not push into each other like some faults; instead, the plates slide along each other, grinding. They mostly slide very slowly, causing deep tectonic tremors, and many minor earth-

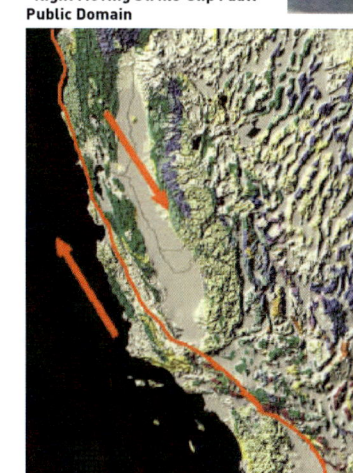

Illustration map showing the "Right Moving Strike-slip Fault" Public Domain

quakes. At times, these earthquakes are felt by people, but mostly not.

Sometimes the plates will lock together, with no movement at all. As they push, the tension builds, and builds until the strain is too strong, and the pressure too great. The plates give way, with a sudden, and violent "slip!" When this happens, one plate slips against the other a few feet all at once, causing a monumental, devastating earthquake.

The San Andreas Fault line runs from north to south in California, as seen on your map. The cities of San Diego, Los Angeles, and Big Sur are on the Pacific Plate, close to the ocean. Whereas, the cities of San Francisco, Sacramento, and the Sierra Nevada mountain range are on the North American Plate. The fault line goes through communities like Desert Hot Springs, San Bernardino, Wrightwood, Palmdale, Gorman, and more.

The San Andreas Fault zone is roughly 1,200 miles long. Plates grind past each other at about 2 inches per year. The fault zone is not one single line for the whole system but instead spreads out like a spider web in certain areas. This area has had only two known major earthquakes along the San Andreas Fault. The first one was in 1906, the second was in 1989. Both were in San Francisco.

Double-decker freeway that ran through San Francisco toppled in the 1989 earthquake. Public Domain

Double-decker freeway collapsed in the 1989 earthquake. Public Domain

The aftermath of the 1989 earthquake at the World Series game between the Oakland "A's" and the San Francisco Giants. Public Domain

Toppled build, squished car, caused by 1989 earthquake. Public Domain

The Gulf of Mexico is a body of water that forms a third of the United States coastline with beaches along Florida, Alabama, Mississippi, Louisiana, and Texas. In Mexico, the Gulf has states that border the water also, like Veracruz and Yucatán. The western end of the island of Cuba also forms a partial coastline, where it joins the Caribbean Sea.

The Gulf of Mexico is oval-shaped and about 950 miles long. For more than 500 years, the Gulf of Mexico has been an essential player in the economic and political development of the United States, Cuba, and Mexico. Exports from the Gulf of Mexico include oil and gas, along with a highly valued fishing industry. This area is abundant with fish because of the deep, cold waters that rise through a process called upwelling.

On October 17th, 1989, the earthquake in San Francisco Bay killed 67 people, and caused more than $5 billion in damage. The double-decker freeway that ran through San Francisco toppled. The upper layer crashed into the lower level, with afternoon commuter traffic going along its way. Many perished.

Although the highways were not as filled as they usually are. A silver lining within this tragedy was that it happened right before the two Californian teams, the Oakland Athletics, and the San Francisco Giants, played for the World Series. Their game was supposed to start at 5:30, and at 5:04 PM, the earthquake rocked San Francisco Bay. The stadium withstood all the shaking, having thousands safely in their seats. Other parts of the Bay were not as fortunate.

Two helpful animated videos are found on YouTube that illustrate what an earthquake is and what a strike-slip fault is.

Check these out!
https://youtu.be/J2yV9PnGeSc
https://youtu.be/dJpIU1rSOFY

Gulf of Mexico shoreline along Florida's coast. Adobe Stock

Upwelling brings cold, nutrient-rich waters to the surface, which encourage seaweed growth and support blooms of phytoplankton, making for a productive ecological system.

In addition, the Gulf of Mexico has also been an important trade route for shipping. There are many key ports, including New Orleans in Louisiana and Houston, Texas.

The waters of the Gulf of Mexico are very warm. These warm waters encourage and intensify tropical storms and hurricanes, commonly entering the Gulf from the Atlantic Ocean. Some hurricanes coming from the Gulf of Mexico have become well-known worldwide due to their massive damage and horrific mortality rates. Recent example are Hurricanes Katrina and Rita in 2005 and Hurricane Laura in 2020, which was the most powerful of the three in recent years. In areas that are prone to hurricanes, homes close to the shoreline are built on stilts to avoid being flooded during the hurricane season.

Satelite imagery with the Gulf Mexico centered. Adobe Stock

Sunset over the Gulf of Mexico, Public Domain

Other characteristics of the Gulf of Mexico shoreline are the barrier islands, which form a chain from Florida to Louisiana, and Texas to Mexico. These islands are separated from the mainland by a narrow body of water. The barrier islands are low-lying and easily flooded in hurricane conditions.

Schools of Fish in the Gulf of Mexico. Adobe Stock

Death Valley is a hot desert located in Southern California in the northern Mojave Desert. Between the major cities of Los Angeles and Las Vegas, this desert contains the most inhospitable land with extreme heat. It has beautiful mountains, sand dunes, salt flats, and a lake that lies below sea level. Death Valley is about 140 miles long and ranges between 5 to 15 miles wide. The lowest point of elevation is called Death Valley's Bad Water Basin, which is 282 feet below sea level. When one stands near this basin, the tallest mountain in the United States, Mt. Whitney, can be seen.

Death Valley received its English name during the California gold rush of 1849. It was called Death Valley by prospectors who crossed the valley on their way to the goldfields. After 13 pioneers died on their way, the valley was aptly named. During the 1850s, gold and silver were found in that valley. In the 1880s, the Borax Mule Train was established, bringing borax, extracted from the land.

Although Death Valley is a desert, there is life made to endure these harsh conditions. Saltgrass, pickle weeds, and rushes are found near spring marshes. Wildflowers watered by snowmelt bloom all over the desert every spring. Visitors come to photograph the wildflowers in this beautiful landscape. There is also animal life. The bighorn sheep, red-tailed hawks, coyotes, and wild burros, to name a few. There are also shallow depressions of water that support tiny fish called pupfish. These fish are unique in that they can live in very hot water!

Mysterious moving rocks in Death Valley - Check it out: https://youtu.be/uyHcs7B27Zk

Black Mountain's Artist's Palette, Public Domain

Amazing sunrise over Death Valley, Public Domain

Darwin Falls in Death Valley

Death Valley, Public Domain

Big Horned Sheep in Death Valley

The highest point in Death Valley is Telescope Peak. The hottest temperature ever recorded was 134°F on July 10, 1913. With Death Valley as a tourist attraction, the park is closed for safety from Memorial Day to Labor Day. All mules and horses are removed from the dessert, due to the extreme heat.

In Death Valley, the Darwin Falls waterfall tumbles 100 feet down into a pool surrounded by willows and cottonwood trees. Scotty's Castle, which is a famous tourist attraction, is built near that waterfall.

Another beautiful area is on the face of Black Mountain, called the Artist's Palette. This display showcases vibrantly colored rocks of various shades. The colors are caused by oxidation of metals within the rocks. It is the most colorful area in all Death Valley.

In one area of the valley there are sand dunes that some believe are fossilized, with visible footprints of dinosaurs in the stone.

The last exciting tidbit... Star Wars film fans listen up! Star Wars scenes from episodes four and six were filmed in Death Valley!

Red Tailed Hawk in Death Valley, Public Domain

Coyote in Death Valley, Public Domain

Sand Dunes in Death Valley, Public Domain

A Closer Look!

at what you have learned in the last 6 lessons!

TrueReview 1

Congratulations!
You are nearing the finish line!
There is no new geography from this point forward, just review!

Previous Learned Geography:

Listed here is the geography learned over the last 6 lessons. All lessons learned before the last 6 lessons are no longer on the map below.

Mississippi River Delta
Mammoth Cave
San Andreas Fault
Gulf of Mexico
Death Valley
Grand Canyon
Black Hills
Ozark Highlands
Okefenokee Swamp
Olympic Rainforests
Niagara Falls
Mojave Desert

Sonoran Desert
Colorado Desert
Painted Desert
Great Salt Lake Desert
Eastern Woodlands
Plains
Plateau
Northwest Coast
California
Great Basin
Southwest
Erie Canal

Pennsylvania Canal
Chesapeake & Ohio Canal
Ohio & Erie Canal
Miami & Erie Canal
Cumberland Road
Santa Fe Trail
Mormon Trail
Gila Trail
Old Spanish Trail
California Trail
Oregon Trail

A Closer Look!
at what you have learned in the last 5 lessons!

TrueReview 2

Congratulations!
You are nearing the finish line! There is no new geography from this point forward, just review!

Previous Learned Geography:

Listed here is the geography learned over the last 5 lessons. All lessons learned before the last 5 lessons are no longer on the map below.

- Mississippi River Delta
- Mammoth Cave
- San Andreas Fault
- Gulf of Mexico
- Death Valley
- Grand Canyon
- Black Hills
- Ozark Highlands
- Okefenokee Swamp
- Olympic Rainforests
- Niagara Falls
- Mojave Desert
- Sonoran Desert
- Colorado Desert
- Painted Desert
- Great Salt Lake Desert
- Eastern Woodlands
- Plains
- Plateau
- Northwest Coast
- California
- Great Basin
- Southwest
- Erie Canal
- Pennsylvania Canal
- Chesapeake & Ohio Canal
- Ohio & Erie Canal
- Miami & Erie Canal
- Cumberland Road

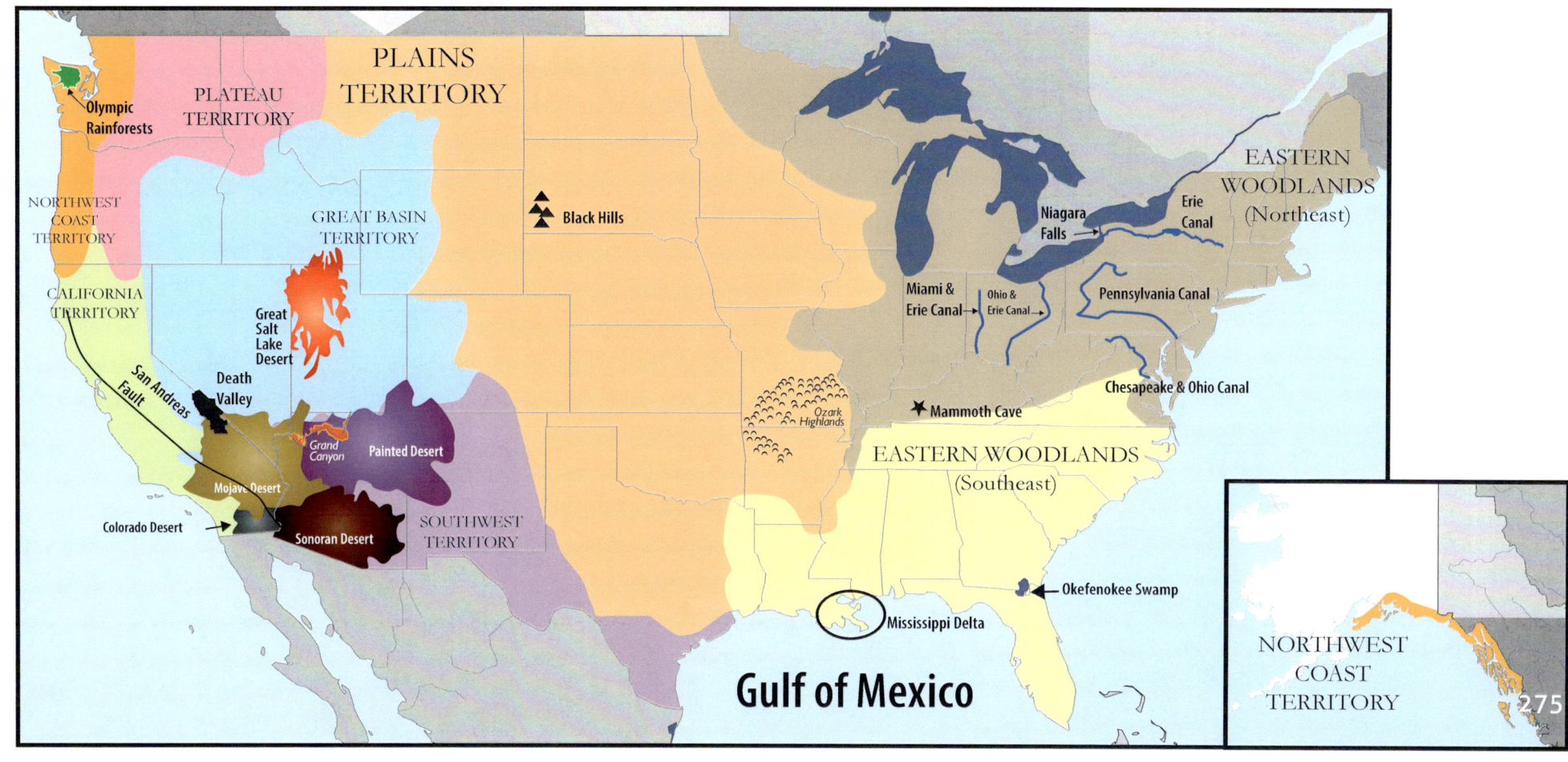

275

A Closer Look!

at what you have learned in the last 4 lessons!

TrueReview 3

Congratulations!
You are nearing the finish line! There is no new geography from this point forward, just review!

Previous Learned Geography:

Listed here is the geography learned over the last 4 lessons. All lessons learned before the last 4 lessons are no longer on the map below.

Mississippi River Delta
Mammoth Cave
San Andreas Fault
Gulf of Mexico
Death Valley
Grand Canyon
Black Hills
Ozark Highlands

Okefenokee Swamp
Olympic Rainforests
Niagara Falls
Mojave Desert
Sonoran Desert
Colorado Desert
Painted Desert
Great Salt Lake Desert

Eastern Woodlands
Plains
Plateau
Northwest Coast
California
Great Basin
Southwest

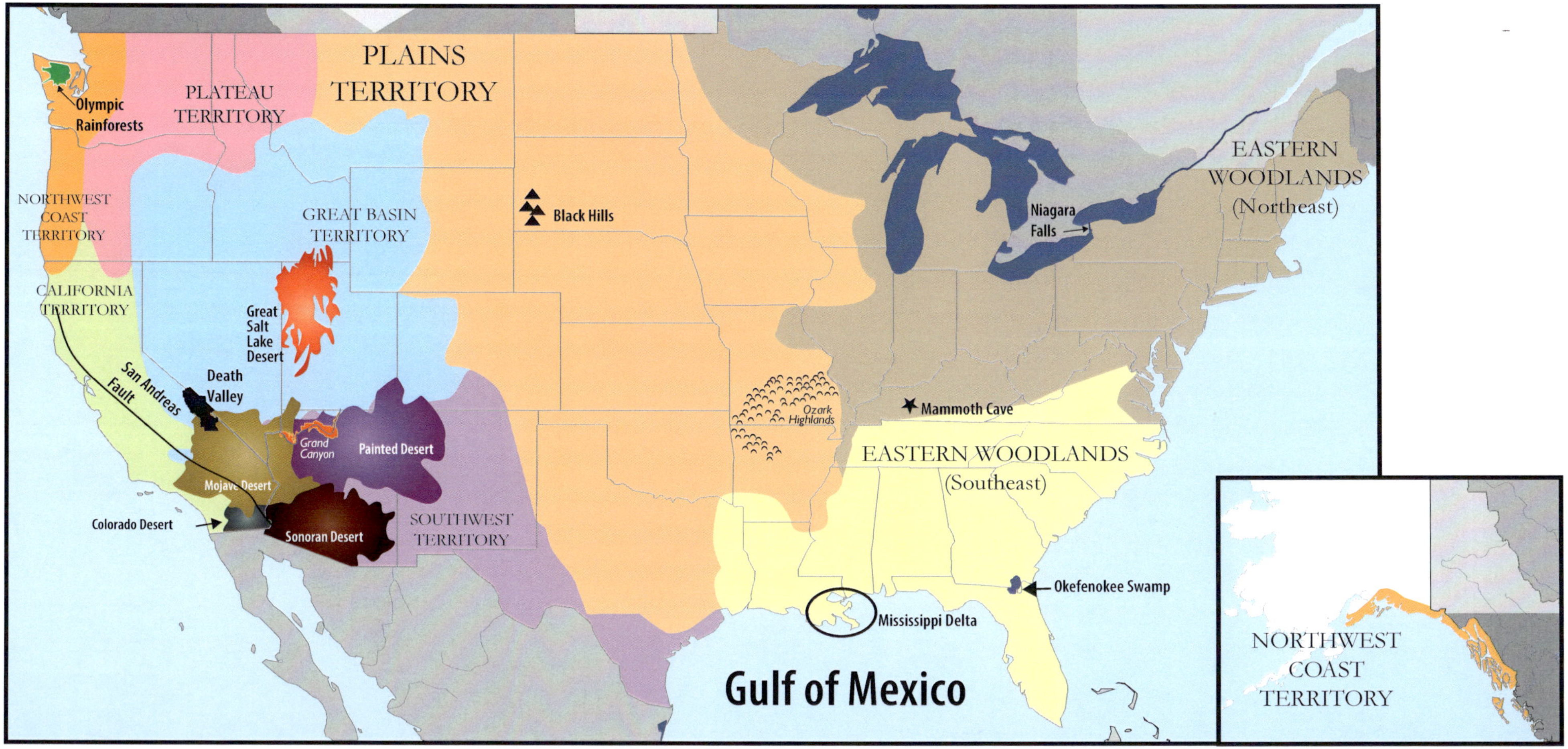

PLAINS TERRITORY

PLATEAU TERRITORY

Olympic Rainforests

NORTHWEST COAST TERRITORY

CALIFORNIA TERRITORY

GREAT BASIN TERRITORY

Black Hills

EASTERN WOODLANDS (Northeast)

Niagara Falls

Great Salt Lake Desert

San Andreas Fault

Death Valley

Grand Canyon

Painted Desert

Mojave Desert

Colorado Desert

Sonoran Desert

SOUTHWEST TERRITORY

Ozark Highlands

Mammoth Cave

EASTERN WOODLANDS (Southeast)

Okefenokee Swamp

Mississippi Delta

Gulf of Mexico

NORTHWEST COAST TERRITORY

A Closer Look!
at what you have learned in the last 3 lessons!

TrueReview 4

Congratulations!
You are nearing the finish line! There is no new geography from this point forward, just review!

Previous Learned Geography:

Listed here is the geography learned over the last 3 lessons. All lessons learned before the last 3 lessons are no longer on the map below.

- Mississippi River Delta
- Mammoth Cave
- San Andreas Fault
- Gulf of Mexico
- Death Valley
- Grand Canyon
- Black Hills
- Ozark Highlands
- Okefenokee Swamp
- Olympic Rainforests
- Niagara Falls
- Mojave Desert
- Sonoran Desert
- Colorado Desert
- Painted Desert
- Great Salt Lake Desert

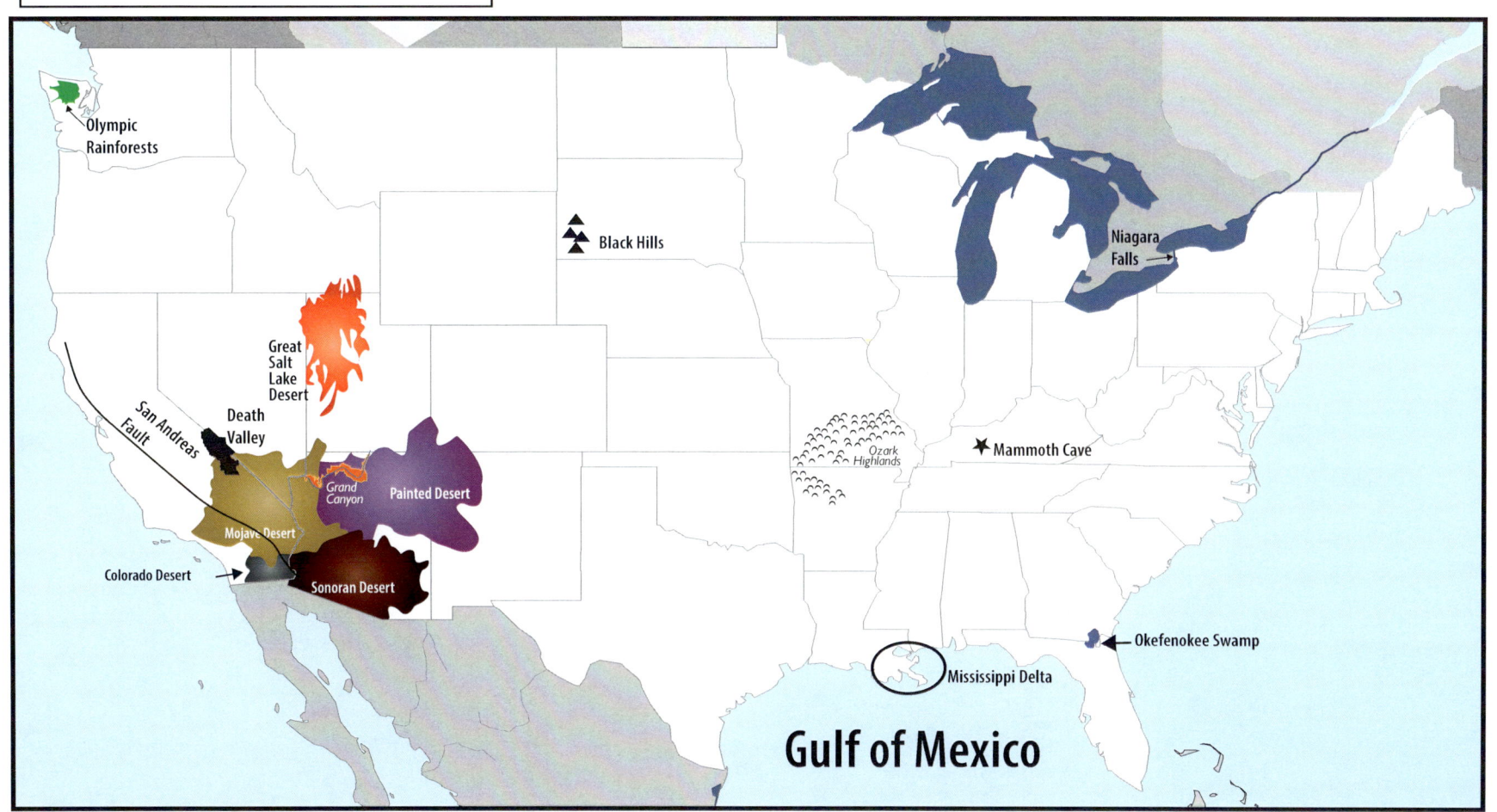

A Closer Look!

at what you have learned in the last 2 lessons!

TrueReview 5

Congratulations!
You are nearing the finish line!
There is no new geography from this point forward, just review!

Previous Learned Geography:

Listed here is the geography learned over the last 2 lessons. All lessons learned before the last 2 lessons are no longer on the map below.

Mississippi River Delta
Mammoth Cave
San Andreas Fault
Gulf of Mexico
Death Valley

Grand Canyon
Black Hills
Ozark Highlands
Okefenokee Swamp
Olympic Rainforests
Niagara Falls

A Closer Look!
at what you have learned in the last lesson!

TrueReview 6

Previous Learned Geography:

Listed here is the geography learned over the last lesson. All lessons learned before the last lessons are no longer on the map below.

Mississippi River Delta
Mammoth Cave
San Andreas Fault
Gulf of Mexico
Death Valley

Congratulations!
You are crossing the finish line!

Blank Black Line Master

281

Geography Books

"Ancient Empires & More!"
(Digital Download & Paperback)

"Europe and Asia, Continents, Oceans & More!"
(Digitial Download & Paperback)

"United States & Capitals PLUS Physical Features" 2 BOOKS *(that work together)***:
Teaching & Student Resource Guide***
Includes the Tid-Bits and Master Maps"
(Digitial Download & Paperback)
Student Map Worksheet Book that includes TrueReview*
(Digitial Download & Paperback)
**Digital and Paperback can be bundled or sold separately.*

Be sure to check out all resources that compliment the "Where in the World?" Geography Series

The Student Workbook for this book can be purchased here:
https://etsy.me/3lFaIv3

Review Games & More

Musical Hop Scotch Mat

Enlarged Map Sets,
Black Line Maps, along with 2 Review Games for these books:

"Ancient Empires & More!"

"Europe and Asia, Continents, Oceans & More!"

"United States & Capitals PLUS Physical Features"

http://bit.ly/WhereInTheWorldGeo